GEORGE WASHINGTON CARVER

GEORGE WASHINGTON CARVER

CARVER

Scientist and Symbol

Linda O. McMurry

OXFORD UNIVERSITY PRESS

Oxford   New York   Toronto   Melbourne

OXFORD UNIVERSITY PRESS

Oxford   London   Glasgow
New York   Toronto   Melbourne
Nairobi   Dar es Salaam   Cape Town
Kuala Lumpur   Singapore   Hong Kong   Tokyo
Delhi   Bombay   Calcutta   Madras   Karachi

and associate companies in
Beirut   Berlin   Ibadan   Mexico City

Copyright © 1981 by Oxford University Press, Inc.
First published by Oxford University Press, New York, 1981
First issued as an Oxford University Press paperback, 1982

LIBRARY OF CONGRESS CATALOGING IN PUBLICATION DATA
McMurry, Linda O.
George Washington Carver, scientist and symbol.

Bibliography: p.
Includes index.
1. Carver, George Washington, 1864?-1943.
2. Agriculturists—United States—Biography.
I. Title.
S417.C3M3   630'.92'4 [B]   81-4896
ISBN 0-19-502971-2   AACR2

ISBN 0-19-503205-5 (pbk.)

All photographs courtesy of Tuskegee
Institute Archives

Printing (last digit): 9 8 7 6 5 4 3 2

Printed in the United States of America

To Mother,
for whom there were no silly questions,
and to Parie,
who reminded me of that.

Preface

George Washington Carver captured the imagination of the American people. The romance of his life story and the eccentricities of his personality led to his metamorphosis into a kind of folk saint both in his lifetime and after. He was readily appropriated by many diverse groups as a symbol for myriad causes. To Southern businessmen Carver was an incarnation of the New South philosophy. Religious leaders embraced the scientist's proclaimed reliance upon God as an inspirational source in an age of materialism. Those struggling through the depression saw Carver as a living Horatio Alger whose story offered hope to those who tried hard enough. To people concerned with race relations Carver's career was either proof of the ability and intelligence of Afro-Americans or an indication that slavery and segregation could not have been too bad if they produced a Carver. And to the general public puzzled by technology that was changing the world with frightening speed, Carver made science seem more human and understandable. Thus, segments of his life and personality were often highlighted and embellished in order to prove a point. The public image that emerged was of a kindly old "wizard," hardly offensive to any believer in the American dream.

Separating the real George Washington Carver from the symbolic portrayals of his life is difficult. Reality and mythology became blurred even within Carver's own mind, and his life did have mythic qualities. Yet Carver was more than a folk saint; he was a real person, with all the complexities and contradictions inherent in human nature, and these were exaggerated by the fact that he was black in a white America. In the end he won international fame for his efforts to find commercial uses for Southern resources and was proclaimed one of the world's greatest chemists. For a variety of reasons both the value of his discoveries and the significance of his role in revolutionizing the Southern economy were considerably inflated.

Carver did not actually assume the role of "creative chemist" until relatively late in his life. Even while still a child, Carver and those around him were aware that he possessed rare and unusual talents. He believed his talents had been given him for some special mission, and he spent many years wandering in search of his destiny. Had Carver been white, his choice of careers would probably have been different. If he had placed his personal desires above his sense of responsibility toward his fellow blacks, he most likely would have become either an artist or a botanist engaged in plant breeding or mycological research. When he accepted Booker T. Washington's offer to come to Tuskegee Institute in 1896, he unknowingly sacrificed these career alternatives but opened the door to his eventual fame.

For almost twenty years, however, Carver remained in the shadow of Washington at Tuskegee, devoting his life to a career of agricultural research and education. When Washington died in November 1915, Carver was in his fifties and had already made many of his significant contributions, but he was still largely unknown and dissatisfied with his life. To some degree this sense of failure was what propelled Carver toward the role of "creative chemist" and international fame after Washington's death.

Myth-making accelerated with Carver's rise to prominence and produced the Carver legend. As a result he became the Peanut Man, a stereotype of an accommodationist achiever that served many symbolic needs. Not only were his weaknesses and failures obscured, but also much of the significance of his vision and work.

All scholars owe large debts to those who preceded them. This is especially true in my case. Much of the Carver story would have been lost without the work of others, especially those at Tuskegee Institute and the National Park Service who interviewed many Carver contemporaries in the 1940s and 1950s. Their investigations into courthouse records and elsewhere saved me much time and effort. Likewise, my work was made easier by the project of microfilming the Carver Papers at Tuskegee, because a thorough search of numerous archives was made and copies of Carver materials were obtained during the course of the project.

I am also indebted to Lucy Cherry Crisp and Jessie P. Guzman, friends of Carver who did extensive research for biographies of the professor. Although their work was not published, their efforts were invaluable to me. Guzman's bibliography of Carver materials was especially helpful.

Published works have also been a great aid. The previous popular biographies of Carver were very helpful, although most were not cited. The two that are cited were written by people who had direct access to Carver or his close friends. Rackham Holt received the cooperation of both Carver and Austin Curtis, among others. Ethel Edwards's book was written in collaboration with Jim Hardwick and Willis D. Weatherford and thus was exceptionally useful on Carver's interracial work. Numerous other uncited monographs, regional histories, and articles were nonetheless essential to understanding Carver and his environment.

In my own research I received both courtesy and substantial aid from the dedicated archivists at the Library of Congress, Iowa State, Simpson College, the Carver National Monument, East Carolina University, the Michigan Historical Collections, and the University of North Carolina. Daniel T. Williams and Helen Dibble at Tuskegee Institute provided so much more than just professional service that I could never adequately express my thanks. Dozens of Carver contemporaries enriched my knowledge and understanding of the professor, although not all are cited. I am especially grateful to John Sutton and Howard Kester, who provided essential information that was not available elsewhere. Vital financial aid was given by Auburn University and Valdosta State College.

Among the numerous individuals who provided help and encouragement are John Blassingame, Pete Daniel, Jim Woodson, Timothy J. Sehr, Sarah Harrison, Mrs. Louis Harlan, Gordon Teffeteller, Raymond Smock, Ann Trice, and T. Albert Davis, as well as Sheldon Meyer and Susan Rabiner at Oxford University Press. My greatest debts are to Allen W. Jones and Richard M. McMurry, as both should be aware.

Contents

GEORGE WASHINGTON CARVER

— 1 —

Wandering in Search of a Destiny

Frederick Douglass once said, "Measure me not by the heights to which I have climbed but [by] the depths from which I have come." While Douglass's humble beginnings had indeed given him much to be proud of, his statement came to be used by turn-of-the-twentieth-century apologists, both black and white, to make a point Douglass had hardly intended. Putting off for later generations the politically fraught discussion of how far blacks might one day be allowed to go, public discussion of black achievement in the early years of the century centered around the more palatable recitation of how far some famous blacks had already traveled. Hence George Washington Carver's early life—how he had managed to climb out of slavery—became useful to those groups that eventually appropriated his story as confirmation of their own contention that blacks who were prepared to pay the price were not unduly deprived of opportunity.

The leading myth-maker in those years, supplying the public with portraits of Afro-Americans who succeeded despite the obstacles they faced, was Booker T. Washington, who wrote the first widely published account of Carver's childhood for his 1911 book, *My Larger Education*. Apparently more interested in using Carver's story to make particular points about the innate abilities of blacks and the value of hard work than in documenting the actual circumstances of Carver's early years, Washington wrote of Carver's childhood in the same directed prose that he had so successfully employed in his own biography, *Up From Slavery*. He noted that Carver "was born on the plantation of a Mr. Carver" and "was allowed to grow up among the chickens and other animals around the servants' quarters, getting his living as best he could." The impression was one of benign neglect by the master of a large plantation. In his later years Carver helped to perpetuate this false impression by continually referring to himself as "a poor defenceless orphan."[1]

Although these and later embellishments distorted the truth of Carver's origins, the real story is certainly grim enough. Southwest Missouri in the 1860s was hardly an auspicious place for the development of black genius. The area was just beginning to advance from its frontier stage. The land in Marion Township, where the Carver farm was located, was first offered for sale in 1843. By that time a few squatters from the East had already begun farming. Moses Carver and his brother, Richard, were among them, migrating to Missouri in about 1838 from Ohio and Illinois. The Preemption Act of 1841, which was passed to encourage small farmers to settle in the West, enabled a person who lived on and improved 160 acres of land for six months to buy it from the government at $1.25 an acre. Like most Western farmers, Moses Carver was not content with 160 acres and purchased a total of 240 acres soon after the land went on sale.[2]

As one of the first settlers, Carver was able to select a good site with an abundant water supply. Two springs and a creek lay near his house, and his acreage included both prairie and timberland. He constructed a rough one-room, hewn-log cabin with one window, one fireplace, and no floor. In this cabin he lived with his wife, Susan, as well as three nieces and nephews who were raised by Moses and Susan after his brother's death in 1839.

The years between 1840 and 1860 were profitable ones for the Carvers and for Newton County. Unlike the frontier areas of the Great Plains, Newton County had adequate water and a terrain suited to farming and livestock raising. During those twenty years the county's population grew from 2,790 to 9,319. With the increased settlement a typical "crossroads village" sprang up near a diamond-shaped grove of trees not far from the Carver farm. Called Diamond or Diamond Grove, the settlement consisted of a general store, a combination blacksmith shop and post office, and one interdenominational church that served as a schoolhouse during the week.[3]

In its first twenty years the Carver farm more than doubled in value. Its 1860 listed cash value of $3,000 was seventh highest in Marion Township. By that time Carver had improved 100 acres, planting mainly Indian corn and lesser amounts of wheat, oats, Irish potatoes, hay, and flax. In addition he had four milch cows, ten other head of cattle, eleven swine, three mules, and fifteen working oxen. He also had an orchard, beehives that produced 200 pounds of honey, and a personal vegetable garden. In other words, he was a relatively prosperous self-sufficient farmer, but certainly not a large planter.[4]

As Carver began to cultivate more of his land and diversify his crops, his need for labor increased. By 1860 his brother's three children were grown and out on their own. Earlier they had probably played the usual role of frontier children by providing a fair amount of labor. Carver soon took on a hired hand and, despite his reputed philosophical opposition to slavery, purchased a thirteen-year-old girl named Mary in 1855. Both Moses and Susan were in their forties and, like many frontier couples, had probably discovered the difficulty of hiring labor when land was still plentiful.

The distaste for buying another human being was lessened by the fact that the purchase was made directly from a neighbor. St. Louis, the nearest major slave market, was filled with the same degrading spectacle that other slave markets offered—the stripping and minute inspection of the "property" and the tears and pleadings of children torn from their parents and men and women separated from their spouses. Mary and Moses were spared that scene.[5]

The slave girl was also not destined for an impersonal life as chattel on a large plantation. Although a number of tobacco and cotton planters had moved to Missouri, having fled the soil deple-

Moses Carver, George Washington Carver's owner and foster father

tion of the upper South, most settled along the Missouri River. About two-thirds of the state's 114,931 slaves lived within twenty miles of the river. In 1860 Marion Township had only five slaveowners with a total of seventeen slaves, including Mary and her baby, Jim.[6]

In other ways the lives of Mary and her children were uncommon. Their owners were certainly not conventional in their attitude toward the "peculiar institution." Although the generation of Thomas Jefferson may have viewed slavery as a "necessary evil," by 1850 the profits from cotton and other cash crops, along with the rise of abolitionism, had converted most slaveowners to the

doctrine of slavery as "a positive good." Moses and Susan, however, remained committed in their basic opposition to slavery and
in their support of the Union all through the decade of rising tension that eventually culminated in the Civil War.

Other factors marked the Carvers as somewhat "different."
Their industriousness and relative prosperity won them the respect of their neighbors, but Moses, especially, was considered
eccentric. He was remembered as having an uncanny rapport with
animals; a pet rooster perched on his shoulders and squirrels ate
from his hand. This talent was put to good use by Moses in training and selling racehorses. He also refused to attend church, although his membership in the Masonic Order suggests that he was
not an atheist. Yet since the church was the center of most social
activities in Diamond, as in other small towns, Moses could easily
have been considered antisocial. The Carvers did like solitude and
built their cabin out of sight of the road. However, Moses was
friendly to visitors, especially children, often providing them with
a treat from his garden or his beehives. He also gladly played his
violin for neighbors, who remembered him as a "good fiddler."
Thus he was labeled "independent-minded" rather than aloof. Susan was considered less peculiar, but rather quiet, withdrawn, and
old-fashioned.[7]

The location of the Carver farm also provided both the black
and white Carvers with experiences different from those of their
counterparts in the older South. In addition to being a largely frontier region, southwest Missouri shared borders with three distinctly different regions. To the south was slaveowning, secessionist Arkansas, to the northwest "Free Kansas," and to the southwest
the Oklahoma Indian Territory. This site was significant in view of
the times.

With the victory for the slave-owning South that passage of the
Kansas-Nebraska Act in 1854 seemed to represent, the willingness
of abolitionist Northerners to continue to compromise on the issue
of the further expansion of slavery seemed to lessen significantly.
That act, which the South had vigorously supported, organized
what had been a vast Indian reservation into the two new territories of Kansas and Nebraska. In both, the issue of slavery was

to be determined by popular sovereignty, with the majority of settlers in the area making the decision. To ensure that their decision would be binding, the Kansas-Nebraska Act nullified the Missouri Compromise of 1820, which had forever banned slavery from the area included in the two new territories.

The hope of those Northerners who had supported the act was that it would appease then-current Southern fears about the booming population growth of the North, which had already brought with it reduced Southern influence in the House of Representatives and more frequent expression of antislavery sentiment. Determined to maintain rough equality in the Senate, the South sought passage of the act to insure that Southern votes would still be sufficient to block any future legislation that interfered with Southern "domestic institutions."

Unfortunately, neither side was willing to leave the Kansas matter to chance. Northerners formed emigration societies to encourage independent farmers to migrate to Kansas; slaveowning Missourians crossed the border to vote illegally in elections, and border warfare soon erupted. For the second time Missouri found itself in the middle of the slavery controversy, but this time debate erupted into violence. Indeed, some historians have described the era of "Bleeding Kansas" as the first stage of the civil war that officially began in 1861.

The tension was felt by everyone along the border, but must have been especially intense for people like Moses Carver who, as slaveowning Unionists, were caught in the middle. From 1854 to 1864 many slaveowners left the area, seeking a refuge for themselves and their "property." Moses Carver, however, was not easily intimidated. He stayed where he was and paid dearly for it during the war.

Although the Carvers were unconventional, in some ways they were quite typical of frontier slaveowners. The increasing prosperity of most early settlers could be measured by the number of progressively larger dwellings on their farm. When a new cabin was built, the older one often served as the slaves' quarters. Thus Mary lived in the original cabin and the Carvers moved into a slightly larger one. Even after Mary was gone and her children had moved into the "main cabin" with the Carvers, the slave cabin was kept as a guest house, probably for the numerous Carver kinfolk, especially those nieces and nephews the Carvers had raised. Moses Carver's reputation for being "tight with his money" is reflected in the fact that a more comfortable frame dwelling was not constructed until about 1890. At that time the two earlier cabins were dismantled so that the logs could be used for other purposes. Moses Carver did not believe in wasting anything.[8]

Frontier slaveowners were also notorious for being haphazard in their recording of slave births. Moses Carver was no exception. It is not even certain how many children Mary bore. There are shadowy references to twin girls who died in infancy, but the only child whose birthdate can be definitely established was Jim. Possibly he was the first child and thus the particulars of his birth were more clearly remembered. At any rate, when Jim died in 1883 during a smallpox epidemic in Seneca, Missouri, Moses provided a tombstone complete with a birthdate of 10 October 1859, which corresponds to the census records of 1860. Yet even for Jim the question of paternity remains unanswerable. Consistently listed as mulatto in census records, his father may have been white. However, any number of whites could qualify as potential fathers—neighbors, the Carver's twenty-two-year-old hired hand or, improbably, Moses Carver himself.[9]

George Washington Carver, on the other hand, suffered the fate of many slaves and, to a lesser extent, the fate of the second-born. Much less is remembered of George's birth. Possibly because he was born during the trying years of the Civil War, George was never certain of his birthdate. In his early manhood he consistently recalled that he was born "about 1865." On several occasions he noted that his birth came "near the end of the war" or "just as freedom was declared." Since Missouri was not in "a state of rebellion" at the time of the Emancipation Proclamation, slavery continued in that state until the implementation of a new constitution on 4 July 1865, a little over a month after the surrender of the Western Confederate forces on 26 May 1865. Although

Carver gave 1864 as his birth year in his later life, it seems likely that he was born in the spring of 1865.

As can be expected, the identity of George's father is also uncertain. He usually named his father as a slave on a neighboring farm who was killed in a log-hauling accident shortly after George was born. Some of George's friends believed that Moses Carver was the father of both boys. However, in contrast with Jim, George was listed as "negro" rather than "mulatto" in the 1870 census, and most of his contemporaries considered him "of pure African descent." If Jim and George had different fathers, this would not necessarily mean that Mary was promiscuous, however. In Missouri, as in other Southern states, slave marriages could not be legalized, and many slave women were victims of unsolicited white lust.[10]

At any rate, neither Mary nor George's father had much influence on his childhood: he never knew his father and his mother disappeared while he was still an infant. The circumstances of his separation from his mother were among the most publicized and romanticized portions of his early life. Dozens of writers recounted and embellished the kidnapping of George and Mary by slave-raiders. Such publicity tended to cloud the truth and warp the recollections of contemporaries. Nevertheless, considering the events of the day, the story appears to be basically true, despite the lack of confirmable details.

Certainly the western border of Missouri was the site of considerable guerrilla warfare and "bushwacker" activity from the time of the election of Abraham Lincoln in 1860 until months after Robert E. Lee's surrender in April 1865. During the rising tide of secessionism in and throughout the war, the people of Missouri were deeply divided in their allegiances. In Missouri, perhaps more than in any other state, the war was literally fought between brothers, and there were even Carvers on both sides. The Confederate states presumed that their sister slave state would join them in founding their new nation. However, between 1830 and 1860 European immigration into Missouri had greatly lessened the influence of the slaveowners, by cutting in half the ratio of slaves to free whites. The strength of Unionist sentiment should have been evident when Stephen A. Douglas carried the state in 1860. Nevertheless the secessionist faction refused to accept the state's 1861 decision to remain in the Union.

Led by Gov. Claiborne Jackson and supported by the Confederacy, the secessionists resorted to force against their fellow Missourians. Located between Unionist Kansas and Confederate Arkansas, southwest Missouri again became a bloody battlefield. Three major battles were fought in the region, and Neosho, the county seat of Newton County, was occupied at various times by both Confederate and Union armies. Indeed, although Neosho was basically a Unionist town, the Confederates briefly established a rebel government there which adopted an ordinance of secession. Throughout the war, area residents were prey to looting and killing by Confederate bushwackers, Union raiders, and ordinary outlaws taking advantage of the unsettled conditions.[11]

As a prosperous, slaveowning Unionist, Moses Carver was a natural target for such activities and appears to have been victimized by raiders on at least three occasions. Sometime during the fall or winter of 1863 a band of men rode onto the Carver farm and demanded all of Carver's money. Characteristically, he refused to reveal its location even after the raiders strung him up from a tree and put hot coals to his feet. Eventually, when searches and torture failed to uncover any money, the band left, but they later returned for a more successful raid. These incidents left Moses Carver with both scars and a distrust of people. Afterwards he kept his money buried in different places all over the farm.[12]

For the rest of that turbulent era Moses doubtless remained alert to any sign of approaching bushwackers. His fears came true near the end of the war when he heard the sound of approaching horses. There was only enough time for Moses and Jim to hide behind a brush pile before the raiders arrived. Mary and the infant George were not as fortunate and were kidnapped and taken into Confederate Arkansas. Mary and her children had become much more than property to both the Carvers and they wanted George and his mother back, even if their freedom was imminent. Fortu-

Carver as a
young boy

nately, a neighbor named John Bentley was in a position to help. As a Union scout stationed in Neosho, Bentley was familiar with the various guerrilla bands in the area and agreed to search for Mary and George. Moses Carver rewarded Bentley with a race-horse when he returned with George; Mary had either died or could not be found. The war was indeed costly to the Carvers.[13]

By the end of 1865 southwestern Missouri, like the rest of the nation, settled down to the tasks of rebuilding, restoring a peace-time economy, and learning to live with the fact of emancipation. Very few people in the war-torn states of the South emerged from the war without feeling its impact. Neither George nor Jim was old enough, however, to realize the momentous changes that were occurring in the nation. Most likely they did not even fully realize the drastic extent to which their own lives had been altered by the war. Freedom and orphanhood are difficult concepts for mere toddlers to understand.

For George, Moses and Susan became the only parents he could remember, as the childless Carvers once again assumed the burden of raising another's children. Moving the boys into the "main cabin" with them, Moses and Susan apparently treated them as blood kin. The Carvers were good parents, and George later recalled that they provided both love and guidance. Nevertheless, George seems to have felt an intense longing, one shared by many adopted children and slaves, to know more of his origins. As a child he pestered Susan to tell him about his mother, but he learned very little because she always started to cry when she talked of Mary. He frequently stood beside Mary's old spinning wheel, as if trying to feel the presence of the woman he could not remember. That spinning wheel and the bill of sale for Mary became two of his most prized possessions as an old man. It was probably unmet psychological needs, rather than physical ones, that led him in those years to refer to himself as "a poor defenceless orphan." The Carvers certainly tried to supply the needs of both boys.[14]

Eventually, of course, Moses and Susan reaped the benefit of the boys' labor as a reward for their efforts. In Jim's case that labor was substantial. He was a tall, robust, and husky youngster who very early assumed a number of chores and was listed as "hired labor" on the Carver farm in the 1880 census, three years before he died.

George, on the other hand, was a frail and sickly child. He suffered from a severe case of whooping cough and frequent bouts of what was called croup. It is possible, however, that his recurrent illness was misdiagnosed and was much more serious than croup. His stunted growth and apparently impaired vocal chords suggest instead tubercular or pneumococcal infection. Frequent infections of that nature could have caused the growth of polyps on the larynx and may have resulted from a gamma globulin deficiency. He sometimes recalled that he could barely talk and could "ride half-fare" until he was in his twenties. Although this was an exaggeration, until his death the high pitch of his voice startled all who met him, and he suffered from frequent chest congestion and loss of voice.

Another explanation has sometimes been given for Carver's high-pitched voice: there are persistent rumors that he was castrated as a boy. Sometimes the kidnappers were blamed for the mutilation, sometimes Moses Carver was named as the villain. Several factors make both versions unlikely. A person castrated before puberty almost never displays any secondary sexual characteristics and seldom grows to normal stature. While Carver's voice never deepened, he reached normal height and grew facial hair. The case against Moses is especially weak since it is doubtful that George would have retained his obvious affection for Moses if he had been responsible for such a deed. After he left Diamond he returned on several occasions to visit the Carvers, even after Susan's death.[15]

The castration story, however, cannot be entirely dismissed. In 1937 Carver, replying to a friend's queston as to why he had never married, referred obliquely to a tragic incident of his past that prevented his taking a wife. He was also very reluctant to discuss the years between his departure from Diamond and his arrival at Iowa State, often declaring that there were some things that he would rather forget. After puberty, castration or testicular failure due to accident or illness would not prevent the development of secondary sexual characteristics, which would explain his mustache. There are, however, numerous other ways to explain his failure to marry. If castration did occur, it provides one more tragic example of Carver's ability to overcome adversity.[16]

Although his terrible bouts of illness left George physically and perhaps emotionally scarred, his curiosity and zest for life were not diminished. His frailty exempted him from the more onerous chores around the farm and led to his being pampered by both Moses and Susan. He was given only light tasks, such as watering the stock and helping Susan with the housework. Otherwise he was allowed considerable freedom merely to be a boy. Hours were spent roaming the woods on the Carver farm, exploring anything unusual and stalking "wild game," usually of the reptile or insect variety. George carefully concealed these and other treasures in his pockets, to be secretly hoarded away in the Carver cabin. After a few unpleasant encounters with George's creatures, and with a milkweed pod that opened at an inopportune moment, Susan required George to empty his pockets at the doorstep. He then built a little pen outdoors for his frog collection and placed his geological finds in a pile next to the chimney. Sometimes the rock pile became too large for Susan's taste, and George would have to decide which treasures to sacrifice.[17]

His other favorite pastimes reflected his frontier childhood. There were few man-made toys, but nature provided rocks to throw, trees to climb, and water to swim in. He liked to fish, but never developed a taste for hunting after he accidentally hit a bird with a rock one day. Holding the bloody mass of feathers and bones in his hands horrified him so much that he remembered the incident the rest of his life. He nevertheless enjoyed the venison and other wild game Moses and Jim brought back to supplement their diet.[18]

Neighborhood children and the Carver's great-nieces and great-nephews provided playmates with which to engage in the age-old childhood games of chase and forfeits. Possibly because of the contrast between his own frailty and Jim's agility and strength, however, George never liked to join in athletic contests. He tended to be rather quiet and shy around other children, becoming easily embarrassed by teasing. Nevertheless he formed bonds of friendship with some of his white playmates so strong that he continued to correspond with them years after he left Diamond. George's acts of kindness, such as whittling crutches for a crippled friend, were fondly remembered decades later.[19]

Nighttime probably brought quiet family gatherings around the fireplace, maybe with music from Moses' violin. Bedtime usually came early on the farm, but George remembered one night when he and Jim furtively explored the world of darkness after the older

Carvers were asleep, only to be discovered by an irate Susan Carver. She wanted to give them both a "switching," but Moses intervened to save them. Later George could recall only one time that Moses resorted to corporal punishment. Both he and Jim received a thrashing for riding some sheep after having escaped punishment for the same offense earlier.[20]

In short, George's childhood was in many ways similar to those of his young white neighbors. Three factors did set him apart from them: his frailness, his genius, and his color. Almost from the beginning he was recognized as being "special." His curiosity seemed to run deeper than average and he quickly mastered whatever was taught him—from the alphabet to crocheting and music. He was especially noted for his ability to care for plants. In a little "nursery" in the woods he carefully transplanted and cultivated most of the native plants. Keen observation born of curiosity led George to an understanding of the needs of each plant and an ability to nurse sickly plants to health. This skill was widely appreciated in the neighborhood and caused him to be called the "plant doctor."[21]

The realization of his special talents probably came to young George before he was aware of the significance of his skin color. Scholars of slavery have noted that house servants and slaves on small plantations tended to internalize more of their masters' values and world view than did the field hands on large plantations. Undoubtedly this tendency was enhanced for Jim and George, considering their particular circumstances. Jim, it was later remembered, sought to become white and was told that the sweat of hard work would wash away his color.[22] Perhaps because he was so much darker, and brighter, George never expressed the desire to be white, but until his death Carver was described by many contemporaries as seeming "more at home" with whites than blacks. Certainly Carver displayed the kind of ambivalence to race that was typical of many educated blacks before the middle decades of the twentieth century. On one hand he rejected the validity of race as a category; on the other he expressed a solidarity with "his people."

Carver and brother Jim

At first, race probably did not seem important to George. His "parents" and his playmates were white. Plantation slaves have noted that they did not really realize their condition until about their tenth year; before then they were allowed to play freely with the masters' children. The same seems to be true for George and Jim. The little Locust Grove church, located about a mile from the Carver farm, opened its doors to both of them. There George received a rather eclectic religious training from a variety of Methodist, Baptist, Campbellite, and Presbyterian circuit preachers, thus acquiring an unorthodox and nondenominational faith that would sustain him for the rest of his life. Part of that faith was a deep belief in divine revelation. Later, when he recounted the numerous revelations he had received from "the Creator" in his laboratory, Carver often referred to his first revelation as a child. As he told it, he had a deep craving for a pocketknife and in a dream saw a vision of a half-eaten watermelon with a knife sticking in it. Early the next morning George eagerly rushed out to the place shown in his dream and claimed his pocketknife.[23]

Ironically, Carver's genius made him aware of racial prejudice. He hungered for more knowledge than the Carvers' old blue-back speller could give. Therefore he and his brother enrolled in the school that met during the week in the same church they attended on Sundays. Apparently they were allowed to enter at first, which would not have been unusual; although teaching slaves to read and write was illegal in antebellum Missouri, after the war a liberal element gained control of the government and attempted to "reconstruct" Missouri by introducing, among other things, free public education. Significantly, the constitution of 1865 made the provision of free schools mandatory for blacks but not whites. Each township was required to furnish a school if it contained more than twenty blacks of school age, which was defined as age five to twenty. Many townships, like Marion, lacked the specified number of black children. With no legal barriers to mixed schools, some allowed blacks to attend white schools. Often, however, local whites demanded the ouster of the black children, and the whites of Diamond were among them. George and Jim soon found the doors that opened for them on Sunday were closed to them during the week.[24]

Their rejection not only taught young George a lesson about the irrationality of racial prejudice, but it also frustrated his attempts to get an education. Neither Susan nor Moses had enough education themselves to answer the multitude of questions that formed in the mind of the precocious child, as George later recalled.

I wanted to know the name of every stone and flower and insect and bird and beast. I wanted to know where it got its color, where it got its life—but there was no one to tell me. I do not know how I learned to read and write, but I did in some way, thanks to the

Carvers. My only book was an old Webster's Elementary Spelling Book. I knew it almost by heart. I sought the answers to my questions from the spelling book, but all in vain.[25]

With the arrival in Diamond in 1876 of a young educated man named Steven Slane, George was privately tutored for a while, but soon the pupil's desire for knowledge outstripped the teacher's ability to supply it. Fortunately there was a school for blacks at the county seat in Neosho, about eight miles from Diamond. As soon as George was old enough to venture out on his own, the Carvers allowed him to move to Neosho and begin his long and often frustrating search for an education. When he left Diamond about 1877, young Carver could not have been much older than twelve. Although he continued to return home on weekends, he never again made his permanent home with Moses and Susan.[26]

In studying the formation of adult personality and character, psychologists generally view a person's early years as a critical period. In Carver's case, clearly, the years at Diamond had been formative. Most of his later interests and values were rooted in his childhood here. From the beautiful terrain of the Carver farm he had acquired a love and understanding of nature, as well as a need for the solitude of the forest; both remained with him the rest of his life. Later in life, his predawn ramblings in the woods would become legendary. From the people of the community he had been bequeathed a mixed legacy. They had led him to the faith that would mold his life and give him a sense of his "specialness," but they had also introduced him to the inhumanity and irrationality of racial prejudice. Finally, his own particular talents and handicaps must have had a significant psychological impact. He was black, gifted, sickly, and orphaned—a unique combination in that frontier town.

His most important formative influence, however, was probably his relationship with Moses and Susan. Not only were they white, but their ages were more appropriate for grandparents than parents. Because of his illness, both pampered George and he was given freedom and encouragement to develop his special talents. His frailty also placed him more directly under the influence of

Susan, who apparently became his most significant role model, teaching him the "womanly" skills of sewing, cooking, laundering, and needlework. Throughout his youth and early manhood, Carver's closest friends were usually older women. Traces of Moses' influence, however, can be seen in George's love of music and his disgust at "wastefulness." More important, Moses' example showed him that a person need not fear being different. Even before he left Diamond, the contours of Carver's life could be glimpsed.

When Carver arrived in Neosho, he entered a predominantly black environment for the first time and acquired his first set of black "parents." Mariah and Andrew Watkins allowed Carver to live with them in their modest three-room frame house in return for helping with the chores. Mariah Watkins was a midwife and nurse with a good knowledge of medicinal herbs. Her skills and deeply religious nature earned her the respect and affection of the white community—a fact undoubtedly noted by the observant young George. His character was shaped by her stern insistence that time should not be wasted. She was a demanding woman, and Carver was remembered running to the Watkins house during the school recess both to do laundry chores and to study. She also further diversified Carver's religious perspective by taking him to the African Methodist Episcopal church, a denomination that had rapidly spread southward during Reconstruction as blacks attempted to control all aspects of their lives, including religious expression.[27]

Carver was willing to work hard for an education, but he soon discovered that his goal was more elusive than he had expected. He was probably filled with eager anticipation as he stepped through the door of the one-room schoolhouse for the first time and met his teacher, Stephan Frost. Disillusionment came rather quickly, however, as he learned that Frost knew little more than he did. Frost could hardly be blamed for his lack of preparation, since no provision had been made for black education prior to the war. In the early stages of Reconstruction white teachers were supplied through the efforts of Northern church and philanthropic groups, the Freedmen's Bureau, and local governments. By the mid-1870s, however, Northerners grew tired of trying to remake the South and local whites began rejecting teaching positions in black schools. Further contributing to the problem was the large number of blacks who flocked to the new free public schools, making the scarcity of qualified teachers acute. Missouri was ahead of most Southern states in the area of black education, but the per-student expenditures were less than those for whites, which necessitated lower teacher salaries, shorter school terms, and few provisions for higher education. There was only one black public high school in the entire state, and Lincoln Institute was the only normal school for the training of teachers. The two institutions could not produce enough teachers to meet the demand.[28]

Although Jim, who briefly attended Frost's school, was satisfied with basic literacy, George was not. When he learned of a family moving to Fort Scott, Kansas, in the late 1870s, he hitched a ride and began the second phase of his quest for knowledge. Knowingly or not, Carver became part of the great black migration to Free Kansas. Blacks from all over the South were growing disillusioned with their opportunities at home. Migrationists such as "Pap" Singleton beguiled them with glowing reports of conditions in the "home of John Brown," and they migrated to Kansas in droves, raising the black population there from 17,000 in 1870 to 43,000 in 1880.

Their numbers were far greater than those of available jobs, and they soon learned, like their earlier white counterparts, that most of Kansas was not a fertile plain but a dry, barren, treeless expanse. At first Gov. John P. St. John tried to alleviate conditions by establishing the Kansas Freedmen's Relief Association. Most Kansans, however, were no more lofty in their racial attitudes than their fellow Midwesterners. The fact that it was a "free soil" state did not necessarily mean that Kansas welcomed black Kansans.

In fact, until after the war Kansas blacks were not allowed to vote or to attend white schools. Indeed, during the bloody struggle to determine the status of slavery in the territory, the majority of both the proslavery and antislavery factions favored excluding free blacks from the state. After statehood was granted in 1861, the heated issue of Negro exclusion melted away only because of the realization that the mere 625 free blacks in Kansas were hardly a threat. The Civil War and the spirit of Reconstruction which produced the Thirteenth, Fourteenth, and Fifteenth Amendments brought some liberalization of racial policy in the Midwest. In Kansas discriminatory legislation began to disappear and black suffrage was allowed. Yet antiblack prejudice still seethed beneath a thin crust of tolerance, and the hordes of black immigrants created cracks in that crust.[29]

As he rode in the back of the wagon along the seventy-five-mile journey to Fort Scott, the teenage Carver was probably unaware of the depth of Kansas prejudice and no doubt daydreamed about the new life he faced. When they arrived in Fort Scott, Carver soon found that the skills he acquired from Susan were very useful in a tight labor market. As he later recalled, "I found employment just as a girl." In exchange for doing the cooking and other chores, he moved in with the family of Felix Payne, a blacksmith. He also found an assortment of odd jobs, working at the Stadden grocery across the street from the Payne house and doing laundry work for the patrons of the Wilder House hotel, the only brick building in town.[30]

Whether or not Carver found his elusive goal of good educational facilities in Fort Scott is unknown. What is certain is that the lesson he remembered had little to do with books. In 1856 a proslavery raid against the detested John Brown had been planned and launched from Fort Scott. Twenty years later the town was still "peopled by the most uncompromising rebels." Although Carver had already encountered prejudice, he was unprepared for what he witnessed on the night of 26 March 1879. At noon that day a black man accused of raping a twelve-year-old white girl was found in an abandoned coal mine and brought to the county jail. Soon after sundown a crowd of about a thousand gathered to watch thirty masked men remove the prisoner, tie a rope around his neck, drag him five blocks, hang him from a lamp post, and then roast him over a fire of dry-goods boxes and coal oil.[31]

Kansas had become accustomed to vigilante action during the frontier era; for many whites lynching was rapidly becoming an acceptable means of controlling the ex-slaves. Even "respected" citizens often condoned the actions of the rabble. As the editor of the Fort Scott *Daily News* noted, "Had this been done quietly . . . no one could have been found to censure, but the unnecessary savagery of burning could well have been omitted." If whites viewed lynching as an act of chivalry, blacks were usually aware that the impunity with which such actions were undertaken by whites against blacks also provided an object lesson in white supremacy. After such occurrences the black population of most towns made itself as invisible as possible. For Carver the shelter of his home was inadequate; he left Fort Scott immediately. "As young as I was," Carver declared over sixty years later, "the horror haunted me and does even now."[32]

Running from that horror, Carver moved to Olathe, Kansas, and entered school at midterm. About fifteen at the time, he had blossomed into a tall, lanky young man who only reluctantly joined in games at recess, preferring to use the free time to examine plants and rocks. He made his home with his second set of black parents, Lucy and Ben Seymour, helping Lucy with her laundry business. In addition he did other odd jobs, shined shoes, and cooked for the family of Jerry Johnson, a barber. On Sundays he taught a class at the Methodist church.[33]

After about a year the Seymours migrated to Minneapolis, Kansas, and Carver moved in with the Richard Moore family in nearby Paola until he followed the Seymours to Minneapolis during the summer of 1880. In late July he borrowed $43.00 from a local Minneapolis bank; by December the loan amount had increased to $156.45. Most likely he used this money to establish the laundry business that he opened in a small shack in a ravine popularly known as Poverty Gulch. For at least part of his four years at Minneapolis he lived with the Seymours. At this time Ben Seymour was farming and Lucy Seymour was nursing patients of Dr. James McHenry, for whom Carver also did odd jobs. McHenry was evidently impressed by the young Carver and lent him books.[34]

The years in predominantly white Minneapolis appear to have been happy and prosperous ones for Carver. He entered the four-room, two-story school, where he impressed his white classmates with his knowledge of history and other subjects. His teacher, Helen Eacker, greatly encouraged him in his studies, and when he left he gave her a gold pin. As was typical of Carver all his life, he became friendly with a number of whites, especially Chester Rarig, often eating Sunday dinner with the Rarig family. He also continued to display diverse talents and to maintain his earlier religious commitment. He painted, crocheted, "fooled around with weeds," and played the mouth harp and accordion at school programs. In July 1883 he was admitted by examination into the Presbyterian church the Seymours attended. Like his other "black mother," Lucy was a very religious and respected person.[35]

In January 1884 Carver purchased two lots of land for $100. A little over ten months later he sold the property for $500 and moved to Kansas City. There he procured a typewriter and a job as clerk at the Union Depot. He also learned another lesson in racial etiquette. One morning he and Chester Rarig went to a large restaurant for breakfast. After they sat down at a long counter, a waiter approached Rarig and announced that he could be served, but his friend could not. They both left the restaurant, but Carver urged his friend to return, saying, "I'll find my breakfast all right." In years to come this scene was reenacted with only minor changes in detail on numerous occasions. Every time Carver seemed to be more embarrassed for his white friends than for himself.[36]

His next encounter with racial prejudice was more painful and costly. He still longed for more education and learned of a small Presbyterian college in Highland, Kansas. After being accepted by mail, he arrived at the school only to discover that it did not accept blacks. He was keenly disappointed and did not even try to enter any school for the rest of that decade.[37]

For about a year Carver remained in Highland and worked for a white family named Beeler, keeping house and doing the laundry. One of the Beeler sons had gone to the newly settled Ness County on the western plains of Kansas, where he opened a store.

The small settlement that grew up around the store came to be called Beeler. The new town seemed to offer great opportunities to young men, so in the summer of 1886 Carver followed Frank Beeler to Ness County and found employment helping a white settler named George H. Steeley.[38]

When Carver arrived, the area was still part of the "sod house frontier." Settlement had begun in the late 1870s, but many had become discouraged and left Beeler before the second great wave of settlers, probably attracted to the area by the building of railroads and the establishment of towns, arrived in the 1880s. Under the terms of the Homestead Act of 1862 a settler could file a claim at the nearest land office for 160 acres of land held by the government under public domain. After five years of residence the purchaser could obtain full title to the land by paying a $24 filing fee. Many settlers, however, were too impatient to wait five years and instead bought their land for $1.25 an acre under the provisions of the earlier Pre-emption Act. Some sold relinquishments to their claim before even securing final title and most claims changed hands several times before permanent settlement was made.[39]

George Carver proved to be a typical settler in almost every way but color. In August 1886 he bought a relinquishment on a quarter section of land south of Beeler. He continued to live with and work for Steeley while he constructed his own dwelling. Lacking native timber on his claim, like most plains settlers, he built a sod house. Such houses were constructed of bricks cut from thick, strong sod from low spots on the prairie. Carver's house was a little smaller than average—only fourteen feet square. When the walls reached the right height, he put in a window and a door and constructed a framed roof over which he placed tar paper and a layer of sod. The walls of sod houses were usually three feet thick and plastered with clay. This made the houses warm in the winter and cool in the summer, but they were also very dark and prone to insect invasions.[40]

Carver's house was completed on 18 April 1887, and two days later he moved in with only a cookstove, bedstead, bed, cupboard, chairs, table, and laundry equipment for furnishings. He had solved one of the three major problems on the plains—the lack of wood. He still had to face the other two: the lack of water and the frequency of extreme weather, ranging from burning droughts to crippling blizzards. He managed to survive a blizzard that struck in the middle of January 1888 and killed over two hundred people along its wide swath from Texas to Canada. On the matter of water he was not as lucky. He tried digging a well in several places but never found water, and had to rely on Steeley's spring about three-fourths of a mile away.

Carver also depended on Steeley for many of his farming implements, since he owned only a spade, a hoe, and a corn planter. Breaking seventeen acres of land, he planted ten in corn, vegetables, and rice corn. He also set out a number of trees and purchased ten hens. His only taxable personal property consisted of his accordion and a silver watch, each valued at five dollars. His 160 acres and homestead may not have amounted to very much, but it was more than he had ever owned before.[41]

The grimness of the frontier usually created a spirit of communal help and friendship among settlers that sometimes partially erased racial barriers. Carver was one of only a handful of blacks in the immediate area. For some reason he always seemed to gravitate toward places with few blacks; there were several black enclaves in the state, but Carver never lived in any of them. In Beeler, as in Minneapolis, his talents and personality soon won him the respect of his white neighbors. Indeed, on the frontier he appeared even more remarkable to those around him and was widely considered to be the best-educated person in the area. He developed an interest in art, taking his first lessons from Clara Duncan, a black woman who had taught at Talladega College in Alabama and later became a missionary for the African Methodist Episcopal church. He also played his accordion for local dances and joined the Ness City literary society, which met weekly for plays, music, and debates. Carver participated in these activities and was elected assistant editor of the group.[42]

The whites of Ness County clearly recognized Carver's "specialness." One later remarked, "When I was in the presence of that young man Carver, as a white man, of the supposed dominant race, I was humiliated by my own inadequacy of knowledge, compared to his." Of interest, the first "embroidered" version of Carver's past appeared in the Ness County *News* in March 1888. The newspaper's brief account of his life included an inaccurate reference to his being a college junior. Why Carver claimed to be more educated than he really was is unclear, since the truth would have made the accomplishments described in the rest of the article even more extraordinary. Noting that his knowledge of "geology, botany and kindred sciences is remarkable, and mark him as a man of more than ordinary ability," the author of the article also discussed Carver's varied talents, including his sketches of "considerable merit" and his large geological collection. Most significant in view of his later career was the mention of his "collection of about five hundred plants in a neat conservatory adjoining the residence of his employer." In conclusion the writer remarked, "He is a pleasant and intelligent man to talk with, and were it not for his dusky skin—no fault of his—he might occupy a different sphere to which his ability would otherwise entitle him."[43]

Probably Carver's desire to "occupy a different sphere" is what led him to continue his wanderings. In June 1888 he borrowed $300 with his land as collateral and paid $200 to secure final title to the land. Soon afterwards he left Ness County, but did not give up his land there until 1891, when he evidently was having difficulty keeping up his loan payments and deeded over the land to his creditor.[44]

His experience in search of an education had already developed in him diverse skills and interests. From his childhood on the Carver farm and his homesteading adventure, he learned many practices of good, self-sufficient farming. Susan Carver, Mariah Watkins, and Lucy Seymour taught him such household skills as cooking, sewing, needlework, and laundering. His curiosity, intuitive grasp, and haphazard education combined to give him a remarkable understanding of natural processes, and he had developed a considerable love of music and art, with some degree of skill at both. Running through all his experiences was a growing religious faith that sustained him and opened the door to several long-lived friendships.

His restless searching brought Carver to Winterset, Iowa sometime between 1888 and 1890. In Winterset he worked at the St. Nicholas Hotel and later opened a laundry. As usual, he became a regular attendant of the local churches. At one church he met a white couple named Milholland. From this acquaintance he at last reacquired a sense of direction in his life, for Dr. and Mrs. Milholland were impressed with Carver's artistic abilities and persuaded him to enter Simpson College, twenty miles away in Indianola, Iowa. On 9 September 1890 he enrolled as a select preparatory student—an indication that despite his accomplishments he had not yet earned a high school diploma.[45]

Simpson College was an ideal place for Carver to resume his quest for an education. It was a small Methodist college with an open-door policy for all ethnic groups. The one black who preceded Carver was already gone by 1890, but there were three Asian students still on campus. The school's religious affiliation provided an environment in which Carver's faith and piety would win respect. As in most church schools, a variety of chapel services were required for all students. Carver eagerly participated in these and in other nonrequired religious activities.[46]

His studies included grammar, arithmetic, art, essay writing, etymology, voice, and piano. More important than any academic subject, however, was a spirit of acceptance that increased his self-confidence. "They made me believe I was a real human being," he noted. One classmate recalled that "in young Carver, as we came to know him, we saw so much beyond the color that we soon ceased to sense it at all," and the surviving information on Carver's career at Simpson College seems to support that assertion. Although he stayed in Indianola for less than a year, he entered into campus life, played ball with the boys, and so won the hearts of the students that they sent him a bouquet of flowers when he later graduated from Iowa State. As usual, however, he was very careful not to cause his white friends any embarrassment. One female classmate remembered how Carver would cross to the other side

Carver in art class at Simpson College

of the street when he saw any of the girls with strangers, so that they would not have to speak to him.[47]

Carver, as always, had to earn the money for his living and educational expenses. He later recalled that when he had paid his college fees, he had only ten cents remaining, with which he bought cornmeal and suet to nourish himself. Whether or not his circumstances were ever that desperate, he soon found a small shack to live in and opened another laundry. When students brought him their dirty clothes, they often stayed to converse. One student remembered, "He had no furniture so we sat on boxes the merchants in town had permitted him to take. I saw the old battered and broken cookstove which he had retrieved from a dump, and the boiler and wash tubs which he had secured on credit." Eventually the students decided to do something about Carver's living conditions. They took up a collection and bought a table, chairs, and a bed, which they placed in his shack while he was away. Later, they also slipped concert tickets and money under his door. No one would ever let on to Carver his or her role in these kind acts.[48]

Carver with one of his paintings

Carver not only made friends on campus, but also became well acquainted with a number of the townspeople. The most significant of these friendships was with W. A. Liston and his wife, the white operators of the local bookstore. Carver spent many hours studying in the bay window of the Liston home. Mrs. Liston, who was also interested in art, adopted Carver as an unofficial member of the family, continuing to call herself "your mother" in the letters she wrote to Carver until her death. She and Carver became very close and shared many interests and outlooks, including a mystical religious orientation that later led her to adopt the Christian Science faith.[49]

Carver had come to Simpson College primarily to study art, and therefore enrolled in Miss Etta Budd's art class. A recent college graduate, Miss Budd was at first dubious of both Carver's artistic abilities and his acceptability to the other students in the all-female art department. His ambition won her over, however, and she soon discovered that "painting was in him" and "was natural for him." Doubts remained in her mind, however, as to whether a black man could make a living as an artist. In addition to his elaborate needlework, Carver sometimes brought plants for her to see that he had cross-fertilized or grafted. When she learned of his love for plants, she encouraged him to pursue a career in botany and suggested that he enroll at Iowa State, the agricultural college at Ames, Iowa where her father, J. L. Budd, was a professor of horticulture.[50]

Her suggestion undoubtedly posed a dilemma for Carver. He loved his work as an artist and was reluctant to put it behind him. But he was over twenty-five years old, and a career in art promised neither immediate personal security nor an opportunity to make a contribution to black welfare. He had already begun to believe that his God-given talents were meant to be used in the elevation of "his people." By becoming a trained agriculturist, he could obviously be of tremendous service, even if he made agriculture only a temporary career.

The decision to leave the security and acceptance he had found at Simpson and to face the unknown once again was difficult for Carver. He had wandered long enough. His journeys had brought valuable experiences and many close friendships, but he had also encountered the dehumanizing force of racism. When Carver left for Ames in 1891, he had no idea what lay ahead. He did not realize that his career at Iowa State would soon bring an end to his restless wandering.

To Be of the Greatest Good

By 1891 Iowa State College of Agriculture and Mechanic Arts had become a leading center of agricultural education and research. Farming had not originally been considered an academic subject, but the establishment of land-grant colleges by the Morrill Act of 1862 gave impetus to the evolution of scientific agriculture. The increasingly national and international nature of the economy, as well as the decreasing fertility of the soil, convinced many farmers of the need for new methods of farming. Individual and group efforts proved insufficient to remedy the ills of agriculture, and farmers began to turn toward the government for answers. After the Civil War, which marked a turning point in the expansion of the activities of the federal government, farmers received a sympathetic hearing in Washington. Both state and federal governments took a larger role in agricultural education and research. The establishment of the United States Department of Agriculture in 1862, the passage of the Hatch Act in 1887 to provide funds for agricultural experiment stations, and the expansion of land-grant appropriations with the second Morrill Act of 1890 meant that agriculture had become a recognized scientific discipline, but one still in its infancy.

Iowa was the first state to accept the provisions of the original Morrill Act, and Iowa State College had an agricultural research program eight years before the passage of the Hatch Act. The faculty in 1891 included men of widely recognized ability, many of whom later left for distinguished careers with the federal government. Three of the nation's secretaries of agriculture in the first four decades of the twentieth century—James Wilson, Henry C. Wallace, and Henry A. Wallace—came from Iowa State. The presence of such men enabled Carver to receive a superior training in agriculture that later proved providential to his career and to Tuskegee Institute.[1]

Despite Iowa State's credentials, Carver may have regretted leaving Simpson College when he arrived. As the only black on the Ames campus, his initial reception was less than warm. On his first day a group of boys shouted derogatory names at him. Living accommodations also proved to be an embarrassment until some of the faculty provided him a room in an old office. Then the dining hall manager made him eat with the help in the basement. Discouraged, Carver wrote Mrs. Liston of his problems. As she later remembered, "I immediately put on my best dress and hat and took the train for Ames." After eating with him in the basement, she "walked out all over the campus with Carver, and stayed with him all evening." He later told her, "The next day everything was different, the ice was broken, and from that on, things went very much easier."[2]

As always, Carver paid his way by doing menial jobs on campus and in town, as well as making and selling lye hominy. Seeking to stretch his meager income, he made some of his clothes and for a time cooked his own meals. His diet was supplemented with wild plants, mushrooms, and banquet leftovers supplied by a cook at the college. He gratefully accepted others' discards, and one student recalled that Carver "would cut up and save used wrapping paper and his classmates would turn their stub pencils over to him for the purpose of his notes in classroom work." At the same time Carver compiled an excellent academic record. Disliking both history and mathematics, he nevertheless struggled through those courses without earning less than a 3.0 average out of a possible 4.0. In botany and horticulture, his favorite subjects, his grades ranged from 3.9 to 4.0. It is interesting to note, in view of his later career, that Carver took only four required chemistry courses and compiled a creditable, but not outstanding, 3.75 average in chemistry. The more practical agricultural courses also did not seem to appeal to him, though he never earned below a 3.20 in any of them. He was remembered by his classmates as the outstanding botany student on campus, but only a little better than average in other courses.[3]

Religion continued to play a significant role in Carver's life and once again helped break down barriers. Soon after his arrival on campus, he and several other students held prayer meetings following the lights-out bell. The number of participants increased until several groups were formed. James Wilson, who had arrived in Ames the same year as Carver to be the director of the Iowa Agricultural Experiment Station, was a devout Christian, so Carver's group began meeting with him in his office on Wednesday nights. The purpose of the meetings, in the words of one participant, was "to pour out to God in prayer our problems, our needs, our hopes, for help." Later some of the same students formed a missionary society.[4]

Religion created a strong bond between Carver and Wilson. "I have been more intimate with Mr. Carver than with any other student on campus," said Wilson, who recalled:

> . . . when students began to come in at the beginning of a new term, Carver and I would sit down and plan how to get boys who were Christians to go down to the depot to meet them, come up with them and help them get registered, help them get rooms, and all that which would establish acquaintance with them and enable young men of Christian leanings to get them into prayer meetings, etc.[5]

Carver was active in the campus Young Mens' Christian Association, serving as missionary chairman for at least two years. In 1893 and 1894 he was selected as a delegate from the campus to the National Students' Summer School at Lake Geneva, Wisconsin. James Wilson and others contributed to a fund to pay the student delegates' expenses. At the conference Carver, the only black delegate, made quite an impression by conducting botany hikes for students from other colleges. A fellow delegate from Iowa State recalled that Carver "had an old metal specimen can, a long tin oval box with hinged cover and a shoulder strap for carrying it, and he was never without it." Not everyone, however, was favorably impressed by Carver's presence. Willis D. Weatherford, who eventually became Carver's friend and coworker for better race relations, later remembered "those of us from the South thought it a little queer that there should be a Negro delegate present."[6]

Carver participated in secular campus activities, too. He helped organize an Agricultural Society, wrote the class poem, drew the class picture, and was a member of the Welsh Eclectic Society, a debating club, as well as the German Club and Art Club. He rose to the rank of captain and was made quartermaster in the school's military division. Though not very athletic, Carver became the first trainer and "rubber," or masseur, for the Iowa State football team. To raise funds for the athletic program various shows were presented, and Carver performed a number of stunts, including a balancing act that involved a hoop and a glass of water.[7]

Carver gladly shared his diverse talents with his fellow students. He played the guitar at Welsh Eclectic Society meetings and gave lessons to a classmate. His horticultural abilities were put to use in creating decorations for the society's banquets, and one student noted how "with the aid of some vines and autumn leaves he transformed the room beyond recognition." In addition, he frequently gave dramatic and humorous readings at the club's meetings. Two favorites were his comic reenactment of "How Rubenstein Played" and a reading depicting a farm scene in which the "calls of the shepherd boy and the caressing language of the milkmaid were imitated in a masterly manner." He did not neglect his art either; he sometimes went on sketching trips, and presented a number of faculty members and students with his paintings.[8]

Because of his wide-ranging abilities and warm personality, Carver was affectionately called "Doctor" by the other students and was well accepted by them as a member of the student body. Many made special efforts to include him in their activities. He

Carver dressed for a role in a play at Iowa State

received a personal invitation to a senior banquet from students who were afraid he would be reluctant to attend. Students also defended Carver when he was refused service at the Highland Park Methodist Episcopal eating house and were enraged when he was heckled and called a "nigger" while serving as part of the Iowa State military escort to the governor at the World's Fair.[9] One student vividly remembered a graphic display of support for Carver.

After Carver became a teacher at Ames, he frequently took his meals with the students rather than with the faculty. He was a great favorite with the students. One day he brought his tray to a table where a student recently come from the South was eating. This student did not relish the idea of eating with a negro, so he expressed his dissatisfaction by rattling his cutlery, scraping his chair etc. and finally gathered up his tray with his provisions and went to an adjoining table. The students at that table had been watching. So when the Southerner came to their table, they rattled their cutlery, scraped their chairs and gathered their trays and went to the table where Carver was sitting.[10]

Although most students tried to protect Carver from racial discrimination, they were reluctant to erase one color line: Carver was expected to refrain from any activity that resembled courtship. In their handling of this taboo, however, the students proved remarkably adept and kind. On one occasion, during Carver's undergraduate days, the all-male Welsh Eclectic Society joined with a women's literary club to give a banquet in honor of the governor of Iowa. For the affair each of the men was assigned to escort one of the young women. To overcome the problem of whom Carver should escort, he was given the honor of accompanying the governor.[11]

To most of the students Carver appeared quiet, unassuming, and gentlemanly, if somewhat eccentric because of his habits of wandering through the woods before breakfast, of always wearing a flower in his lapel, and of speaking in a high-pitched, effeminate voice. With a few students, however, he let down the barriers of restraint and dignity and engaged in boisterous horseplay and footraces across campus.[12] After Carver left Ames, one student wrote:

I often look back upon those miserable days when you bossed us around, and wonder how I ever lived through it. Do you remember the time you chased me all around the backyard with a great butcher knife which you pretended to use in digging up plants? If you had ever caught me and severed my juglar vein with that monstrous weapon, I never would have forgiven you. I hope you have reformed and turned over a new leaf ere this, and no longer chase defenceless Freshmen around with knives.[13]

As at Simpson College, the affection Carver won from members of the campus was expressed in their desire to help him participate in activities which he was unable to afford on his limited budget. In December 1892 an exhibit of the paintings of Iowa artists was held in Cedar Rapids. Several people encouraged Carver to enter a few of his works in the show, but he insisted that the trip would be too expensive. A group of students then practically kidnapped Carver, took him to a store, bought him a new suit, and handed him a ticket to Cedar Rapids. Their efforts were rewarded when Carver's "Yucca and Cactus" was one of the paintings selected to represent Iowa at the World's Columbian Exposition in Chicago.[14]

In addition to his other activities, Carver engaged in scholarly pursuits. While still an undergraduate, he published an article entitled "Grafting the Cacti" in the *Transactions* of the Iowa Horticulture Society. This 1893 article expressed a philosophy espoused by Carver the rest of his life.

> The earnest student has already learned that nature does not expend its forces upon waste material, but that each created thing is an indispensable factor of the great whole, and one in which no other factor will fit exactly as well.
>
> Now the cacti is [*sic*] one of those factors, with doubtless their widest range of usefulness as yet locked up within them waiting for the kindly hand of man, prompted by the necessities of the age, to wave his magic wand over them that they may show forth their long hidden usefulness . . .[15]

During his senior year, Carver presented a paper on "Best Bulbs for the Amateur" at the annual meeting of the Iowa Horticulture Society. In his bachelor's thesis, "Plants as Modified by Man," Carver described the work done by himself and others in grafting and cross-breeding such plants as plum trees, geraniums, and amaryllis to improve their fruit, vigor, or appearance. He noted that "man is simply nature's agent or employee to assist her in her work" and to bring order to the random processes of nature. In his rambling conclusion Carver blended his reverence for nature with his artistic temperament.

Why should not the horticulturist know just how to build up size, flavor, vigor and hardiness in his fruits and shrubs, and the florist know just how to blende [sic] and perfect the color of his flowers, producing not only harmony, but a glorious symphony of nature's daintiest tints and shades, with just as much certainty as the artist mixes his pigments upon the palette, and the novice go on with his new creations until nature refuses to indulge him any longer?[16]

The practice of hybridization to enhance the desirable features of plants eventually helped create the "green revolution" by producing incredibly high-yielding crops that were resistant to disease and drought. In the 1890s, however, scientific alteration of the genetic properties of plants was a relatively new field, based upon the discoveries of Charles Darwin and Gregor Mendel during the 1860s and 1870s. Not until about 1900 was the importance of Mendel's work in heredity widely accepted. The public was still suspicious of scientific "meddling" with the forces of nature, and this attitude might explain the defensive tone in the conclusion of Carver's thesis.

Carver's ability to raise, cross-fertilize, and graft plants won him the respect of the faculty. One professor noted that Carver was called the "green thumb boy" and had a natural instinct for plants. Thus at the end of his senior year Carver was persuaded to pursue postgraduate work and was appointed to the college faculty as an assistant in botany. Placed in charge of the greenhouse, he was freed from constantly seeking menial jobs to support himself. His greenhouse work also sustained his interest in horticulture, and he contributed two horticultural articles entitled "Best Ferns for the North and Northwest" and "Our Window Gardens" to Iowa's Agricultural Experiment Station bulletins.[17]

For his postgraduate work Carver was assigned to L. H. Pammel, a noted authority on mycology. Under Pammel's influence, Carver developed a life-long interest and expertise in the study of fungi and plant diseases. Although recognition and classification of fungi and other plant diseases dated back to the eighteenth century, mycology as a scientific field was established by the work of two Germans, Anton de Bary and Julius Kuhn, in the second half of the nineteenth century. Thus Carver's second major area of interest was also a relatively new branch of science. Both hybridization and mycology were still largely in the experimental stages and the major breakthroughs which revolutionized agriculture were decades away. The first hybrid seed corn was not available to farmers until the mid-1920s, and effective synthetic fungicides did not appear until after World War II. The many later demands of a more practical nature at Tuskegee Institute, however, prevented Carver from ever making any significant breakthrough in these fields.[18]

While he was at Ames, Carver's mycological skills were as widely recognized as his abilities at plant breeding. He was noted for his "instinct for nature," which allowed him to spot likely habitats for various species of fungus. This talent allowed him to find numerous rare and new species and caused Pammel to call him "the best collector I ever had in the department or have ever known." While he was a postgraduate student, Carver's skill was displayed by his collaboration on three mycological articles and his contribution of about fifteen hundred specimens to the college herbarium. Two of the articles indicate that he was engaged in research in fields that were very popular at the time: inoculation and comparative studies of the use of *Bordeaux mixture* as a fungicide.[19]

In addition to his research, Carver was also given the responsibility for some freshmen biology courses and apparently won the respect of his white pupils. One, who later became a professor in the College of Agriculture at the University of Wisconsin, wrote a letter of gratitude to him in 1941. He thanked Carver for interesting him in botany and noted that he seldom saw a certain plant without remembering him. Later he declared that Carver was his best teacher and displayed an unusual gift for guiding students to discover things for themselves, rather than telling them everything.[20]

Carver's ability to inspire and instruct extended beyond the students under his immediate charge. One of his professors,

Henry C. Wallace, had a precocious six-year-old son also named Henry. Carver allowed the boy to go with him on his rambles through the woods and shared with him the mysteries of nature. The young Wallace, who later became renowned for his plant breeding and for his service as secretary of agriculture and then vice-president under Franklin D. Roosevelt, credited Carver with giving him his first and life-long interest in plants. He called Carver the "kindliest, most patient teacher I ever knew" and declared, "He could cause a little boy to see the things which he saw in a grass flower."[21]

Nearing the completion of work for his Master of Agriculture degree in 1896, Carver discovered that he had a number of options for his future. In November 1895 representatives of Alcorn Agricultural and Mechanical College, a Mississippi school for blacks, asked him to join their faculty. At the same time the faculty at Iowa State made it clear that they wanted to retain Carver there. President William M. Beardshear wrote, "We would not care to have him change unless he can better himself." Professors Pammel and Budd noted that Carver had been reappointed to his position at a salary as large as Alcorn College was offering. It was James Wilson, however, who wrote the most eloquent letter, declaring.

In cross-fertilization . . . and the propagation of plants, Carver is by all means the ablest student we have here. Except for the respect I owe the professors, I would say he is fully abreast of them and exceeds in special lines in which he has a taste.

. . . We have nobody to take his place and I would never part with a student with so much regret as George Carver. . . . I think he feels at home among us, but you call for him to go down there and teach agriculture and horticulture . . . to the people of his own race, a people I have been taught to respect, and for whose religious education we consider it a privilege to contribute. I cannot object to his going. . . . It will be difficult, in fact impossible to fill his place.[22]

While Carver seriously considered accepting the offer from Alcorn, he did not wish to leave Iowa State until he had completed his postgraduate work. In the meantime, Carver received a more tempting offer from Booker T. Washington. By 1896 Washington was well known both for his leadership in guiding Tuskegee Institute to prominence among black normal and industrial schools and for his speech at the Atlanta Exposition in 1895. In that address he espoused what became known as the "doctrine of accommodation," proposing that blacks cooperate with white Southerners and "cast down their buckets" where they were, using vocational education to climb the ladder of economic success. Economic prosperity and education were of great importance to both black and white Southerners; thus, they should cooperate in these spheres, instead of battling over less important issues of political and civil rights or social equality. When blacks became an indispensable part of the economy, political rights would naturally follow, according to Washington. The biracial popularity of Washington's speech in an era of increasing racial tension marked the beginning of his rise to a position of leadership.

Indeed, Washington's leadership reflected the conditions of his era in much the same way that Frederick Douglass's had been a symbol for his. The militancy of Douglass was compatible with the abolitionist spirit of the Civil War and Reconstruction periods, when blacks won many victories for civil and political rights. But even before the end of Reconstruction in 1877 those rights were being chipped away. The abandonment of the "Negro cause" by the North and the federal government, as well as the Southern political turmoil of the Populist era, accelerated the pace, and by the 1890s blacks were losing rights on an almost daily basis. Black protest was met with white violence, and lynching became rampant. Both sides were terrified by the prospect of racial warfare, and were reassured when Booker T. Washington asserted that blacks and whites could still work together.[23]

With his background, Carver could readily appreciate the ideas of self-help and interracial cooperation. He had made himself useful and had found acceptance. He agreed with Washington's insistence on the fundamental importance of economic development in uplifting the former slaves. Early in his career at Iowa State, Carver had told James Wilson that he had given up his cherished work as an artist because "it would not do his people as much good as a thorough knowledge of the sciences of agriculture, which he might impart to them."[24]

On 26 March 1896 Washington offered Carver a chance to do such work. But Carver's 3 April reply was hesitant, noting his Mississippi offer and his desire to complete his work at Iowa State. Two days later, however, he had second thoughts and wrote that he "might be induced to leave" for a "satisfactory position" before he got his master's degree. Finally, on 12 April 1896, Carver enthusiastically declared that "it has always been the one ideal of my life to be of the greatest good to the greatest number of 'my people' possible and to this end I have been preparing myself for these many years; feeling as I do that this line of education is the key to unlock the golden door of freedom to our people."[25]

In reply to Carver's letter of 12 April, Washington explained that the board of trustees of the John F. Slater Fund had decided to establish an agricultural school at Tuskegee, but had doubted that he could find a black man to head it. "You perhaps know," he added "that at the present all of our teachers are of the colored race." Stressing his desire to retain an all-black faculty, Washington lamented, "If we cannot secure you we shall be forced perhaps to put in a white man." To prevent this, he offered Carver $1,000 a year plus board "to include all expenses except traveling." After describing Tuskegee's "policy of trying to get teachers who come not only for the money but also for their deep interest in the race," Washington then revealed his determination to secure Carver by declaring that if the terms were not satisfactory, "we shall be willing to do anything in reason that will enable you to decide in favor of coming to Tuskegee."[26]

Carver replied that he had received better offers elsewhere, "but I expect, as I have already stated, to go to my people and have been looking for some time at Tuskegee with favor. . . . Therefore," Carver continued, "the financial feature is at present satisfactory." He then listed his course work in agriculture and noted that he had "been for several years making large collections along economic lines" which he planned to bring with him. If his training was satisfactory for the planned course of study at Tuskegee, Carver declared, "I will accept the offer."[27]

By 6 May 1896 all matters relating to Carver's employment at Tuskegee were settled. Washington agreed to allow Carver to finish his work at Iowa State before coming to Alabama, and Carver pledged "to cooperate with you in doing all I can through Christ who strengtheneth me to better the conditions of our people." Carver wrote Washington that he had read his "stirring address delivered at Chicago" and "said amen to all you said" for this was "the correct solution to the 'race problem.' "[28]

Carver spent the remainder of the summer completing the requirements for a master's degree in agriculture and finishing some experimental work assigned to him. Leaving before the graduation ceremony, he arrived in Tuskegee in October 1896, filled with missionary zeal. Carver firmly believed God had given him unusual talents because of a divine plan for his life. His experiences seemed to support his belief, for he had indeed proved his intuitive abilities in a number of fields—from art to botany—even before receiving much formal training. To Carver there was no explanation of his remarkable skills except his close rapport with the Creator.

With a classmate at Iowa State Carver had dreamed of becoming a missionary to Africa.[29] Although in going to Tuskegee he did not leave the continent, he still conceived of himself as a martyr who had left security, success, and happiness to uplift a backward people. These were noble ideas, and blacks in the "shadow of the plantation" in Black Belt Alabama certainly needed help to rid themselves of the legacies of slavery: poverty, ignorance, inefficiency, and economic dependence. Yet a sense of mission has its dangers. It can easily lead to feelings of self-importance, especially when it is coupled with sentiments of martyrdom.

With God behind him and Washington begging him to come, Carver believed himself a very special faculty member. In 1896 he was the only member of the staff to hold an advanced degree from a white college. The majority of the teachers were graduates of

black industrial schools, and a large number of them were educated either at Tuskegee or Hampton Institute, the black industrial
school in Virginia which was Washington's alma mater. If Carver
felt somewhat superior to his fellow teachers, many of them were
suspicious of a man who had little "practical experience." A spirit
of rivalry, which was not always friendly, bloomed under Washington's demanding leadership. Some members of the faculty resented Carver's "exorbitant" salary of $1,000 a year, since the av-
erage salary in 1893 was less than $400. His darker color may have
also influenced the reactions of some, since most of the faculty and
students at Tuskegee were light-skinned mulattoes, and until the
"black is beautiful" movement, color prejudice was common in
many black communities. At any rate, Carver did not receive the
reception he expected.[30]

Moving from Iowa State College to Tuskegee Normal and Industrial Institute required a number of adjustments, many of
which Carver did not make very gracefully. He left a predominantly white environment for a black campus community, and his
experiences in acquiring an education had probably better prepared him to live with whites than with blacks. He moved from a
college to a normal and industrial school that combined the functions of an elementary school, high school, and vocational school.
At Tuskegee such abilities as breeding delicate flowers and collecting rare fungi were not as highly prized as basic survival skills.
Furthermore, Carver had never lived in the deep South, with its
dismal poverty and peculiar social institutions. Macon County, of
which Tuskegee is the county seat, was typical of the central, Black
Belt area of Alabama in the 1890s. Within a plantation economy a
white minority exercised economic and political domination over
the black majority. In many ways Tuskegee Institute was an en-
clave of independence in an area where most blacks were dependent upon white landlords and creditors. The founding of the Institute in 1881 had largely been the result of the political clout of
the then enfranchised black community. By 1896, however, only
the economic usefulness of the school and the diplomacy of Booker

T. Washington made such independence acceptable to the whites, and even at the Institute life for blacks was more precarious than it would have been in Iowa.[31]

At first Carver accepted these conditions as an inspiring challenge to the success of his mission work. If much of his environment was discouraging, Alabama, with all its unfamiliar flora, was a botanical paradise. In March 1897 he wrote Pammel, "This is indeed a new world to Iowa. Very poor to be sure but many things to make it pleasant. I like it so much better than I thought I would at first." The letter stressed the weather and flora of Alabama, however, not Carver's work.[32]

Carver viewed Tuskegee not only as his mission field, but as a temporary one. After spreading enlightenment he planned to move on to greater things. Such an attitude was probably apparent to his coworkers as soon as he arrived. If the arrogance inherent in his assumptions was suspected, hardly a month after his arrival Carver confirmed suspicions in a letter to the Institute's finance committee. Unhappy that his request for rooms did not receive immediate attention, he wrote:

Some of you saw the other day something of the valuable nature of one of my collections. I have others of equal value, and along argicultural lines.

You doubtless know that I came here [solely] for the benefit of my people, no other motive in view. Moreover I do not expect to teach many years, but will quit as soon as I can trust my work to others, and engage in my brush work, which will be of great honor to our people showing to what we may attain, along science, History, literature and art.

At present I have no rooms even to unpack my goods. I beg of you to give me these, and suitable ones also, not for my sake alone, but for the sake of education.[33]

The tone of the letter angered some of the faculty and failed to have completely satisfactory results. As late as 1901 Carver was still discontented with his accommodations and requested two more rooms. He apparently still had not learned to temper his

Carver, ca. 1897

arrogance, for he stated, "I desire a place to do some historic painting. I greatly desire to do this that it may go down in the history of the race."[34]

Eventually Carver received both adequate office space in the Agricultural Building and living facilities in two rooms of Rockefeller Hall, a boys' dormitory. Because of the crowded housing situation on campus, the fact that a bachelor had received two rooms caused continued resentment, and Carver remained somewhat aloof from the social life of the campus. Although he engaged in friendly banter and even a few practical jokes with his dining hall tablemates, many of whom were women teachers, Carver rarely attended campus social functions. Throughout his long tenure at

Tuskegee he formed few social relationships with faculty members and almost never made visits to the homes of fellow teachers.[35]

The austerity of Carver's social life resulted from more than strained faculty relationships. The demands on his time were enormous. What spare time he salvaged from his hectic schedule usually went for the pursuit of the loves Carver had sacrificed—botany and art. In addition, he had the withdrawn, reserved temperament of a loner. His nomadic early life taught him how to form friendships of rare spiritual depth and intensity in a short time, but not how to sustain these relationships on a daily basis. It was probably for this reason that Carver's only courtship failed to result in marriage.

The courtship may have been painful for Carver, as he was reluctant to speak of it in later years, and thus few details are known. He did seriously think about marriage in 1905, for he wrote Mrs. Liston for her advice. The most likely candidate for the prospective bride is Sarah L. Hunt, the sister-in-law of the Institute's treasurer, Warren Logan. According to Carver, he and the lady realized that they did not share the same goals. Numerous other factors may have played a role in his failure to marry. In addition to his being a loner, Carver's work and religion absorbed most of his time and energy. He dedicated his life to the church. Of course, the remote possibility of a physical disability could also have influenced him. At any rate, despite numerous match-making efforts by his friends, Carver never seriously considered marriage again.[36]

While Carver's preoccupation with his work led some to view him as unfriendly, those who approached him found him both warm and intensely interested in them. His extraordinary gift of making individuals feel special and important led many to believe that their closeness to Carver was unique. Actually Carver had many close friendships. But a barrier to his inner self always remained, and few, if any, were ever allowed to penetrate it. Significantly, most of his intense personal relationships were sustained by correspondence, not daily contact.

Many of Carver's close friendships were also with whites. Even more than Booker T. Washington's, his childhood and youth had been dominated by the influence of whites. Moses and Susan Carver were the only parents the young George Carver had ever known. The Milhollands, the Listons, the Budds, and the Pammels all considered Carver an unofficial member of their families. All of Carver's classmates and teachers at Simpson and Iowa State were white, and with men like James Wilson, Carver had established relationships that went beyond that of teacher and student.

It was only natural that Carver soon developed a warm relationship with whites in the town of Tuskegee. Many no doubt interpreted his naturally reserved and unassuming personality as an endorsement of the racial etiquette they expected. His sense of being an agent for the divine produced not only a certain arrogance, but also a certain humility. If he was special, Carver constantly declared throughout his career, it was because God had made him so. God deserved the credit, not Carver. In addition Carver quickly learned, as all Tuskegee teachers did, that he was expected to place the school's welfare above his own and refrain from any action that could jeopardize the crucial white support it received. The era was one in which such a school in Black Belt Alabama could not possibly survive without white blessings.

Tuskegee whites were attracted by more than just Carver's humility. They recognized and valued his talents and skills, perhaps even more than Carver's fellow blacks did. In *My Larger Education* Washington marveled over Carver's ability to make "the acquaintance of so many of the best white as well as colored people in our part of the country" in spite of his "timidity." Washington then quoted Carver's explanation:

Shortly after I came here I was going along the woods one day with my botany can under my arm. I was looking for plant diseases and for insect enemies. A lady saw what she probably thought was a harmless old colored man, with a strange looking box under his arm, and she stopped me and asked if I was a peddler. I told her what I was doing. She seemed delighted and asked me to come and see her roses, which were badly diseased. I showed her just what to do for them—in fact, sat down and wrote it out for her.

In this . . . and several other ways it became noised about that there was a man at the school who knew about plants. People began calling upon me for information and advice.[37]

While both Washington and Carver sometimes embellished the truth for symbolic purposes, the essence of this story is probably true. Throughout his career Carver was indeed often consulted by Tuskegee whites on everything from plants to art. He even made "house calls" to perform such services as dipping the tips of a prematurely pruned tree in paraffin to save it. Washington realized the value of Carver's friendships in the white community and sometimes asked him to represent the school's interests to prominent whites with whom he had especially good relationships. For example, in 1914 Carver was asked to request Cora Varner, whose lands adjoined the Institute's property, to cease thinning her forest lands since the removal of the trees was impairing the appearance of the campus.[38]

After Carver came to Tuskegee Institute, he did not break his ties with the white friends of his childhood and youth. He continued to correspond with the Listons, Milhollands, and Pammels, and with many of his classmates and teachers. He did lose contact with Moses Carver for a short period and even hired a lawyer to find his foster father, who was finally located in Galena, Kansas. Moses, who was ninety in 1905, had left the old homestead after the death of Susan to move in with some relatives there. From Galena the relatives kept Carver posted on his health and activities. In 1908 Carver returned home for his last visit with Moses, who died in 1910 and was buried in a pair of trousers Carver had sent him.[39]

One of Carver's old friendships proved to be especially valuable to Carver and Tuskegee. The year after Carver left Iowa State, James Wilson was appointed secretary of agriculture by President William McKinley. Wilson did not forget the former pupil with whom he had been so close. When Tuskegee's new Slater-Armstrong Memorial Agricultural Building was completed in 1897, James Wilson attended the dedication exercise, becoming the first cabinet officer to visit the Institute. Wilson undoubtedly also encouraged McKinley to accept Washington's invitation to Tuskegee, and on 16 December 1898 McKinley became the first president of the United States to come to the school.[40]

These visits were symbolically important, but Wilson also aided Tuskegee in more practical ways. To Carver he wrote, "Call on me freely for any help you need in the line of seeds or anything of that kind and I will lean your way heavily." Because Wilson remained the secretary of agriculture throughout the McKinley, Roosevelt, and Taft administrations, this offer of aid could have been significant. To some degree, however, Wilson's hands were tied by the nature of the Department of Agriculture's authority and its relationship to state governments. Although he significantly extended the scope of his department's activities, the actual administration of most departmental funds remained with the states. This filtering process for these and other federal funds usually meant that blacks received a disproportionately small share of such money. Thus Wilson was unable to grant some of Carver's requests, like that for the establishment of a demonstration farm at Tuskegee. Nevertheless the United States Department of Agriculture, under Wilson's guidance, aided the agricultural work at Tuskegee Institute in every possible way.[41]

Carver's ability to attract white interest and support for the Institute became more important the more he learned that Booker T. Washington was a hard man to please. When Carver first arrived in Alabama in 1896 he probably felt invincible. His abilities had impressed some of the leading agriculturists of the nation. But Carver soon learned that although his abilities also impressed Washington, he lacked one skill that was highly prized by the principal—a talent for administration.

Trouble on the "Tuskegee Plantation"

When he arrived on the Tuskegee campus, Carver saw himself as a partner with Booker T. Washington in "lifting the veil of ignorance." If he had envisioned a harmonious and equal working relationship, he was quickly disappointed. In reality, despite enormous mutual respect and the increasing fame that Carver's work won for both himself and Tuskegee, the two men's relationship remained periodically stormy from Carver's arrival in 1896 until Washington's death in 1915.

One basic problem was that Carver's expectations and priorities did not coincide with Washington's. In 1896 the Alabama legislature enacted a law establishing an agricultural experiment station on the Tuskegee campus and appropriating $1,500 for its operation.[1] On the basis of his experience at Iowa State, Carver expected the experiment station to be a central feature of Tuskegee's agricultural work. At both Iowa State and Alabama Polytechnic Institute in Auburn, near Tuskegee, research was given high priority. There were fundamental differences, however, between Tuskegee and those two land-grant colleges, and Carver never entirely adjusted to Tuskegee's uniqueness. Both the Ames and Auburn experiment stations had legislative appropriations at least ten times larger than that given Tuskegee,[2] and Booker T. Washington placed little value on pure research. He was more interested in those things that directly benefited the farmer and enhanced the image of Tuskegee Institute. In the face of these and other limitations Carver did a remarkable job with his experiment station work.[3]

Although Carver's many talents aided Tuskegee's work, he was almost completely inept at administrative duties. This was a disastrous shortcoming to Washington's mind, for several reasons. In theory agriculture had been a cornerstone of the Tuskegee program since its 1881 origin; in reality the money to establish a separate Agricultural Department had not been available until the 1896 grant from the Slater Fund.[4] Thus both a new department and a new experiment station had to be created, and Washington was counting on Carver to display the necessary organizational skills.

Washington was also exceedingly sensitive about the impression that Tuskegee Institute made on outsiders. In his mind his own success and that of his school became a crucial test of the abilities of Afro-Americans in an age of racism. Even the smallest detail that detracted from the Institute's image of perfection was of utmost importance to Washington. A horse barn was to "be built with an imposing front," and a scrap of paper on the ground was considered a major blight. The school not only had to be effective in its activities, but it had to give the appearance of being run efficiently.[5] Smooth, efficient operating procedures require personnel with a high degree of managerial skill, and Carver did not fit the pattern.

If Carver's administrative shortcomings were not enough to cause friction between Washington and himself, their personalities ensured a stormy relationship. Carver was a dreamer and idealist; Washington was preeminently a realist and pragmatist. Outward appearances meant little to Carver; he seemed to derive a kind of perverse pleasure from dressing beneath his social and economic status. In other ways, however, similarities between Carver and Washington caused problems. Both men were exceedingly sensitive to criticism, filled with a sense of mission, and anxious to prove their own merit. Washington ran his school like the "master of a plantation," but Carver refused to play the role of humble slave. The result was mutual respect for each other's abilities and aims, coupled with bitter clashes over policy and procedures. Carver's chosen "mission field" proved to be considerably less than a paradise.

One of Carver's first complaints was the scope and extent of his duties. Being the head of a new agricultural department and director of a new experiment station was enough to occupy a full workday, but Washington demanded more. In addition to teaching, extension work, and research, Carver had numerous administrative duties and miscellaneous chores. He was held responsible for all phases of Tuskegee's agricultural work, including two school farms, the barns and livestock, the poultry yard, the dairy, the orchard, the beehives, and the pastures. Since the school had no veterinarian when Carver first arrived, he served in that capacity also. Outside of these responsibilities and the usual duties of an academic dean, Carver was given an odd assortment of other chores: planning and supervising the beautification of the school grounds; looking after the "closets" and other sanitary facilities; doing analysis work for the purchasing agent and others; and even looking after "the matter of reckless driving about the grounds."[6]

Some of Carver's extra duties derived from his membership on the Institute's Executive Council, which was composed of the heads of departments and served as an advisory body to the principal. Members were not only asked to take on additional responsibilities and to serve on various "investigative committees," but the council meetings themselves were a drain on their time. The council usually met twice a week, and Carver complained several times that these meetings, combined with general faculty meetings and departmental meetings, kept him sitting in meeting rooms when he had other work to do.[7]

Carver's dissatisfaction sprang from more than just having too many responsibilities. He also believed he did not receive the cooperation and support that his work required. He persistently complained about not being supplied with enough men to do various jobs, and he often had little freedom to choose the people for whose work he was held responsible. He also deplored the lack of necessary equipment and the frequent substitutions made in his purchase orders without his knowledge. Even getting a rope to hoist the weather flag and the water for his laboratory proved difficult.[8]

Such impediments were irritating, but Carver was more seriously disturbed by conflicting orders and shifting priorities. In 1903 he implored Washington to "map out a well defined policy and not deviate from it unless careful consultation were held." Less than a year later he reiterated his plea, noting that the school "would thus avoid all of the very costly mistakes made this year."[9] A major part of the problem stemmed from Washington's desire to maintain personal supervision over even trivial campus activities. With so many matters on his mind, Washington often shifted priorities and changed orders, according to what was in the forefront of his attention. He demanded perfection in first one area and then another, sometimes without giving his people the means or freedom to meet his demands.

For Carver, as well as others, the problem was compounded by Washington's frequent absences. Although Washington continued to command even when away from campus, he sometimes had to act through agents. One of these agents was his brother, who served as the superintendent of industries. John H. Washington had little respect for Carver or his abilities. The two clashed often, and Carver chafed under the orders of the superintendent.[10] As early as 1898 he declared, "Mr. Washington I wish you could be here more than you are and look into matters yourself, and not take peoples' word for it."[11]

While Washington's style of leadership affected all the Tuskegee faculty, Carver appeared to be less able to restrain his frustration and bitterness. He often wrote letters bristling with resentment. A little more than a year and a half after his arrival, he penned a report to Washington that emphasized both his own sacrifices and the lack of support from the Institute. He noted that he "labored early and late and at times [beyond] my physical strength." He had given up his "partial arrangements" to enter the Shaw School of Botany in St. Louis to acquire his doctorate, "a degree that no colored man has ever taken," in order to study the "food question" at Tuskegee and to attempt to cut losses on the school farm. Yet he was not even given a private secretary. What bothered Carver most, however, was Washington's policy toward the experiment station. Carver stressed that he was "working with the smallest and most inexperienced staff of any Station in the U.S." and that it was impossible "to do this work without men and means." In view of these difficulties, he resented Washington's attitude toward the work of the station, and declared:

> Now Mr. Washington, I think it ludicrously unfair to have persons sit in an office and dictate what I have to do and how I can do it. . . . If I thought things were to run as they have always run I would not stay here any longer than I could get away.[12]

Disturbed about actions taken by the Executive Council and John H. Washington in 1902, Carver wrote the principal:

> From causes which I am wholy [sic] unable to dicipher [sic] I feel that I do not get the cooperation of the council. Many times no attention is paid to my wishes and things are passed over my head which work contrawise to my efforts to carry out the school's wishes. . . .
>
> I shall endeavor to carry out the school's wishes to the letter, but I do not like this decision. My work has been hampered the entire school year from similar reasons. . . .
>
> I want it understood that this is in no way rebellious, but a plain statement of facts as I see them.[13]

Despite persistent and rather thinly veiled threats to leave, Carver was still at Tuskegee in 1904, facing the identical obstacles of his earlier days. Failure to get proper stenographic help prompted him to pen a bitter picture of his predicament in January.

> I fully appreciate the necessity of not increasing the school's expenses a single dollar or even less, but my work is of such a nature that I cannot do it without help regularly. I beg to say that this is my seventh year's connection with the school. I have not asked for

an increase in salary or a vacation each year, and I have been wholly unobservant of office hours, beginning early and working late, also every night, for the school in one way or another.

My correspondence is constantly increasing, two bulletins are now ready except the typewritten work, and one has been on hand since last spring. Today my classes run thus: 8:00 to 9:00, agri. chemistry; 9:20 to 10:00, the foundation and harmony of color to the painter; 10:00 to 11:00, class of farmers, and one period in the afternoon. In addition to this I must try—and rather imperfectly— [to] overlook seven industrial classes scattered here and there over the grounds. I must test all the seeds, examine all the fertilizer— based upon the examination of the soil of the different plots. I must also personally look after every operation of the ten acre experiment station. I must endeavor to keep the poultry yard straight. In addition to the above I must daily inspect 104 cows that have been inoculated, looking carefully over the temperature of each one, making comparisons and prescribing whatever is necessary, besides looking after the sickness of other animals.

Again, the museum and laboratory (which hardly have an equal in the South for their specific work) are almost wholly the work of my own efforts, giving many things from my own private collection and securing others from various sources. If money were my only object I could not afford to stay at Tuskegee. I came here with the one idea of assisting you in building up the most difficult division of your great scheme. I came knowing that I would encounter more difficulties in the way of proper sympathy and support. I knew it would not be an easy life to live. I am not seeking that just now, neither am I seeking personal aggrandizement. I only want to give the school my best service.[14]

While belligerent and whining letters did little to endear Carver to Washington, the principal's dissatisfaction ran deeper. Part of the problem stemmed from Washington's unrealistic expectations from his faculty, but the school's trustees were also particularly anxious for Tuskegee's agricultural work to be an unmitigated success. Washington was under constant pressure to put agriculture on a paying basis as a good example to black farmers.[15] Combining effective agricultural education and profits was probably an impossible dream, but Carver's administrative shortcomings heightened the problem. The result was a pattern of ultimatums from Washington and resignation threats from Carver that continued until the principal's death.

Several of Washington's complaints concerned externals that affected Tuskegee's public image. For example, he rebuked Carver for not seeing that the agricultural machinery was put away. This practice could harm the implements, but Washington seemed more concerned that it appeared "like the common country people." Carver was also told to straighten the pictures, maps, and charts in the Agricultural Building and to see that signs were kept up to date and in place at the experiment station. Washington noted that the weakness of the signs was "especially noticeable" the day of the governor's visit.[16]

Much more serious were Carver's difficulties with personnel management. He seemed to have trouble delegating authority and securing the cooperation and support of some of his employees. He admitted that he was "frequently obliged to stop and do work that belongs to someone else." At the root of some of Carver's problems was the lack of adequately trained men and the reliance upon student labor. He sometimes failed to take into account the depth of ignorance of many of the students. One group of students, for example, misunderstood Carver's directions for the preparation of a dip for sheep. The first sheep died almost immediately after it was dipped, but the students continued to dip about a dozen more before deciding they should check to see if something was wrong.[17]

Carver's Agricultural Department, like the rest of the campus, suffered from divisive rivalries, which he was inept in handling. Some of the rivalry centered on Carver himself. A number of his men resented the attention his laboratory work received at the expense of their own work. A few were hurt by Carver's failure to take them into his confidence regarding his discoveries and hinted that he was masking fraudulent research by refusing to disclose how he got his results. Interdepartmental strife became especially acute with the arrival of George R. Bridgeforth in 1902. Carver was less than enthusiastic about hiring Bridgeforth for his department, and in time Carver woefully regretted his reluctant approval of the young man. A classic battle of two strong wills, resembling that between Carver and Washington, ensued. In the end Carver lost both battles.[18]

George R. Bridgeforth was the temperamental opposite of the quiet, secretive Carver. He was a big, energetic, blustery man with a flair and a taste for administrative power. He considered himself vastly more able than Carver to head Tuskegee's agricultural work and at times did not bother to conceal his disdain for Carver's ability. Writing both Carver and Washington long letters that were really lectures on what was wrong in the Agricultural Department, Bridgeforth quickly won enmity from Carver and admiration from Washington.[19]

As Bridgeforth's star rose with Washington, Carver became more and more resentful of both Bridgeforth's flagrant assaults on his authority and Washington's failure to support him as the head of the department. The Carver-Bridgeforth disputes became bitter and petty, demeaning both men. In 1904 Carver reduced the number of teams of horses allowed to Bridgeforth for his "Short Course in Agriculture." Bridgeforth wrote Carver a belligerent letter stating, "I do not intend to spend my time running around getting orders to work when one manly order would save all trou-

Carver and the agricultural faculty at Tuskegee

ble and hard feeling." He also declared that he would be forced to go to the principal.[20] Carver replied that Bridgeforth's attitude "has been and is yet very unsatisfactory to me and, of course, cannot continue." He went on to issue an ultimatum.

> As to the reduction of the teams, I did that because I thought it wise; and I shall never consent to have no say in the matter as long as I am head of the Department. . . . I have no objection to your taking up any matters you desire with the Principal; but there are certain courtesies which I demand, and will have, if the person stays in my employ. I want it clearly understood that I am not going to put up with such notes as this coming into my office from you.[21]

Bridgeforth completely ignored the ultimatum and asserted that Carver's notes were "in every respect laughable." Indeed, Bridgeforth issued his own ultimatum.

> I shall not stand another bit of this bluff and you must do business like a man and take some interest in the things that pertains [sic] to school. You seem to have lost all interest in all things at the school as it is noticed by all. . . . I am here to work as a man and I expect to be treated as such. I am not to be intimidated by your recent threats.[22]

Carver sent Washington a copy of Bridgeforth's original note and his own reply and noted, "I am sorry to have to trouble you with these matters but they have reached the limit of my endurance, as he does not improve." Washington replied with homilies about getting along with people, but he added, "I shall expect that respect and obedience must be given to the heads of the departments."[23]

Nevertheless, less than three months later friction again erupted between the two men, this time over Bridgeforth's title for the school catalog. Bridgeforth asked to be listed as Carver's assistant, and Carver forwarded his request to Emmett J. Scott, Washington's secretary. When Scott questioned the appropriateness of the title, Bridgeforth blamed Carver for not aggressively supporting his claims and wrote, "Let us be men and face the truth." This dispute prompted Carver to request that a committee be established to "consider very seriously whether Bridgeforth is a fit person to be connected with Tuskegee." An appointed committee, however, recommended that no transfer be made, and Carver was once again forced to swallow his pride.[24]

Carver's major problem in his conflicts with Bridgeforth was his position as the unsuccessful incumbent. He had already displayed his inability to meet the principal's demands; Bridgeforth appeared both willing and able to do so if given the opportunity. After disappointing Washington in numerous minor ways, Carver was especially vulnerable in one area under his responsibility: Washington was outraged by the professor's total lack of success at raising chickens. For some reason the poultry yard moved from one catastrophic crisis to another under Carver's direction, and no amount of attention or money seemed to make the chickens produce as they should. Unfortunately, Carver's "chicken problems" began at the very time Bridgeforth was maneuvering to enhance his position at the expense of Carver's.

In a sense it was one of the ironies of fate that led to Carver's downfall due to chickens. In 1903 the poultry farm had been under Bridgeforth's direction, but the lack of satisfactory results led Carver to shift responsibility for the yard to Columbus Barrows sometime in 1903 or early 1904. A report on conditions in the poultry yard in May 1904 indicated an increase in fowl during the year, but noted that the care of the chickens and the quality of instruction had deteriorated under Barrow's supervision. A crisis came 22 September 1904, when a new committee made its report to the Executive Council. The report charged that everything in the yard was in "very bad condition," and that the daily poultry reports "are not true ones." Barrows was quoted as saying that whenever a large number of fowls died, he was "instructed not to report them all at one time as Mr. B. T. Washington would tare [sic] him to pieces." After the report was read, Barrows was summoned to the council meeting where he testified that he was told by the director of agriculture to make false reports. In rebuttal

Carver replied that he did not "recall having given such injunctions."[25]

Bridgeforth knew when to strike, and early the next month he and several other members of the Agricultural Department submitted a proposal for the department's reorganization. Their plan called for making John Washington the director of agriculture instead of Carver. The department was also to be divided into five divisions, a move that would give most of them equal footing with Carver as division head. Two days later Booker T. Washington told Carver "that the position in which you are placed is an awkward and serious one" and stated his own view of the incident: "There is no doubt in my mind . . . a mistake has been made on your own part either in the direction of carelessness, . . . or in the direction of being a party to the deception." Washington then asked Carver if he was willing to make a serious and determined effort to bring complete reformation and change in his department.[26]

Carver replied by giving a catalog of his achievements and declaring, "Now to be branded as a liar and party to such hellish deception it is more than I can bear, and if your committee feel that I have willfully lied . . . my resignation is at your disposal." Accusations appear to have grown even more bitter. Several days later Carver attempted to refute charges that his own report and a personal check to cover some of the losses were attempts to cover up what had happened. He also pledged never again to "be duped and fooled" and to approach the management of the poultry yard "with renewed vigor." Washington's reply was less than enthusiastic. He reminded Carver that he had already made clear "just what I wish you to do in order to put yourself in the attitude of being in a position to remain in the permanent employ of the Institute," and noted that any reorganization or change in Carver's status would be decided after a committee was appointed to study the matter.[27]

On 3 November 1904 Washington sent Carver a copy of the committee report and indicated his general agreement with its recommendation to divide the agricultural department. Since

Carver's best work was in the areas of teaching and experimentation, Washington suggested that the committee's proposed title for Carver of "Director of the Experiment Station and Agricultural Instruction" seemed appropriate, as did the title of "Director of Agricultural Industries" for Bridgeforth. Before making a final decision, however, Washington requested Carver's opinion of the report.[28]

Carver willingly gave his opinion in a long letter on 8 November 1904. He most vehemently expressed dislike for the new title because it was "too far a drop downward" from director of agriculture and would never be understood by the public. In addition, Carver averred that splitting the theoretical and practical teaching would "result in constant turmoil and final failure" and that removing a single department head would create "a flimsy organization which cannot stand and will furnish data for outside criticism." Carver was especially hurt by the accusatory tone of the committee report and asked Washington to accept his resignation.[29]

Carver and students with a cow skeleton at Tuskegee

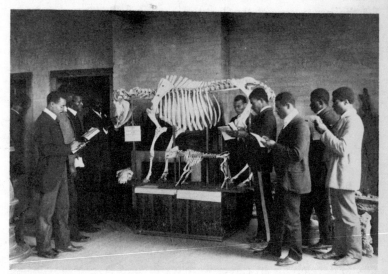

About a week later Carver penned another letter that seemed both to give his conditions for staying and to catalog his grievances. Among his chief complaints was being bypassed on farm matters despite his overall responsibility for them. "I have spent much time in writing out suggestions and recomandations [*sic*]," he declared, "to be ignored afterwards." The problem, Carver believed, resulted from the lack of a clearly defined agricultural policy and the failure to include him in all meetings pertaining to the farm. "My assistant," Carver wrote, "was consulted freely and frankly and sometimes brought into meetings where I should have been." This treatment was especially galling since the subordinates who were consulted frequently had to obtain the requested information from Carver.

Carver's demands included a reduced teaching load, more support in getting subordinates to do such things as attend department meetings, at least part-time stenographic help, and, stubbornly, retention of responsibility for the poultry yard. Carver also presented his own reorganization plan. It logically proposed a "training farm in connection with the Experiment Station" for the education of professional agriculture students and a separate farm for the production of the Institute's needed food supplies to be "operated mainly by hired labor and night students."

Carver's letter also alluded to an "unanswered and unsolicited letter" which offered him a new job elsewhere with a $200-a-year increase in salary "besides other tempting advantages." Although he claimed he was bringing the letter to Washington's attention "for no other purpose than to prove my interest in Tuskegee," [30] Carver was in fact seriously considering accepting the offer as late as the following February. During his college days, Carver had met Ralph W. McGranahan, a white man who in 1904 was serving as president of the black Knoxville College in Tennessee. For several years Carver had gone to Knoxville College to lecture at the school's summer session, and now McGranahan had written asking Carver to come there as a full-time faculty member of both art and agriculture. Although an annual salary of $1,200 and an opportunity to develop his art career were tempting, Carver was reluctant to leave his experiment station work at Tuskegee. The desirability of Knoxville College therefore hinged on whether Carver could get his old friend James Wilson to establish an experiment station there. When Wilson was unable to meet this request, Carver decided to stay at Tuskegee.[31]

The decision to remain in Alabama was probably made easier by the fact that Carver won the initial skirmish of the reorganization battle. For the time being he was allowed to keep both his title and the poultry yard. He had been given an opportunity to reduce his outrageous workload, but he was apparently too proud to accept the "demotion." His desire to have another chance to make the poultry yard successful proved to be an especially serious mistake.

For the next few years conditions at the poultry yard improved, but by 1908 Carver was receiving more and more criticism about his operation of it. In 1908 Bridgeforth became Carver's equal by his promotion to head the new Department of Agricultural Industries. Carver's title was changed to "Director of Agricultural Instruction and Experiment Station," the identical label he had rejected four years earlier. The worst was yet to come, however, because conditions at the poultry yard steadily deteriorated.[32]

In 1909 the accuracy of the poultry yard reports was again questioned. When a shortage of fowls was discovered, the yard manager claimed that a number of chickens had been sold to a "travelling poultry peddler." Washington reacted with skepticism, and the man was discharged. Carver once again dipped into his personal funds to replenish the losses and considered leaving Tuskegee, but he was advised by James Wilson to stay.[33]

Washington's comments about the poultry yard became increasingly hostile and skeptical, often questioning the accuracy of Carver's explanations of losses and discrepancies. By May 1910 Carver was so frustrated that he again turned to James Wilson for a way out, inquiring if the secretary of agriculture could not recommend his being sent to Liberia. In this venture Carver had Washington's blessing, but the request could not be filled by Wilson.[34]

By 20 October 1910 conditions at the poultry yard reached crisis proportions, with 765 chickens "wholly unaccounted for." Again reorganization of the agricultural work was discussed, with John Washington and Bridgeforth recommending that the two departments be reunited and split into two divisions. Although Carver had opposed the original separation, he now objected to the reunification because the head of the new department was to be Bridgeforth instead of himself.[35] Washington attempted to find a face-saving alternative for Carver, while stripping him of his remaining authority in the Agricultural Department.

According to Washington's plan, Carver was to retain his department-head status as director of the experiment station, and Bridgeforth was to be named director of the reunified department. To assuage Carver's feelings he was to be given the title "Dean" in the Agricultural Department, but the title was merely honorific. Although Carver was to have titular authority over the teaching function of the department, Washington made it clear that Carver was Bridgeforth's subordinate and that in "all matters of difference" Bridgeforth had the "authority to decide." The poultry yard was to be removed from Carver's jurisdiction, but as compensation he was to be given better laboratory facilities.[36]

Despite Washington's efforts, Carver was not appeased and quickly tendered his resignation.[37] As before, he turned to James Wilson for employment prospects. Tuskegee's internal politics were clearly an enigma to Wilson, who replied to Carver's query:

> What in the world they want to put anybody over your head for is more than I can understand, unless you are developing characteristics that are new to me. You will have to be the judge of what is wise for you to do. I do not happen to know of a place where your services would be wanted at the present time, but nobody has ever suspected that you would care to leave there.[38]

Washington was reluctant to give up his experiment station director, who had won wide acclaim for his work, so the principal went back to the drawing board to devise another plan. He appointed a committee and apparently accepted its recommendations. Under the new proposal the work of Carver and Bridgeforth was completely separated, with Carver as director of the department of research and experiment station. Carver's duties included only operating the experiment station, publishing bulletins, conducting bacteriological and other analysis work, delivering special lectures, and retaining control of the poultry yard. The committee further recommended that a "first class laboratory be fitted up for Prof. Carver" and that Carver teach agricultural classes only "if he desires." The plan astutely recognized that Carver could not tolerate being subordinate to Bridgeforth in any sense.[39]

Unfortunately, neither Bridgeforth nor Carver could refrain from badgering the other, since each was allowed to think he had won a victory. Carver promptly notified Bridgeforth that he did not desire to teach certain classes and insisted that he needed their shared stenographer all day. John Washington tried to mediate the dispute, but eventually the matter was referred to the principal, who held a meeting with Carver and a few other interested parties in his office on 21 February 1911 to find a solution. Distressed over the outcome of the meeting, Carver wrote Washington the next day expressing his dissatisfaction and pointing out that former promises were not being kept.[40]

Washington's patience had worn thin by this time, and he responded with an explicit five-page ultimatum. "Perhaps in the past we have done ourselves as well as you an injustice by pursuing a policy of trying to please everybody," Washington declared. The school could no longer permit Carver "to argue at length every order that is given, and lay down the conditions upon which you will [obey]." Carver had to realize, Washington asserted, that the school was a large organization which required teamwork. The school gave Carver a wide latitude of freedom and financial support, but when given a direct order, he balked. "Instead of complying with this order in a sympathetic and prompt manner," Washington charged, "you are dilly-dallying with it, and have tried in many ways to bring influences to bear through officers of the school and students to get us to change this order."

In the ultimatum Washington not only listed the charges

against Carver but he also gave an interesting assessment of Carver's abilities.

> When it comes to the organization of classes, the ability required to secure a properly organized and large school or section of a school, you are wanting in ability. When it comes to the matter of practical farm managing which will secure definite, practical, financial results, you are wanting again in ability. You are not to be blamed for this. It is rare that one individual anywhere combines all the elements of success. You are a great teacher, a great lecturer, a great inspirer of young men and old men; that is your fort [sic] and we have all been trying as best we could to help you do the work for which you are best fitted and to leave aside that for which you are least fitted.
>
> You also have great ability in original research, in making experiments in the soil and elsewhere on untried plants. You have great ability in the direction of showing what can be done in the use of foods and the preserving of foods.

In spite of these talents, Washington informed Carver, he had developed two attitudes the school could not tolerate. His desire to have a laboratory fitted up for his exclusive use and to be relieved of teaching could not be permitted. "We are all here," Washington declared, "to help the students, to instruct them, and there is no justification for the presence of any teacher here except as that teacher is to serve the students." After reaffirming the need for Carver to obey orders, he closed by declaring, "I repeat that all of us recognize your great ability, recognize your rare talents in certain directions, and we should all be sorry to part with your service, but the time has now come for perfect frankness and for definite action." [41]

If Washington had any thought that the chastised Carver would now swallow his pride and bend himself to the school's demands, the principal was quickly disappointed. Carver had been forced to accept numerous unwanted changes in his status. He was left with two slender victories—the promise of a well-equipped laboratory and another chance to prove himself in the poultry yard. Carver believed that he was engaged in experimental work that would prove to be of vast economic importance, and obtaining delivery of the promised new lab equipment also became crucial to his self-respect. The result was continuous bickering over supplies for the laboratory. In addition, his final chance for success with the poultry yard was a dismal failure and continued to be a source of friction between Carver and Washington until the yard was finally removed from his control in 1913.[42]

Carver's failure to hold on to his two minor victories seems to have made him more hostile, bitter, and sensitive to criticism. These feelings interfered with the effectiveness of his work, especially his teaching, since Bridgeforth did not make much effort to be tactful in his handling of Carver. Carver's wounded vanity was probably the root of his problems, as can be seen in his reaction to the news that he was to be laid off one month during the summer of 1914. The layoff was an economy measure by the school, but Carver considered it a personal affront. Despite the fact that he had sizable savings and rarely spent but a fraction of his salary, Carver declared, "I can never consent to work only part of the year as long as I am able to put in full time." Such treatment, Carver asserted, forced him "to seek a place where I can have some assurance of being cared for when I reach the point where I am not so vigorous as I am now." This was the third resignation threat since the reorganization of 1910, and, like the others, it was not carried out.[43]

Washington alternated between trying to placate Carver and issuing new ultimatums. The principal discovered that removing Carver did not solve the Agricultural Department's problems. Bridgeforth proved as unable as Carver to put the agricultural work on a paying basis.[44] Nevertheless, Carver persisted in a habit Washington found very hard to tolerate; the professor continuously questioned the principal's decisions and orders. Washington insisted upon loyal deference. As he explained to Carver, his suggestions were in most cases "but a polite way of giving orders" and the Executive Council was not intended to be "a debating club."[45] Thus Washington was torn between his respect for Carver's natural genius and his irritation at Carver's uncooperative spirit. The stormy relationship that developed between these two strong-willed men meant that Carver's chosen "mission field" gave him a taste of hell as well as paradise. Although the individual disputes were petty, their combined influence on Carver and his work was enormous. Increasingly he retreated from his Tuskegee duties and focused his efforts where they were appreciated—away from Tuskegee. It is also likely that his administrative failures and humiliations drove him to prove to himself and to others that he did have a special, God-ordained role to play in the destiny of his people.

The Need for Scientific Agriculture

In 1896 George W. Carver's "mission field" in Black Belt Alabama offered numerous challenges. Called to teach agriculture to "his people," he quickly learned that Southern farmers, both black and white, suffered from all the ills of Northern agriculture and more. Various forces trapped most Southern farmers in grinding poverty, which brought apathy, despair, and a sense of being the victims of some vast conspiracy. In assessing the situation, Carver wrote:

> The average Southern farm has but little more to offer than about one-third of a cotton crop, selling at 2 and 3 cents per pound less than it cost to produce it, together with the proverbial mule, implements more or less primitive, and frequently a vast territory of barren and furrowed hillsides and wasted valleys.
>
> Another mortgage may have been added as an unpleasant reminder of the year's hard labor. The Southern farmers, as a whole, have been too slow to admit that the old one-crop and primitive implements are quite out of harmony with the new, and up-to-date methods and machinery. Indeed, many are not aware that such conditions exist, and are patiently waiting, starving—blindly and stubbornly refusing to believe that their ills and misfortunes are not due to legislation or social reforms.[1]

Actually, legislation did have something to do with the plight of the farmer. State contract and debtor laws, coupled with a lack of adequate credit facilities, led to the evolution of the crop-lien system and various forms of peonage. The Civil War had brought a transformation, but not the elimination, of the Southern plantation system. Land was still concentrated in the hands of a relative few, only now the landlords were frequently absentee landowners. Without land to mortgage, farmers resorted to mortgaging their future crops to landlords or merchants. These creditors usually insisted on the planting of the favored cash crop—cotton. At the end of the year it was a rare tenant farmer or sharecropper who had grown enough to start the new year free of debt. Usually each year the crushing burden of debt increased, leaving the farmer in a state of semislavery.[2]

Other factors worked to the detriment of the small farmer. Fluctuating agricultural prices, unfair taxation policies, lack of adequate transportation facilities, deflation, and poor marketing conditions all played a role in the chronic ills of agriculture. Yet at the root of the problem was the failure of farmers to adjust to a changing market economy. Tradition and superstitious individualism helped prevent the farmer from assuming the role of businessman in an era of rapidly developing industrial capitalism. In the South, reliance upon the almost exclusive cultivation of cotton meant overproduction of a commodity that frequently declined in price but not in the cost of production. In fact, the depletion of the soil by the constant planting of cotton forced farmers to cultivate more and more acres at less and less profit.[3]

The problems of agriculture were complex, and the farmers were bewildered. The Populist party had seemed to offer a political solution to their desperate plight, but the collapse of the party by 1900 meant that farmers had to turn elsewhere for help. To many trained agriculturists, scientific agriculture seemed to promise salvation. By applying scientific methods the farmer could learn how to cut production costs and how to provide goods for which there was a market demand. Carver was expressing the spirit of the age when he wrote *The Need of Scientific Agriculture in the South*.

The virgin fertility of our soils, and the vast amount of unskilled labor, have been a curse rather than a blessing to agriculture. This exhaustive system for cultivation, the destruction of forests, the rapid and almost constant decomposition of organic matter . . . make our agricultural problem one requiring more brains than that of the North, East, or West. By the advance of civilization, the markets have become more fastidious; and he who puts such a product upon the market as it demands, controls the market, regardless of color. It is simply a survival of the fittest.[4]

The faith of Carver and others in the power of scientific agriculture was somewhat exorbitant and typical of the optimism of the emerging progressive period. If scientific methods of farming could not single-handedly solve all the ills of agriculture, they could help alleviate many of the problems. In the 1880s agriculture had just begun to emerge as a scientific discipline, and much remained to be learned about all phases of farming. The average farmer obviously had neither the time nor the means to engage in costly experimentation. The nature of research demands failures as well as successes, and few farmers could afford the risk of failure. As a result, government began to assume responsibility for agricultural research.

The idea of government-funded units for the sole purpose of agricultural research has long roots, but the first distinct organization of this nature was established in Connecticut in 1875. Other states adopted the idea of agricultural experiment stations, and the popularity of such stations continued to grow. Finally, in March 1887, President Grover Cleveland signed the Hatch Act, which recognized federal responsibility for subsidizing agricultural research.[5]

The Hatch Act was a creature of the land-grant colleges. The administrative heads of these colleges formed a loose association in the mid-1880s that undertook as its first campaign the passage of the Hatch Act. The resulting legislation bore the marks of its creators. A federal research grant of $15,000 per state was to "be divided between such institutions as the legislature of such State shall direct." In the South the Hatch funds went the way of the land grants of 1862—exclusively to whites.

Theoretically the Southern land-grant institutions served all, but their doors were closed to blacks. In 1887, dividing Hatch funds between white and black land-grand colleges would have been impossible. Black land-grant colleges were not "separate but equal"; they were nonexistent. By 1890 the complete abandonment of black farmers began to trouble the Northern conscience, and when the second Morrill Act was passed to increase the funding of the land-grant colleges, a provision for the establishment of black land-grant colleges was tacked onto it.

Some seventeen "1890 colleges," as they came to be called, were established. The label was significant, because the differentiation between the white 1862 colleges and the black 1890 colleges went beyond mere names. The 1890 colleges received a dismally low percentage of federal and state funds and were not allowed membership in the increasingly powerful National Association of State Universities and Land-Grant Colleges.[6]

Since blacks were barred from the Southern white land-grant institutions, obtaining adequately trained teachers for the new 1890 colleges posed a serious problem, which was compounded by the meager salaries carved out of limited funds. Under these conditions, Washington's begging supplication to Carver in 1896 is easy to understand. Washington was ever eager to secure more for his school and in 1890 had tried unsuccessfully to obtain the land grant provided by the second Morrill Act. Instead the grant went to the state school at Huntsville, headed by W. H. Councill.[7]

In 1896 both Councill and Washington wanted the Alabama legislature to provide funds for an experiment station at their schools. Although Councill was willing to "out-accommodate" Washington, by this time Washington had a number of factors in his favor. His Atlanta speech had won national recognition for him and increased contributions for the Institute, making possible the construction of the new Agricultural Building. He had carefully cultivated the friendship and support of a number of prominent politicians in Alabama and knew the arts of political bargaining. If this were not enough, Washington led a group of legislators on a tour of his campus, where they met his impressive new head of the Agricultural Department, and also went to Montgomery to lobby for the interests of his school. Washington outmaneuvered

Councill and won the battle for the experiment station, even though the land-grant college was the more logical place for such a facility.[8]

The two men were battling for a crumb. Typically, the financial support provided by the act to establish the station was rather token. Whereas the experiment station at Auburn received $15,000 of Hatch Act money each year, Tuskegee's station annually received $1,500 of state funds. There were also no provisions for land or buildings, which were to be supplied by the Institute. Nevertheless, Washington could claim a symbolic victory in obtaining the first all-black experiment station in the United States.[9]

Other features besides black administration and low funding set Tuskegee's experiment station apart. Its failure to receive any Hatch Act funds placed it in a kind of stepchild relationship with the United States Department of Agriculture (USDA). The Hatch Act established an Office of Experiment Stations within the USDA to oversee the stations receiving federal funds. These stations were required to file annual reports to justify the use of their appropriations and in turn received advice and aid from the USDA. Tuskegee's station might have been completely ignored by the federal government had it not been for Secretary of Agriculture James Wilson. Instead, Alfred C. True, the director of the Office of Experiment Stations, included Carver's station in the activities of the office, asking him to file voluntary reports and sending him all the office's publications. True also included the Tuskegee station in his reports, although he apparently received with some degree of incredulity Carver's assurances that $1,500 constituted all the station's funding.[10]

Under Secretary Wilson the USDA tried to aid Carver's work by enlisting him as a collaborator in research projects directly under the department's control. Usually such aid came in the form of sample seeds, fertilizers, or equipment to be tested, not monetary grants. Because most of the USDA's research funds went to state legislatures and not the research units themselves, Carver's share remained exceedingly small. For example, when the Adams Act of 1906 increased the federal research funds from $15,000 to $30,000 per state, all of Alabama's increase went to the Auburn station, so that Carver's station now received one-twentieth, instead of one-tenth, the funding given the other station. Actually the discrepancy was even greater, because Auburn's station received other state and college funds, while Tuskegee's did not. By 1912 Auburn's annual funding had reached $69,439; Carver's appropriation remained $1,500 for as long as the station existed.[11]

Although James Wilson was unable to give Carver much substantial help, he was a continual fountain of encouragement. In 1901 he wrote Carver of a request from the North Carolina College of Agriculture asking the secretary to recommend someone for a professorship at a salary that more than doubled Carver's. "I said at once," Wilson declared, "I would have George Carver go there but that I can't take him away from Tuskegee, where he is doing his life work." More realistically, Wilson continued, "It is true that God in His wisdom has tinted your skin. In His wisdom, mind you; there is no mistake in His work. You could probably not get this $2,500 on that account." Five years later Wilson assured Carver, "You are probably doing more good to the southern people than any other man in the South; and I write this with deliberation." If so, Carver was doing this service with incredibly limited resources.[12]

In some ways the Tuskegee station resembled all the others in organization. It had a director and a Board of Control. The board was composed of the state commissioner of agriculture, the president and the experiment station director of the agricultural college at Auburn, and the members of the board of trustees of Tuskegee Institute who lived in Tuskegee. While it was given the power to supervise the work of the Tuskegee station and to suggest experiments, the board never played a very active role. In reality Booker T. Washington was a one-man Board of Control.[13]

Washington was greatly interested in the work of the experiment station because, like everything else connected with Tuskegee, he was anxious for it to be a credit to the Institute and to blacks. Again his expectations were exorbitant. He wanted the station to be the equal of the white ones, while often ignoring the fact it received only a fraction of their support, financially and otherwise. Carver rightfully resented impossible demands that were frequently not backed by any significant financial support.

Yet Carver wanted the station to be a success probably more than anyone else did. He entered the work with an enthusiasm typical of a man who had often won despite the odds. Many of the experiments he conducted on the ten-acre experimental plot were similar to those at other stations. Indeed, a great deal of duplication of effort occurred in the early days of American experiment station work. Carver made no revolutionary departures from standard procedures, and none of his findings had a radical impact on the practice of scientific agriculture. The emphasis of his work, however, was decidedly different from that of most stations. Actually his lack of funds may have been a blessing in disguise, for most of his results were within the reach of the "man fartherest down," the black farmer.

Many of the standard practices of scientific agriculture were sound in theory but could not possibly be duplicated by impoverished sharecroppers and tenant farmers. Partly by intention and partly because of its limitations, Carver's station became more of a "little man's station" than others. Even though his experiments were aimed at all levels of farming, Carver spent significantly more time on projects that required hard work and the wise use of natural resources rather than expensive implements and fertilizers.

In his first experiment station bulletin, published in 1898, Carver set forth the goals of his station, declaring that "neither time nor expense will be spared to make our work of direct benefit to every farmer." He specifically promised to investigate soils and how to improve them, fruits and vegetables best suited for home and market, forage plants, and livestock raising. Expressing a desire not to duplicate the efforts of other stations, he noted that he would quote from other stations' bulletins when "their work bears directly upon our interests" and acknowledged he had "freely used the ideas and, in some cases, without especial reference [the] language" of other bulletins.

Carver made it clear in his first bulletin that he intended the station to serve as an advisor and consultant to farmers, writing that "we not only invite, but urge, every farmer to send samples of soils, grains, fertilizers, fodders, grasses, insects, feeding stuffs, etc." to the station for analysis. In addition Carver invited "every farmer within reach, to visit our Station frequently and come in more direct touch with us." Although this kind of invitation was fairly standard among experiment stations, black farmers likely felt more comfortable in accepting an offer from Carver than one from Auburn.[14]

Carver promised to issue a bulletin about once a quarter and, as far as possible, to provide them free of charge. Publishing bulletins was considered one of the major functions of experiment stations. Often these early publications reported the findings of station experiments and were directed more at other researchers than at farmers. Thus many employed careful scientific language that described results, but only hesitantly suggested applications of those results. Carver, on the other hand, promised that "few technical terms will be used, and where such are introduced, an explanation will always accompany them."[15] As a result, while Carver's bulletins rarely contained radically new scientific ideas, they were usually more simply written and readable than most. In the production of bulletins, as well as many other areas of his career, Carver often played the role of interpreter rather than that of innovator.

Carver fell far short of his optimistic projection of four bulletins a year. During Washington's lifetime he averaged only a bulletin and a half each year, which provided another source of conflict between Washington and himself. The principal was concerned about the unfavorable comparison that could be made between the volume of Carver's production and that of other stations. The station at Auburn did outproduce Carver several times over, but such a comparison was unfair. With two exceptions Carver personally produced all the thirty-one bulletins written by 1916. By 1905 the Auburn station staff numbered thirteen men, more than half of whom held advanced degrees. Few of the thirteen could have had outside demands on their time comparable to those under which Carver labored.[16]

Nevertheless Washington relentlessly pressured Carver, complaining in 1909, "I cannot feel that your department is doing justice to the matter of getting out the Bulletins." In the same letter he reluctantly granted Carver's request for a stenographer to help with the bulletins but warned him not to "make a mistake of becoming dependent upon this kind of help." Carver was expected to conduct the research, prepare the manuscript, and do the typing, but he was not provided with a printing press. Consequently, although Washington demanded more bulletins, when a finished manuscript was submitted to the school's printing office, Carver was often told there were no funds to print it. On several occasions he had to resort to begging for appropriations, and at least one bulletin was never published. At one point, after Carver had waited six months to get three different bulletins printed, he expressed his bewilderment to Washington. "I do not understand where the Experiment Station appropriation goes," he wrote; "I am very confident I have not used it." He had cause to be suspicious, for a public accountant sent in 1907 to examine Tuskegee's use of the experiment station appropriation found charges against the account by other departments.[17]

Usually between two thousand and five thousand copies of a bulletin were printed. It rarely took long for the supply to be exhausted, and getting money for reprints was even harder than for the first printing. This was frustrating to Carver, for he was delighted by the growing demand for his bulletins. He took special pleasure in informing Washington of such praise, perhaps to show that his work was appreciated elsewhere, if not at home. For example, in 1911 Carver sent Washington a copy of a letter which he declared "was not intended to reach our eyes and ears." In the letter the Deputy Commissioner of Education for Massachusetts recommended Carver's bulletins as "among the very best."[18]

Carver believed the demand for his bulletins resulted from his unique "threefold idea" in the writing of some of them. Rather than aiming these bulletins at other researchers, Carver sought to supply three different groups with valuable information about one crop in one publication. Thus several of his bulletins contained simple cultivation instructions for farmers, a "little of the history, botany, entomology and fungus diseases" of the plant for teachers, and recipes for housewives. Actually this was only one of the many kinds of publications produced by Carver. His bulletins covered a wide range of subjects and utilized various styles, from simple farming instructions to, in one case, a mycological treatise.[19]

Both the variety of subjects and the multileveled approach of Carver's bulletins illustrated his unique position among agricultural researchers and educators. Other experiment station staffs included separate chemists, botanists, entomologists, and mycologists. At the Tuskegee station all these positions were filled by one man—Carver. This had its advantages and disadvantages. Obviously the division of Carver's labors made it practically impossible for his original research in any one field to measure up to that of specialists. Yet more than his working conditions pushed Carver toward the role of generalist in an age of increasing specialization. He viewed the world as an organic whole and was interested in all facets of nature and the relationships among them. Being a generalist meant Carver did not excel in any single branch of science, but his combined knowledge of the various branches was exceeded by few. The scope of his knowledge was a decisive factor in his becoming one of the most effective agricultural educators and scientific popularizers of his era.[20]

The wide range of Carver's interests and his concern for the "little man" were apparent in his research work at the experiment station. From the first he simultaneously undertook a variety of projects that reflected his various interests. Some were continuations of earlier work. Very soon after his arrival in Tuskegee, Carver cooperated with F. S. Earle of the Auburn experiment station in compiling a preliminary list of the fungi of Alabama, contributing sixty-four specimens to Earle's list, which was published as Bulletin 80 by the Auburn experiment station. During his second year he conducted cross-breeding experiments with amaryllis.[21]

At the Tuskegee station Carver divided the ten-acre experimental field into a number of plots and proceeded with several experiments. He selected one acre of the poorest land on the farm for a soil-building experiment. Using good cultivation practices and rotating soil-enriching plants like cowpeas and velvet beans, he was able to increase dramatically the productivity of the soil without heavy use of commercial fertilizers. In 1897 the yield of the one-acre plot resulted in a net loss of $2.40, but by 1903 Carver was able to produce a net gain of $94.65 from the same acre. The results of this experiment were published in 1905 in Bulletin 6, *How to Build Up Worn Out Soils*. The bulletin stated that the experiment was conducted "keeping in mind the poor tenant farmer with a one-horse equipment" and that "every operation performed has been within his reach." As Carver noted, "This seemed desirable, because the majority of the Negro farmers in the vicinity of Tuskegee are men of small means and are under the necessity of earning a living while bringing their land up to a condition of productiveness."[22]

In 1897 Carver also conducted an experiment on sweet potatoes, which fit the mold of standard fertilization experiments and was therefore aimed at the farmers who could afford to purchase commercial fertilizers. He marked off sixteen plots of one-half acre each and planted them with three varieties of sweet potatoes. Using fertilizers supplied by the German Kali Works of New York, he tested the effect of various combinations and amounts of fertilizers, as well as the lack of fertilizer. The results, set forth in Bulletin 2, *Experiments with Sweet Potatoes*, were surprising only in the degree of difference per acre in production—40 bushels to 266 bushels. The poor quality of the original soil was probably responsible for this incredible difference. Carver's careful cultivation of the soil, however, aided in producing "the largest yield ever made in the state." His success was met with some disbelief, and Carver disgustedly declared that some of the teachers "want to deny the yield because they would not go out to see it."[23]

During the first year Carver experimented with stock feeding with the goal of reducing dependence on expensive commercial stock foods. He tried a mixed diet of corn and acorns on hogs.

Some people on campus thought Carver was "going crazy" when he offered to buy acorns from nearby farmers, but Bulletin 1, *Feeding Acorns*, received praise from other experiment stations. In the bulletin Carver extolled the "beautiful Southland of ours, with so many natural resources" and noted that "the great quantity of acorns produced in our oak forests . . . have been heretofore practically a waste product."[24]

Beginning in 1898 Carver initiated a series of experiments on forage plants to determine "the best ones for soil builders and forage purposes" in the locality. Six varieties of cowpeas, velvet beans, and five kinds of corn were tested the first year. Later sorghum, soybeans, and various grains were tested. Many of the grains were not usually grown in Alabama, and Carver was trying to encourage their use. In 1906 he published Bulletin 8, *Successful Yields of Small Grain*, to demonstrate that good results were possible with proper cultivation of the soil. His findings preceded by four years a similar report by the Auburn station.[25]

In addition to trying out plants rarely cultivated in Alabama, Carver also experimented with livestock of the same category. Sheep-raising experiments in 1898 showed that although sheep could be profitably raised in Alabama, parasites were a major problem. Experiments in beekeeping were not very successful for a variety of reasons, and Washington remained unhappy with Carver's efforts in this area.[26]

Carver began asking for various kinds of aid from the USDA, headed by his old friend James Wilson as secretary of agriculture, and whenever possible Carver's requests were granted. In 1899 he asked for the establishment of a voluntary observer's weather station at Tuskegee. Such a station was opened, and Carver was given weather reporting equipment by the Weather Bureau of the USDA.[27]

As Carver became involved in more and more different projects, Washington expressed concern that the experiment station consumed too much time and land when "we consider the small amount of money we are getting from the state." The principal feared that "the mere fact that this large field is called an experiment field prevents it being used in producing crops that we need." Evidently Washington believed research should be profitable and was reluctant to admit that failures are a necessary part of experimentation. As in all other areas of campus activity, he issued contradictory suggestions and orders. While chastising Carver for "clinging too closely to methods formerly used," Washington insisted that he was not spending enough time experimenting on the one most widely tested crop in the South, stressing in 1910 the importance of raising at least an acre a year of cotton, "since that is the principal industry in this part of the country."[28]

Carver had tested thirteen varieties of cotton in 1899, but he increased his cotton experiments under Washington's pressure and had issued five bulletins on cotton by 1915. Washington, the realist, was correct in believing that farmers would continue to rely on cotton and thus needed help with that crop, especially with the approach of the boll weevil. Yet Carver, the dreamer, was more interested in finding something to end this debilitating reliance on cotton.[29]

James Wilson shared Carver's dream and in 1901 thought he had found an ideal occupation to supplement cotton growing—the cultivation of silk. He wrote Carver in November, telling him of the USDA's request for a $10,000 appropriation from Congress to study silk culture. Asserting that the occupation would be ideally suited to Carver's region and race, Wilson wrote that he wanted some of this money to go to Tuskegee.[30]

Carver grasped the opportunity with enthusiasm and obtained Washington's consent for the project. Admitting he knew little about silk culture, he requested information and a list of things needed to prepare for the experiment. A food supply for silkworms was necessary, so Wilson had 300 cuttings of mulberry sent for Carver to set out. The cuttings did well, and a small-scale effort was made in the spring of 1902 with about twenty-five silkworms. Carver was encouraged by the initial success and declared that Tuskegee was honored to take part in the project because "something is going to be done for our people which will be far reaching and of lasting benefit to them."[31]

Dr. L. O. Howard of the Division of Entomology in the USDA was also enthusiastic and imported two modern reels and an expert reeler from Europe. One reel was to remain in Washington; the other was to be sent to Tuskegee. The USDA evidently decided to make Tuskegee the center of this enterprise and paid Carver's way to Washington, D.C., in early 1903 to discuss the project. During the spring of 1903 efforts centered on raising the silkworms and expanding the mulberry grove, and USDA officials made several trips to Tuskegee to inspect the results. Then in the fall of 1903 Carver and a "bright advanced student" went to Washington to watch the setting up of a reel and learn the art of reeling.[32]

The glowing hopes for silk culture began to fade in the face of practical difficulties and waning interest, and the project quietly collapsed within a few years. Four decades later Carver recalled that the work "was not attractive to my people who know nothing of sericulture. . . . We are cotton growers."[33] While silk culture was an unrealistic means for economically uplifting black farmers, the project likely suffered also from a trait of Carver's personality which marked much of his research work. He was an impatient dreamer who sought a dramatic breakthrough to end the cycle of poverty in the South. His interest in any venture rapidly waned after the first success and seldom could be maintained long enough to bring an idea to fruition. Instead, a new idea would grasp him and he would move on to a new project. "I am not a finisher," he often said in later years.[34] A few of his dreams served as catalysts for increased interest and research in some areas. Many, however, were born prematurely and died.

Carver did maintain a steady interest in mycology throughout his career. At Iowa State he had developed a talent for collecting specimens, but mycology is a scientific discipline that requires a high degree of training and sophisticated equipment for the proper identification of the multitudinous species of fungi, and Carver had neither the training nor the equipment. Nevertheless, his mycological efforts were among his significant scientific contributions.

Quick to exploit the ideal collecting conditions of warm, humid Alabama, Carver compiled a list of *Cercosporae* he found in Macon

County and published it in the organ of the Iowa Academy of Sciences in 1899. The list was also published as Bulletin 4 of the Tuskegee Experiment Station. In the bulletin, *Some Cercosporae of Macon County, Alabama,* Carver expressed his gratitude to L. H. Pammel and J. B. Ellis, another prominent mycologist, for their help. He had reason to be grateful, since his own equipment for identification consisted of little more than a microscope that had been given him by the students and faculty of Iowa State. Throughout his career he sent specimens to specialists all over the nation for verification. While his preliminary identifications were remarkably accurate, considering his training and equipment, Carver's real talent was for finding rare and new species.[35]

J. B. Ellis was grateful for Carver's talents. He received many valuable specimens in return for aiding Carver in identification, several of which were noted in articles on new species by Ellis and others in the *Journal of Mycology.* In 1902 Ellis collaborated with B. M. Everhart on an article entitled "New Alabama Fungi" which listed sixty important species he had received from Carver. Included in the list were two new species named for the Tuskegee scientist.[36]

Carver was also in touch with other mycologists, who often requested his help in locating material and acknowledged his aid in articles. He corresponded with and sent specimens to several mycologists and plant pathologists in the USDA. Although these activities hardly had the dramatic qualities of his peanut research, Carver's efforts were valuable and marked him as a man who could have had a significant career in mycology if conditions had allowed it to become more than a hobby. The idea of being a mycologist, however, died with Carver's dreams of getting his Ph.D. in botany.[37]

The years from 1902 to 1905 were devoted to finding crops that would both build up depleted soil and be attractive to farmers. With the cooperation of the USDA, Carver experimented with sugar beets and a new variety of cowpea.[38] Then in 1903 he began "making a pretty thorough test of the Spanish peanut." Although he continued to experiment with new crops, such as rice and Cuban sugarcane, he gradually focused his attention on three crops that seemed most promising to him: cowpeas, sweet potatoes, and peanuts.[39] He realized that while farmers were desperate for help, they were also reluctant to try anything new. He therefore embarked on a program to convince them of the value of these crops. To do this he stressed not only the soil-building qualities of the plants, but also how the crops could help make the farmer more self-sufficient by meeting needs that previously required purchased goods.

Carver began with an investigation of possible uses of the cowpea. In 1902 he informed Booker Washington that cowpeas could be grown in abundance and would meet many of the needs of the school. Bulletin 5, *Cow Peas*, was published in November 1903, and in it Carver stressed that although cowpeas were not quite as good as alfalfa in nitrogen gathering, they provided "much nutritious and palatable food for both man and beast." To prove his point he gave twenty-five recipes for the use of cowpeas, including directions for making coffee, griddle cakes, soup, pudding, salad, and croquettes. The bulletin was so popular that it was revised and reprinted in 1908. It was followed by a more complete bulletin on cowpeas in 1911, which embodied Carver's "threefold" idea of simultaneously speaking to the needs of farmers, teachers, and housewives.[40]

Sweet potatoes seemed especially attractive to Carver because they could be cultivated relatively easily and stored for use during the winter months. In 1906 he issued a bulletin on methods of preserving sweet potatoes and another of his "threefold" bulletins in 1910. Bulletin 17, *Possibilities of the Sweet Potato in Macon County, Alabama*, included information on the history and varieties of sweet potatoes, their cultivation, insect and fungus problems and their treatment, harvesting, storing, canning, and preparation of sweet potatoes for stock food and for human consumption. Few of the ideas were original with Carver; he openly acknowledged that many of the recipes were taken verbatim from a USDA bulletin. But he combined his experiences with existing knowledge to produce a readable bulletin popular enough to require several reprintings.[41]

The peanut, the crop that eventually won Carver his fame, was the last of the three to receive his attention. It captured his imagination originally because in addition to its easy cultivation and soil-building properties, it also provided a much-needed source of protein. Carver was deeply concerned about nutrition and realized that meat was a luxury beyond the economic reach of the impoverished sharecroppers. His plot work with peanuts, which started in 1903, convinced him that the cultivation of the crop was uniquely suited for the needs of small Southern farmers. He began collecting data and recipes for a bulletin on peanuts. The final product, Bulletin 31, *How to Grow the Peanut and 105 Ways of Preparing It for Human Consumption*, was published soon after Washington's death and proved to be one of Carver's stepping stones to fame.[42] Although earlier USDA publications had recommended the planting of peanuts and suggested numerous possible uses for the crop, Carver's bulletin was the first to give specific recipes.

In 1904, however, Washington was still concerned that Carver was not giving sufficient attention to cotton, and he turned nine additional acres over to Carver for cotton experiments. The nine acres were planted rather late in 1905 with several varieties of cotton. By July 1905 the plot was reported to attract "the attention of everyone who passes the field" because the cotton "is extremely well bolled and is growing very fast, due largely to the careful and thorough preparation of the soil."[43]

One of the varieties of cotton being tested was "Carver's Hybrid," the product of cross-breeding experiments by Carver. He continued crossing and hybridizing cotton with the view of producing a long staple and a more prolific upland variety, as well as one that matured rapidly before the boll weevil could do much damage. Some of his hybrids drew favorable comment, but none became established as a major new variety. The farmers who received the improved seeds free at the annual Farmer's

Conference, however, probably did not care if Carver's cotton did not appear on the various lists of major varieties. One Baldwin County farmer, for example, claimed that his Carver's Hybrid was "the best looking cotton in the county."[44]

Although Carver practically had to be forced to grow cotton originally, the publicity given to his results increased his interest. He was informed that his cotton experiments had been highly commended at a meeting of experiment station workers in Germany, and German officials asked him to make a list of cotton seeds best adapted for East Africa. Italian officials requested similar help for Somalia. Carver's abilities also received recognition closer to home. A Montgomery cotton merchant sent him some cotton seed from India to test, noting that "with your watchful and talented attention, something for the good of all may be developed." Another cotton factor to whom Carver sent a bale of cotton declared that if all the cotton of the section was of equal staple and as carefully harvested and ginned, it would bring an additional $1.25 per bale. As Carver quickly pointed out, this increased market value on an average crop would bring in an additional $39,000 to Macon County alone.[45]

What especially delighted Carver was the success he had with cotton he grew without the use of commercial fertilizers. He used two methods of fertilization that were, he declared, "the cheapest and most effective way of reclaiming barren land." The first of these methods was the green manuring system, where "heavy growths of cowpeas, velvet beans, grass, etc." were plowed under in the fall and "rye, wheat, oats, barley, vetch, etc." in the spring. The second method employed a compost made of leaves, mulch, and barnyard manure. By this method Carver was able to grow numerous bolls of "unusually large and healthy development" on ordinary cotton stalks.[46] Obviously, if a tenant farmer could reduce his need for commercial fertilizer, the chances of lifting his burden of debt improved.

Ironically, as Carver's interest in cotton grew, Booker T. Washington's seems to have declined. By 1908 conditions in the Agricultural Department at Tuskegee had reached a crisis, and Washington's confidence in Carver had been shaken. The result was not only a reorganization of the department, but also an increased interest in and attention to the experiment station by the principal. His criticisms and suggestions grew more frequent until he was dictating station policy to Carver. For his part, Carver resented the interference in his work and Washington's continually changing orders. In addition, while his workload was decreased by his removal from the Agricultural Department, he was only given one postgraduate student to assist him in his station work, although his bulletins continued to list Tuskegee's entire agricultural staff on the masthead.[47]

Carver's frustration with Washington's fluctuating priorities was vented in a bitter letter in February 1911. He reminded the principal of his orders in 1910 to turn the station into a "sort of demonstration" farm for the growing of vegetables. Seeds had been ordered and planted when Washington decided that grasses and soybeans should be grown instead. Carver was glad to cease growing vegetables, "except in an experimental way," since the marketing procedures of the school required him to sell his produce through the school truck garden at a loss. He also agreed that soybeans and grasses should be tested, but insisted upon the need to continue cotton experiments, declaring that:

> so long as we have an experiment station, we ought to grow such an important crop as cotton—at least enough of it to show something of its culture and management, as I do not see how the public could excuse an experiment station that did not grow cotton, and especially now, in the most critical time, since the boll weevil will reach us in a very few years. In fact we should stand at the forefront at fighting this pest.[48]

Carver, however, as well as Alabama farmers, soon grew disillusioned with cotton production when the boll weevil rapidly defeated the efforts to stop its spread. First entering Alabama in 1910, the weevil had infested 51,300 square miles of the state by 1921.[49]

Actually, by 1910 Carver's interest in the entire Tuskegee experiment station was declining, and he turned more and more to the laboratory and lecture circuit, where he did not have to rely upon cooperation from Bridgeforth's department. Charges of neglect began to arise. Carver had to depend on student labor supplied by Bridgeforth to cultivate the experimental fields, and sometimes he failed to supervise these students sufficiently. One investigative committee reported discovering a boy applying some kind of fertilizer to plants in the station plots. When he was questioned, the boy admitted he knew nothing about the fertilizer but had decided to try it, without consulting Carver, after reading about it in the *Southern Cultivator*.[50]

During the later years of Washington's administration, only three new plot work experiments really aroused Carver's interest. As usual when Carver was excited about something, he was able to interest others. The first of these projects was a cultivation technique—natural fertilization. The other projects concerned new crops for Alabama—soybeans and alfalfa.

Organic fertilization, both by plowing under vegetable matter and by using composts and manure, seemed to answer a crying need for small farmers. Carver first tried the methods on cotton crops and produced a high yield—about a bale and a half per acre. He then extended the experiment to other crops and got phenomenal results. Not only were such techniques cheaper, but they also increased the resistance of the land to drought and excessive heat and did more permanent good in enriching the soil than did commercial fertilizers, Carver contended. His faith in organic fertilization place him outside the mainstream of then current scientific doctrine, which advocated the increased use of synthetic fertilizers. Few shared his enthusiasm until the needed resources for the synthetics proved to be limited. With his methods and natural "green thumb," Carver was able to produce vegetables of gigantic size, which apparently aroused some degree of envy on campus. He urged the principal to be careful in passing on his ideas to the men on the Tuskegee school farms. "I think the effect will be better," he cautioned Washington, "if you leave my name off this report, if sent to the farms as [my report] the management resents it."[51]

Soybeans and alfalfa were only two of several crops tested by Carver, often in cooperation with the USDA. Strangely, he failed in his attempt to cultivate kudzu, but he was especially delighted with the soybean results because the crop provided abundant forage "of the nicest possible kind." His interest was increased by the visit of a Northern agriculturist to inspect Tuskegee's soybean work, and he was intrigued by the growing interest in soybeans as a source of vegetable oil. In 1914 he expanded his soybean experiments in cooperation with a New Jersey paint company and tested five varieties to determine the tonnage of forage, number of bushels of beans, quantity of oil, and fertilization properties each variety yielded.[52]

His alfalfa experiments were conducted in collaboration with both the USDA and Alabama's state commissioner of agriculture. Despite poor weather conditions, Carver was able in 1912 to get a prolific yield of alfalfa on two acres without commercial fertilizers; each acre produced three tons of hay. He wrote James Wilson that there was "no reason why alfalfa should not be grown very generally over the South." "Anyone who sees this plot," Carver declared, "I think will have no skepticism about it." State Commissioner Reuben F. Kolb was so impressed with Carver's data that he sent them to the Montgomery *Journal* for publication.[53]

Washington was also impressed and decided that Carver should grow more alfalfa. Carver, however, balked at the idea of becoming an alfalfa producer instead of an experimenter. Some of his objections were practical. Tuskegee's Agricultural Department had the teams, labor, and tools necessary to cultivate the desired twenty acres of alfalfa; the experiment station did not. He only hinted at his fears of further conflict with Bridgeforth, writing that the "persons who are to receive the benefits from [the experiment] must be in sympathy with it, since after all I must depend upon them for all the labor of every description."[54]

This conflict and other similar ones decreased Carver's taste for experiment station work. He continued to be plagued by drafts against his budget by other departments.[55] The basic problem, however, was that Carver was not a "finisher" and Washington was mainly interested in final products. In his plot work, as well as his later career, Carver conceived of himself as a "trail blazer" who pointed the way and inspired others to complete and expand his ideas. Given his limited funds, equipment, and time, perhaps Carver was a greater realist than Washington. Unfortunately, most agricultural researchers were heading in another direction. Increasing amounts of federal and state funds were piped into mechanization and efficiency projects that aided the big agribusiness units, not the small farmer.[56] Had there been more men like Carver and had they been given adequate funding, perhaps both the decline of the family farm and the mass exodus to the cities could have been slowed.

The Process of
"Understanding Relationships"

Agricultural education was obviously the ultimate goal of Tuskegee experiment station work, for even the most significant findings of agricultural research were of little practical value until communicated to farmers. But in many ways discovering what farmers should be doing was much easier than persuading them to accept and use new techniques. This task was especially difficult in the early days of agricultural education. The merits of modern practices were not so obvious then, and many farmers were illiterate and superstitious. In most of them there was an ironic combination of spirited individualism and economic dependence. Even if their suspicion of "book learning" was overcome, many farmers were tightly reined in by their landlords and creditors. Self-sufficient farming and crop diversification, two of the major tenets of early agricultural education, often contradicted the interests of landlords and creditors, who preferred a cash crop and a dependent labor force.[1]

These conditions affected all nonlandowning farmers, but the black farmers suffered the most. A smaller percentage of them owned the land they worked, and they were further handicapped by the legacies of slavery. Freedom was a decided improvement over bondage, but liberty could not buy land, food, or clothes for the propertyless ex-slaves. Although Southerners declared slavery a great civilizing and educational force for the uplift of blacks, the "peculiar institution" did not always prepare slaves for effective independence. Slavery left many freedmen with little more than a knowledge of cotton cultivation and a distaste of manual labor.

Illiterate, propertyless, and usually lacking experience in farm management, blacks soon saw even their newly won freedom slipping away. Soon after the end of the Civil War, Southerners began evolving patterns of repression to keep the valuable black labor force in a condition of unofficial slavery. Though this policy was not entirely successful, the South effectively closed enough doors of opportunity to keep a large majority of blacks not only on the farm, but on someone else's farm. The rising tide of racism and white supremacy made exploitation easy, even of black landowners. Regardless of their position, most black farmers lived bleak and precarious existences in the land where cotton reigned supreme.[2]

Because the white power structure was unlikely to radically alter the prevailing economic status of black farmers, many black educators assumed the responsibility for alleviating their plight. These men took on a gigantic responsibility with incredibly limited resources. To obtain the needed funds many, such as Booker T. Washington, were forced to use devious and demeaning tactics. After all, beneath the veneer of rhetoric they were asking whites to act against perceived economic interests. Aiming at economic independence for their race, Washington and others promised an efficient labor force. In an era when white supremacy was a national doctrine, Washington's success at selling himself and his ideas was miraculous, although he sometimes became so enmeshed in political manuevering that he lost sight of his goals and made unnecessary and detrimental compromises.[3]

One of the keys to Washington's success was his ability to recruit highly competent blacks. Without the aid of such men as Carver, Washington could never have led Tuskegee Institute to the place of prominence it held by the time of his death. Their talents served both the school and the race, as they became the vehicles for implementing Washington's noblest visions.

Because of the large numbers of blacks engaged in farming,

either by choice or because of the lack of alternatives, Washington had long realized the importance of agricultural training. Lacking both men and means prior to 1896, he had to rely on informal educational efforts in agriculture. When he obtained funds then to establish a separate department of agriculture at Tuskegee, he needed a man of exceptional talents to head the department. Carver may have fallen short of Washington's demands as an administrator, but few excelled him as an educator.

Even at the height of Washington's exasperation with Carver, the principal admitted that Carver was "a great teacher, a great lecturer, a great inspirer of young men and old men." Numerous elements of Carver's personality combined to make him a tremendously effective educator and speaker. He did not possess polished oratorical skills, but he did have a highly developed sense of showmanship. Usually speaking in a plain, conversational tone, both in public lectures and in the classroom, Carver sprinkled his talks with subdued humor and understated dramatic examples. The impact of his speeches was often incredible. One listener vowed, "You are the most seductive being I know, capable of making yourself loved by all the world when you choose."[4] Actually it was this remarkable talent as much as his scientific achievements that brought Carver international fame. In the beginning, however, this gift, like Carver's other talents, was directed toward helping the "man furtherest down."

When Carver arrived on the Tuskegee campus, he was armed with an advanced degree and teaching experience from one of the nation's leading agricultural colleges. He quickly learned, however, that Tuskegee Normal and Industrial Institute was considerably different from Iowa State. Iowa State was a college that accepted only high school graduates; Tuskegee's students' previous background ranged from fifth grade through high school education, and many were barely literate. Carver's curriculum at Iowa State was heavily weighted in the sciences and theory courses. Washington believed academic classroom work should be secondary to and supportive of the actual practice of a vocation. In Washington's

Carver in classroom at Tuskegee

educational scheme, the students were not only to get experience in their trade, but their work was also to supply the physical needs of the school.[5]

After the Civil War, many Southern blacks were eager to taste the forbidden fruit of education and made significant sacrifices to educate themselves and their children. Many of the more gifted and fortunate could and did benefit from higher education, but many were so enmeshed in poverty and ignorance that they had to be taught basic survival skills first. The teaching methods used at Iowa State were hardly appropriate for this task, and it is a measure of Carver's greatness as a teacher that he was able to be as effective under the conditions at Tuskegee as he had been at Iowa State.

At the heart of Carver's success was his enthusiasm for his subject and his unusual perspective on it. Whether his course was labeled botany, chemistry, or agriculture, what he taught was an appreciation of the miracles and beauties of nature. To Carver the great creative forces of the universe were divine in origin, and the man who attuned himself to these forces could harness their power and become an agent for the creation of the miraculous. To study agriculture was to study one means of harnessing the forces of nature for the benefit of man. Carver's lectures on even the most mundane subject became religious as well as educational experiences.[6]

In Carver's philosophy nature was a great teacher. An understanding and appreciation of natural phenomena and forces led to a clearer perception of all great truths. Nothing existed in a vacuum; everything was an integral part of the great whole. Therefore, when a student really undertood one phenomenon, he could easily be led to understand all related phenomena. Learning, Carver stressed, should be structured to lead a student from what he already knew to the "nearest related unknown." Education was merely the process of "understanding relationships."[7]

Carver believed the best means of teaching relationships was the "group method." Students were not taught abstract, isolated precepts of the various sciences, instead, one particular object, like the cowpea, was studied in depth, and the student was shown how the various natural forces that were usually studied separately under such headings as chemistry, meteorology, botany, and entomology, came together in the production of this single plant. When a student thoroughly understood the processes that created a cowpea, he could readily grasp how these forces affected other phenomena. Even his approach to teaching displayed Carver's self-ordained role of generalist in an age of specialization. Such an approach was highly effective in meeting the needs of the average Tuskegee student.[8]

Another effective ingredient in Carver's teaching formula was his belief that a student could more easily understand what could be seen and touched than an abstract idea. Every day before breakfast Carver went rambling in the woods and fields. On these trips, he declared, he communed with his Creator. He also collected specimens of plants, fungi, and minerals that were often used as classroom examples. Many of the specimens were placed in the agricultural museum, which was used by Carver and others in their teaching. Since at some point he had acquired taxidermic skills, animal specimens joined the plants and minerals.[9]

These and other physical objects were used to illustrate natural processes; for example, the roots of the cowpea were employed to explain nitrogen fixation. This kind of prop was fairly obvious, but Carver was often ingenious in his use of objects to convey abstract ideas and values. One of the key ideas in Carver's philosophy was that nature produced no waste, therefore so-called waste products resulted from man's failure to apply his intelligence to the use of natural resources. To illustrate this idea, Carver sometimes displayed a mass of tangled, knotted string that had been discarded as useless. He would then produce another batch of old string that had been neatly tied and wound, able to be used again for its original purpose. Ignorance, Carver would declare, was like the tangled mass of string, while intelligence brought order and usefulness.[10]

Carver also believed the best teacher was a guide rather than a dispenser of knowledge. Students should be inspired to learn on their own by actively engaging in the educational process; learning in this way became a lifelong adventure. His botany classes competed against one another in collecting specimens of species within a generic family. Students were encouraged to conduct experiments and engage in special projects on their own. Some, like Thomas M. Campbell, took up Carver's challenges with enthusiasm. Campbell, who later became the first black demonstration agent,* put together a hog skeleton for the agricultural museum in his spare time.[11]

Carver especially urged students to collect and identify various kinds of specimens, because he wanted them to observe and learn from the things around them. Students often brought their specimens to Carver for identification and explanation, and they were continuously astonished at the breadth of his knowledge. It became a kind of game to try to stump the professor. Finally one

---

*The USDA hired demonstration agents to induce farmers to try new methods of farming. They are what is known today as "county agents."

group of boys decided to trick Carver by constructing a new species of insect from miscellaneous parts of various bugs. "The most
pious looking fellow in the group was chosen to make the presentation in the pretended search for new entomological light," one of
the conspirators recalled. To their delighted dismay, the professor
quickly identified it correctly: he pronounced it a "humbug."[12]

Above all else, Carver's reverence for the miracles of nature
inspired students. Things once taken for granted became exciting
and miraculous when explained by Carver. On botany hikes students listened not only to generic identifications but also to reci-
tations from Greek poetry. Carver's enthusiasm was genuine and
infected those around him. One time he stayed up all night to
witness the flowering of a rare-blooming plant. His message was
clear: beauty and meaning are within the reach of even the most
impoverished.[13]

The effectiveness of Carver's classroom techniques led Washington to call upon him frequently to lecture to his fellow teachers on
how to improve their teaching methods. Once the principal even
asked him to meet with the day laborers on campus to instruct
them and inspire them to better service. Carver was also encouraged to explain his methods in writing for the use of others.[14]

His ideas were outlined in several nature study leaflets that
gave simple instructions for teaching nature study courses in rural
schools. "In the beginning," the first leaflet stated, "every teacher
should realize that a very large proportion of every true student's
work must be outside the classroom." Describing his "group
method" for presenting the parts and the families of plants, Carver
suggested many practical exercises to get students to observe their
surroundings and to think for themselves. In 1910 he again incorporated his ideas in a bulletin, *Nature Study and Gardening for
Rural Schools*.[15]

He preached that a garden should be connected with every
school and that every child should be involved in the study of nature or agriculture. "Nature study is agriculture, and agriculture is
nature study—if properly taught," he declared. Learning about
plants and how to cultivate them was valuable for everyone, for

"even if the child does not become an agriculturist, or a farmer, these things all have a tendency to make the child think, and that is what we are trying to teach him—to think."[16]

The nature study leaflets and bulletins brought Carver widespread praise, and their success induced him to embark on a large task, the writing of a botany text. James Wilson encouraged Carver in this endeavor and the resulting draft, "Suggested Outlines for the Study of Economic Plant Life," elaborated his "group method" and his emphasis of the economic importance of plants. The draft's simplified techniques for teaching were highly commended, but money was never found for its publication.[17]

Despite all of Carver's efforts to make agriculture exciting and stimulating, most of Tuskegee's students came to school to escape from the farm and preferred to study other trades. Tuskegee officials tried many tactics to get students into the Agricultural Department. Thomas M. Campbell recalled that when he first arrived at Tuskegee, the registrar attempted to interest him in farming.

> I told him promptly that I had worked long enough on a farm and did not care to learn anything more about it. He then asked me if I would like to take agriculture. I said that I thought I would like that very well. So he assigned me to the livestock division. Imagine my surprise when I learned that agriculture was farming.[18]

Such ploys were coupled with publicity attempts to glamorize agriculture and the weighting of student wage scales to favor agricultural students. Still, the number of professional agricultural students remained lower than Washington desired under both Carver's and Bridgeforth's administrations, as well as those of their successors.[19]

Carver faced other problems in trying to make his teaching effective. Most serious was the multitude of demands on his time. In addition to his administrative and other duties he was expected to teach an average of four to five classes a day. During the first years at Tuskegee his teaching consumed at least the entire morning. At first Carver sacrificed other duties to his teaching, telling Washington, "In regard to the teaching I have always felt as you do about it, and therefore have stuck with it at the expense, frequently of the other, and more practical part, but I think I see brighter days ahead, if the Lord spares you to engineer this great work."[20]

Carver's optimism began to wane when he found his load undiminished and his failure at the "more practical part" severely criticized. By 1906 he was so frustrated that he turned to his old friend James Wilson, who offered no more than sympathy and understanding:

> It is evident you need help, that is all. All these things you can manage if you can have subordinates enough to help you out. It is utterly out of the question that you can teach so much and take charge of all these other things. . . . About half that amount of teaching would be abundant, and someone else should take the other half.[21]

But Wilson was not Booker T. Washington, who was attempting to build something great from practically nothing.

Of all the rivalries on campus, the most intense was between the academic and industrial departments, which represented the "two phases" of Tuskegee's work. As these two divisions jockeyed for power, the students sometimes suffered. For example, Carver informed Washington in late September 1897, "I have as yet had no classes" because the head of the Academic Department declared that such classes "interfere with the academic work and he is not going to change the schedule." Such conflicts and the heavy workloads of all the teachers often made scheduling difficult. In 1901 Carver lamented, "At one time we have a class room, at another, none. Sometimes the teacher is present, other times absent." Clearly Tuskegee teachers had to make "bricks without straw" in more ways than one.[22]

Carver always considered teaching conditions less than ideal, but they became intolerable when Bridgeforth became the head of the Agricultural Department. Having suffered a humiliating loss to his worst enemy, Carver was definitely not prepared to be Bridgeforth's humble subordinate. For his part, Bridgeforth moved quickly to establish himself as department head in fact as well as in name. In the resulting conflict Washington encouraged the victor to treat the vanquished Carver with tact and sympathy. "You will have to bear in mind that Mr. Carver has conceded a good deal," Washington wrote, "and it will not pay just now to irritate him further." The intense rivalry did not abate, however, and the real losers were the students. They begged Carver to teach them, but Carver was only willing to conduct classes held within his own department. He wrote Washington that he could not adjust to anything that placed him under Bridgeforth.[23]

Washington was well acquainted with Carver's stubbornness and frantically sought to negotiate a settlement to win his cooperation. He apparently tried once more to make both men feel they had won a victory. Privately the principal told Carver that his classes would be sent to him and would be totally under his control. Washington failed, however, to make this point clear to Bridgeforth, and Carver begged him to "make it definite, after the classes are sent to me, that there will be no interference, as no longer than yesterday I received dictations from Mr. Bridgeforth as to what I was to do."[24]

Although Carver warned of "trouble again" unless satisfactory arrangements were made, Washington left campus with matters still unsettled. Conditions grew steadily worse during his absence, and Warren Logan, the school's treasurer, tried to calm Carver's growing indignation. He pleaded with Carver to reconsider his decision to resign, since the school needed his valuable services. Logan asserted that the lack of "official word" placing his classes under "his exclusive control" was merely an "oversight."[25]

Upon his return Washington pieced together a settlement, but a year later the truce was crumbling. Carver was unhappy, and Bridgeforth was complaining that Carver's teaching was "disconnected and miscelaneous [sic]." Having decided upon a new strategy, Washington placed Carver's classes under the Academic Department rather than the Agricultural Department. Bridgeforth was irate over the separation of what he called the "Kid Glove part of agriculture" from the practical work. The arrangement was indeed artificial and did not stop disputes over such issues as teaching loads and the location of classes.[26]

The final result of all the bickering was Carver's retreat from teaching duties. Washington was willing to make many concessions to Carver, but he would not allow him to forego teaching. Under Washington's successor, Robert Russa Moton, however, Carver finally got his way and was relieved of all teaching except in the summer school. Tuskegee's summer session was devoted to giving advanced training and encouragement to men and women who taught during the year in black schools all over the South. Carver continued to inspire and instruct these teachers during the summer for at least ten years after Washington's death, and his services were cherished by men and women who confronted numerous handicaps in bringing enlightenment to their people.[27]

Although Carver's vanity led him to desert his regular teaching duties, he never ignored the students of Tuskegee. From the beginning his relationships with students were not restricted to the classroom, for he was one teacher who took seriously Tuskegee Institute's goal of educating the total person. Tuskegee's early students were the grandchildren of slavery. Most of them needed to be taught much more than botany or chemistry; they had to be taught the essentials of living in a hostile world.

Carver often stressed the teacher's duty to take a personal interest in students, especially those "who seem rather dull and are from any cause behind in their studies." Practicing what he preached, his interest extended far beyond the classroom and included all students, not merely those in agriculture. His residence in Rockefeller Hall made him accessible to all boys in curricula from printing to plumbing. Many students availed themselves of this opportunity, and they usually found Carver a warm and willing listener to their problems. As one student noted, "When advice is sought by the humblest student there is no 'red tape' to encounter in entering his office." Carver even helped to cut the red tape students encountered elsewhere, as when he asked for relief from a school hospital bill for a crippled student.[28]

His advice was given with so much love, understanding, and

humor that it was long remembered by students. Asked about marriage, for example, he would tell the boys to "get your bird cage before you take unto yourself your canary." At the core of his advice, however, was his admonition to be "as wise as a serpent and as harmless as a dove." He tried to get "his children," as he called them, to learn to respect themselves and others. He told each to become a person "who neither looks up to the rich or down on the poor" and "who takes his share of the world and lets other people have theirs."[29]

Self-respect requires living up to one's potential, and Carver employed a number of devices to encourage students to be their best. His love and faith in them were powerful influences, but he also used wit to break down their barriers to self-fulfillment. Constantly teasing them about their "worthlessness," Carver often hinted that he might be forced to take "drastic action" if they did not improve.[30]

"His children" frequently were handicapped by poverty and discrimination, but Carver believed limited vision and narrow horizons were just as seriously restricting and could be more easily changed. He wanted students to look beyond the known and seek new answers to old problems. "This old notion," Carver wrote, "of swallowing down other peoples' ideas and problems just as they have worked them out, without putting our brain and origionality [sic] into it, and making them applicable to our specific [needs] must go. And the sooner we let them go the sooner we will be a free and indipendent [sic] people."[31]

Espousing the doctrine that achievement helped to bring acceptance, Carver constantly urged young blacks to do the "common things in an uncommon way." He lamented the fact that too few blacks had made themselves important economic and social forces in society and encouraged them to change that condition.

We must get hold of the soil and work ourselves into an indispensable part and parcel of this great body politic. At the present time we are too parasitic. If we should drop out of existence, the world would not be sufficiently jarred to cause much of a tremor. We must change that so that if such a jar should come upon us that the whole world would feel it and suffer accordingly.[32]

Carver realized that many obstacles to black success resulted from white racism, not black weakness, but he warned not to use this as an excuse for failure. In a 1908 article he restated Washington's "cast down your bucket" philosophy.

In these strenuous times, we are likely to become morbid and look constantly upon the dark side of life, and spend entirely too much time considering and brooding over what we can't do, rather than what we can do, and instead of growing morose and despondent over opportunities either real or imaginary that are shut from us, let us rejoice at the many unexplored fields in which there is unlimited fame and fortune to the successful explorer and upon which there is no color line; simply the survival of the fittest.[33]

Significantly, the article urged blacks to engage in plant breeding to develop improved species. Carver's own success in this field made him optimistic; if blacks were directed to explore the unknown, they could win the Darwinian struggle for survival.

Carver was a dreamer, and his optimism reflected the spirit of the age. Although confrontation with the harsh realities of racism later dimmed his optimism, he could never shed entirely his faith in a just universe. Such a belief was central to his religion, and it was this vision and faith that Carver sought most earnestly to impart to "his children." His was a joyous religion of love that went far beyond the Protestant work ethic or the fear of eternal damnation. As a result, students who had previously found religion repressive sought out Carver for Bible discussions.

Carver's Sunday evening Bible class grew out of this student enthusiasm. In February 1907 seven students asked Carver to help them organize a Bible class to be held during the thirty-five minute break between Sunday supper and evening chapel services. When the first meeting convened in a room at the library, about fifty students came to hear Professor Carver discuss the creation story. The creation was explained in the "light of natural and revealed religion and geological truths," using maps, charts, plants, and geological specimens as illustrations.[34]

Three months later the attendance had climbed to over a hundred and continued to grow during the thirty years Carver taught the class. Although students at Tuskegee had very little free time and were required to attend several religious services on Sunday, many boys began rushing through supper in order to get good seats for Carver's voluntary class. The class to which they hurried was obviously not a typical Bible class. One student, who reluctantly attended the first time, later recalled that upon entering the room "smiling faces . . . created an atmosphere of welcome" and for the "first time in my life I was witnessing no gloom surrounding the Bible."

> I began to feel as I had back home when we went to a candy-pulling party—happy that I had come. But perhaps this happy feeling that I had now would leave, and fear and gloom descend on me again as soon as discussion of the Bible started.[35]

Fear and gloom, however, were not part of Carver's religion. He spoke of a beneficent Creator who brought happiness in this life to all who attuned themselves to His messages. Students were puzzled by Carver's failure to mention "God" and asked the professor if "the Creator" was the same as God. He assured them God and the Creator were one and the same and explained that

> our Creator is the same and never changes despite the names given Him by people here and in all parts of the world. Even if we gave Him no name at all, He would still be there, within us, waiting to give us good on this earth.[36]

Carver's Creator could not be limited and circumscribed by man's labels; neither could He be threatened by the discoveries of science. To Carver there was no conflict between religion and science. Indeed, the Creator revealed Himself in His creations. Thus the more man learned about the universe, the more clearly he could perceive his Creator. If Carver's Creator was different from the old man in the sky of his students' previous religious training, his explanation of heaven and hell was especially enlightening to boys raised on fire and brimestone.

> When our thoughts—which bring actions—are filled with hate against anyone, Negro or white, we are in a living hell. That is as real as hell will ever be.
>
> While hate for our fellow man puts us in a living hell, holding good thoughts for them brings us an opposite state of living, one of happiness, success, peace. We are then in heaven.[37]

To Carver the Creator was good, and evil was the result of man's failure to open himself to this good. Evil was man's creation; goodness and love were God's. Therefore love was a more powerful force than hate. Such a philosophy was central to Carver's approach to racism. To return hate with hate seemed to Carver only to compound the problem and make its solution more difficult. For this reason, and not because he accepted Southern "racial solutions," Carver persistently refused to express bitterness toward the white South.

When his Bible students confronted him with statistics of racial hatred and violence, Carver responded with the story of David and Goliath to illustrate the power of love to vanquish hate.

> Fear of something is at the root of hate for others and hate within will eventually destroy the hater. Keep your thoughts free from hate, and you need have no fear from those who hate you. . . .
>
> David, though small, was filled with truth, right thinking and good will for others. Goliath represents one who let fear into his heart, and it stayed there long enough to grow into hate for others.[38]

Undoubtedly Carver was an idealistic dreamer whose optimistic faith sometimes put him out of touch with reality, about both race relations and the economic possibilities of some Southern resources. Yet to blacks grappling with the bleak conditions of an era called the "nadir of black existence," he offered a spark of hope and a reason to continue to struggle.

To a large number of students Carver gave more than inspiration. Many students might never have completed their studies at Tuskegee without the aid of loans he either made personally or cosigned with them. Carver spent little money on himself, preferring to wear old clothes and make many needed articles from waste or natural materials. Consequently he always had a large reserve of cash. With this reserve he preferred to make loans rather than gifts, as the money went further that way and did not sap the initiative of students, but he frequently made small monetary donations to those he felt needed such help. His generosity extended to nonemergency situations also, as when he donated a piano to a girls' dormitory.[39]

A student's graduation did not mean the termination of Carver's help and support. "His children" continued to turn to him for financial aid. One asked his "father" to talk to "Santie Claus" about a uniform he needed at his new school. Another wrote that he had passed the state exams and was ready to practice medicine, but he needed an instrument for reading blood pressure.[40]

More important than direct financial aid, however, were Carver's efforts to get students good jobs or further education. He operated to some degree as a one-man employment bureau, using his contacts to obtain positions for worthy students. For the brighter students he sought to secure scholarships to allow them to get a college education, and several attended his alma mater, Iowa State.[41]

In addition to such aid, Carver continued to advise and inspire students long after they left Tuskegee. He encouraged "his children" to keep in touch with him through correspondence. The many who wrote him soon learned that they would receive a prompt response. Despite his busy schedule, he always found time to pen a personal reply to all such letters.

It was not unusual for Tuskegee faculty to urge former students to report their successes and problems, and many students wrote Washington and others. Since Tuskegee strove to educate the whole person, teachers often became surrogate parents. Student letters to Carver, however, reveal a very special relationship.

Carver obviously embodied the warmth and love of parenthood more than the authority.

One Puerto Rican student wrote, "I have not forgotten you because I remember the many times you played with me and made my life while in Tuskegee happy" and closed the letter with "Goodbye old top." Another student, whom Carver had encouraged to go to Iowa State, opened his letter with "Hello Prof" and declared, "You see I'm pretty near being a scientist myself and as I have always had a hankering for being familiar with great folks I take this liberty in addressing you. Look out! I'll be calling you 'George,' first thing you know." [42]

Writing of his intention to come to the Farmers' Conference, one "child" threatened to bring a "gang" and "sit in a position facing you so I can make faces at you." As he was bringing his wife along, he declared his intention "to be 'dignified' if possible" and warned Carver, "If you start anything my gang will take care of you." [43]

Even the respect students felt for Carver's genius was tempered by affection and warmth. In a letter to the professor one student described his ambition.

> With all my boasting of you I must be frank and tell you that you are a most discouraging fellow. You see while at Tuskegee we were constantly urged to pick out some great soul whom we should strive to emulate. Unfortunately for me I picked you out, and have been working my head off to get somewhere in sight of you but every time I round a big bend and get a glimpse of your coat tail nothing possesses you but to double your speed and finally emerge on the peak of some distant, inaccessible mountain. Now young man I'm getting good and tired of it and if you want me to follow you any further you'll just have to slow down to some reasonable pace that's all!! [44]

Many letters mentioned spankings, beatings, or thrashings. "I suppose you really and truly feel like giving me a good spanking," wrote one student; "well, your 'use-to-be *boy*' is now at home with his wife and feels that it would take a pretty good man to handle him." What such letters referred to were Carver's constant teasing threats to "beat" his "bad boys." Occasionally he actually administered a mock thrashing by gently scuffling with "his children."[45]

Such horseplay was not very dignified, and some faculty members regarded the activity with distaste. A few even hinted that Carver's relationship with his boys was tainted with homosexuality. Carver did display an intensely warm and caring feeling for "his children" that was more typical of a mother than a father. After all, such women as Susan Carver, Mariah Watkins, Lucy Seymour, Mrs. Liston, Mrs. Milholland, and Etta Budd had played key roles in his developing self-image. His gentleness, religious nature, and appreciation of beauty are traits labeled feminine in Western culture, and the pleasure he took in cooking, sewing, and needlework served to enhance suspicions. Yet the persistent rumors of homosexuality most likely resulted from failure to understand an orientation to life that deviated from the norm.

Carver's gentleness was also extended to the actual children on campus. For many years he taught classes at the Children's House, a school for the sons and daughters of the faculty. Children were fascinated by Carver's lab and often stopped by to see what the professor was doing. After cautioning them to keep their hands behind their backs, he would lead them on a tour of his laboratory, explaining all the mysterious apparatuses. Sometimes he took groups of children on botany hikes.[46] When Thomas M. Campbell acquired a family of his own, Carver was often invited to Thanksgiving and Christmas dinner.

> He always came early and brought pocketsful of peanuts. He romped and played with the children and allowed them to climb upon his knees and get the peanuts out of his pockets. After dinner he would say, "Well, I'm going to leave this 'boiler factory' now."[47]

Carver acquired many favorites among the campus children and kept in touch with them after they grew up and left Tuskegee. He took special interest in his namesakes, such as George Carver Campbell, remembering their birthdays and graduations with small checks to go toward their education. Eventually, however, his namesakes grew too numerous for his bank account.

Whether "his children" were named for him or not, Carver gave them a far greater legacy than small checks. All, regardless of race or age, were taught to dream of a better world and were inspired to work at making their dreams come true. Even the practical Washington realized this gift of inspiration was too precious for a price tag.

Making Education Common

At the heart of the "Tuskegee ideal" was Washington's belief that education should be "made common," that is, related to the needs of the masses. He was striving to make the meager funds available for black education perform the monumental task of elevating an entire race. Tuskegee students were taught from their arrival to their departure to dedicate the opportunities provided by their education to the betterment of their people, not merely to personal success. Each graduate was to become a missionary spreading enlightenment to the masses of Southern blacks trapped in ignorance and poverty.

In the Washington era the need for such enlightenment was obvious in the South. Large numbers of blacks were not only illiterate, but superstitious and ignorant of even the basic knowledge necessary for survival. They had little conception of nutrition or the causes of disease, and their dismal ramshackle shanties were virtual germ factories. Most were farmers, many of whom "planted with the moon" and had scant understanding of the actual forces that controlled their harvests.

Ignorance was not limited to blacks. In the antebellum South education had been difficult for any but the affluent to obtain, and illiteracy was not unusual among whites also. As the progressive spirit swept the South at the turn of the century, programs of public education bequeathed by the Reconstruction governments were again emphasized. Great educational reforms began, and increasing amounts of money were poured into education. Unfortunately, white supremacy was a copartner of Southern progressivism. In state after state the education of black children was slighted to provide better opportunities for whites, in an open perversion of the Supreme Court's "separate but equal" doctrine.

The relative neglect of black education had at least two roots, both economic. Budget-conscious state legislators realized that with the limited resources of the South an equal per capita appropriation would probably mean poorer education for whites. Second, there was a widespread belief that blacks did not need an education and might even be spoiled as a source of cheap labor by too much learning. Thus blacks had to supplement meager state appropriations for their education with personal sacrifice and appeals to Northern philanthropy.[1]

It is hardly any wonder that Washington struggled to get the most from every dollar. Carver accepted wholeheartedly the need for "making education common" and sought to imbue his students with the missionary zeal of the "Tuskegee Ideal." He was largely successful, with some help from a perhaps less than idealistic attitude on the part of some students. Student distaste for farming made it difficult to keep agricultural enrollment high, but the fact that large numbers of Tuskegee's agricultural graduates preferred to become teachers rather than to return to the farm meant that their knowledge was diffused all over the South.

When these students left Tuskegee to work in established black schools or to found new ones, they often wrote Carver of their successes and problems. In addition to teaching such practical matters as the use of cold frames and hotbeds for winter gardening, many graduates endeavored to impart a new spirit to the disheartened peoples of their communities. Frequently their efforts met with some success, as a report from one graduate in Mississippi indicated.

Well, Prof., I hope you won't get angry with me because I state this business. Bad disease is breaking out in this community, and it is all laid on me. You know I always tried to be a good boy, and I am about to get trapped. I might as well tell you what this dis-

ease is so you will know all about it. This disease is "Self-Reli-
ance." I have been working hard to make these people depend
more on themselves, and I am certainly seeing the fruits of my
labor. When I first came down here all the community flocked to
me for cabbage plants. I told them they could raise them themselves, but they said they couldn't. As I would sell out some plants
I would tell him how he could depend upon himself along this
line. In many cases they would say they would rather buy them
than to raise them themselves. I kept after them until now, when
these people not only can sell plants, but any quantity of vegetables.[2]

While such efforts were indeed important in the lives of many
individuals, Washington had long realized more was needed to
reach enough farmers to make a dent in mass ignorance. Almost
from the day his school was opened, Washington sought to extend
its influence into the rural communities of Macon County. As
usual, his motives were mixed. He felt a genuine concern about
the plight of impoverished rural blacks, but he also realized that
their backwardness would discredit Tuskegee Institute. Out of
these concerns grew the school's extension programs.

At first Tuskegee's extension work consisted of little more than
Sunday afternoon rides by the principal into the countryside. On
these trips he sought to establish a rapport with the black farmers.
Once their trust and friendship was won, he would advise them on
how to improve their living conditions. In these efforts Washington was aided by the superintendent of the school farm, Charles
W. Green.[3]

Gradually the Institute's activities in the community grew, until the school became unofficially responsible for black education
in Tuskegee and Macon County. Numerous local schools were
opened under Washington's influence, but he sought new methods
of reaching the adult farming population. Thus in 1892 he held a
Farmers' Conference on the Institute grounds. Expressing a faith
in the "common sense" of the illiterate black farmers, Washington
believed they could make great strides if given a forum for their
problems and a source of guidance. He therefore issued about sev-

enty-five invitations to "farmers, mechanics, school teachers, and ministers to come and spend a day at Tuskegee, talking over their conditions and needs."[4]

A surprising crowd of four hundred people arrived on campus 23 February 1892 for the meeting. Instead of hearing lectures on agriculture, the farmers were encouraged to describe both their failures and successes. From the discussions a consensus emerged that the major problem of black farmers was economic dependence. When Washington asked how many owned their homes, only twenty-three raised their hands. Many admitted they often bought articles they could produce themselves, which added to their crushing burden of debt. Several farmers related how they had been able to free themselves from debt by carefully handling their limited resources, and all joined to adopt a set of resolutions in which they vowed to work for economic independence and the improvement of their homes, schools, and churches.[5]

The enthusiasm at the first Farmers' Conference persuaded Washington to make the meeting an annual affair. Attendence doubled the next year and continued to grow, until thousands were attending. Washington decided to lengthen the conference to two days, with the first day being the Farmers' Conference and the second a Workers' Conference. After the farmers had discussed their problems and what they could do for themselves, educators, ministers, and others interested in the betterment of the race would meet the next day to talk over what they could do to help the farmers in reaching their desired objectives.[6]

After Carver's arrival the conferences continued to grow and drew farmers and workers from all over the South, as well as interested whites from both the South and the North. The Farmers' Conference was as much a source of inspiration as of education, and the numerous stories of success encouraged many to sacrifice immediate wants to eventual economic independence. One farmer reported, "I was twenty years old at Emancipation. I didn't have shifting clothes, besides I was lame," but for a year "I ate water and bread" and now "I have 1,300 acres of land." Each year more and more farmers proudly announced that they had bought land and built homes, and one farmer declared, "I thank God on my knees for these Conferences. They are giving us homes."[7]

Under Carver's leadership the activities at the Farmers' Conferences increased. Most importantly, he was able to procure free garden seed from the USDA. Such seed had originally been distributed through United States congressmen to their constituents and frequently went to farmers who could help the congressmen get reelected, not to those who most needed them. By the direct grant of seeds to Tuskegee for distribution at the Farmers' Conferences, the USDA made it possible not only to encourage farmers to grow their own food stuffs and "get away from the living-out-of-the-store habit," but also to provide the means of doing so. By 1903 the USDA was supplying 2,500 packets containing ten packages of various kinds of seeds to the Tuskegee Conference. Carver also distributed seeds harvested from the experiment station plot, such as those for Carver's Hybrid cotton.[8]

The experiment station was used for practical demonstrations of what improved cultivation techniques could produce. Farmers were taken on tours of the station plots, where the various experiments were thoroughly explained to them. "They openly expressed themselves as feeling more encouraged than they had ever felt before," Carver declared, because "they could see the actual work upon the ground." Carver wanted to expand the Conference further by providing overnight accommodations to farmers who came great distances and by giving prizes as an incentive to further improvement, but apparently these ideas were considered too costly.[9]

While Carver doubtless realized the value of inspiration, as a trained agriculturist he also recognized that some problems could not be overcome without additional education. To him the conditions were truly deplorable. Much of the soil of the deep South "was practically a pile of sand and clay, making a yield far below the cost of production" because of years of soil erosion, poor land preparation, and no crop diversification. Most farmers had "practically no live stock" and "poor gardens, if any at all." As a result the food of most families was "as a rule meager, of the worst type, and poorly prepared." The remedy for such problems required more instruction than could be given in one day a year.[10]

Iowa State College had long held monthly Farmers' Institutes to meet the educational needs of the farmer, and in 1897 the idea was transplanted to Tuskegee by Carver. On 11 November 1897 the first Farmers' Institute was organized at Tuskegee, and Charles Green was elected president. Instead of yearly meetings, the Farmers' Institute met monthly in the Agricultural Building at times which would allow farmers in the immediate area to attend the session and return home by nightfall. The Institute differed from the Conference in that its members received specific agricultural advice, rather than merely inspiration and general suggestions. They were taught such things as "the kind of fertilizers to use, the kinds of crops that are adapted to particular kinds of soils, how to build up worn out soil, the rotation of crops, [and] the proper time for planting." In short the members became students while remaining full-time farmers.[11]

Attendance at the meetings was voluntary, and twenty-five to seventy-five farmers were usually present. They were encouraged to bring samples of crops, soils, and fertilizers with which they had experienced either success or failure. Employing his knowledge and abilities at analyzing soil, Carver was able to explain the causes of their results. Often the farmers were taken out to the experiment station plots where they could witness for themselves the value of scientific agriculture. Sometimes they were given samples of such things as sugarcane to try for themselves. On these tours Carver was pleased that the "questions asked were most intelligent ones and you could see that the people were asking for information." Some of the farmers also accepted Carver's invitation and began visiting the experiment station between the monthly Institute meetings.[12]

Soon many of the wives started coming to the meetings with their husbands, and Carver was delighted. He realized "the average housewife knew but little about the nutritive value of foodstuffs, economy in selection, and palatable and attractive preparation" of meals. The Farmers' Institute offered one means of correcting this deficiency, and Carver arranged for some of the senior girls at Tuskegee to prepare cooking demonstrations for the meetings.[13]

One outgrowth of the Farmers' Institute was a yearly fair on the Tuskegee campus. The first Farmers' Institute fair at Tuskegee was held in 1898 to provide a place where the farmers and their wives could display the fruits of their labor. Both the quality and quantity of the exhibits increased until highly commendable samples of all kinds of livestock and crops, as well as needlework and prepared foods, were displayed. Attendance grew from a few hundred in 1898 to thousands by 1915, and the fair was extended from one day to several days in duration. The success of the Tuskegee fair attracted the attention of local whites, and in 1911 the white and black county fairs were combined to produce one fair under the direction of the biracial Macon County Fair Association. The union of the fairs was of symbolic importance to Tuskegee blacks, but as was typical of most interracial activities of the era, certain concessions had to be made to white racial sentiments in the fair's organization and accommodations. The major concession was the provision for separate facilities, such as ticket booths.[14]

From the fair's beginning Carver recognized that it served a variety of purposes. Claiming that from the exhibits alone a "family may get a liberal education during the few days the fair is in session," Carver described the fair as a source of "strength, information, inspiration and encouragement." The gathering was immensely important for "few, if any, realize the wealth within our county and the ease with which we can, not only live, but can accumulate much above a living," he explained, "until we see and study such a collection of evidence." Knowing that the bleak and dreary existences of many farmers often led to discouragement, Carver considered "the chance to meet many old friends and form new acquaintances as well as to enjoy a good laugh" equally important benefits of the fair.[15]

Despite the success of such projects, Carver believed still more could be done for local farmers, especially "during the dull winter season." In early December 1903 he suggested that a "lecture course and some practical work" would be valuable to the farmers in the county. As a result the first "Short Course in Agriculture" was held at the Agricultural Building for six weeks in January and February 1904. The short course, which was later shortened to two weeks, was designed as a school for farmers during the winter months when many had idle time on their hands. It sessions ran from midmorning to midafternoon to allow farmers to come and return home the same day. Later, inexpensive accommodations were provided for those who lived too distant for daily travel.[16]

The sessions were provided free to the farmers and their wives and were usually held during the two weeks preceding the annual Conference. The short course got off to a slow start, with fewer than twenty farmers attending in each of the first two years. Publicity efforts in various school publications and at the Conference and the Institute were successful, and by 1912 over 1,500 were enrolled. During the two-week sessions simple and practical instruction was given by Carver, Bridgeforth, and other members of the agricultural faculty. The men were given demonstrations in "ploughing, seed testing, the use of machinery, stock judging, milk testing," and other phases of self-sufficient agriculture, including methods of organic fertilization. The women were taught poultry raising, sewing, cooking, and procedures for making dairy products. At the end of the course a "commencement" was held, featuring competitions among the students for monetary prizes and such speakers as the editor of the *Southern Cultivator*.[17]

Just as Tuskegee's regular students were implanted with a missionary zeal, farm families attending the Farmers' Conferences, Institutes, and short courses were urged to share their knowledge with others in their communities. They were encouraged to hold local institutes and conferences, and Tuskegee staff members often went to various communities to aid in organizing such activities. The impact of Tuskegee spread even more widely when Carver and others were asked to provide such help in Georgia, Florida, Mississippi, Louisiana, South Carolina, and other Southern states. Black normal schools everywhere in the South began holding their own conferences, institutes, and fairs, frequently featuring Carver as the star attraction.[18]

The enthusiasm of Southern blacks for such activities was rejuvenating to Carver and kept alive his faith and hope for the salvation of his people. Despite the other demands on his time, exhausting traveling conditions, and sometimes wretched accommodations, he attended a growing number of farmers' meetings all over the South. His trips were valuable to the cause of agricultural education, but Carver also learned a great deal. Not all of his enlightenment was inspiring, however.

The nature of the Tuskegee campus community created a rather idealized environment where one could easily insulate oneself from the degradations of racism. Not until Carver began his travels outside Tuskegee did he witness the brutal side of Southern race relations.

For example, in November 1902 he set out for a farmers' exhibit at a small black school in Ramer, Alabama, twenty miles from Montgomery. The Ramer school's two teachers, Nelson E. Henry and Ada Hannon, were well respected by the local white community, but only received $36 a year from the town for their work. Moreover, the rural town maintained rigid control over the outlying black population; no blacks were allowed to live inside the town.

Carver was accompanied by Frances Johnston, a renowned white Northern photographer who was making a photographic study of black educational efforts in the South. He and Miss Johnston arrived at the Ramer depot at night and were met by Henry, who had arranged for the photographer to stay with a black family. After they all left town in a buggy, however, Johnston decided it would be wiser for her to board with whites. Consequently, Henry returned with her to town about 11:00 p.m. By this time only three young men remained at the depot, and they welcomed the returning party with gunfire. Henry fled to Montgomery and Johnston returned to the house where Carver was staying. After taking her to the next train station, where she left on the morning train, he walked "all night . . . to keep out of [the white's] reach," but returned the next day to observe the situation.[19]

Washington was in Boston at the time, and Emmett J. Scott, his secretary, immediately launched an investigation and sent a delegation, including Johnston, to discuss the matter with the governor. When other Ramer whites learned of the occurrence, they assured the governor and Tuskegee officials that the actions of the three "desperadoes" did not reflect the sentiment of the town. Johnston, whom Carver called "the pluckiest woman I ever saw," wanted to press charges, but Tuskegee officials preferred to negotiate so that the school could be reopened. Although they received assurances that Henry and Hannon could safely return, both were reluctant to do so, and Ramer blacks feared the consequences of their return. Asserting the need to "stand by Henry and all these out of the way places," Institute agents therefore began making arrangements to move the school farther from Ramer and hire two new teachers.[20]

"This lesson shows us," declared one investigator of the incident, "that we have not yet got to the point, everywhere, where we can act without great prudence and forethought and in view of the actual conditions in a given community." He also recommended that "hereafter those who go out in any way as representatives of the school must be guided by its judgement or go out on their own responsibility." For Carver, it was a graphic lesson in the precariousness of black existence in the rural South. He described the event as "the most frightful experience of my life" and declared "it was a very serious question indeed as to whether I would return to Tuskegee alive or not."[21]

Generally Carver's travels were more successful and enhanced his reputation among both blacks and whites. His appearances at farmers' meetings also multiplied the demand for his bulletins. To meet the need for simplified publications on scientific agriculture for distribution to black educators and farmers, the Tuskegee experiment station issued several bulletins with easy-to-read instructions on such topics as dairying and poultry raising.[22] Smaller

Farmer's Leaflets were also printed and distributed. A good example of these publications is the *Farmer's Almanac*, originally published in 1899. This six-page leaflet contained brief descriptions of appropriate activities for the farmer each month of the year. For example, in October the farmer was urged to:

> Continue to set strawberries, and the sowing of turnips, mustard, lettuce, radish, rutabagas, etc. See that all the garden and farm tools are repaired and made ready for spring work.
>
> Give attention to the manure heaps and see that they are not heating too much or the elements of fertility washed out by the heavy rains. Begin digging sweet potatoes. Save seed. Sow oats and rye.[23]

In addition to keeping the language of such publications simple, Carver also tried to reach the small farmer by showing how he could improve the quality of both his farming and his family's life through the wise use of natural resources. Such publications as *Saving the Wild Plum Crop* and his bulletins on soil building through green manuring and organic fertilization illustrate Carver's efforts to get farmers to decrease their dependence on purchased goods. His emphasis on the use of natural resources and waste materials reflected Carver's faith that the Creator provided for His children if they would but "Look unto the hills from whence cometh thy help."[24]

Carver's artistic temperament made him yearn for more than full stomachs and secure houses for his people. He wanted their drab existence to be enriched with an appreciation of beauty. He preached the joys of nature study, but he also provided practical suggestions for the impoverished sharecropper to beautify his dismal surroundings. Few could afford to paint their shacks or landscape their barren yards, which more often than not did not even belong to them. They could not afford such improvements, that is, if they relied upon merchants for their materials, but the Creator provided materials free of charge.

In Bulletin 21 Carver gave detailed descriptions of how native clays could be prepared for white and color washes to enhance both the exterior and interior of houses. All shades of red, yellow, and white could be made directly from the clays, and even blues and greens could be produced with the addition of a little laundry blue. To prevent interior color washes from rubbing off, one could add glue, well-boiled starch, flour or rice paste, or specially prepared milk. Red clays worked best for exterior use, but white ones worked as well as lime whitewashes. For greater permanence, linseed oil could be used instead of water to thin the clay. The bulletin, Carver declared, was intended to aid the farmer in "making his surroundings more healthful, more cheerful, and more beautiful, thus bringing a joy and comfort into his home that he has not known heretofore."[25]

To landscape a yard one did not have to rely on an expensive commercial nurseyman. Carver explained in Bulletin 16 that by turning to the native plants of Macon County one "can find flowers of rare beauty and fragrance, foliage unsurpassed in richness, and fruits, berries and other forms of seed capsules possessing a richness of color and gracefulness of form, which well nigh approaches the ideal in beauty and grace." The bulletin, *Some Ornamental Plants of Macon County, Alabama*, related where to find and how to care for numerous wild trees, shrubs, vines, and ornamental grasses. With only the expense of labor, a yard could be transformed into a beautiful garden.[26]

In an effort to make his ideas more widely available, Carver also wrote articles of advice for various school publications, which played a vital role in the school's extension activities. In addition to the Tuskegee *Student*, which had a large circulation among alumni, Washington established a local farmers' weekly in 1905. Under the editorship of Clinton J. Calloway, the *Messenger* was directed toward the teachers and farmers of surrounding counties and was distributed to schools, local conferences, and institutes. It contained "Suggestions to Farmers" written by Carver and other agricultural faculty members.[27]

After the financial collapse of the *Messenger* in 1913, a new paper edited by Issac Fisher was established in 1914. The *Negro Farmer*, which later became the *Negro Farmer and Messenger*, was closely affiliated with Tuskegee but had no official connection. During the lifespan of the paper, from 1914 to 1918, a number of articles by Carver were published. In "Being Kind to the Soil" he gave simple plowing and cultivation instructions to transform a "soil robber" into a "progressive farmer." An article entitled "The Fat of the Land—How the Colored Farmer Can Live on It Twenty-One Times Each Week" reflected Carver's interest in nutrition and gave daily menus for a week. With the exception of a few staples each menu was composed of foods a farmer could produce for himself.[28]

By 1906 the various extension activities of Tuskegee Institute had grown considerably. In addition to its own conferences, fairs, institutes, and short courses, the school was sponsoring similar activities throughout the region. A "conference agent" had been employed to devote his attention to various local meetings, and in 1901 an extension division was established within the Agricultural Department "to put within the reach of farmers such pamphlets, leaflets and bulletins as will help them." In 1904 Clinton Calloway, the extension secretary, optimistically reported, "To get the average 'black belt' farmer to think seems to be a herculean task but we are sure of signs of a great awakening."[29]

The major problem with this optimistic report was that the "average 'black belt' farmer" was still not being reached by the extension efforts of Tuskegee. Usually only the more knowledgeable and ambitious farmers took advantage of Tuskegee's programs. Many isolated farmers remained only dimly aware of either Tuskegee or scientific agriculture. It was these whom Carver tried to reach by continuing Washington's weekend rides into the countryside. Loading up a wagon with "a few samples of farm products and other demonstration materials," he would venture out to round up a group of farmers for a practical demonstration. Often he would go to rural churches and talk to the crowds after the services. Apparently he was tremendously effective in capturing the interest and attention of these illiterate farmers. Such spare-time efforts, however, could hardly reach more than a small fraction of those who needed agricultural instruction.[30]

The problem of reaching more farmers was shared by other agricultural schools, and a growing awareness of the inadequacies of the traditional approaches to agricultural education led some agriculturists to advocate new methods of taking instruction directly to the farmer. Many farmers were simply not taking advantage of the existing programs. Illiteracy prevented the use of even Carver's simplified bulletins among large numbers of farmers. Local institutes were probably the most effective, but they were too few and too widely scattered to reach all who needed them.

"Movable schools" and demonstration work were the methods that evolved to solve these problems. Tuskegee Institute had already been firmly in the mainstream of agricultural education with the establishment of conferences, institutes, fairs, and short courses, and now the school became one of the leaders in the developing field of demonstration. Agriculturists in Europe had experimented with movable schools, but not until 1904 did Iowa State initiate the movement in the United States with "Seed Corn Gospel Trains," which carried lecturers and demonstration materials to railroad stations to meet with crowds of farmers. In 1904 Washington suggested to Carver that a wagon be outfitted as a "traveling agricultural school" to make regular trips into the countryside under a full-time operator. The idea probably grew from the success of the sporadic weekend trips and from a letter from Roscoe C. Bruce of Tuskegee's Academic Department, which pointed out the use of movable schools in Europe.[31]

Carver declared the idea "a most excellent one" and immediately submitted a proposal for such a project. Included in the proposal was a rough sketch of a wagon that would open up to display all kinds of dairy equipment and large charts on "soil-building, orcharding, stock raising and all operations pertaining to the farm." Carver also suggested lectures on various phases of self-sufficient farming and soil examinations to determine the best methods of cultivation and fertilization as well as the most suitable crops for the various soils.[32]

Washington obtained money to equip and operate such a wagon from Morris K. Jesup, a New York banker and philanthropist, and the John F. Slater Fund. Named the "Jesup Agricultural Wagon," Tuskegee's movable school began its work on 24 May 1906 with Bridgeforth as its operator. The wagon, which was made by students at Tuskegee, carried all kinds of farming equipment. Through individual contacts and open-air meetings "at the end of some cotton patch, corn field, cross roads, country store, or any place . . . most central for all concerned," the Jesup Wagon reached over two thousand people a month during the summer of 1906.[33]

Often Bridgeforth obtained farmers' consent to use their land for a demonstration of new techniques and machinery. This phase of the Jesup Wagon's work especially interested Seaman A. Knapp when he visited Tuskegee in 1906. Knapp, a special agent for the USDA, had pioneered in farm demonstration work while trying to combat the boll weevil in Texas. He would select a typical farm, guarantee payment for any loss, and get the owner to follow government instructions for dealing with the boll weevil and increasing the production of his farm. The success of the "cooperators" convinced their neighbors of the benefits of scientific methods better than any lecture could have. The effectiveness of Knapp's methods led to his being hired by the USDA as "Special Agent in charge of the Farmers' Cooperative Demonstration Work," with the duty of establishing such programs elsewhere.[34]

Washington was quick to exploit Knapp's interest and suggested that the Jesup Wagon be made a part of the USDA program. Knapp agreed, and on 12 November 1906 Thomas M. Campbell was notified of his appointment as the first black demonstration agent. Campbell, who was plowing when he learned of his new position, had been recommended by both Carver and Bridgeforth and was to be paid jointly by the General Board of Education, a Northern philanthropic fund for education, and Tuskegee Institute. He received a token dollar a year from the USDA to give him the official status of a federal employee.[35]

In operating the Jesup Wagon, Campbell used Knapp's methods, selecting a typical farm to be renovated through the work of neighbors who thus learned methods of improving their own

homes and farms. The graphic display of the possibilities of cooperative action was as valuable as the teaching of new methods.
Under Campbell the Jesup Wagon significantly expanded the
range of Tuskegee's impact, as his travels took him farther and
farther away from the Institute.[36]

Campbell's success was duplicated by John B. Pierce, a Tuskegee graduate and a Hampton Institute man who was appointed
as the second black demonstration agent shortly after Campbell's
appointment. The effectiveness of these two was very gratifying to
Knapp and paved the way for the subsequent appointment of numerous other black agents. Writing to Carver, Knapp expressed
his faith in the importance of demonstration work.

> If a few of the millions that are spent, and I think sometimes par-
> tially wasted, on the wealthier classes, in so called higher educa-
> tion, could be spent remodeling the homes of the poor and chang-
> ing their view points it would be a great and lasting benefit to the
> world![37]

Others shared Knapp's enthusiasm for demonstration work,
and as a result the Smith-Lever Act was passed in 1914 to increase
federal appropriations for demonstration work through county
agents. Although 846 black agents were eventually appointed, the
program was largely administered through the white 1862 land-
grant colleges. Thus in 1950 the average annual salary of a black
extension agent in Alabama was $2,752, while white agents earned
an average of $5,011. The same kind of discrepancy was found in
the other Southern states, and as late as 1971 a study found "widespread discrimination in both the services and the employment
practices of State Extension Services."[38]

The white domination of the programs of the USDA played a
significant role in limiting the legacy of Carver and Washington's
extension activities among black farmers. Economic, social, and
technological forces operating to weed out the small farmer from
American agriculture received a boost from the land-grant complex's increasing orientation toward large agribusiness units. The
aim of Carver's work was the improvement of the quality of life

among black farmers, but the evolving system of American agriculture has made the small farming operation economically untenable, so with each day that passes there are fewer and fewer people to whom the legacy of Tuskegee's extension work is applicable. Such changes might have come even if all levels of government had made a concerted effort to maintain a viable rural community. The point remains, however, that Tuskegee and other institutions whose work was directed toward the small and landless farmers received but a pitiful fraction of the support that state and federal governments lavished on the agricultural research units that developed the technology to make the family farmer obsolete. As early as World War I blacks began migrating to Northern cities in search of the economic opportunities they could not find in Southern agriculture. Urban ghettos filled with displaced rural families ill-equipped for city life was a high, and perhaps unnecessary, cost to pay for agricultural efficiency.

Other factors made the impact of Tuskegee's extension work difficult to assess. Numerous visitors to Alabama during Washington's lifetime noted extraordinary improvements in the living conditions of blacks around Tuskegee Institute. True, Washington and Carver were unable to change the fundamental pattern of white economic dominance in the Black Belt, but individual blacks were able to improve their homes, diets, educational facilities, and social life, as well as obtain a larger degree of economic independence. Many of these gains, however, were erased during the grueling years of the Depression, and a study of Macon County in the 1930s was able to find only lingering traces of the influence of Tuskegee in the countryside.[39]

Nevertheless, the combination of Washington's ambition and Carver's advanced agricultural training placed Tuskegee Institute in the mainstream, and sometimes the forefront, of early agricultural education. Their relative success in the face of incredibly limited resources was a tribute to the ability and dedication of Afro-Americans and was therefore of tremendous symbolic importance. The lessons Carver taught were not radically new ideas, but the staples of scientific agriculture, combined with a plea for the wise use of natural resources. Like his white counterparts, he often found segments of his audience unreceptive. Yet to thousands of blacks in the South, Washington and Carver brought the means for a better life, and this is both an intangible and a significant legacy.

Undeveloped Southern Resources

One of the major promises extended to Carver when he was forced
to accept Bridgeforth as head of the Agricultural Department was
a "first-class laboratory." This concession reflected the direction
Carver's interests had steadily been taking. The reorganization of
1910 merely accelerated the trend of his activities as he began to
feel more and more like an outsider in Tuskegee's agricultural education and extension programs.[1]

Carver was not hired as a chemist, and a laboratory was not
provided him in 1896. Convinced that a laboratory was an essential
part of agricultural research, he more or less constructed his own.
"I went to the trash pile at Tuskegee Institute," Carver recalled,
"and started my laboratory with bottles, old fruit jars and any other
thing I found I could use." His early efforts, he declared, were
"worked out almost wholly on top of my flat topped writing desk
and with teacups, glasses, bottles and reagents I made myself."[2]

Gradually Carver expanded his laboratory, drawing on supple-
mentary appropriations for the expansion of the Agricultural Building from the Slater Fund, gifts from friends and companies, and
small appropriations from the reluctant Finance Committee of the
Institute. By 1910, however, the laboratory was still crude by contemporary standards. Nevertheless, through his basic knowledge
of chemistry Carver was able to provide valuable services with his
makeshift lab. Like the chemists at the Alabama Polytechnic Institute in Auburn, Carver analyzed soils and fertilizers for farmers

and others in the vicinity of Tuskegee. When his students graduated and spread out across the South, they encouraged farmers to send soil samples to Tuskegee for analysis. After Carver analyzed these samples, he would inform the senders what the soil needed to become more productive. These services were provided free of charge and appear to have consumed considerable time. Soon other concerns led him into further areas of investigation.

From his childhood Carver had been keenly interested in the nutritive and medicinal value of plants. Mariah Watkins taught him a great deal about medicinal herbs, and Carver frequently treated himself with such remedies as the "liquor of pine needles for colds." His awareness of nutrition's importance increased in the face of the terrible blight of malnutrition in the South. Widespread research in the twentieth century brought a growing realization that the lethargy of Southerners was due to more than a backward social order. The scourges of tuberculosis, hookworm, and malaria were gradually diminished through sanitation and medical crusades, but the fourth "lazy disease," pellagra, was harder to overcome. Its elusive cause was finally discovered in 1915, when the debilitating disease was found to result from the nutritionally deficient diet of salt meat, meal, and molasses that dominated the tables of poor Southerners.[3]

While Carver's dietary work preceded the discovery of the cause of pellagra, he had enough basic knowledge of nutrition to realize the shortcomings of the Southern diet. Vitamin deficiencies were more easily overcome than the lack of protein, as small gardens were not costly, but meat and other recognized sources of protein were beyond the economic reach of many. Carver turned to his laboratory for the answers, and much of his early work was what he described as "cookstove chemistry." The first step was to find good sources of protein within the budgetary limits of impoverished sharecroppers. In his search he analyzed various plants for their protein content, giving particular attention to crops that could be easily and cheaply cultivated and would help to enrich depleted soils.[4]

Carver's investigations led him first to cowpeas, then to sweet potatoes, and finally to peanuts. Once he discovered a crop with the desired combination of properties, he turned his attention to finding attractive uses for it. At first these were merely recipes. By 1920 he had worked out dozens of ways to cook cowpeas, but all were simple processes any cook could duplicate in a kitchen. Some were imaginative, however, especially the recipes based on pea meal, which Carver explained could be made with an ordinary coffee mill. Meat substitutes were provided in pea meal recipes for cowpea loaf and croquettes.[5] Such dietary research spanned the first twenty years of Carver's career at Tuskegee.

To encourage the use of his recipes Carver publicized them in bulletins, lectures, and exhibits, and in the agricultural museum at Tuskegee. The interest displayed in the unusual recipes eventually led Carver to seek more exotic uses for his three favored crops. After 1910 flattering publicity helped to transform Carver from a "cookstove chemist" to a "creative chemist," whose work was less directed toward the masses.[6]

Prior to 1910, however, most of his work remained simple enough, like his recipes, for an illiterate farmer to duplicate. For example, Carver advocated the use of waste plant fibers to make rugs and other everyday articles.[7] At the heart of his activities were the ideas that nature produced no waste and even the poorest man could improve his living conditions through the proper use of natural resources. These ideas were certainly not original, but Carver was a remarkably successful and effective publicist of the philosophy.

Native clays were the only natural resources that interested Carver from a commercial standpoint during the first two decades of his work. As early as 1899 he suggested that the clay of Macon County contained ocher of quality equal to those used as pigments in paint manufacturing. While he advocated the crude use of native clays in beautifying farmhouses with color washes, he remained intrigued with the possibility that paint production could become a leading industry for the area and made several unsuccessful attempts to arouse interest in the commercialization of Alabama clays.[8]

In 1902 Carver thought his dreams of a paint industry were about to be realized. Late in 1901, while investigating a cattle herd near Montgomery with a "wealthy white citizen," Carver spotted some interesting clay along the roadside and "sprang out of the buggy" to collect some of it. Bringing the clay back to Tuskegee, he extracted numerous oxides that produced a variety of colors. The land belonged to a Montgomery business firm, and upon Carver's request a representative of the company, Alva Fitzpatrick, sent him additional samples of clay. Fitzpatrick was enthusiastic over the possibility of a great discovery from "the bosom of our red hills."[9]

The two most encouraging pigments were "a beautiful carmine" and a "rich Prussian blue." The company's officers had previously believed the clay might be valuable but had not been encouraged by their investigations. With Carver's results in hand, they went to both a local paint dealer and an artist for their opinions of the professor's sienna and Prussian blue pigments. Both assured them of the commercial value of the sienna deposit and declared the Prussian blue to be the richest they had ever seen. On the basis of these recommendations a prospectus for the Montgomery Paint and Dry Color Works was printed, offering 10,000 shares of stock at a dollar a share.[10]

For his efforts and advice Carter was to receive "a nice complimentary block of stock." Whether or not Carver intended to keep any profits for himself or turn them over to Tuskegee Institute, Washington was clearly interested in the development of the company, either for financial or publicity reasons. He sent his secretary, Emmett J. Scott, to talk to the officials of the Mongomery firm and made a dramatic announcement of Carver's discovery at the 1902 Negro Conference. The Tuskegee *Student* hailed the fact that "a black man is the one who has opened up what promises to be a large and new market for a splendid product." The Atlanta *Constitution* picked up the news item and reported the "claims that the dyes are superior to any on the market and that the reduction can be made on a commercial basis."[11]

Almost as soon as the prospectus was printed, however, the

owners received discouraging reports about samples that had been sent to commercial chemists and paint companies in other parts of the country. The reports scared off a few of the initial investors, but Alva Fitzpatrick was convinced the poor test results were caused by an "absence of information as to the cost of producing our stuff" and asserted one "could only expect discouragement from patented competitors." He was confident that Carver could overcome their objections and Carver's response greatly encouraged him. Yet despite Fitzpatrick's personal confidence in the product, he had difficulty raising the needed capital to begin operations.[12]

Finally on 14 January 1903 the incorporation of the company was announced, and Carver was requested to send all sample products and painted and stained boards to aid in the sale of stock. A new prospectus listed the authorized capital stock at $50,000, of which $30,000 had been already subscribed. It contained endorsements of the commercial value of the pigments from Carver and several painters and merchants. An exhibit of the materials was set up in an office, and a home in Montgomery was painted with the pigments.[13]

By the summer of 1903 the remaining stock was still unsubscribed, but an offer was received from the Ohio Paint and Varnish Company to exchange $10,000 of the Ohio company's stock for $10,000 of the Alabama company's stock. Whether or not the deal was consummated, the Montgomery Paint and Dry Color Works Company had progressed by January 1904 to the point of hiring a plant manager. The manager wrote Carver for an estimate of what his services were "worth up to the present time" and asked how much time he was prepared to give "in getting up formulas for different grades of paint" after the machinery was installed.[14]

Carver was unprepared to be treated like a common employee of the company and wrote Fitzpatrick, who assured Carver that 1,000 shares of "fully paid-up stock" had already been allotted to him and would be sent as soon as the company's books were received and its stock issued. Less than two months later, however, Carver received a cryptic note stating that the paint enterprise was "hanging fire and may fall through" and offering the chance to buy the land containing the deposits. What happened to the company is unclear, but Carver's dream of spearheading the development of a new local industry was crushed.[15]

Clearly Carver relished the role of "discoverer" and the publicity and admiration the paint enterprise brought him. In his mind the wise use of undeveloped Southern resources offered the key to the South's salvation and to a better life for all Southerners. He wanted to show the South the way to economic rejuvenation, but skeptics wanted proof of the validity of his vision. Obvious and tangible results, like a paint factory were highly prized by the pragmatic Booker T. Washington. The commercial development of one of Carver's products could prove that the professor was not merely an unrealistic dreamer. After the humiliations of the 1910 reorganization, Carver naturally turned his attention again to the development of marketable products.

The delivery of the promised first-class laboratory was crucial to Carver not only because of his wounded pride, but also because he was certain that the Creator was leading him to important discoveries. Even prior to the reorganization controversy, Carver requested equipment for the laboratory as part of the plans for a new Agricultural Building. The blueprints called for a research room, which Carver understood "was to be a private laboratory, where more technical work would be done in connection with foods, water, minerals, diseases, etc." When the room was not developed according to Carver's ideas, he reminded Washington that Tuskegee "is recognized as a very high authority on these subjects." "I have done this work under very unfavorable conditions," Carver declared, "and successfully competed with laboratories with splendid and throughly up-to-date equipment." The requisitioned apparatus was basic, the largest item of expense being gas connections to replace "the old, antiquated, crude and dangerous methods of the work with alcohol and gasoline." He cautioned Washington, "I am sure you would not have us to attempt to fool the public by just filling the room with something and calling it research apparatus when in point of fact it is not."[16]

Even a small requisition was a drain on Tuskegee's limited resources, and no action was taken until the reorganization crisis. With Carver threatening resignation, a committee was appointed to study the role Carver should play in the Institute. It recognized that the title "consulting chemist" and the laboratory would be the greatest balms to his ego and the greatest inducements for him to stay.[17] Washington agreed with the committee's report, and Carver was temporarily appeased. In fact a letter from James Wilson indicated that the provision for a laboratory enabled Carver to claim that he had in fact been promoted. Wilson's letter of 10 December 1910 offered congratulations.

> I am very much pleased with your letter, and to find that you have been promoted to a higher class of work. Research, of course, is the highest class of work connected with agriculture. Your abilities that were brought out through your education at Ames are now fully recognized and it will place you in the corps of experimenters of the whole country and the whole world. I have no hesitation in concluding that you will add to the sum of human knowledge along these lines, very materially and very promptly.[18]

Although Wilson's letter inspired him to thoughts of new service and fame, Carver realized by February 1911 that Washington's conception of a first-class laboratory varied considerably from his own and expressed his concern that the new Department of Research was "not going to receive the sympathy or the support of the school." Even before the letter was received by Washington, the latter had realized the professor's dissatisfaction and penned a promise to ask the trustees for $1,300 at their February meeting and an additional sum at the June meeting.[19]

During the next few years Carver was repeatedly disappointed by the progress of the laboratory. The Board of Trustees failed to act on some of the requests, and the Finance Committee returned requisitions for lack of adequate appropriations. To expedite matters Carver drew up a list of needed equipment in September 1911 with a statement of the purpose of each. The list contained many basic items, so Carver obviously still lacked much standard laboratory equipment. After each setback Washington proclaimed his support and promised rapid completion of the new lab. Carver's hopes would soar as he envisioned saving the school thousands of dollars and bringing the Institute new stature. Although bits and pieces of equipment were delivered, Carver complained as late as December 1912 that much of the apparatus was useless because it lacked connecting pieces. "I do not think it fair to deceive ourselves that we have a workable laboratory," Carver protested, "when we have not." [20]

Nevertheless the facilities were far superior to Carver's "trash pile" laboratory, and he was determined to prove that the expenditures had been wisely made. One of the ways the lab was to pay for itself was by enabling Carver to do various kinds of analyses for the school. Very early Washington discovered that even the prestigious Tuskegee Institute was not exempt from exploitation by white merchants. It became Carver's routine duty to examine products ordered by the school's business agent to determine if they met the standards the merchants had promised. With the school physician, Carver also periodically examined the school's water and milk supplies for bacteria. In addition Carver analyzed varied kinds of materials, including rocks, blood, and plants, for both employees of the school and others who brought or mailed in samples. [21]

Outside the laboratory Carver was given miscellaneous investigative duties. Even prior to the reorganization he had tested all seeds before planting. To this chore was added the task of keeping a check on the "ashes and cinders from various furnaces in order to determine coal wastes, if any." Later he was asked to make a thorough inspection of the sanitary facilities on campus. [22]

One of Carver's strongest arguments in favor of a better lab was the possibility of expanding his soil analysis work. Not only could he better handle requests from farmers, but he promised to make an extensive survey of Macon County soils. The results were published in 1913 as Bulletin 25, *A Study of the Soils of Macon County, Alabama, and Their Adaptability to Certain Crops*. Identifying eleven different kinds of soils and their locations, Carver explained how each should be cultivated and fertilized and listed the best crops for each.[23]

The new equipment also rekindled Carver's interest in the possibilities of native clays. In April 1911 he informed Washington that his chemistry classes were working with him to show how the clays could be used for interior and exterior decoration and exclaimed, "I am sure no one realizes what a wealth we have in these clays." After examining Carver's work, Washington was apparently convinced of its value and asked Carver to prepare an exhibit of the stains and paints for the Tuskegee post office. His confidence was not shared by his brother John, who wrote Carver that he hoped that the post office exhibit would be "more comprehensive" and use "better labels" than Carver's exhibit at the school. He was especially anxious for Carver to be specific about the practicality of the paints. "It is easy to get up a few samples of things which can never be made practical," he wrote. "My point is that whatever we advertise it should be something that can be put into commercial form and sold in competition with such material as is produced in other sections of the country."[24]

The criticism led Carver to reiterate the purpose of his work. Carver admitted that he had not determined how cheaply his paints and stains could be manufactured because the focus of his attention had been elsewhere. "When I began this work," Carver asserted, "I had in mind primarily the rural school-teacher and farmer [and] how easily, effectively and inexpensively" schoolhouses, homes, fences, and barns could be beautified. He was certain his results would form the basis of an important bulletin and would save the school "several hundred dollars a year" in paint costs.

Carver sensed, however, that Booker Washington, as well as his brother, was more interested in the commercial aspects of the clay experiments, largely because commercial development would bring the school favorable publicity. Therefore, Carver also noted that two white gentlemen from West Point, Georgia, had examined his exhibit and exclaimed, "My! what a blessing to the whole South!" When his new lab was completed, Carver promised to "have an exhibit ready for the state and various fairs that will be the biggest drawing card put on exhibition in recent years." The durability of the paints and stains had already been proven, he explained, since some of the samples in the recent exhibit were over eight years old, and he pledged to "give more attention to the practical and commercial side" after the exhibit was completed.[25]

Over the next few years Carver fulfilled several of the promises he made to Washington. Bulletin 21 was published in 1911, giving simple instructions on white and color washing with native clays. Several students tried color washing their dormitory rooms, with success. His wood stains received a trial when a new Episcopal church for whites was built in Tuskegee. All the interior woodwork was stained with a "dark mission" stain which he supplied at one-tenth the cost of equivalent commercial stains. Carver was elated, claiming that "this practical demonstration will remove any skepticism," and he sent Washington a copy of a letter from a church member who declared, "Everyone who sees this stain is wonderfully impressed with its beauty, and it is hard to make some believe that it is a home product."[26]

After the successful demonstration at the Episcopal church, various people in the community began using Carver's products in their homes. In July 1912 Carver also began to supply the school's paint division, and his stains and calcimines were used in the girls' practice cottage, Dorothy Hall, the teachers' dining hall, the Academic Building, and several teachers' cottages. By January 1914 he was able to announce that during six months his laboratory "did $339.53 worth of business and has a net credit of $177.63." Later that year he reported that he had furnished the school and "a few outside sources" with 452 gallons of calcimines and 48 gallons of paints and stains since the preceding June.[27]

Still, Carver felt the need of demonstrating the market value of his products. When an article appeared about his stains in an edition of the Montgomery *Advertiser*, Carver wrote Washington, "You will note that persistence and perservereance [*sic*] is getting [the stains] into workable shape." From the beginning of his renewed interest in clays in 1911, Carver was convinced that he could disprove John Washington's assertions of the impracticality of commercial development and persuaded Emmett Scott to join him in manufacturing some of his clay products. For at least a year the two men planned their commercial venture, evidently in secret. In a letter to Scott dated 9 September 1911, Carver recounted the comment of a prominent white that "mills would spring up within a few years to manufacture these clays" and declared, "Now I am ready to go in with you on such a propposition [*sic*] any time. Just keep it *mum* and we will divide up."[28]

Scott and Carver planned eventually to manufacture various kinds of paints and stains, but they decided to start with a commodity that cost less to produce. In his experiments with clay, Carver had also made several kinds of talcum and face powders, and they believed that less than two thousand dollars would be needed to begin manufacturing those products. They checked the cost of packaging and the applicable provisions of the Pure Food and Drug Act of 1906, but their plans for production were held up by delays in the completion of the new laboratory. Without certain pieces of equipment Carver was unable to verify the purity of his powder and was therefore afraid to put it on the market.[29]

While he and Scott were making their plans, Carver received a proposition from an Arkansas drug company that also manufactured paints. The company wanted to send an expert to Tuskegee to investigate the minerals of the county and to consider the advisability of purchasing some stock in a local company to manufacture clay products. Carver sent copies of the correspondence to Scott and noted at the bottom of one letter that he told the company's representative, "I would entertain no proposition." This decision may have been a mistake, since Scott and Carver's plans evidently never came to fruition for some reason, and Carver was once again disappointed in his attempts to prove that his ideas were commercially feasible.[30]

The school's savings in painting costs was almost as impressive to Booker Washington as a successful commercial venture would have been. It was probably for this reason that Carver turned his attention to discovering other substitutes for items in the Institute's budget. The desire to reduce Tuskegee's expenses was partly responsible for Carver's increased interest in organic fertilization between 1910 and 1915. He also sought to find minerals in Macon County to replace lime and other commercial soil preparations. Apparently he had some success, for the Institute's business agent was asked to consult with Carver about eliminating all purchases of commercial fertilizers in 1912.[31]

Other substitutes Carver developed were a laundry bluing agent, a powder for polishing metal, and bedbug poison. He sent trial samples of the first two to prominent Tuskegee citizens, who testified to their efficacy; one imaginative recipient tried the laundry blue in his fountain pen and reported that it made a fine ink. The bedbug poison, which Carver declared would save the school $44 annually, was tested in the school's dormitories. While the poison was initially effective, it lacked residual properties, and the bedbugs returned. Evidently Carver was unable to overcome this failing, for as late as 1919 bedbugs remained a problem at Tuskegee.[32]

Hopes of reducing Tuskegee's food costs helped to increase Carver's interest in investigation of foods, and he submitted money-saving but nutritional menus to Washington. However, studies in the second decade of the twentieth century showing the effects of malnutrition also spurred Carver's food research. Perhaps to convince Washington of the significance of dietary investigations, he directed the principal's attention to an article on "how certain foods produce fat and make one lazy and therefore sleepy" and reminded him of his own earlier statement "upon this point," concluding, "There is probably no subject more important than the study of foods."[33]

The first problem for a nutritionist in the South was to persuade Southern farmers to diversify their crops so that they could diversify their diets. Thus Carver spent considerable time collecting and developing recipes for the preparation of cowpeas, sweet potatoes, and peanuts—the three crops he had determined would provide nutritional supplements and could also be easily and cheaply raised by the average farmer. He demonstrated the versatility of the peanut by having his class of senior girls prepare a "peanut luncheon" in Washington's honor in 1911. All the courses on the menu were based on peanuts, including the "meat." Numerous other exhibits showing various ways to cook the three crops were constructed by Carver, who with his flair for the dramatic made the possibilities of the crops seem miraculous in an effort to capture the attention of his audiences.[34]

One reason for Carver's interest in sweet potatoes and peanuts was the keeping qualities of the crops, which, like the grains he also encouraged farmers to grow, could be stored easily for use throughout the winter months. Preserving the fruits of summer's labour for winter's use was a major problem in the improvement of the diets of those too poor to purchase food without going deeper into debt; therefore Carver had long investigated methods of food preservation, the results of his early experiments were published as Bulletin 10 on saving the sweet potato and Bulletin 12 on preserving the wild plum crop.[35]

After 1910 Carver expanded his efforts in the area of food preservation. In 1911 he investigated methods of meat curing and pickling at the Auburn experiment station and the Armour packing plant in Montgomery, with the idea of developing an inexpensive method of preserving meat during the warmer seasons of the year. In early October Carver sent Washington a sample of meat he had cured. Washington congratulated him for his "great achievement" and urged him "to go ahead now and try the same experiment on half a dozen or more pigs."[36]

The experiment had a pleasant side effect for Carver: Washington asked Bridgeforth to work as a subordinate partner in the research, doing the actual work of slaughtering and preparing the meat in the pickling solution according to Carver's directions. Bridgeforth evidently balked at the order, which provoked Washington to write that the "records in my office show that I spend more time in dealing with your Department and trying to get orders carried out . . . than I do with all the other departments combined." [37]

Carver's small victory over his adversary was followed by the success of his pickling formula. Samples of the pork pickled in 1911 were found to be in "excellent condition" in August 1912, and Washington urged the cancellation of all purchases of canned meat since Carver had proved that pork could be prepared in almost any season of the year and preserved. As soon as a pig was full-grown, it was to be slaughtered and prepared by Carver's methods to save the costs of continued stock feeding, as well as the expense of purchased meat. In order to make such savings available to farmers, Carver published Bulletin 24, *The Pickling and Curing of Meat in Hot Weather*. Of course Carver had grander visions of "a revolution in the pork industry here in the South" which would "start from the Tuskegee Institute," but there is no evidence that his methods were adopted by any commercial meat packers. [38]

Carver's interest in food preservation was also reflected in his 1915 publication of *When, What and How to Can and Preserve Fruits and Vegetables in the Home* as Bulletin 27. More important to his later fame were his investigations into methods of drying foods. His success at drying fruits and vegetables became significant with the shortages of World War I. Carver developed the drying techniques to lower the cost of food preservation, but the war made his dehydration experiments extremely timely, as Carver noted in a 1917 leaflet. "The shortage of tin cans, glass containers, [and] the high price of sugar . . . make it emphatic," Carver wrote, "that we have some other method [than canning] within the reach of the humblest citizen." [39]

Carver's work with foods—his "cookstove chemistry"—was not entirely original, because many other scientists were investigating nutrition and food preparation. The focus of his early laboratory work, however, was somewhat different from that of most other researchers, just as his plot work differed from other experiment stations. In the beginning he had aimed his efforts towards "the humblest citizen." After 1910 he was apparently seduced by publicity and praise into more exotic fields of investigation. Nevertheless, through Tuskegee Institute's varied extension activities his advice reached thousands and improved the diets and lives of untold numbers of farmers in the South.

The Wizard of Tuskegee

Tuskegee Institute's extension efforts benefited Carver as well as black farmers. The Farmers' Conference, fairs, articles, and bulletins gave Carver a platform for displaying his talents to a wide audience of blacks and whites. In these activities he used the force of his personality and his flair for the dramatic in the cause of agricultural education. These gifts also helped win him the growing recognition that provided a foundation for his later fame.

Booker T. Washington's stature focused international attention upon the activities at Tuskegee Institute. Many prominent people from all over the nation came to Tuskegee for the yearly conference or commencement exercises, or just to visit. During Washington's lifetime he was given most of the credit and publicity for any success at Tuskegee, regardless of who was personally responsible. Although Washington's lieutenants remained somewhat in his shadow, the magic of his name provided valuable contacts for men like Carver. The doors that opened to a representative of Tuskegee were especially important in Carver's case, for he had a rare gift of turning acquaintances into friends. In addition, his abilities proved impressive to those who shared his interests and opened more doors to an increasing network of professional contacts.

As director of the Tuskegee experiment station, Carver met the white agriculturists at Auburn, and at least two of these men became his personal friends as they exchanged ideas and services. In 1897 Carver's aid to F. S. Earle in his study of Alabama fungi formed the basis of a relationship that lasted the entire time Earle was at Auburn. In 1901 Earle wrote Carver of his disappointment that the Tuskegean did not stop by to see him on a visit to Auburn. "I am always glad to see you," he declared, "and would have liked to show you the additions we have made to our collections." Tuskegee's lack of a veterinarian caused Carver to consult frequently with C. A. Cary, the veterinarian on the Auburn staff and a fellow alumnus of Iowa State. The 1887 Iowa graduate was obviously impressed with Carver's training and abilities and gladly gave his services to Tuskegee, both in the diagnosing of livestock and in lecturing to students.[1]

Since Carver's station was considered an unofficial member of the white experiment station complex under the direction of the Office of Experiment Stations in the USDA, Carver was also able to become personally acquainted with agriculturists all over the nation. He attended the 1902 meeting of the National Association of Directors of Experiment Stations in Atlanta and brought a number of the directors to Tuskegee for a visit after the meeting. In the summer of 1904 Carver reciprocated with visits to several of the Southern stations. Most important, Carver's work was reported in the annual report of the Office of Experiment Stations, and he participated in the exchange of bulletins among stations. Thus Carver's work came to the attention of the nation's leading agriculturists. Indeed, the uniqueness of his black skin among station directors probably enhanced the interest of his efforts.[2]

Washington's status with the Republican administrations of McKinley, Roosevelt, and Taft, as well as Carver's friendship with the secretary of agriculture, meant that Tuskegee was included in the activities of other divisions of the USDA. Carver served as the Institute's representative in agricultural affairs and in the interest of Tuskegee went to the national capital on several occasions, where he became personally acquainted with many members of the USDA. These contacts were expanded by cooperative projects between the department and Tuskegee and numerous visits from USDA officials. Many were impressed both by Carver and his work, and Tuskegee Institute was quick to publicize favorable comments like that of C. R. Ball of the USDA's Division of Agrostology who, on a visit in 1901, was "very greatly surprised at the extent of the work being performed in the Agricultural Department and especially at the Experiment Station."[3]

Carver's work also caught the attention of various state officials in Alabama. An especially friendly relationship developed between Carver and ex-Populist Reuben F. Kolb when the latter became the state commissioner of agriculture. The two men corresponded, exchanged several visits, and collaborated in an alfalfa experiment. Common interests also brought together Carver and Hubert H. Smith, the curator of the Alabama Museum of Natural History, and they exchanged ideas and handmade Christmas cards.[4]

The significance of Carver's relationships with agriculturists and scientists at the land-grant colleges, with the USDA, and with prominent citizens in Alabama was that many of these men recognized Carver as an equal partner in research work. Such recognition from fellow researchers was the first he received at Tuskegee. Given the dominance of white supremacy in that era and Carver's incredibly limited resources for research, their acknowledgement was meaningful, but it was hardly the stuff of which national heroes are made. The names of few agricultural researchers become household words in America.

Recognition by researchers, however, helped open the door to contacts with other groups interested in agriculture. James Wilson's friendship was probably instrumental in getting Carver an invitation in 1904 to join the American Breeders' Association, of which Wilson was president. Carver's relationship with C. A. Cary led to an invitation to read a paper at the Alabama Live Stock Association's 1903 meeting in Birmingham. Carver was delighted by this invitation from Cary, who was president of the group, and declared that the request was "quite unique as [the Association] is a distinctly Southern organization."[5]

At the meeting Carver spoke on the livestock work at Tuskegee, and Cary followed him to the podium to "most heartily endorse every word" and to urge all to visit Tuskegee. The Birmingham newspapers described Carver's speech as "one of the most interesting of the addresses delivered." As Carver was leaving the next day, however, Cary admitted that he had been "very fearful at first" about the reaction of the all-white group to his invitation but had decided to "make the venture as someone must at some-time, somewhere." The group's response was "a great and agree-able surprise" to Cary, since almost every man had come and "per-sonally thanked him for the inovation [sic]."[6]

Carver's abilities also brought him into contact with white lay-men who were interested in agriculture. An example of this kind of relationship was the friendship between Carver and H. G. Has-tings of the Hastings Seed Company in Atlanta, Georgia. In Sep-tember 1910 Hastings came to Tuskegee to examine the cotton breeding experiments at the experiment station. Hastings, who was planning to establish a cotton breeding farm himself, wanted to learn more about Carver's work. Impressed with what he saw at Tuskegee, he asked Carver for hybrid cotton seed and recommen-dations of competent men for the Hastings breeding farm. A per-sonal attraction between the two men led to a sporadic but lifelong correspondence between them.[7]

The relationship with Hastings was typical of numerous others that Carver cultivated. Carver had a rare gift for making people feel a special bond with him, regardless of their race or economic class. He was indeed "seductive," as one of his admirers labeled him. His position at Tuskegee provided access to numbers of whites, and drawing on his earlier experiences, he gradually built up a network of biracial friendships. Although some of these rela-tionships retained a paternalistic cast typical of Southern race re-lations, many were evidently "color-blind."

Very early in his Tuskegee career Carver realized the impor-tance Washington attached to such interracial relationships. After all, no amount of black achievement could reduce racial prejudice unless it was recognized and accepted by whites. In the 1890s even many of the black man's "best friends" in the white commu-nity accepted social-Darwinist ideas that implied the innate inferi-ority of Negroes. In addition, many of the bridges of communica-tion between blacks and whites were breaking down. Hence,

Carver was quick to inform Washington of any recognition he received from whites. In 1897 he noted that "several leading white men" examined his sweet potato experiment and said "in all their experience they have never seen anything like it." A year later Carver related the desire of another white man to come to see Carver as often as possible and to have Carver come to his farm for consultations.[8]

As Carver became better known in the area, numbers of whites began to attend his farming lectures in the surrounding countryside, and he received frequent invitations to visit white farms and plantations, even some that were closer to the better-staffed Auburn station. The value whites placed on either Carver's knowledge or his ability to communicate it to their black field hands led to some relaxation of Southern mores. In 1903, for example, Carver made the incredible announcement to Washington that on one trip to an Alabama plantation he had spent the night at the home of the white farm manager. Such incidents convinced Carver of the appropriateness of Washington's approach to race relations. It appeared that economic usefulness would indeed bring acceptance.[9]

During Carver's first ten years at Tuskegee his research and extension work brought only limited recognition to him among fellow researchers and Alabama farmers. With the expansion of Tuskegee, graduates had established numerous "little Tuskegees" all over the South, which were quick to adopt successful programs of the parent school. Many turned to Tuskegee for aid in setting up their own farmers' conferences, institutes, and fairs, and Carver increasingly took to the road to attend such affairs in all the deep South states. These travels brought him to the attention of numerous whites as well as blacks, because the "little Tuskegee" school presidents usually followed Washington's policy of cultivating the friendship of prominent local whites.[10]

On the lecture platform Carver preached conventional agricultural wisdom, but he did it in a most unconventional way. His high-pitched voice would startle his audience to attention, and then his enthusiastic reverence for his subject would enrapture the group. A subtle blend of humor and drama enlivened the conversational tone of his lectures. His greatest ability, however, was to infect his audience with the same childlike awe he felt for the miracles of nature. One listener tried to describe the magnetic quality of Carver's lectures.

> The most striking thing about him is his eyes, which are deep black but which seem to have two gleaming coals of living fire behind them. His skin is extremely dark, but when he begins to talk, race and color are lost sight of and one hears a wonderfully soft, musical voice telling a story of God's bounty and of man's indifference to the great gifts spread before him on every hand.[11]

An example of Carver's blend of humor and religion in an agricultural lecture is a speech he delivered in 1908 at Homer College in Louisiana. Asked to help initiate a farmers' organization and annual conferences, he spoke on the need for black farmers to organize and cooperate to improve themselves.

> I would have you to know that we belong to a very powerful race or in other words, we can become very powerful if only we would organize. There is not a single object in all the realm of animate nature that is not organized. Indeed the work of creation was a work of organization. We are told that in the beginning all was void and darkness covered all things and that our Creator and Father began his work by setting all things in order or organizing them. And as He proceeded with his work, it was with deliberation and by well ordered degree. Not one of all the millions of things He made was left until it was pronounced "very good." What an example for us! And yet how different is our way of doing our work. How differently would we have gone about such a stupendous work! We would no doubt have made MAN first, without a place for him or food for his subsistance. I hold before you my hand with each finger standing erect and alone, and so long as they are held thus, not one of all the tasks that the hand may perform can be accomplished. I can not lift. I can not grasp. I can not hold. I cannot even make an intelligible sign until my [fingers] organize and work together. In this we should also learn a lesson.[12]

Carver's effectiveness on the podium made him a drawing card at farmers' meetings, and his appeal was increasingly exploited by black agricultural schools. "His name attached to a placard or bulletin announcing a proposed farmers conference," declared an official of a black school in South Carolina in 1918, "will draw a larger number of interested individuals—both white and black—than the name of any other speaker who may be secured." Invitations to conferences and to meetings of black teachers' associations began to pour in from across the South. By 1915 the volume became so great that Carver apparently felt overwhelmed. Washington insisted that all invitations be answered, however, and assured Carver of the school's willingness to excuse him from his duties to attend as many conferences as possible.[13]

Each year the number of lectures given and the size of the crowds grew, sometimes reaching into the thousands. More and more white faces appeared in the audiences, and their reaction was gratifying to Carver. As early as 1903 Walter B. Hill, chancellor of the University of Georgia, attended a farmers' conference at the state normal school for blacks in Savannah and heard Carver speak. Afterwards Hill proclaimed, "That was the best lecture on agriculture to which it has ever been my privilege to listen. The speaker has not only shown himself a master of the subject, but is also possessed of pedagogical ability to impart it clearly and forcibly to others—a combination which is possessed by only five or six men in the entire country." Naturally, both Carver and Tuskegee officials were quick to publicize such comments, and the remark was repeated in newspapers as far away as New York.[14]

At first the topics of Carver's lectures were of a general nature, such as "Does Scientific Agriculture Pay?" and "How to Build Up Worn Out Soils and Make the Farm Pay." Generally he would bring examples of such things as crops and soils so the farmers could see for themselves the results of good farming methods. In addition to lecturing, Carver also made himself available to farmers at the meetings for consultation. They were encouraged to bring soil and crop specimens and ask him about their specific problems.

The combination of his dramatic lectures, the graphic displays of experiment station results, and his ability to pinpoint the mysterious causes of crop failures seemed nothing short of miraculous to his uneducated audiences. Soon announcements of farmers' conferences were billing Carver as the "wizard of Tuskegee."[15]

This aura of the miraculous was enhanced around 1910 when Carver began focusing his lectures upon one or more of the crops he was trying to encourage farmers to plant: cowpeas, sweet potatoes, and peanuts. These lectures followed somewhat the format of his "threefold" bulletins, discussing the properties of the plant, its cultivation, and its uses. Carver realized that general lectures on diversified farming seldom created a large enough spark of determination in the listeners to be translated into action. He tried instead to show farmers in concrete terms the value of growing something besides cotton, and he had the ability to make even the lowly cowpea appear to be God's answer to the farmers' ills. His listeners sat in awe as Carver demonstrated how the versatile cowpea could yield everything from soup to coffee, and were dazzled by the large number of dishes he concocted from this common pea.[16]

His lectures on the cowpea, sweet potato, and peanut combined two of Carver's talents very effectively. Not only was he a compelling speaker, but his artistic temperament had long enabled him to construct eye-catching exhibits. Whatever the theme, Carver could display his subject to maximum effect. He was frequently asked to prepare exhibits for conferences, commencements, and fairs at Tuskegee, and eventually he received requests from other fairs and conferences. At first the exhibits were rather conventional, often displaying large and magnificent vegetable and fruit specimens that had been produced and preserved through the application of scientific methods. Even these simple demonstrations were dramatic enough, however, to become one of the central attractions at the state fair in Montgomery and to receive favorable comment in the press.[17]

Probably because of the interest created by his exhibits, Carver received an invitation to place one in the state capitol in 1903.

Carver exhibit of preserved foods in 1916

From Montgomery he excitedly wrote Washington of its success, saying that "from early morning until late at night it has been thronged with prominent people, both ladies and gentlemen." He noted that the governor had been to see it twice and that several legislators "say it is the best and most catching [advertisement] the school has ever made and told me to tell you that if you wanted the [legislature] to do anything for you to let them know." Carver also included a quotation from a less prominent visitor who exclaimed, "I tell you we've got to climb, the niggers are ahead of us."[18]

After the reorganization at Tuskegee in 1910 Carver spent more time in the preparation of exhibits to demonstrate his work with natural resources and food products. One of the more popular displays centered on his clay products. In 1911 the Montgomery *Advertiser* described Carver's exhibit at the state fair. It included fifteen distinctly different wood stains, thirteen calcimines of such colors as lavender, green, yellow, and dark blue, and also white and buff toilet powders. A wooden box stained "mission oak" adorned the front of the booth, and the clay from which each product was made was shown in its untreated state, just as it had been dug from the earth.[19]

Although his clay products attracted the most attention at first, Carver had a number of other displays that stressed the theme of the wise use of nature's bounty. A stock food exhibit showed the uses of Macon County grains, grasses, and weeds; another featured various products from native stone. The imagination reflected in these displays was insignificant, however, compared to that which inspired the feather exhibit. Composed of fifty-three different products made from the feathers of domestic fowl, it reflected both Carver's enthusiasm and his ability to lose touch with reality. In 1914 Carver claimed that "this exhibit when finished will show that last Thursday alone we threw away more than $50.00 worth of feathers besides the lucrative employment it would give to many girls here." Despite Carver's excited assurances that the feather exhibit "will be the most valuable and astonishing of any Tuskegee has attempted," no great chicken feather industry sprang up in Alabama.[20]

Much more significant to Carver's later fame were his nutritional demonstrations. In 1914 he began preparing an exhibit of food products, as well as medicinal vegetables, fruits, and herbs, that could be grown in Alabama by the average farmer. His purpose was to show "how farmers can live comfortably [in the] winter" from their own farm products. Presented at the Macon County Fair in 1915, the display included a showcase filled with home-grown foods "cooked and prepared temptingly in a dozen different styles" and jars of products dried, canned, pickled, and preserved. "To cap it all," the Tuskegee *Student* noted, "he served a cup of delicious coffee made with dried kidney beans." As a reporter from the Montgomery *Advertiser* declared, to see Carver's multiple products from common plants "makes one wonder why he has been so blind to their use for so many years."[21]

Carver's work made him known to farmers, researchers, businessmen, and educators in the South. The recognition by these groups also led to interest from another—the press. Until Washington's death, newsmen devoted most of their attention to the principal in their coverage of Tuskegee affairs, but articles by and about Carver appeared from time to time. Generally these were not found in national publications, but in Iowa or Alabama papers, where Carver was personally known. For example, the Montgomery *Advertiser* occasionally cited his work in such features as "They Teach Farming by Farming at Tuskegee."

Often Carver's friends were responsible for his early publicity. James Wilson, in an interview with *Technical World Magazine*, stressed Carver's sacrifice of an art career for a life of service to his people. One newspaper column on Carver, drawn from an interview with an unnamed friend, had been published as early as 1900 in the Des Moines *Daily News*. It was a long and flattering but inaccurate account of Carver's life and work and was reprinted in the Tuskegee *Student*. The reprinting of the article without corrections was typical of Carver's later relationship with the press.[22]

When errors and exorbitant claims were made in articles about him, Carver laughingly disavowed the statements but did not take steps to have the mistakes removed from the public record. Such actions later encouraged the invention and repetition of numerous myths. Instead of specific corrections, Carver maintained a general posture of self-effacing denial of his worthiness for his many honors, which merely served to create the most popular myth of all, that of his deep humility. He was indeed humbled by his faith in the Creator, but it was a humility based on the arrogant assumption of being an agent of the divine. His self-effacement was probably based on this concept of his role and most likely reflected some degree of guilt about the falsehoods in his public record. Contrary to Southern opinion, his humility was evidently not a deferential response to white supremacy, for the tone of his speeches and letters remained the same whether his audiences or correspondents were black or white.

Carver did not shy away from publicity; instead he relished and actively courted it. His humiliations at Tuskegee may have magnified his need to be reassured of his worth and to show people like John Washington and George Bridgeforth the error of their belittling assessments of his ability. In addition, publicity was highly prized by Booker Washington in his battle to obtain funds and prove the abilities of Afro-Americans. To seek recognition was therefore not entirely self-serving, but also benefited the school and other blacks. At any rate, Carver was not above actions like sending a copy of a personal and highly complimentary letter from James Wilson to the *Southern Ruralist* in Atlanta, then basking in the glory of its publication together with an editorial note declaring the letter to be "merited recognition of services which have meant much for the welfare of the colored race, but will mean more for all Southern agriculture" and labeling Carver "a real factor in agricultural progress."[23]

At first Carver's articles on agriculture only appeared in Tuskegee publications or in Hampton Institute's *Southern Workman*. From his personal acquaintance with Lou Sweet, however, came a request in 1902 for an article for publication in the *American Monthly Review of Reviews*, which Sweet edited. Later Carver was delighted to receive requests for material from such sources as the Shreveport *Times*, New Orleans *La Hacienda*, and the agricultural magazine of Langston University in Oklahoma. Usually he promptly notified Washington of these indications of his spreading recognition.[24]

In general, the publicity most cherished by Washington was praise from prominent whites. Thus the comments in 1910 of Sir Harry Johnston in his *The Negro in the New World* carried special weight with the principal. The English nobleman toured the United States and spent some time in Tuskegee. In a paragraph designed to illustrate the accomplishments of Afro-Americans of unmixed blood, Johnston wrote of Carver,

> He is, as regards complexion and features, an absolute Negro; but in the cut of his clothes, the accent of his speech, the soundness of his science, he might be professor of Botany not at Tuskegee, but Oxford or Cambridge. Any European botanist of distinction, after ten minutes' conversation with this man, instinctively would deal with him "de puissance en puissance."[25]

Although other writers echoed Johnston's appraisal of Carver's unmixed ancestry and scientific ability, most described Carver's appearance as being more like a field hand than a professor, which was more correct, considering his usual attire of worn and mis-matched trousers and coat. Indeed, his eccentric habits in haber-dashery drew considerable comment from the press until his death. Descriptions of his "floppy cap," "well-turned" collars, and homemade ties embarrassed some Tuskegeans, but through the decades Carver proudly announced on special occasions that the suit he was wearing had been given to him by his fellow Iowa State students when he graduated from college. Comfort and thrift were greater virtues to him than external appearances. Once he de-clared, "I don't want to wear shoes, but I do it—to escape unde-sirable publicity." It was one of his few concessions to the sartorial suggestions from colleagues.[26]

Significantly, the year after the publication of the *Negro in the New World* Booker T. Washington gave the first lengthy account of Carver and his career in *My Larger Education*. In his earlier books Washington had practically ignored Carver, but in this book he quoted Johnston's evaluation of Carver in full, translating John-ston's French to read "would treat him as a man on a level with himself." Instead of describing Carver's efforts to improve the lives of impoverished sharecroppers, Washington cited the recognition Carver had received from whites. He told of Carver's relationship with James Wilson, of his being the only black invited to a meeting of leading teachers in Alabama, and of a visit by the colonial sec-retary of the German Empire to examine Carver's cotton experi-ments. Washington's purpose in stressing this kind of achievement was made evident in his conclusion. "I have always said that the best means . . . for destroying race prejudice is to make [oneself] a useful and, if possible, an indispensable member of the commu-nity in which he lives," Washington wrote. "I do not know of a better illustration of this than may be found in the case of Professor Carver."[27]

In 1914 another long article about Carver appeared in a Tus-kegee publication. Entitled "The Latest Contribution to Negro Progress," the article was published in the *Tuskegee Alumni Bul-letin* and discussed Carver's work with native clays instead of his educational efforts. Stressing the commercial value of Carver's paints, stains, powders, and cleansing agents, the author stated that the "Alumni Bulletin takes pride in presenting this discovery to its readers, as it is signally a contribution to a race, a country, and an age in which discovery and invention are the keynote."[28]

In "an age in which discovery and invention are the keynote," Carver's visionary preaching to poor black farmers of a better, more self-sufficient life through the wise use of nature's bounty received only limited praise, and he remained in Washington's shadow. Almost all the fame Carver had earned, outside of a small circle of agricultural researchers and educators, resulted from either white acceptance of him or the possibility of the commercial development of his products. A human desire to prove his personal merit gradually led him to succumb to the temptation to give the public what it wanted, while rationalizing his change of emphasis as an expansion of his basic vision. By the time of Washington's death Carver was moving toward the role of "creative chemist," exploring the sweet potato and peanut not for their nutritive potentials, but for their commercial possibilities.

— 9 —

The End of an Era

During a Northern tour in the fall of 1915, Booker T. Washington became ill and was brought back to Tuskegee, where he died on 14 November. His death marked the end of an era both in race relations and in the career of George Washington Carver. During the next year a series of events brought Carver out of the shadows and into a place of national prominence that rivaled Washington's.

For a few months after Washington's death, however, Carver felt only depression and despair. His bitter exchanges with the principal seemed to haunt him, making him forget the letters of support and affection he had also written. He had frequently asserted his faith in Washington's vision when it was criticized and sent him small gifts and flowers. Nevertheless, after giving half a year's salary to the Booker T. Washington Memorial Fund, Carver dejectedly wrote Emmett Scott, "I am sure Mr. Washington never knew how much I loved him, and the cause for which he gave his life." Too distraught to teach his classes, he was given the duty of supervising "study hour" and was an object of pity on the campus. Only when he became involved in raising money for the memorial fund was the paralyzing burden of grief eased.[1]

Robert Russa Moton's succession to the principalship of Tuskegee also brought brighter days for him. Unlike Washington, Moton treated him as a treasured partner. Partly because Carver had already won recognition outside the Institute, and partly because of the differences in the personalities of the two principals, he soon held a much more exalted position on campus.

Carver continued on occasion to write quarrelsome letters that stressed his heavy demands and sacrifices, and there were a few declarations such as, "I do not get to enjoy any outing because I must work night and day trying to keep up my work altogether." Moton's response, however, was considerably different from Washington's replies. Instead of issuing ultimatums, Moton tried to meet most of Carver's demands, and when he could not, he used tact and flattery to win cooperation. For example, soon after Washington's death, Carver notified the head of the Academic Department of his inability to teach his usual classes in botany in the fall.[2] Instead of rebuking him for shirking his duty and stressing the need to justify his salary, as Washington probably would have done, Moton wrote:

> I wish you would withold your definite decision until I have a chance to talk with you. . . . I need not tell you that it will be impossible to get anybody to teach this subject as you have done, and I do not like to think of the students losing the inspiration and help that would come by your teaching.[3]

A year later Carver again tried to escape teaching, and Moton's response was even more flattering and pleading. In this letter Moton appeared to be siding with Carver in his appraisal of Bridgeforth.

> I am very anxious that you have definite, organic touch with the Agricultural Department, . . . for reasons that I am sure must be obvious to you.
> I hope it may be possible for you this year to take at least one period, selecting any subject that seems to you advisable. I know how taxed you are, and I hesitate to add anything to your already very heavy program, but I am anxious to have as many students as possible come in direct contact with you. I know of no other persons who can give the inspiration, saying nothing about the technical instruction that you can give.[4]

Evidently Bridgeforth was not very happy with the new situation. In May 1918 he left his position as head of the Agricultural Department to take a less prestigious job as a county demonstra-

tion agent. Since Emmett J. Scott had already departed in 1917 to
become a special assistant to the United States secretary of war,
Carver was one of the few remaining links to the early Washington
administration at Tuskegee. This role and the focus of Carver's
work both enhanced his value to the Institute. His attempts to find
substitutes for wartime shortages interested the USDA and led to
cooperative efforts. Under Washington's leadership Tuskegee had
benefited from collaboration with the Republican administrations
of McKinley, Roosevelt, and Taft. Democrat Woodrow Wilson's
victory in 1912 brought a decline in the Institute's political influence, and Washington's death left Carver as one of the strongest
surviving bridges to the federal government.

To some degree Carver's rise in stature on campus was also the
result of his truly international recognition in 1916. With almost
uncanny timing, two invitations were issued to him during the first
autumn after Washington's death. A request to serve on the advisory board of the National Agricultural Society was followed by an
invitation to become a fellow of the Royal Society for the Arts. The
British invitation was especially effective at getting Carver more
publicity, for the contrast between his slave origins and his membership in a royal society proved irresistible to most newspaper
reporters.[5]

These two honors were stepping-stones to fame, although this
was not readily apparent. In December of that year the editor of
the *Southwestern Christian Advocate* asked Tuskegee for information about Scott, Moton, and Carver to be used in a weekly series
entitled "Men Making Good." Convinced of the suitability of Scott
and Moton, the editor declared, "I am not absolutely clear about
Mr. Carver but it seems to me he has made distinct contributions
to the life of the race." Obviously his name had hardly become a
household word. In fact how and why Carver's name came before
the Royal Society is an intriguing question. Carver believed his
friend Sir Harry Johnson was responsible, but Royal Society officials later stated that his selection was based on his membership in
"kindred societies" in the United States. Nevertheless, the honor
impressed people both on and off campus.[6]

Carver's increased status was reflected in Executive Council meetings at Tuskegee. Instead of the earlier castigations of Carver for failures, by 1916 the minutes were filled with statements of praise and commendation for his work. There was also a discussion of how he could be freed from "minor things" in order to have "sufficient time to do justice to his work." Carver became the only council member to be addressed with the prestigious title of "professor" rather than "mister," and in 1919 Moton gave him an unsolicited increase in salary. The increase, Carver's first raise in over twenty years, was a symbolic gesture rather than a reflection of his need for a higher salary, although five years before his salary had been among the lowest for Tuskegee administrators.[7]

Throughout Moton's tenure as president to 1935, he and Carver remained close, and those years were perhaps the happiest ones for Carver at Tuskegee. In 1919 he even refused a job offer that he had solicited a few years before from the black state college in Greensboro, North Carolina.[8] Moton's handling of him produced a decidedly more harmonious relationship between professor and principal, but harmony came at the cost of a severe diminution of Carver's campus duties.

After a few years Carver successfully limited his teaching to the summer sessions for teachers. For six to ten weeks each summer he met with schoolteachers from all over the South who came to the Institute for refresher courses and advanced study. Serving as a source of inspiration as much as information, Carver was active in the summer school until his health began to fail in the 1930s. Theoretically he taught agriculture, but, as in the past, his approach was often unusual. Carver's flair for the dramatic at its best illuminated a vision of rare scope and depth. At its worst, his showmanship degenerated into petty, ego-bolstering exhibitionism, as when he would play the piano, paint, and recite poetry simultaneously.[9]

Letters from his summer students indicate that they valued the opportunity to study with "the professor," as he continued to be called. Many noted their newfound appreciation of nature and revitalized spirit of dedication. "I caught some of your spirit while there," one declared. "I noticed you were always busy preparing something for your classes or someone. Now I value my spare moments more." Others detailed how Carver's course had materially helped them. One wrote that when the Atlanta school board had finally provided a black summer school for remedial work, he had been selected as one of twelve teachers.[10]

Occasionally, the students sought tangible ways to express their appreciation. In 1921, for example, they presented Carver with a cut glass vase filled with handmade flowers and a poem written by one of them. As with his earlier undergraduate students, he developed a playful and affectionate relationship with these grown men and women. They, too, were subject to teasing threats of "thrashings."[11]

The demise of Carver's regular teaching did not end his contacts with undergraduate students. He continued to meet his Bible class for as long as he was physically able. The assembly room in Carnegie Library was usually filled to capacity for the Sunday night meeting. Often more than a hundred boys attended, and in November 1920 over two hundred were enrolled. The Bible class students often became "adopted children" and wrote back to their "father" for years after leaving school. From New Jersey one student wrote, "I have received more real help from our Sunday evening lessons than any other subject I took while I was in school." Others echoed this theme.[12]

Continuing to live in Rockefeller Hall, Carver also became confidant and counselor to numerous boys in the dormitory. For some, like Clarence Hart, he became a substitute father. Hart turned to Carver frequently for advice and aid and remembered him every Father's Day. John Sutton, who came to Tuskegee in 1916 to do postgraduate work under Carver, was also profoundly influenced by the professor all of his life.

Most Tuskegee students had been shielded from the cruel realities of the racial caste system by loving parents and continued to live rather sheltered lives in the black community at Tuskegee. After they left and were confronted with the full force of racism, they often turned to Carver for advice and comfort. Their experiences as soldiers during World War I were especially enlightening, and their growing disillusionment with the quality of democracy in America was reflected in their letters. One wrote, "There is much I should like to tell you about Camp Jackson. I should not like to write it as it sounds too much like German propaganda." Another told of scoring 58 out of a possible 60 on an examination for a commission in the regular army, only to be told that there was no suitable vacancy. "Of course," he wrote, "this simply means no vacancy for *Black Officers.*"[13]

Carver could offer little more than the soothing balm of loving concern for the wounds of racism. In other ways he continued to offer more tangible help, still serving as an "employment bureau" and a source of financial assistance. Carver left the role of classroom teacher but did not cease to be an "inspirer of young men."

After Carver abandoned the classroom, he gradually deserted the plot work of the experiment station as well. In 1916 only two projects were undertaken outside the laboratory. In one entitled "Making of a Living on a Small Plot of Ground," five acres were planted with corn, peas, velvet beans, hay, and other vegetables to demonstrate the profitability of diversification and were fertilized with a homemade mixture of "two loads of muck and leaves from the swamp and the woods, and one load of barnyard manure." The other project was the cultivation of cotton under boll weevil conditions. One acre was planted and yielded a little over a half a bale of cotton, which Carver declared was sufficient to "meet demands, and allow us to clear the land and put in another crop." As he noted, no commercial fertilizer had been used on the field for over nine years and each operation was "kept within the reach of the one-horse farmer."[14]

For the next few years the plot work remained essentially the same. In 1917 Carver named as his three main lines of investigation clays, sands, and vegetables grown in Alabama, particularly peanuts, velvet beans, and sweet potatoes. Of these only the vegetables required plot work, and even there the major focus was in finding uses for the crops. By 1923 the only new crops listed in his experiment station reports were Napier and Merker grasses for pastures, and none of his bulletins after 1916 focused on new plot work.[15]

Few were surprised when in 1925 Carver announced that he was "dispensing with the plot work of the Experiment Station" but would continue the "laboratory work, bulletins, and other forms of cooperative activities." Apparently his decision was accepted, for no charges were made against the station after 1925 and the Chambliss Children's House was built on the station plot in the late 1920s.

Since Carver was in his sixties in 1925, the plot work under his direction would have ended soon under any circumstances. However, his stated reasons indicate the changing focus of his efforts after Washington's death. "I am away from the school so much," he declared, "that it is impossible to conduct a scientific experiment of value." He also noted that there were "so many agencies in operation all through the country doing more effective work" of this kind that the land could be "used to much better advantage." Agricultural research was indeed booming, but few investigators focused on the problems that Carver had.[16]

Actually there were other factors preventing effective plot work by Carver: low funding and no staff. The entire budget for all of Carver's work was never more than $3,351. Of this amount, almost $2,000 went for salaries and only $2,076 was furnished by the school and state appropriations. Credits for goods produced on the station land and in the laboratory brought in the other $1,275. Carver's staff consisted of himself and a part-time stenographer.[17]

Of course the experiment station had never had a large budget or staff, so the major reasons for the end of plot work were probably Carver's age, his commercial endeavors, and his vastly expanded lecture schedule. As early as 1917 he was spending almost as much time at other campuses as at his own. For example, in February 1917 he attended more than one farmers' conference a week in four different states. His lectures became yearly features at such schools as Utica and Vorhees. By 1925 his lecture schedule also included tours of white colleges, speeches sponsored by civic and commercial groups, and special fairs and conferences from

Carver exhibit, ca. 1920

Texas to the Atlantic Ocean. Black schools found it harder to obtain Carver's services and frequently rescheduled programs so he could attend. As one black principal wrote, "We do not want to leave 'Hamlet' out of the play."[18]

When he was on campus, Carver spent more and more time in the laboratory rather than the station fields, which was reflected in his bulletins. After 1916 only one even mentioned new plot work. Without Washington's continual prodding, his production of bulletins also drastically declined. The two that appeared in 1916 were the results of earlier work. One, significantly, was his "three-fold" bulletin on the peanut. The other, *Three Delicious Meals Every Day for the Farmer*, gave wholesome menus that could be prepared with few purchased goods. The next year three bulletins appeared, but two were merely expansions of previous ones. *43 Ways to Save the Wild Plum Crop* expanded a 1907 bulletin and gave recipes for wild plums. *How to Grow the Cow Pea and Forty Ways of Preparing It as a Table Delicacy* converted a 1908 bulletin to the "threefold" approach. Carver's only other bulletin in 1917 provided general advice on many subjects, such as the control of the boll weevil, the preparation of homemade fertilizer, and the desirability of new money crops, specifically corn, velvet beans, peanuts, sweet potatoes, and cowpeas. Carver tacitly recognized that the demand for these crops was still weak and suggested, "If a paying market cannot be had for the raw product, they should be fed to stock and turned into milk, meat, butter, eggs, lard, etc."[19]

In 1918 only two bulletins were issued: a "threefold" pamphlet on the tomato, with "115 ways to prepare it for the table," and a six-page treatise on *How to Make Sweet Potato Flour, Starch, Sugar, Bread and Mock Cocoanut*. After these publications three years passed until another bulletin was printed; then a five year gap followed, broken only by the reprinting of old bulletins. Thus in the ten years after Washington's death only eight new bulletins appeared, of which three were expansions of previous works. During the last seventeen years of Carver's life, from 1927 through 1943, only five new bulletins were issued.[20]

The years under Washington's leadership had been hard but productive ones for Carver. With limited time and money he had provided outstanding service as an agricultural researcher and educator. But this work left him largely unknown to the general public. Even before 1916 he had begun the metamorphosis to "creative chemist," and Washington's death accelerated this change. Moton allowed Carver to retreat from his campus duties—his predecessor probably would not have. Moton also did not have the charismatic appeal of Washington; therefore his lieutenants received more attention. As always, Carver's numerous "products" and their possible commercial value were the center of that attention. After years of relative obscurity, he began to give the public what it wanted.

In his continued quest for commercial success, he submitted to Emmett J. Scott a list of fifteen products "now ready for the market" in December 1916. Scott was intrigued with a rubber substitute derived from the sweet potato and declared, "I think I see a

lead." Carver, however, believed that the rubber was not sufficiently proven at the time and reasserted his belief that his wood
stains were the products "cheapest, easiest and best to go into with
small capital." He also recommended his calcimines, toilet powders, cleansing agents, and feather products, all of which he had
developed before Washington's death. The ten other products
were additional discoveries that foreshadowed later work: plant fiber products, dyes, sand products, "artificial hair products," and
items made from the sweet potato, peanut, cowpea, soybean, velvet bean, and other vegetables.[21] Evidently Scott's "lead" failed to
materialize, and in February 1917 Carver enthusiastically announced a proposed local company to market a mixed stock food
he had formulated.[22] It also failed to come to fruition.

Although these developments must have been discouraging,
new interest in Carver's laboratory work was sparked by World
War I. As the conflagration engulfed most of the world, international trade was disrupted and agricultural production plummeted
in the war-torn states. Even before the United States entered the
war in 1917, Americans were experiencing shortages of certain
goods, which became more acute as the nation mobilized for war.

Calls for conservation and searches for substitutes made
Carver's work more timely. Like most Americans he joined wholeheartedly in the war effort, urging farmers to plant more wheat
and touting dehydration and other methods of food preservation to
prevent waste. He even discouraged Institute students from pull-
ing the wild peach and plum blossoms. In the face of shortages
some products that under normal circumstances had not been
commercially feasible now became attractive alternatives. Special
interest was shown in Carver's vegetable dyes and the rubber
substitute from sweet potatoes. The Germans held a near monop-
oly in the production of some dyes and kept their methods a carefully guarded secret. Carver was convinced that his dyes could easily replace the German ones immediately. His rubber, on the
other hand, was still in the experimental stage, but he believed in
its future potential. Neither, however, was utilized before the end
of the war brought the end of the shortages.[23]

Carver's answer to the wheat shortage received the most attention and came the closest to fruition. To save scarce wheat he induced the Institute dietician to use two cups of sweet potatoes for every six cups of flour in preparing bread for the school. This recipe did not call for sweet potato flour, but Carver's work in vegetable drying led him naturally to its development. Any palatable way to make bread with less wheat appealed to the federal government, and the USDA asked Carver to come to Washington for consultation in January 1918.[24]

A meeting was held in the office of David Fairchild, chief of the Bureau of Plant Industry, and Carver exhibited his sweet potato products for a number of interested parties from the USDA and private business. Immediately Fairchild declared some of them to have great commercial possibilities, especially the sweet potato flour, several breakfast foods, and a mixture for making bisque and candies. Carver then supervised the baking of a loaf of bread, which was sliced and eaten. After the meeting, he excitedly reported to the Institute what had happened.

> I really never felt so much like praising God for what appears to be coming to us as a race than now. Not one time has colored been mentioned, but, every man talked business as he saw it, and every possible courtesy has been shown to your representative, so much so that I have been hardly able to get away from some of their special food conservationists. They not only showed me their products but asked me to criticise them, and they seemed especially pleased when I would make suggestions for their improvement.[25]

The next day the men met again and decided:

1.) That the drying of the sweet potato possesses great possibilities in the way of conserving the crop, ease of transportation, and storage.

2.) That efforts must be made at once to get the farmers in the South to greatly increase their crop.

3.) That an immense drier be secured and put in some ideal place in the South where 10,000 bushels of potatoes can be secured and run through the drier as a trial venture.

Carver hoped that the drier would be located at Tuskegee and was pleased when Fairchild requested several pounds of the mixture for bisque and fifty copies of the leaflet on breadmaking with sweet potatoes. The meeting ended with Fairchild "bringing his fist down with a heavy thud on the table" and declaring, "We must do something now, we have fooled [around] long enough." [26]

For the next few years the USDA proceeded with sweet potato drying experiments. Carver was disappointed when the drier was placed at Arlington Farm instead of Tuskegee, but he was delighted to be frequently consulted. Federal employees and others wrote and visited with him to exchange ideas. Finally in November 1919 a three-pound sample of sweet potato flour was sent to Carver by H. C. Gore, the USDA chemist in charge of the Fruit and Vegetable Utilization Laboratory. Gore described the process for making the flour and added, "You will notice that this method is practically identical with that described in your Bulletin No. 37." [27]

Carver's contributions to the USDA experiment received publicity through the efforts of both the school and Carver himself. When he went to the farmers' conferences, he mentioned his trip to Washington and urged the farmers "to go back to their homes, organize, and not let one single potato go to waste." He further instructed them "to erect community and individual sweet potato 'driers' and dry their sweet potatoes, sack them, and in this way be rendering an invaluable service to the Nation in its efforts for conservation." His leaflet How to Dry Fruits and Vegetables provided them with the necessary specific information. To provide further uses for their crop, How to Make Sweet Potato Flour, Starch, Sugar, Bread and Mock Cocoanut gave simple instructions that required no more than a "clean coffee mill, spice mill, or any type of mill that will make wheat flour or corn meal." At later conferences he often displayed a small mill that could be purchased for $3.50. [28]

Carver also wrote several articles touting the commercial possibilities of sweet potatoes and continued to expand his list of products. In 1918 he seemed well on his way to becoming the

"Sweet Potato Man." Later, although he did not desert this work, the end of the war soon brought an end to the interest in sweet potato flour. Meanwhile, on 22 September 1919 Carver sent Moton word of a discovery that ultimately shaped the course of his career. "I am sure you will be pleased to know," wrote Carver, "that I have today made a delicious and wholesome milk from peanuts." About a week later Walter M. Grubbs of the Peanut Products Corporation in Birmingham, Alabama, heard of the discovery and wrote Carver for details. Carver assured him that the milk tasted as good as cow's milk and had been successfully used as a substitute in baking and in making dairy products such as cheese. He also declared, "I think I am conservative in my statement when I say that it is without a doubt, the most wonderful product that I have yet been able to work out, and I see within it, unlimited possibilities." Grubbs came to Tuskegee to investigate and departed dazzled by both Carver and his many peanut products.[29]

Believing that Carver's work would have a great impact on the rapidly growing peanut industry, Grubbs urged the professor to "make a few remarks" in Enterprise, Alabama, at the dedication of a monument honoring the boll weevil for its role in curing the South of cotton dependency. This invitation marked the beginning of Carver's adoption by the peanut industry. Despite later claims that he almost singlehandedly transformed the peanut from an inconsequential crop to a multimillion-dollar enterprise, a sizable, well-organized, and increasingly powerful peanut business existed even before Carver became its symbol. Indeed, if the sweet potato industry had been as well organized Carver might never have become the Peanut Man.[30]

Peanut production had grown rapidly in the decade before the 1916 publication of Carver's bulletin on peanuts, and several USDA bulletins had already stressed the potential of the crop. Nevertheless, for a period after World War I the peanut business suffered from growing pains and other problems. Both producers and processors quickly realized Carver's value as consultant and publicist, especially after his appearance at a convention of the United Peanut Association of America in Montgomery. As the editor of the *Peanut Promoter* noted, when he first arrived at the 1920 meeting there were "doubts lingering in the minds of the audience as to the advisability of having one of the Negro race come before them." Doubts may have arisen in Carver's mind as well when he was forced to ride the freight elevator to the meeting room. Once inside, however, he again displayed his power over audiences. As they listened to him describing his work and realized "its full bearing upon the peanut industry," they soon forgot about color. "Dr. Carver verily won his way into the hearts of the peanut men," the editor declared. Their appreciation was expressed in a unanimous resolution to aid him in securing his patents.[31]

During 1920 articles about Carver's peanut milk were published in newspapers and national magazines such as *Popular Mechanics, Good Health,* and *The Liberty Bell.* This publicity was negligible, however, compared to the bountiful harvest of goodwill for both Carver and peanuts that resulted from his appearance before the House Ways and Means Committee tariff hearings in 1921.

For years the United States had imported sizable quantities of peanut products, and peanut organizations lobbying for protection paid Carver's way to testify before Representative Joseph W. Fordney's tariff committee. Since Carver persistently refused to wear the gifts of clothing that were often given him for such occasions, the committee was apparently somewhat bewildered when an immaculate but shabbily dressed black man stepped forward as a witness.[32]

At first it appeared that Carver would not be taken seriously. The committee members watched with amusement as he pulled samples out of his "Pandora's box" and laid them on the stenographer's desk. This activity consumed several of his allotted ten minutes, and he had barely begun to show some of the uses of crushed peanut cake and peanut hulls when the chairman cracked, in a reference to Prohibition, "If you have anything to drink, don't put it under the table." Carver quickly replied that the drinks would "come later if my ten minutes are extended." The room filled with laughter, but John N. Garner of Texas, later Franklin D. Roosevelt's vice-president, admonished, "Let us have order. This man knows a great deal about this business." He continued to support Carver throughout the proceedings and later recalled the presentation as "one of the most interesting talks I had ever heard before the committee and one of the most effective."[33]

The next outburst of laughter came when Carver displayed a breakfast food with the remark, "I am very sorry you can not taste this so I will taste it for you." After sampling the product he explained that the cereal combined sweet potatoes and peanuts, which were "two of the greatest products God has given us" and could provide "a perfectly balanced ration" if all other vegetable foodstuffs were destroyed. "Do you want a watermelon to go along with that?" asked Representative John Q. Tilson of Connecticut. Carver replied that watermelon was a good dessert, "but you know we can get along pretty well without dessert. The recent war has taught us that." Rep. Tilson made no further remarks during the presentation.

Carver proceeded to show samples of stock food, flour, ice cream flavorings, dyes, milk, instant coffee, Worcester sauce, cheese, oil, and other products made from peanuts. His time was repeatedly extended until at last the chairman declared, "Your time is unlimited." At one point Carver was sidetracked into a discussion of the value of chinaberries, which opened the door for Representative Henry T. Rainey, an opponent of tariff protection, to attempt to trap Carver into an admission that peanuts did not need protection by comparing them to chinaberries which obviously did not require a protective tariff. A spirited debate followed. Rainey asked, "Could we get too [many peanuts], they being so valuable for stock foods and everything else?" Carver responded, "We could not allow other countries to come in and take our rights away from us," and asserted that American peanuts were superior. If that was true, Rainey replied, "then we need not fear these inferior peanuts from abroad." Using butter and oleomargarine as an example, Carver declared, "Sometime you have to protect a good thing." Rainey immediately seized the opportunity to point out that there was no butter or oleomargarine tariff. Garner once again rescued Carver by noting that special taxes had in fact put butter "out of business." The exchange finally came to an end amid sustained laughter with Carver's frank admission, "That is all the tariff means—to put the other fellow out of business."[34]

Carver's showmanship and humor captivated the congressmen and the spectators, and he "soon had them each and every one leaning over the railing to see what was coming next and to get every word spoken." When he finished, applause filled the hearing room, a rare occurrence indeed at a tariff hearing. More important, as a peanut industry spokesman proclaimed, "He not only pleased the committee, but convinced them in no uncertain way that the peanut industry was worth protecting and preserving for American farmers." The representatives "wrote into the Fordney bill the highest rate that the peanut industry has ever had," he declared, "three and four cents per lb., unshelled and shelled respectively." In less than an hour Carver had won a tariff for the peanut industry and national fame for himself.[35]

Trudging through the countryside to bring a better life to black sharecroppers was not good copy for the press, but impressing congressmen and winning a protective tariff for an industry were. Hundreds of newspapers across the nation carried the story of Carver's testimony. More important, the peanut industry had found its patron saint. Four months after the tariff hearings Carver discussed "The Potential Uses of the Peanut" at the United Peanut Association convention in Chicago. The next year he carried his peanut exhibit to the Greater Four County Fair in Suffolk, Virginia at the expense of the Peanut Growers' Exchange. While there he was housed and entertained by the Suffolk Negro Business League, probably to the relief of the white fair managers. By this time his identification with the peanut was so well established that the League presented him with "a hand painted china set made to imitate the peanut shell."[36]

Carver also served the peanut industry by regularly contributing articles to various trade publications and by advising individuals and companies. He was consulted by various peanut producers and processors on a wide variety of problems, from the separation of oil in peanut butter to the suitability of "Pickaninny" for a trade-mark. On the latter question, Carver replied, "Now, my people object seriously to . . . being called 'Pickaninnies' " and suggested another name be found.[37]

Although Carver's advice and help, which was given without charge, continued to be sought in the years to come, the free publicity Carver brought to the peanut industry was probably more valuable. In practically every one of his speeches the peanut was profusely mentioned, and by 1923 he was talking before a wide variety of religious, educational, civic, and farming groups. In addition, increasing numbers of articles about him in national publications invariably alluded to the "lowly goober." After all, it seemed uniquely appropriate to the white press that the son of a slave should be an expert on such a "lowly" plant. Few could resist the temptation to use imagery linking the "humble Negro" with the "humble peanut."

The creation of the Peanut Man began with the discovery of peanut milk, and Carver had great hopes for its commercial success. He envisioned it not as a substitute for cows' milk, but as a "distinct product in the diet of the human family" with unique qualities and uses.

> Peanut milk is a perfect emulsion of the oils, fats, proteins, carbohydrates and some of the ash of the peanuts. Many different kinds of milk can be made by controlling the proportions of carbohydrates and proteins and scientifically diluting the product. Its keeping qualities are about the same as those of cow's milk. It makes splendid bread, rich in flavor, and is excellent for creaming vegetables. Since it is a purely vegetable drink, it forms body building nourishment for invalids or children.[38]

Carver also believed that peanut milk provided a cheap source of protein, for a pint could be made from only a "3 ounce glassful of peanuts." Indeed, he claimed that his method of making milk was more efficient than that of a cow.

> It takes the cow twenty-four hours to make milk. I can make from peanuts better, cleaner and more healthful milk in five minutes. The cow simply takes out of the food she eats what is soluable.

Which is the cleaner process, that of grinding, moistening, heating and filtering in a machine or pan, or passing cereals, vegetables or the vegetable matter a cow eats through her stomach?[39]

Others seemed to agree that peanut milk was a viable commercial item, but Carver's dreams of finally providing a practical product were dashed when he learned that an Englishman had already patented a process for making peanut milk in 1917, two years before Carver's announcement to Moton. In 1921 Carver considered taking "out a patent over his by proving my process is superior in many ways," but he never did, and the Englishman was unable to exploit the patent profitably, possibly because he demanded $150,000 and a 3 percent royalty.[40]

In reality, the patent was not important anyway, for it was Carver's personality, not his milk, that excited the peanut industry. Their enthusiasm did not diminish; the Peanut Man was producing huge amounts of free publicity instead of milk. The relationship was mutually beneficial. By 1922 Carver had overcome the relative obscurity of his earlier years and entered a new era in his life.

No longer engaged in most of the activities that had filled his first twenty years at Tuskegee, Carver gradually became known as a "creative chemist." In 1922 the North Carolina Negro Farmers' Congress presented him with a silver loving cup for "Distinguished Scientific Research," instead of for his many years of educational efforts.[41] Articles began to appear in newspapers and magazines that established the essential ingredients of his new folk hero status. Practically every one mentioned his slave origins, his being captured and "swapped for a $300 race horse" as a child, and his hardships while getting an education. Also popular were his election to the Royal Society and his appearance before the House tariff committee. Many were impressed by a reported job offer from Thomas Edison that Carver declined; the proffered salary varied with the author of the story, but was always high. The sheer number of his products and their humble origins dazzled, without giving clear insight into the value of his work. In short, the exotic qualities of his life and work were highlighted and often distorted, and what emerged was an image of Carver singlehandedly remaking the South.

The precise role Carver played in this myth-making process is difficult to determine. He undoubtedly relished and courted publicity. Some of the news items were probably drawn from the vast store of anecdotes Carver used to illustrate points in his speeches. Apparently these stories were based on fact, but they tended to be embroidered as time passed. Almost everyone is sometimes guilty of subtly improving a story. Carver's improvements, however, were published and never specifically corrected by him.

A good example is the Edison offer. As early as March 1917 Carver obliquely referred to it in a speech at a black college, but it was not widely publicized until later. When asked for more specific information, Carver always replied that he had promised to keep the details of the negotiations confidential. Yet he continued to mention the incident frequently in speeches, often to tout the potential of the South. "The possibilities in New Jersey [where Edison's lab was] are not what they are in the South," he proclaimed in a 1923 speech. "The South is going to come into its own, and is destined to be the richest section of the whole United States. This part of the country is undeveloped and has peculiar possibilities on account of its climate and soil." Thus Carver implied that he had nobly stayed at Tuskegee to serve his region and his people.[42]

Occasionally Carver supplied a few details in response to inquiries about the Edison offer. He usually blamed an indiscreet taxi driver for the breach of confidentiality, and he sometimes admitted that there were "six figures in the offer." After the amount had been reported as $200,000 by Ripley's "Believe It or Not" in 1936 and as $100,000 in a 1937 Readers' Digest article, the curator of the Edison Laboratory wrote to Carver about the numerous requests to confirm the offer he had received. "I do not know why confirmation should be required of us when the story was apparently told by you to the writer of the article," he continued, "as it seems to be altogether consistent with Mr. Edison's ways, but it occurred to me that it would be interesting if we could get the story direct from you for our files."[43]

Carver replied with a two-page letter describing the circumstances of the offer but still refusing to disclose the amount. According to Carver, he received a telegram "shortly after the opening of the World War" which invited him to Orange, New Jersey for a conference with Edison. It was sent by a Mr. Hutchinson for Edison, and Hutchinson later came to Tuskegee to see Carver about joining the research staff, since his boss was busy checking the electrical system in a submarine. The chauffeur who brought Hutchinson to Tuskegee overheard the conversation and "gave out the statement," which Carver asserted "would never have been known if he had not given it out." [44]

It is very unlikely that Carver would have fabricated the entire story, but he was never able to locate the telegram, and the Edison Laboratory has been unable to document the offer. Whatever the circumstances, the incident appears to have impressed Carver and the public more than it did Edison, because when he wrote to Tuskegee in 1927 seeking botanists for some field work the letter was addressed to the "Agricultural School" and did not mention Carver. [45]

Even if the story was essentially true, Carver's attempt to blame a "taxi driver" or a "chauffeur" for publicizing the event is clearly a distortion. A third party may have first mentioned the offer, but Carver was responsible for spreading the story. The temptation was too great. Although Edison was in many ways also an eccentric dreamer, his success lent credibility to his evaluation of commercial possibilities. Thus his endorsement seemed to provide proof that Carver was not an impractical charlatan, as George Bridgeforth, John Washington, and others had charged.

By 1922 the Royal Society invitation, the tariff hearings, the support of the peanut industry, and the Edison offer finally brought Carver the recognition which he had so long sought. Nevertheless, he still cherished the dream of playing a concrete role in the remaking of the South through the utilization of its undeveloped resources. Much of his time during the next few years was devoted to realizing that dream.

Dawning of the New South

Carver had long dreamed of his products proving to be commercially valuable. His hopes had soared with each new manufacturing suggestion, but repeated failures had brought discouragement and despair by 1917. Carver's rise to fame, however, renewed his visions of factories springing up throughout the South to manufacture his discoveries. Not a man of small dreams, he naturally saw himself as the vanguard of not merely new industries, but indeed of a new South.

Revealing his strongly mystical nature, he often told of a vision he experienced on his first day at Tuskegee in Booker T. Washington's office. While listening to the principal, he gazed out the window and suddenly saw the barren clay and dismal poverty of central Alabama transformed into rolling green hills dotted with neatly painted farmhouses and enjoying obvious prosperity. He knew that somehow he was to play a major role in the transformation.

At first he had turned his attention to the small farmer, preaching diversified farming and the wise use of natural resources. Eventually he stressed the cultivation of two crops—peanuts and sweet potatoes—to bring redemption to the South. After he began to focus on commercial uses for these crops, he added an anecdote to his repertoire to explain his changing emphasis. As he told it, he was stopped in downtown Tuskegee by a prominent white lady one day. She commended him for urging farmers to plant something besides cotton, but she asked a very disturbing question:

"What are the farmers supposed to do with all their peanuts and sweet potatoes when there is no real market for them?" He realized then, he would say, that the answer to the South's poverty lay in the answer to this question.[1]

Although these stories are possibly apocryphal, they reveal Carver's changing pattern of thought. He did not view his new focus as a departure from his original mission. The truth that he had preached to the poor black sharecropper was valid for the entire South, and indeed for the entire world. The Creator provided man with the resources needed to meet all his needs, but man was blind to some of their uses. For illustration Carver often quoted such scriptural passages as "Look unto the hills from whence cometh thy help," "There is much food in the tillage of the poor, but there is that which is wasted for want of judgement," and "God said, Behold, I have given every herb bearing seed, which is upon the face of all the earth . . . to you it shall be for meat." All man needed to do to eliminate poverty and hunger was to harness the forces of nature and use wisely the bountiful resources of the world.[2]

Applying these ideas to the problems of the South, Carver believed the region, like the sharecropper, would have to become less dependent upon others for its needs. Rather than importing items that were scarce in the area, the South had to learn to exploit what ever resources were plentiful. Thus Carver saw commercialization of his ideas as a first step in remaking the South by eliminating its colonial economic status.

By 1923 he had ample cause to believe that his discoveries were valuable. Letters poured in from all over the nation with manufacturing proposals. Much of the early correspondence concerned peanut milk, but when the Englishman's patent eliminated that as a viable product Carver turned the bulk of his attention to breakfast foods and diabetic flour. Neither was a new discovery, but his interest was rekindled by manufacturing inquiries. Both products combined the sweet potato and the peanut, because, as Carver declared before the tariff committee, "The peanut and sweet potato are twin brothers, and can not and should not be separated."[3]

As early as 1919 a Chicago man expressed interest in manufacturing Carver's breakfast foods. Although the initial arrangements seemed very promising, nothing developed from the proposal. In April 1922 William H. Danforth, president of Ralston-Purina, wrote that he had heard of the breakfast foods and would like to learn more. By that time, however, the formation of a company to market the products was being explored, and Carver's response was deliberately vague.[4] His reluctance to pursue such promising leads reflected one of the major barriers to the manufacture of his products. He simply did not want to be trapped into the daily grind of solving all the production problems that would inevitably arise. He was, after all, a dreamer, whose restless mind preferred to tackle new ideas and explore new discoveries. He did not even bother to record most of the processes he used. Later some claimed that his products had been stolen by others and placed on the market without giving him credit. Yet in most cases there was apparently little to steal but an idea.

Carver sometimes appeared to want the credit without the tedious work entailed in actual production. A good example is his handling of the diabetic flour. At Hampton Institute he met Stephen H. Blodgett, a physician interested in diabetes. Blodgett wondered if Carver's peanut and sweet potato flours could supplement the starch-free flour manufactured by Lister Brothers, which several of his patients found unpalatable. An analysis of the peanut and sweet potato flours revealed that they both contained about 10 percent carbohydrates, which seemed acceptable for many diabetics without severely restricted diets. Blodgett pressured Carver to approach Lister Brothers with his ideas, but the professor delayed taking any action for over a year. In the meantime, however, he freely mentioned his work with a "diabetes specialist" and the flours' great promise, without giving many specifics.[5]

Carver's desire to remain unentangled with the "business end" of his discoveries prevented him from exploiting the interest of

Carver in laboratory at Tuskegee

men like Danforth and Blodgett. After all, he had been made painfully aware of his managerial shortcomings at the Institute. For years he had sought someone to handle the "practical" side of his work—men like Booker T. Washington, Alva Fitzpatrick, and Emmett J. Scott. In the early 1920s Carver at last found someone eager and willing to devote his time to arranging for the exploitation of Carver's discoveries. Ernest Thompson was a young man from a prominent white Tuskegee family who was blessed with a comfortable inheritance. Carver had known Thompson for some time, and as early as 1913 Thompson had supported Carver's work with a donation of fertilizer to the experiment station. In the 1920s Thompson assumed the role of Carver's business manager.[6]

Thompson, who had little experience to qualify him for this position, was probably chosen because he shared Carver's grandiose vision. The professor was flattered by the interest of successful, established businessmen but could never become truly enamored with anyone who considered his work merely a business venture.

Thompson, on the other hand, described their proposed company as a "lasting monument to you" and a "benefit to mankind for years to come." To the future detriment of both men, Carver chose a fellow dreamer to handle his affairs.[7]

Thompson undertook the task with the gusto of one who knew he was helping to remake the South. All expressions of commercial interest were referred to him. Realizing the need for adequate financing, Thompson enthusiastically invited promising parties to Tuskegee to examine Carver's work. Problems quickly arose, however. Some inquirers proved to have insufficient capital; others were not adequately convinced of the feasibility of the products. Carver's reluctance to reveal his unpatented processes hampered efforts to market them. Neither Thompson nor Carver was willing to finance the procuring of patents until a company was formed to defray the costs. As a result businessmen were asked to buy ideas without knowing precisely what they were getting. The response was often skepticism.

For example, Carver declared one of his paints to be a "sextuple oxide," a term that bewildered chemists. Later he became defensive about the label and wrote Thompson:

> What difference does it make if the blue is an oxide-sulphate, or choride, so it does the work. I call it sex-tuple oxide, because after years of work (three years), I am able to produce this beautiful blue only by oxydizing six times. I may find another way when I get time to try it out, after we protect our formulas, I will be glad to show them everything I know about any of it. . . . For the sake of the organization, suppose we stop calling the blue anything but a *very fine* Prussian Blue.[8]

Apparently Carver's defensiveness about processes prevented any arrangement with Ralston-Purina or Lister Brothers. He turned the matters over to Thompson, who reported that the companies wanted samples, which should not be supplied until patents were obtained. Thus two promising leads were not pursued.[9]

For almost two years Thompson repeatedly proclaimed that he had at last procured the "right contacts" and that formation of a company was imminent. When the plans floundered, he reaffirmed his faith in his and Carver's shared vision and declared "better men" would be found to help them realize their goals. One of the biggest disappointments came from his contact with Sears, Roebuck's Julius Rosenwald, a firm supporter and trustee of Tuskegee Institute as well as a personal acquaintance of Carver. Rosenwald could provide both adequate capital and merchandising skills, so after an investigative trip to Tuskegee by Sears representatives Thompson eagerly awaited some encouraging word. Day after day passed without any response. Thompson then hoped that Carver could influence Rosenwald at the 1922 Founder's Day and trustees' meeting. Soon, however, Thompson and Carver gave up on the Sears connection, and Thompson began bringing more interested parties to Tuskegee.[10]

Finally, in early 1923 Thompson recruited the help of some executives of the Atlanta and West Point Railway, who scheduled and paid for an exhibit of Carver's products at the Cecil Hotel in Atlanta during March, both to net publicity for the railroad and to test the interest of the city's financial community in the products' development. They were very successful in meeting the first goal. Their publicity agent reported, "The newspapers gave us fine publicity and [Carver's] entire stay was in the nature of an ovation" because "he made friends here by his ready wit, fine delicacy of refinement, pleasing manners and humble demeanor." Under the headline, "Tuskegee Scientist Makes Lasting Paint From Mud; Was Ancient Egyptian Art," the Atlanta *Journal* extolled Carver's work in a manner that scarcely dampened his belief in its importance. His peanut, sweet potato, and clay products, the paper declared, "constitute a trilogy that in import to this section and to this country, has never been approached to date."[11]

Significantly, Carver's mysticism and religious vision had captivated the reporter as much as the commercial possibilities of his products had. The professor's view of his work had always differed from the boosterism of the New South leaders who soon adopted him as a symbol. For him the products resulted from a larger divine revelation concerning man's place in the universe. For example, the paper reported his response to questions about the permanency of his paints.

> "Why should they not be permanent?" asks Dr. Carver, simply.
> "God made the clays in the hills; they have been there for countless generations, changeless. All I do is to prepare what God has made, for uses to which man can put it. It is God's work—not mine."[12]

Indeed, one of the ironies of Carver's career was his identification with the so-called New South movement. Every generation after Reconstruction proclaimed the dawning of a new South, and the slogan meant different things to different people. But the most successful version in Carver's time was that of the white Democrats who overthrew Republican rule in the 1870s. Called Redeemers or Bourbons, their ideology was best expressed by Henry W. Grady, the editor of the Atlanta *Constitution* from 1879 to 1889. According to their view, the South would again rise to a position of national leadership by showing the world how to industrialize humanely and solve racial problems. The South had the necessary ingredients: climate, resources, labor, and, of course, a superiority in the art of "civilized" living. All that was needed was to marshal the great abilities of Southerners and to induce capital investment in the region.

Sometimes wrapping themselves in the mantle of the "lost cause," these New South leaders actually advocated a real departure from the old order. The place of the planter was to be usurped by the merchant and manufacturer. Agrarian ideals were to be replaced by the work ethic and businessmen's values. They advocated diversified and scientific farming, but farmers were to play only a supportive role, and become businessmen who produced agricultural products for a world market. Prosperity, they argued, would bring racial harmony, but blacks were to be kept permanently subordinate, a source of cheap labor. The racial cooperation they espoused was based on a paternalistic view of themselves as guardians of the rights and interests of a "lesser people."

On the surface this New South vision was compatible with Booker T. Washington's accommodationist program of black education and economic development, and he and the Bourbon Democrats did cooperate in many mutually beneficial ways. After Washington's death, Carver's advocacy of Southern industrialization made him the logical successor to the role of black symbol of the New South. His need for recognition by practical men, however, blinded him to the basic contradictions between his visions and theirs. For Carver, industrialization was to play the supportive role, providing a viable means to prosperity for the small farmer. While this difference seems a minor theoretical technicality, in reality Carver's ultimate goals were incompatible with those of the Bourbon Democrats.

In almost every Southern state the Bourbons' rise to power was accompanied by policies detrimental to small farmers and blacks. Often economically tied to the railroads, the Bourbons furthered their interests at the expense of the small shipper. As businessmen they sought to make government serve business through corporate tax incentives that led to retrenchment and decreased social services. To provide cheap labor they became involved in the scandalous convict-lease system. Merchants and creditors were aided by state contract and debtor laws, as well as tight-money policies, that helped to fasten an almost insurmountable burden of debt on the small farmer, causing many to lose their land through foreclosures and tax auctions. In short, Bourbon policies helped eliminate the independent family farmer—the very people Carver was trying to preserve.

Blacks suffered doubly, from their status both as marginal farmers and as the major source of convict-lease labor. In addition, the Bourbons exploited racial prejudice to maintain political power. Their policies hurt the majority of Southerners, and they met challenges to their rule with cries of "white supremacy." When the Populist party tried to create a political union of black and white farmers in the 1890s on the basis of mutual economic interest, the Bourbons crippled the third party movement by arousing fears of "Negro rule" and then, with amazing skillfulness at the strategy of divide and conquer, presented themselves as the best protectors of blacks from the lynch-mob mentality of the white lower classes. Such wiliness, coupled with Carver's desperate need for business allies, blinded the professor to the irony of his adoption by the second-generation New South spokesmen.[13]

The need for such recognition presents one of the most puzzling paradoxes of Carver's career. How could a man so imbued with a sense of divine destiny continue to feel so vulnerable to the doubts of his fellow man? Yet questions about the failure to manufacture his products obviously struck a painful nerve. The *Journal* article also contained a patent distortion of the truth, apparently by Carver himself. The reporter noted:

> For a generation, the work of this remarkable man has been pursued with the patience characteristic of a true scientist, who works for the love of it; his light has been under a bushel of his own modest device; fifteen years ago Booker T. Washington was begging him to spread his achievements before the world, only to be denied again and again.
>
> "I am not ready yet," he said always. "When I reach the third or fourth series of by-products—then we'll see."[14]

By 1923 there could be little doubt that Carver was "ready," and the Cecil Hotel lectures finally provided the spark for forming an actual company. Invitations were sent by the railroad to the "most prominent business men." Their enthusiasm was so encouraging that in less than a week Thompson wrote Carver, "You can talk as much as you like in Tuskegee. It's all over now."[15]

Actually many details remained to be settled, but the wheels were started toward incorporation. The principal figures involved were Charles W. Wickersham, president of the Atlanta and West Point Railway; Scott W. Allen, vice-president and general manager of the L. W. Rodgers grocery store chain; Hugh M. Dorsey, a former governor of Georgia; and J. P. Billup, the general passenger agent of the Atlanta and West Point Railway. All appeared to be sincerely concerned with the future of the South. Dorsey had written a pamphlet on peonage in Georgia which caused the formation of a "Dixie Defense" committee in outraged response. Allen had helped to prepare a booklet entitled "Helping Georgia Help Herself." If these men seemed to share Carver's vision, however, they also shared a certain degree of inexperience with this kind of organization. In addition, none was free to devote his undivided attention to the company.[16]

In spite of these shortcomings, matters moved swiftly and smoothly at first. A meeting was held in Atlanta late in March. Much to Carver's delight, a private railroad car was sent to Tuskegee to provide both his transportation to Atlanta and his lodgings in the city. Such small gestures seemed to please him greatly, and he mentioned the private car quite frequently in letters to friends. By mid-April he was also able to report, "The organization seems to be moving along nicely. Those who have given it careful study seem to feel that it will revolutionize economic conditions here in the South."[17]

Two issues had to be settled before incorporation: patent protection for the processes and the relationship of Tuskegee Institute to the company. C. W. Hare, a Tuskegee attorney, was dispatched to Washington, and patent application for "Paint and Stain and Process of Producing the Same" was filed on 13 June 1923.[18] Matters were not so easily handled at Tuskegee. Evidently Institute officials wanted to share the profits from processes developed with their laboratory equipment. Thompson wrote to Carver:

> Dr. Moton sent Mr. Wickersham the agreement or contract that Mr. Merrill had prepared for you to sign—it is about the same as the one Mr. Hare had—So you do not want to sign it. I am sure Mr. Hare will advise you to this effect. Things are going too fine now to have them spoiled.[19]

Although the details of the financial agreement with the Institute are unknown, the matter was apparently settled. The manner of Carver's compensation is also unclear, but one newspaper reported that he would receive 10 percent of the company's net income.[20]

At a June meeting Dorsey and Thompson were authorized to proceed with the incorporation of the Carver Products Company, and application for charter was filed with the clerk of Superior Court of Fulton County, Georgia, on 21 August 1923. The function of the company was to be "buying, selling and dealing in formulae and patented processes for the development of various and sundry products, such as food, dyes, stains, paints and other like products from the sweet potato, the peanut, the pecan, the okra, the dandelion, the black oak, the sweet gum, the willow, the swamp maple and other like native growths; and also from wood ashes and all clays, toilet powders, face creams, cleansing powders and other like products."[21] The list of products was grandiose and testified to Carver's wide-ranging research interests, but the aim of the company was quite limited. It was a kind of holding company that manufactured nothing; other companies were to be sold the processes outright or on a royalty basis.

With Wickersham as president, Allen as vice-president, and Thompson as secretary-treasurer, the company was to be capitalized at $125,000, which was divided into shares of stock priced at $1.00 each. How much of the stock was subscribed to by the founders is unknown, but Carver began to refuse to grant loans, declaring that his money was all tied up in the company.[22]

Even before incorporation, a prospectus, company stationery, and advertising matter were printed. The company also reprinted two flattering articles about Carver from *World's Work* and *Success* magazines, along with a number of endorsements, in a small pamphlet that Carver later used to reply to requests for more information about himself. He was delighted to receive the first letter on company stationery in August 1923 and soon used it for all his letters to friends.[23]

With incorporation came new publicity. The Atlanta papers told of the company and quoted Thompson's prediction that "diversification of crops, with subsequent escape from 'cotton bondage' will follow the new venture." The Baltimore, Maryland, *Manufacturers' Record* noted, "The Southern farmer will benefit greatly by the new markets opened for [Carver's] products by this company, which expects to be in actual operation in a short time."[24]

This prediction depended upon the raising of sufficient capital and the formation of companies to do the actual manufacturing. All that the incorporation of the Carver Products Company had changed was the number of people sharing the expense of patent applications and promotion. It merely took over as a corporate body the role that Thompson had played as an individual.

Carver's paints and stains were considered the most promising items for rapid development, and promotional efforts were undertaken. Wickersham suggested that a practical test of the usefulness and durability of the paints be made by painting half of a railway car with regular paint and the other half with Carver's. Carver was unable to match the colors perfectly, however, so an entire car was painted instead. An exhibit of the clay products was also installed in the company's headquarters at the Healey Building in Atlanta, and invitations were mailed to possible manufacturers in February 1924.[25]

The first manufacturing venture took place closer to home, however. The incorporation aroused new interest among Tuskegee businessmen who had previously been timid about getting financially involved, much to Carver's hurt and disappointment. Also, a good deposit of the needed clays was found in nearby Notasulga. For these reasons, plus the ready availability of Carver, it was decided that the first manufacturing plant would be opened near Tuskegee. An engineer was retained to survey the deposits and design machinery. By early May 1924 he had drawn up specifications for the plant and predicted it could be ready for operation in about ninety days. Carver delightedly wrote to a friend, "You will be pleased to know that the plans are perfected for a $27,050.00 paint plant to be erected about two miles up the creek from Chehaw."[26]

Financing still remained a major problem, though. The amount raised by the company's officers, the Tuskegee businessmen, and the sale of stock was inadequate. Many potential investors wanted a guaranteed market before proceeding. To meet these needs the Carver Products Company turned to Robert Woodruff of the Coca-Cola Company. Several meetings were scheduled and an agreement was reached to try the paint in Coca-Cola's barrel painting operations. Evidently the overtures to Coca-Cola were unsuccessful, for Carver Products continued its quest for financial backing.[27]

In spite of the numerous problems, Carver was still optimistic in September 1925, when he wrote, "I have practically retired from the nominal work of the Institute and will devote the remainder of my life trying to get these industries going and leave them for the benefit of the younger generation of our race especially, I hope." Three months later he notified the business committee of the Institute that he was "dispensing with the plot work of the Experiment Station."[28]

Carver seemed willing to stake his future on the Carver Products Company, but by February 1927 he was forced to admit that it "has really never functioned and I believe that they will be called to surrender any claims they may have upon the sweet potato products." After about four years the company's only fruits appear to have been three patents and several disgruntled small investors. The patents covered two paint processes and one process for the making of cosmetics from clay and peanuts, which were applied for in 1923 but not issued until 1925 and 1927. Although Carver later claimed to have "many patents" and "others applied for," these in fact remained the only ones.[29]

For several years Carver and Thompson sought unsuccessfully to get the paints manufactured. Cosmetics and food products always remained another possibility, but problems arose in that area too. Many of his peanut products could probably be profitably manufactured only in conjunction with other kinds of processing, such as the making of oil. Peanut cake and meal were waste products in this established industry, but Carver had difficulty in obtaining them. A number of previous similar patents were also discovered, and the food and cosmetic products were abandoned.

One discovery, however, did get on the market in the 1920s. In 1922 Carver developed an emulsion of creosote and peanuts that he called Penol. At that time creosote was a recognized base in patent medicines for respiratory problems. Carver believed that peanuts enhanced creosote's palatability and medicinal value because of their nutritive properties. In a widely publicized New York speech he mentioned Penol and its great potential. A newspaper account implied that he had developed a new cure for tuberculosis, which provoked a great deal of interest and a rather angry letter from a manufacturer of another creosote preparation. In reply Carver explained that the papers had erred in their comments and that he would not assert Penol's superiority until after thorough medical tests.[30]

Nevertheless, Carver believed his discovery was very valuable and was delighted by testimonials from doctors and patients who tried Penol on an informal basis—the only "medical tests" that were made. After he received an inquiry from the advertising firm that handled Phillips' Milk of Magnesia, Bayer Aspirin, and Fletcher's Castoria, Penol began to appear to be the perfect item to manufacture. It both utilized a Southern crop and would relieve ailing individuals. Carver could not let go of the dream of being the agent of the divine in bringing a lasting and significant transformation in the quality of life for mankind.[31]

Sometime in 1925 or 1926 the Carver Penol Company was founded by Thompson and a number of prominent Tuskegee businessmen, including a physician, a druggist, and several bankers. According to the printed stock offering, it was incorporated under the laws of Delaware with 150,000 shares of stock to be issued. The *Peanut Journal* reported that Carver was not actively involved except in a scientific way. "I have nothing to do with it," he claimed, "more than to endeavor to keep them straight in its manufacture." Yet at times he indicated a personal financial interest in the company as an excuse to deny still numerous loan requests.[32]

By May 1926 Carver reported that a factory was being fitted up with plumbing and machinery to begin operations within a few weeks. A factory was indeed started, but on a very limited scale. It was described the next year as a "small temporary factory" consisting of "a small Coles motor which furnished power for simple machinery," a "barrel of peanuts in the corner," and a "small table with bottles of Penol." Characteristically, its walls were covered with Carver's paints.[33]

In spite of its size, Carver claimed the company was launching a $35,000 advertising campaign. It did print a small pamphlet that declared that Penol was "composed of some of the best known and most proven remedies for Coughs, Sore Throat, Bronchitis, Catarrh, Pulmonary and Stomach Troubles." The booklet also claimed that Penol was a "Tissue Builder, Intestinal Cleanser, Germ Arrester, Nerve Food and Intestinal Antiseptic" that would not irritate or nauseate.[34] The "medicine" was copyrighted but not patented, and by 1929 there were complaints about its quality. Thompson began looking for someone to take over the operation. One man he approached wrote Carver about a letter "from Ernest Thompson saying that he wanted to sell out cheap as he realized now that he was not the man to handle your products at all." Nevertheless, the company continued to limp along, issuing a new invitation to purchase stock in April 1930.[35]

By late 1931 Carver was naming R. H. Powell, a Tuskegee attorney, the agent for his products, but Thompson evidently retained proprietorship of Penol. Finally in 1932 he found a Danville, Virginia firm to handle it on a royalty basis. The company, headed by J. T. Hamlin, Jr., distributed two other preparations— an "herbal extract" and a laxative. On 29 March 1932 Hamlin signed a contract that gave him the right to produce and sell Penol for a monthly fee of $100 and a royalty of two-and-a-half cents per bottle.[36]

Hamlin was enthusiastic and changed his firm's name to the Herb-Juice-Penol Company. Although he quickly lined up Sharpe and Dohme pharmaceutical laboratory to manufacture his new product, it took two years for them to perfect the process. During this time Carver came to Virginia to aid in solving the production problems, and a very friendly relationship developed among all the concerned parties. Hamlin seemed to have been able to satisfy Carver of the sincerity of his "vision."[37]

Penol was not a great success. As early as July 1932 the contract was renegotiated to reduce the monthly payments to $50 because of low sales volume. Advertising in publications such as *Drug Topics* did not help substantially. By 1937 the monthly payments were again reduced, and finally discontinued. In August Hamlin reported repeat orders of only about two dozen bottles a month and wrote Carver that Thompson was "very much discouraged."[38]

The next month Thompson's discouragement was expressed in a letter from his attorney that charged Hamlin with breach of contract and demanded $2,100 in back payments, a full accounting of all sales, and a check to cover the royalties due. The company would then decide about its option to cancel the contract. The letter ended with a threat of "immediate legal action on our part."[39]

Hamlin was "shocked and surprised." He could not understand how the friendly relations had deteriorated, and wrote:

> Surely you can see we have had the worst end of the bargain all the way through, however, we have worked every minute with the thought that you two gentlemen, as well as Dr. Carver were well aware of just what we have been up against and would at least show appreciation for the work we have done.[40]

The major problem was Thompson's desperation. His inheritance and fifteen years of his life were spent following an elusive dream. In the end he settled for security and more limited horizons in a post office job. Penol remained with Hamlin because small royalties were better than none.[41]

During these sordid negotiations Carver remained aloof and noncommital. Hamlin kept pressuring him, however, for advertising pictures, the rights to other Carver products, and a new formula to make Penol "more palatable." Carver replied politely, but he was tired of the entire matter.[42] He wrote Thompson that Hamlin was "worrying me about Penol" and declared, "Penol is your personal property. I gave it to you with the hope that it might be a nice little compensation for you and your wife as the years multiply." Thompson should therefore handle Hamlin, Carver argued, but he refused to lend his name to the product if the formula were changed.[43]

Hamlin's complaints were justified. He had paid for advertising and for perfecting production by Sharpe and Dohme, and by 1936, when the payments were discontinued, he had sent Thompson over $1,000 plus royalties. All of these expenses came out of a sales volume that never exceeded $5,000 a year.[44]

Hamlin, who had an obvious stake in the success of Penol, doggedly continued his efforts on its behalf even during the Depression. By the time the nation's economic troubles began to ease and brighter days were expected, however, great pharmaceutical advances had occurred, and the federal government was cracking down on patent medicines, including Penol. Hamlin's problems with the Food and Drug Administration (FDA) caused him to continue to worry Carver about Penol. By then Carver's dreams for the medicine were dead, and only the bitter taste of failure remained, so each new challenge by the FDA must have opened a painful wound.

In 1937 the FDA reported that an analysis of Penol invalidated the medicine's nutritional claims and its description as "a perfect emulsion which would carry creosote through the system without irritation and nausea." At first only the claims for the peanut portion of the formula were refuted. Three years later the FDA questioned the value of creosote as well, following the publication of an article that condemned creosote as practically worthless in the treatment of respiratory disorders. The government also charged that Penol contained insufficient creosote to be effective. Weary of the whole affair, Carver offered Hamlin little encouragement or aid.[45]

Evidently Hamlin settled matters with the government, for in December 1941 he unsuccessfully sought Carver's permission to use his picture on the cartons and in advertising matter. Still holding on to the dream, he declared:

> This would be of an untold advantage to the product and would definitely tie you and your life's work into this most meritorious product which we want so much to pass on to the suffering humanity and we do not want to lose sight of that even though it is of necessity that we receive proper renumeration in so doing.[46]

Hamlin was more stubborn than Carver or Thompson in pursuing success for Penol, but the product eventually died a quiet death in the face of failure and the competition of superior products.

Carver continued to show sporadic interest in the manufacture of his products, despite such disclaimers as, "We manufacture nothing. We simply work out formulae. After that I do not follow them up. I do not know who manufactures them. In fact it is of no interest to me who manufactures them after I get through."[47] He remained defensive about the lack of commercial development of his products, but he had been badly burned and refused to get directly involved again in similar ventures until he saw them as a way to finance the Carver Foundation in his last years.

In retrospect all the manufacturing attempts were ill-funded and poorly organized. The question, therefore, remains whether any of Carver's discoveries could have been commercially successful with proper handling. Penol was based on ingredients that have since been proven ineffective. The only detailed processes for which records remain are the patented ones, and from their description they seem more appropriate to small-scale production and not developed to the point of commercial feasibility. The cosmetic patent, for example, calls for a "quantity of salicylic acid substantially the size of a small pea, 10 drops of benzoin and three to four drops of any desired perfume."[48] It should be remembered, however, that Carver was working before the major synthetic and pharmaceutical breakthroughs of the twentieth century. Obvious weaknesses in his products were not so clear then. Also, commercial development had not been the original intent of his work.

Among his religious friends, Carver admitted in the 1930s that he had been diverted from his real mission by these manufacturing endeavors. He deceived himself through vanity about the divine plan for his life. Considering the circumstances, he can perhaps be excused for his blindness. In other ways he was more successful in ushering in a New South. To some that slogan meant an era of racial brotherhood, and Carver aided their attempts to realize those dreams through his interracial work in the 1920s and 1930s.

Breaking Down Barriers

The years between Carver's arrival at Tuskegee in 1896 and his rise to fame were among the bleakest in Southern race relations. During his first year there the United States Supreme Court issued its momentous decision in the case of *Plessy* v. *Ferguson*, which sanctioned "separate but equal" facilities for blacks. The decision did not originate segregation, but it provided a legal basis for its institutionalization. In the next two decades hundreds of Jim Crow laws were adopted at all levels of government throughout the South, solidifying old racial barriers and creating new ones. By 1916 sporadic discrimination based on custom had been replaced by systematic repression based on law.

During World War I, black participation in the "war for democracy" raised hopes for democracy at home. Blacks came back from Europe determined to "win on the home front," only to be met with a wave of violence that reached its bloody peak in the Red Summer of 1919 with the lynching of seventy blacks and the occurrence of twenty-five race riots. In these circumstances Afro-Americans of all classes viewed the improvement of race relations as crucial.[1]

Carver's rise to fame took place in this era of racial violence. He probably believed that God intended to use him to calm the troubled waters. His work with the United Peanut Association and the Carver Products Company provided bridges between blacks and whites. Two new honors also seemed to support his view of the significance of this dimension of his work.

During the 1923 exhibit at the Cecil Hotel, Carver received a highly symbolic endorsement. The Atlanta chapter of the United Daughters of the Confederacy (UDC) adopted a resolution to send "a written expression of their interest and appreciation" to Carver. The newspapers naturally reported the resolution, which was interpreted a little differently in the black and white communities. Blacks emphasized its recognition of black ability, while whites viewed the UDC action as an indication of the reasonableness and fairness of Southern race relations. The UDC president claimed, "As a southern organization, we naturally feel an interest for the negro that people of other portions of the country do not either feel or understand."[2]

The UDC resolution was a conservative Southern endorsement. The same year Carver was recognized by a group with a radically different view of Southern race relations, the National Association for the Advancement of Colored Peoples. The NAACP was organized in 1909 during the heyday of Jim Crow legislation as an alternative to Booker T. Washington's accommodationist program. Because of its roots in the anti-Washington Niagara Movement of W. E. B. DuBois and William Monroe Trotter, the NAACP's relations with Tuskegee Institute remained strained during the principal's lifetime. Friction also resulted from the competition between the two institutions for acceptance as the legitimate voice of Afro-American aspirations. By 1923 the NAACP was winning the battle for leadership, and its endorsement of Carver can be considered as symbolically important as was that of the UDC.

The Spingarn Medal of the NAACP was one of the most coveted awards among American blacks. For several years Carver's friends lobbied to get him the medal, which was given to the individual who had most advanced the black cause during the year. In June 1923 the awards chairman notified Carver that "the award was made to you for your achievements in agricultural chemistry."[3]

Apparently, W. E. B. DuBois, the editor of the NAACP publication *Crisis*, was not wholly convinced that Carver's major contribution was in "agricultural chemistry," and wrote him for "further details concerning the commercial value of your chemical discoveries" to use in an article about the award. He also indicated that he wished to stress "the impression that you have made upon the white South."[4]

In the end the official citation reflected DuBois's emphasis, declaring that the award was made "in consideration of [Carver's] services in agricultural chemistry, his recent recognition by a British Royal Society, and for lectures on agriculture during the last year before white and colored audiences, particularly in the South, where his clear thought and straightforward attitude have greatly increased inter-racial knowledge and respect."[5] This was a more legitimate basis for the award, but it still tended to reinforce the impression that Carver's most significant work occurred during the second phase of his career. Thus his commercial endeavors, instead of his educational efforts, brought black as well as white recognition.

Receiving the Spingarn Medal not only delighted Carver but also inspired him to seek yet another honor. For some time the white South had addressed him as "Doctor," probably to avoid breaching the taboo against calling blacks "mister." Many came to assume he actually did possess a doctorate, which occasionally caused embarrassment. Carver notified his Iowa State professor, L. H. Pammel, of the NAACP award and suggested that the school might want to send a representative to the Kansas City presentation ceremony. In describing his response to the medal, Carver noted that only an honorary doctorate from his alma mater would mean more. Pammel correctly interpreted the hint and made an appeal to college officials for such a degree, without success.[6]

The other two honors, however, established Carver as a force for better race relations. Although his interracial contacts spanned his entire carer, his new fame provided new opportunities. Invitations from white organizations and schools dramatically increased, bringing him to the attention of a growing number of white moderates and liberals who were working to improve conditions for blacks in the South.

The South has always had its "forgotten voices" of dissent on racial matters, but the intensity of their cries and the receptiveness of their listeners have varied according to historical circumstances. The lynchings and riots of 1919 sparked the consciences of some white Southerners. The massive northward migration of blacks during and after the war alarmed others who feared the loss of cheap labor. Therefore, after several decades of relative silence voices of dissent were once again raised to question the South's solution to the "race problem."

As always, the Southern men and women who undertook to improve race relations had widely varying goals. Some merely wanted to reduce the abuses of Southern racial patterns without destroying the system of segregation or the premise of white supremacy. To them even a "lesser race" deserved the protection of the law against lynching and peonage. They wanted to cleanse the system, not change it. Others, however, believed the system itself was both evil and based upon falsehoods. In their minds blacks were their equals and any racial barriers were artificial and dehumanizing to all. While differing in goals, the two groups differed little in method. Even the most moderate spokesmen for racial justice realized that their words often fell upon hostile ears. All felt as if they were walking a thin tightrope of conscience. To say too little was to imply consent. To say too much was to lose one's audience and perhaps provoke more violence. Thus all sugarcoated their words to appeal to Southern vanity as well as conscience.

The similarity of methods meant that both groups could work through the same organizations. During the period after World War I many channeled their efforts through the Atlanta-based Commission on Interracial Cooperation. The CIC had as its premise that dialogue between the races was necessary to improve conditions. It therefore sought and won the support of moderate Southern black leaders. Because Tuskegee Institute was an active participant in this movement, many CIC leaders had an opportunity to meet George Washington Carver.[7]

Some of these leaders were especially interested in the invitations Carver received to speak at Southern white colleges, for the organization saw education as the essential first step in its work and believed that little could be changed until the falsehoods that supported discrimination were exposed. Although many adult education projects were undertaken, Southern youth was seen as the key to real change. During the college years their minds were more open to new ideas. In fact, in colleges across the South various campus organizations, especially Young Men's Christian Association groups, were seeking more knowledge on race relations. The YMCA leadership was quick to exploit such interest and found the CIC willing and able to finance efforts in this area. The first steps taken were rather timid. Each summer regional student conferences were held throughout the country. In 1920 the Southern regional conference at Blue Ridge, North Carolina, invited Robert Moton to address the students. Moton was housed and fed separately, but his warm reception by the students convinced many that contacts between young people and educated blacks would produce beneficial results.[8]

At this time Carver was proving this ability to reach young people. In August 1920 he spoke at Mississippi State College at the invitation of its president. During the next two years he was asked to lecture at Mississippi College in Clinton and at Clemson College in South Carolina. These invitations convinced Will W. Alexander, a guiding light behind the CIC, of Carver's usefulness in promoting racial understanding. Alexander was also very active in the Methodist church and arranged two appearances by Carver before large church assemblies in 1922. His reception reaffirmed Alexander's belief that the professor's magnetic, compelling personality might be able to break down racial barriers that others had been unable to penetrate.[9]

In 1923, with church invitations coming in and Carver's life story being used in church literature, Alexander decided it was time to bring Carver into the joint CIC-YMCA youth work. He arranged for Carver to be invited to the Blue Ridge conference that summer. As it turned out, the director of the camp, Willis D. Weatherford, and Carver had met years before when they were both student delegates to a YMCA summer camp in the 1890s.

Weatherford was delighted to have Carver, but embarrassed by the provision of separate accommodations for the professor. A Southern aristocrat from Weatherford, Texas, he remembered his own initially angry reaction to Carver's presence thirty years earlier, and now he was afraid that if too many racial concessions were forced upon Southern youths they would close their minds and hearts. He painfully and awkwardly explained to Carver why he hoped this limited contact would allow more bending of racial etiquette in the future. With his typical kindness, Carver assured him that he was quite comfortable.[10]

When the time came for his presentation, Carver undoubtedly felt the weight of an awesome responsibility. From his talks with Alexander and Weatherford he knew that they considered his success crucial to the future progress of their student work. He intended to use an indirect approach, as always, never mentioning race relations at all. Instead he described the miracles and beauties of nature and how natural forces and resources could be harnessed for the benefit of man. To illustrate his point he displayed samples of his products made from sweet potatoes, peanuts, Alabama clay, and other "underutilized" resources. The indirect lesson was that creative genius could be encased in black skin. When he finished the applause was long and hard. A number of the young men came up to shake his hand; for some this must have been a significant gesture.[11]

Carver always scanned his audiences to spot those he considered most responsive. One young man had caught his eye because of his rapt attention. Carver longed to meet him and was delighted when he made his way forward with the others. Weatherford introduced him as Jim Hardwick, a young man who had been captain of Virginia Polytechnic Institute's football team and was now training for YMCA work. Carver immediately offered to make Hardwick one of "his boys." The young Virginian did not know how to interpret this remark and became guarded in his responses. Before Carver's stay was over, however, he sought out the professor to ask what he had meant. Carver told how he endeavored to help young men to seek the truth. As he did not have any children of his own, he called them his "adopted boys." Hardwick, the descendant of slave owners, asked the ex-slave to let him into the "family." In the years that followed many more whites would join that family, but Carver always called Hardwick his "oldest Blue Ridge boy."[12]

Being one of Carver's boys meant receiving continuous letters of support and encouragement. The professor's gift for making people feel special and important is revealed in his letters to young Hardwick. In October 1923 he wrote:

> God has so willed it that there were always a few good friends to encourage and strengthen me when the burden seemed greater than I could bear. God gave you to me for courage, strength, and to deepen and indelibly confirm my faith in humanity, and oh how I thank Him for you, you came to me when I needed you most.[13]

The letter probably referred to a rather nasty situation that had arisen in Tuskegee over the new Veterans' Hospital there. The year 1923 witnessed Carver's smashing success at Blue Ridge, the Spingarn Medal, and the incorporation of the Carver Products Company, but the furor over the Veterans' Administration (VA) Hospital served as a counterweight to his rising hopes of a new and better world.

The federal government decided to open a hospital for black veterans because of the discrimination they faced at the existing facilities. Tuskegee was selected as the site, and area whites were assured that the facility would be white-controlled. Moton, however, wanted the hospital to be black-run, both to provide jobs for the increasing number of black doctors and nurses and to demonstrate black managerial ability. With the aid of such organizations as the NAACP, the Urban League, and the black press, he pressured VA officials and President Warren G. Harding to hire blacks.

Tuskegee whites quickly mobilized to ensure that the original promise of white control was realized. When the hospital opened they seemed to have won, for it was staffed mainly by whites. Even white nurses were hired, and because they were forbidden by Alabama law to touch black patients, the acual work was done by poorly paid black maids. Black protest accelerated, resulting in increased racial tension in Tuskegee. Moton left town and went to work behind the scenes, as Washington often had in civil rights matters.

President Harding and the new head of the VA supported Moton's position and ordered the immediate hiring of blacks. When the first black to hold a managerial position arrived in July 1923, a Klan march was the response. News of the impending march brought blacks from all over the state to defend the Institute. As a result the march did not cross the campus, but did cause the new black employee to leave town. In the end, however, the march, further lobbying and threats of violence did not halt the transition to an all-black hospital, which was completed on 7 July 1924. It was a significant victory for black power and illustrated the growing clout of black organizations.[14]

As often happened, Carver's loyalties were probably torn between his white and black friends. Officials of the Carver Products Company urged him to come to Atlanta during the furor, but he later claimed that he believed he should remain with "his people" at Tuskegee. Nevertheless, a number of his closest white friends, such as W. W. Thompson and C. W. Hare, were involved in the white lobbying effort. Hare's role did not prevent his becoming the attorney for Carver Products, and Carver maintained good relationships with white Tuskegee generally. The incident, however, must have exposed the duality of his response to race, wavering between a sense of racial solidarity and the rejection of race as a valid category.[15]

The VA Hospital episode was discouraging, but Carver could find solace in the aftermath of his Blue Ridge trip. Invitations to speak in white colleges began arriving in floodlike proportions. Students who had heard him at Blue Ridge wanted Carver to come to their campuses. The volume of requests necessitated some kind of coordination, and Will Alexander assumed the job of organizing a tour. As Carver explained, "So many calls are coming in; some to me personally and a number to him, that I thought it wise to turn the whole matter over to him."[16]

In the fall of 1923 Carver was not well. He had been overburdened with a hectic schedule and was probably near exhaustion. In his earlier trips to appear before white audiences most of the arrangements for travel were left up to him. Whites just did not seem to realize what burdens were imposed by Jim Crow laws, such as the lack of sleeping cars on railroads and hotel and restaurant facilities for blacks. Traveling in the South required careful planning by blacks. Fortunately, when Alexander organized a tour of South Carolina colleges for November, Carver was able to get J. T. Hodges, the president of the black Tillotson Teachers College in Texas, to accompany him. By making transportation, lodging, and meal arrangements, Hodges was able to reduce some of the burdens on Carver, and the trip was an overwhelming success.[17]

In less than a week Carver and Hodges made the rounds of six colleges. The expenses for the trip, which were less than sixty dollars, were paid by the CIC. The Clemson student paper noted that his speech marked the first time a black had spoken in the college chapel and remarked, "He is probably the one colored man out of a million who could have held the attention of the Clemson boys." The CIC and YMCA hoped that Carver would not be the last black to speak at these schools and anxiously solicited reports of his speeches from school officials.[18]

There must have been a great feeling of relief and then exaltation when the responses began to arrive. From Clemson came the report, "To see a man as black as Doctor Carver and yet as able as he is, comes as a distinct shock to Southern boys, and jars them out of their conviction of the negro's absolute inferiority." Likewise the president of Erskine College asserted that "there is no better way to create a proper relationship between the two races." "The direct appeal to the white man is good," he declared, "but there's something winning in the indirect method which makes the appeal not of word but of objective life."[19]

There was only one minor criticism among the glowing reviews. A generally favorable letter noted that Carver's voice was "bad that morning" and that he took "a little long to get into his subject." Characteristically, Carver felt compelled to respond and explained that he was "trying to warm up an unresponsive audience." His apparent inordinate desire for unmitigated acclaim was rooted in more than his previous frustrations and humiliations. As he explained to Jim Hardwick, "It is important to know what people think of you. They must love you and have confidence in you if you are to help them."[20]

If Carver had any doubts, the responses convinced both Alexander and Weatherford of his gift for breaking down racial barriers. They were joined by Robert B. Eleazer of the CIC and J. W. Bergthold of the YMCA in their desire to exploit this talent as much as possible. Weatherford brought a group of seniors from Vanderbilt to Tuskegee in February 1924. In March Eleazer wrote an article about the "Goober Wizard" for the *Intercollegian*, a magazine "devoted to the concerns of the Student Christian Movement." They hoped to arrange another college tour in the spring, but Carver's health and schedule would not permit it. He was also invited to attend the YMCA southwestern regional conference in Hollister, Missouri, as well as to return to Blue Ridge.[21]

Carver was unable to go to Hollister that year, but he did go back to Blue Ridge and enjoyed the benefits of the doors he had opened the year before. In 1924 he did not sleep in isolation. Howard Kester, a remarkable young man who was with a delegation from Lynchburg College in Virginia, invited Carver to share a cottage with the two dozen young men in his group. It was the beginning of a friendship between the two that lasted until the professor's death.

One barrier was crossed, but others remained. Carver still did not eat in the dining hall; food was brought to him by his "Virginia boys." When it was announced that Carver would speak at the conference, two student delegations from Florida and Louisiana stated their intention to walk out as soon as he began his speech. After he was introduced by Alexander and began to speak, however, "an almost unbelievable silence fell over the auditorium" and not "a soul budged." At the end of his speech, the leader of the Florida delegation rose and "stated in a loud, clear voice" what he and his fellow delegates had planned to do. Then he extended an apology to Carver on behalf of the group. The professor had worked his magic again.[22]

To capitalize on Carver's ability to make friends he was invited to stay at the camp for several days so that the students could meet him personally. So many wanted a chance to talk with him that someone had to be designated to make appointments. The interviews were limited to fifteen minutes each, but Carver was still kept busy from four in the morning until midnight. In addition to the personal interviews, Carver was asked to meet with several state delegations in their cottages. At these meetings he was often begged to visit campuses, and four delegations urged him to stay in their cottages the next summer at Blue Ridge. These contacts led to further "adoptions," and during the following month Carver received more than forty letters from his "Blue Ridge boys."[23]

As Carver's family grew, many followed the lead of the "eldest son," Jim Hardwick, and came to Tuskegee to visit Carver. For some the decision to come was costly. When Howard Kester went to Tuskegee, his father told him not to return home. Nevertheless, many came to feel that, as one son declared, "To me Tuskegee has come to be a mecca to which I must make my annual pilgrimage for mental and spiritual substenance."[24]

Both the YMCA and the CIC wanted to exploit the interest Carver had created and were eager to arrange more opportunities for students to meet him. Groups in North Carolina, Kentucky, and Tennessee pleaded for lectures on their campuses. The demands upon Carver's time and energy, however, were starting to overwhelm him. One of the demands for which he had little enthusiasm was a fundraising campaign for Tuskegee Institute. He believed the publicity from his interracial work would benefit Tuskegee more than direct appeals for contributions. He therefore asked Bergthold to inform Moton of the value of his work and request that the professor be relieved of some of his Institute duties. Bergthold agreed, and wrote Moton that "Dr. Carver has exerted such a wholesome spiritual influence in his personal contacts with students, that I believe in all sincerity he is making one of the finest and most far-reaching contributions to right racial relationships of any man now before our students."[25]

To capitalize on this influence, Bergthold arranged for Carver to appear before a statewide gathering of Kentucky YMCA college groups in December 1924. In November, however, an event occurred that shook Carver's confidence and made him wonder if he could continue to render "valuable service."

He was invited to speak to the Women's Board of Domestic Missions of the Reformed Church in America at its meeting in New York City. As he had never been there, he apparently looked forward to the trip with a mixture of excitement and uneasiness.[26]

He was allotted twenty minutes to talk before a crowd of five hundred in the Marble Collegiate Church on 18 November. This was less time than he usually liked to speak, but he quickly launched into an abbreviated version of his familiar lecture and presentation. Displaying his various products, including the new Penol, he reiterated the theme of his reliance upon God for his discoveries. "No books ever go into my laboratory," he told his listeners. "I never have to grope for methods; the method is revealed at the moment I am inspired to create something new." Without God to "draw aside the curtain," he said, he was helpless.

In the middle of the lecture Carver glanced at his watch and abruptly stopped, but a disappointed sigh from the audience led to his recall. When he finished, applause filled the church, despite some hesitancy because of the setting and the fact that no other speaker had been applauded. Carver must have gone to bed that night relishing another triumph. He had woven his magic spell once more.[27]

There was, however, one member of the audience who remained unenchanted. A reporter from the *New York Times* was appalled by the description of Carver's methods and wrote an editorial entitled "Men of Science Never Talk That Way," which deplored his "complete lack of the scientific spirit."

> Real chemists, or at any rate other real chemists, do not scorn books out of which they can learn what other chemists have done, and they do not ascribe their successes, when they have any, to "inspiration." Talk of that sort simply will bring ridicule on an admirable institution and on the race for which it has done and still is doing so much.[28]

Carver was deeply stung by these words. It seemed as if whenever he became convinced that he had discovered God's plan for his life, something occurred to trigger the nagging self-doubts of his earlier Tuskegee days. Even mild criticism could reopen painful wounds, and this editorial implied not only that his work was not legitimate, but that he was actually causing great harm to the Institute and to his race. The blow was softened by friends and strangers who rallied around him, filling his mailbox with letters of support. He penned a reply to the *Times;* when it was not published, friends circulated copies, and other newspapers declared their support and printed his response.[29]

In the end the incident reaped more publicity for Carver and led to his adoption as a religious symbol. His life story appeared in increasing numbers of church publications, and quite a few clergymen sought him out. By January he was able to assert that "I did indeed feel badly for awhile, not that the cynical criticism was directed at me, but rather at the religion of Jesus Christ. . . . I [now] believe through the providence of the Almighty it was a good thing."[30] Nevertheless, Carver appears to have become even more sensitive about questions regarding his methods.

After Bergthold assured Carver that he should continue his work "in faith with unabated enthusiasm," he agreed to attend the Kentucky meeting and went on a tour of North Carolina colleges in January. On that tour, which included the University of North Carolina and the women's college at Greensboro, his presentations were again highly praised except on one occasion. A professor at the university, who did not attend the lecture, insinuated that Carver was a faker and expressed doubt about his membership in the Royal Society of London. The author of a student editorial, however, indicated that his fellow students were incensed by the remark and declared that the professor who questioned Carver's integrity had taken a "tumble from the high position I had always accorded him."[31]

In spite of numerous invitations, Carver did not speak at any more Southern colleges that year. He did venture north to appear before a student body, however. A young white man, Charles W.

Hyne, whom he had met at Utica Institute, was attending Cornell University in Ithaca, New York, and arranged for Carver to give four lectures at the school. At the Cosmopolitan Club Carver gave one of his very rare speeches directly concerning race relations. "Without genuine love for humanity," he declared, "it is impossible to accomplish much in this question of the races." He asserted that "differences are bound to be adjusted more and more as time goes on, and as we come to realize that each individual, no matter what his color or creed, has his particular task to do in life."[32]

Hyne was pleased with the reception of the speech but disappointed when his social fraternity refused to invite Carver to dinner. "Most of the fellows were for it," he wrote, "but a few were dead set against it. I did not wish to make an issue of it and knew you would not want to come under such circumstances." Thus even in the midst of success Carver was painfully reminded of the importance of skin color, even in New York. His young white friends sometimes deferred to social pressure, but they often asserted their desire to take a different course. Hyne later wrote, "I should very much like to go to Montgomery with you. Suppose the crackers would stand for it? Well maybe [they] would have to."[33]

Although Carver did not attend the Blue Ridge conference in 1925, the impact of his two previous visits was still felt. By March 1926 he had received some 470 letters from his "Blue Ridge boys."[34] One, Howard Kester, wrote a tribute to Carver for the April edition of *World Tomorrow*, which stated "the man who has been and is to this day the greatest inspiration in my life is a Negro."

In the whole life of this saintly man I see the future of a great race. In his eyes I see the soul of a people who experienced God and understand the meaning of the Cross.

The unique contribution George Carver has made in the field of science and religion is symbolical of the contribution the Negro race is destined to make to our civilization if all unequal relationships are abolished and the Negro is given every opportunity fully to develop his personality.[35]

The previous fall Kester had visited Carver at Tuskegee, and the two excitedly wrote and mimeographed a charter for the George Washington Carver Fellowship. The avowed purpose was "to unite all kindred spirits, whatever race, religion or nationality, who behold in the universe the most sublime expression of Love, Truth and Beauty, through which the Great Creator eternally speaks concerning the things that He has created." By then the Carver Products Company had not lived up to its promise, and Carver shifted some of his attention to recruiting new members for the fellowship. Although the group never officially functioned, the dream of an interracial movement to change the world remained with both men.[36]

In the summer of 1926 Carver was finally able to attend the Hollister conference, where his reception was similar to that at Blue Ridge, and numerous boys were adopted into the "family." In the fall he made a twelve-day tour of Virginia colleges, but was forced to cancel a planned tour in Tennessee due to sickness and exhaustion.[37]

Significantly, by 1926 the student interracial movement encouraged by the CIC had become too "radical" for some CIC members. Inspired by the Student Volunteer Movement Quadrennial Convention at Indianapolis in 1923, as well as CIC and YMCA efforts, students had established interracial forums on campuses across the South. Joint meetings were held with students from neighboring black colleges, and some members, including several of Carver's "boys," renounced any form of segregation, even to the point of having biracial luncheons with members of both sexes present. While some of the CIC leaders, like Will Alexander, had themselves spoken out against Jim Crow laws, this was not the official policy of the CIC.[38] Therefore at a meeting of the CIC in 1926 a delegate raised the issue of whether the CIC should support the student forums. As a reporter noted, "There was frank uneasiness lest the meeting of young people of both sexes and both races in communities where sentiment is still so inflammable might give rise to gossip which would jeopardize the entire program of the commission." A compromise was reached with the decision to "note with interest and encouragement the progress of the forums" and to express the hope that they would be carefully supervised by college authorities.[39]

The suspicion of adults probably only heightened the interest of the students. In fact, their letters to Carver often revealed a kind of conspiratorial thinking, as they plotted what they could get away with next. They seem to have pictured themselves as Davids facing the Goliath of race prejudice and gloried in their victories, large and small.

If some CIC members had doubts about the student forums, they were still convinced of Carver's value to the movement and anxious to arrange a college tour for him in the winter of 1927. Student organizations in a number of states were begging for Carver, but it was decided that his presence was most needed in Mississippi. Unfortunately, there was a breakdown in communication between the CIC and the local organizer and Carver's appearances before the white colleges were canceled because of a misunderstanding. When something similar happened to a proposed tour of Atlanta colleges in April, Carver became discouraged and feared that racial prejudice was increasing in the colleges. The YMCA student secretary of Virginia, Forrest D. Brown, was one of Carver's "boys" and tried to reassure him that conditions were not growing worse. To prove it he issued an invitation to come to Virginia in 1928.[40]

Brown seemed determined to make the tour successful and carefully arranged for engagements in Virginia and Tennessee. He also accompanied Carver on the entire two-week tour and took care of all the accommodations, which included dinners in the homes of whites along the way. Carver was again a smashing success, winning over a dubious chemistry professor at Washington and Lee, adopting new members of the "family," and provoking a student editorial against racism at Maryville College in Tennessee. The CIC paid all the expenses of the tour.[41]

Although invitations continued to arrive, Carver's health and schedule did not permit anything more than a speech at Birmingham-Southern in 1929. The next year Forrest Brown was in Pennsylvania and arranged some lectures at Northern schools for Carver. That same year Jim Hardwick became the student secretary of the Southern region for the YMCA and was headquartered in Atlanta. His friendship with Carver was reinforced with frequent visits to Tuskegee. Together they plotted a "Good Will Tour" for the spring of 1931 under the auspices of the YMCA. In April, after a lecture in Atlanta, they visited YMCA and YWCA groups in several Virginia and North Carolina colleges.[42]

The success of this tour prompted them to attempt another, to begin at Birmingham on May 7 and end at New Orleans on May 19 of 1932. At first all went well, but when they arrived at the Women's College in Columbus, Mississippi, the president of the college informed them that the engagement had been canceled. Hardwick was indignant and insisted that Carver would speak somewhere. After being rebuffed by the local white churches, he was told that Carver could use the auditorium of the black high school. The women at the college were invited to attend the hastily improvised lecture, but they were denied permission to go. Although tension was rising in the city, fourteen faculty members braved criticism to attend.[43]

Some of the young women at the college were furious at the turn of events, and one registered her complaints in an article in the student newspaper. A week earlier she had written an editorial hailing the decline of prejudice in the South; now she bitterly retracted her praise of the "superficial coating of tolerance" around her. "Some of us are inclined to tuck our heads with shame and deplore the fact that we dwell in a state so backward in some respects as Mississippi," she declared. "It is right that we should be ashamed . . . , but instead of sitting down and blushing, we should be up and doing something about it." She lambasted the college officials and townspeople for their treatment of Carver and learned the cost of "being up and doing something": she lost the scholarship that she had won as an honor student.[44]

No problems were encountered at the University of Mississippi, Mississippi State College, or at several small schools, and despite the setback in Columbus, Carver could rightly call the trip "our triumphal march with God through Mississippi." His family now had some Mississippi "children," and Hardwick decided it was time for a "family reunion." In October he began planning a surprise testimonial dinner for Carver, to be held in Atlanta during the Christmas holidays. He wanted to present the professor with a bound copy of letters of appreciation from those whose lives he had touched. In response to his request some four dozen letters were received and bound in blue and white, Carver's favorite colors.[45]

The "family" excitedly made plans to surprise Carver at the banquet. Unfortunately the day Carver was to come it rained heavily and the Chattahoochee River flooded. Carver was forced to wire his regrets, not realizing that he was the guest of honor. Later, after the book was delivered to him, he wrote, "I can so thoroughly understand now why the high waters cut me off, so I could not get to the meeting. I am sure I would not have exhibited much composure, I am quite sure I would have collapsed."[46]

The great love expressed in those letters would have deeply moved even a less emotional man than Carver. Many echoed the words of one in describing Carver's impact on their racial attitudes.

> You have shown me the one race, the human race. Color of skin, or form of hair mean nothing to me now, but length, and width, and bredth [sic] of soul and loving kindness mean everything.[47]

Several emphasized that it was Carver the man, and not Carver the scientist, whose friendship they treasured. "To the world you are known as one of the greatest of all scientists," one wrote, "but to your boys you are known as the spiritual guide to whom each can turn in times of doubt or discouragement." Likewise Howard Kester declared, "Marvelous are the miracles you have performed in the laboratory but more marvelous still are the miracles you have wrought in the mind and heart of hundreds of men and women."[48]

During the next year Carver made two major speaking tours to white colleges, one to Georgia schools, the other to Eastern colleges from the Carolinas to Connecticut. Both were successful, but soon afterwards Carver became increasingly involved in the development of a peanut oil massage therapy for infantile paralysis, and the demands on his time led to a tapering off of his college tours. Until 1936 he occasionally gave single lectures at nearby colleges, but a serious bout of pernicious anemia in the late thirties put an end to such engagements. [49]

Even after he could no longer make extensive tours, Carver continued to correspond with his "family" until his death in 1943. The impact he had on the lives of the young men and women he met through the CIC and YMCA is one of his greatest legacies. His influence went far beyond that of the average chapel or assembly speaker for a number of reasons. First, he insisted upon settings in which he could have personal contact with the students. "Please make it clear," he wrote regarding one tour, "that we prefer to meet the students rather than a small group of the *elite* at a dinner engagement." [50] In addition, he truly liked young people and could effectively communicate his affection and interest to them. To be sure, they respected and admired Carver, but they also liked him. He was not merely a hero figure or a token black; he was a friend with whom they felt at ease.

Their letters reflect the absence of barriers in their relationship with Carver. They poured out their most secret and personal problems and fears, knowing they would be heard sympathetically. They also felt free to tease the famous scientist, often poking fun at both his inventiveness and his saintliness. For example, one declared:

> I believe if you were marooned on a desert island, you would be busy teaching the fish to swim better or making vanilla ice cream out of sandspurs. It's a good thing you have peanuts, sweet potatoes, etc. to work with, otherwise you would certainly be in more mischief than a half-grown puppie. [51]

Another wrote in mock anger of his intention to provoke Carver to "soil his saintly lips by murmuring 'Damn' and 'Hell.' " [52]

Those who had traveled with Carver had especially fond re-

membrances. On most of the tours in the late twenties and thirties
Carver was accompanied by Brown or Hardwick and their friends,
both male and female. This arrangement eased some of the burdens of travel, but created special problems. All travel had to be
by automobile, and the cars were not always reliable. "We have
trusted ourselves to old automobiles," Hardwick recalled, "in some
situations in which it seemed only a miracle could get us where
we wanted to go. A time or two it seemed that our only hope lay
in your extracting some gasoline from nearby vegetation."[53]

Another difficulty was getting something to eat along the way.
The solution was picnic lunches that usually ended in nature lessons by Carver. On one occasion a pond was nearby and the sev-
enty-year-old scientist joined his young colleagues in swimming
and the splashing that inevitably followed. Often the schedule was
too hectic to allow stopping at all, and one participant later reminded Carver of "our sandwich lunches in the Buick at 50 mi.
per hour—Jim driving (swinging the old stirring [sic] wheel right
and left), you yelling for sardine sandwiches, and me struggling in
the backseat trying to spread the butter."[54]

These trips forged bonds of friendship that went beyond mere
respect for Carver's genius. Traveling with a black also provided
the "boys" with firsthand knowledge of discrimination, making
them aware, as Hardwick noted, "of the many doors that neither
you nor any member of your race could enter." Friendship with
Carver not only opened their eyes to discrimination, but also created in many the determination to take a stand against it. As one
of his "Hollister boys" wrote, "It has been hard at times to face
the crowd—to stand alone and fight for the thing I thought was
right, but always there comes the assurance you have created in
me."[55]

From all over the South students wrote Carver of their efforts
for racial justice. For example, one of Carver's "girls" led the formation of a biracial study group at the Women's College of North
Carolina and wrote him of her hopes that it would "act as a leav-
ening lump in the student body."[56] Often the students wanted to

go further than the college administrators would allow. From Texas Tech came one such report.

> We have been informed by the President of the College that it is all right to discuss *justice for* the Negro, but that we must be careful about discussing justice *with* the Negro; . . . that would be admitting equality which will not do in this part of the country.[57]

Significantly, many of the "family" continued to work for racial justice long after leaving school. Several became liberal ministers. One argued for greater appropriations for black education in the Texas state legislature. Another wrote a prize-winning editorial for the Roanoke, Alabama *Leader* in 1956, urging his readers to remember the precepts of Christianity in the midst of racial turmoil in that town. Numerous other "children" took stands, both large and small, against racial intolerance, and at least one risked his life for his beliefs. Howard Kester embarked on many dangerous missions for brotherhood through his affiliations with the Fellowship of Reconciliation, the Socialist party, the NAACP, and other organizations. He investigated lynchings and helped black and white sharecroppers found the biracial Southern Tenant Farmers' Union in Arkansas. His life was in jeopardy on so many occasions that Carver once told him how to prepare a suicide powder from a common plant. Fortunately, he never had to use it, and until his death in 1977 he still considered Carver "one of the greatest influences on my life."[58]

It is true that Carver's "children" and the other young adults who became involved in the interracial movement represented only a small minority on the Southern campuses of the twenties and thirties. Yet their letters reveal that they were not social outcasts; rather, in many cases, they were popular student leaders. They did not remake the South, or for that matter even their own campuses, but they did speak out and were tolerated to a remarkable degree. The continued support of the CIC even when the students became "too radical" suggests that the leadership of that organization was not as conservative as the official policy implied. Just as the Southern abolitionist movement of the 1820s and 1830s was eventually silenced in the 1850s, the "forgotten voices" of these Southern young people became lost in the rise of "massive resistance" in the 1950s. The complexity of Southern race relations and traditions can never be fully appreciated, however, until all the voices of dissent are no longer concealed by the myth of the solid South.

— 12 —

The Peanut Man

In the 1920s it seemed that developments in technology, mass production, and marketing would usher in a new millennium of prosperity and abundance. No one doubted that the United States was the richest nation in the world. Science and business worked together to create and sell new products, and encouraged by installment credit, consumers eagerly bought mass-produced goods. Most viewed the future as bright with promise.

The prosperity of the twenties was uneven, however. Some segments of the economy, such as the textile industry, did not share in the boom. Near the bottom was agriculture. For most of the decade overproduction and declining prices brought farmers a preview of the depression that would spread to others in the thirties. Because the Southern economy was still largely based on agriculture and textiles, the region fell further behind the North materially. It was against this backdrop that Carver had sought to launch manufacturing concerns for his products. Although he failed, by 1924 he was firmly established as the Peanut Man, and peanut growers and processors exploited his expertise and promotional skills in their efforts to unseat King Cotton. Carver's interests and activities remained diverse, but he devoted a significant amount of time to acting as consultant and publicist for the peanut industry. From 1924 to 1938 he served the industry as technical adviser, lecturer, and prolific contributor to trade publications.

As a recognized peanut expert Carver was consulted by a diverse group of individuals and institutions. In 1924 he answered inquiries from two graduate students at the University of North Carolina and from the chemist-in-charge at the Protein Investigation Laboratory of the USDA. Several manufacturing concerns also sought Carver's advice. The most important was the Tom Huston Company. Although Carver reported that 198 "factory problems of many kinds have been worked out" in his laboratory in 1924, the Tom Huston Company was apparently the only peanut processing firm to benefit substantially from Carver's advice.[1]

Located in nearby Columbus, Georgia, the company was rapidly expanding when Tom Huston wrote Carver in 1924. He was interested in a new method for salting peanuts "without having to use oil in an effort to stick salt on the outside" and offered to pay the professor for his help. Carver arranged to meet Huston at the Montgomery State Fair in November to discuss the matter. That meeting started a long-term relationship. For years Huston continued to write for advice, and Carver visited the plant on numerous occasions.[2]

In 1929 the company decided to expand its research facilities and apparently asked Carver to join its staff. Although he was evidently tempted by the offer, Carver declined and listed his reasons for doing so. Among the reasons he noted, "My work is a great publicity asset for the school and my race," he noted and later added, "I, with others, am clannish enough to want my people to receive credit for my work." He continued, however, to advise Huston in the establishment of the laboratory and to provide guidance to the chemist who was hired.[3]

Beginning in mid-1930 Carver provided the Tom Huston Company and the entire industry with one of his greatest services. During that year's growing season two company employees, Bob Barry and Grady Porter, experimented with planting Virginia-type peanuts in Georgia, Alabama, and Florida. They selected ten farmers to plant ten acres with two varieties of Virginia peanuts, which brought a higher price than varieties usually planted in that region. They solicited information and advice from experiment stations in the three states but received very little aid or encouragement. When several stations reported that their staffs had unsuccessfully tried such experiments earlier, Barry and Porter sent them a printed questionnaire about their methods and results. Only one station returned it. Nevertheless, the Huston employees continued the project despite such discouragement.[4]

At first the experiment looked promising, but when the peanuts were harvested it was found that many had failed to mature or had rotted in the shell. This made Barry and Porter suspect the presence of plant disease, and their investigations convinced them that fungi were decreasing the production of the usual varieties of peanuts as well as the Virginia type. Although the Tom Huston Company was a buyer of peanuts, not a supplier, Huston and his employees shared a genuine concern for the plight of Southern farmers. Indeed, the company used cotton stationery during the 1930s to show support for the hard-hit cotton planters. Always seeking to aid farmers, Barry and Porter approached the experiment stations again with their evidence of plant disease.[5]

Although several stations were cooperative, most concluded that disease was not a major problem. They were following the lead of W. R. Beattie, a peanut expert who was senior horticulturist at the USDA. In August 1930 he asserted that the disease was the effect and not the cause of the failure of the Virginia-type peanuts to mature. Barry and Porter remained unconvinced and turned to Carver.[6]

After visiting some infected fields, Carver agreed that fungi were causing problems and made a preliminary identification of several that were producing both root rot and leaf spot. Faced with Carver's report Barry admitted that his mind was "going around in circles" as he tried to decide what to do.

Possibly some high official in the Department of Agriculture in Washington could be startled into an appreciation of the seriousness of the situation. He could call a meeting of the agricultural powers of the Southeastern States and learn all the details of your discoveries. It might be the rest of them would boo at the situation because somebody else found it out. Then too people in political jobs are not looking for hard work as a rule. If they did attempt to

do something the chances are they would scare the farmer to
death and cause him to reduce his peanut acreage unreasonably.
As Grady Porter puts it, it would be like running a bear out in
front of him without giving him anything to shoot with.[7]

In the end Barry and Porter decided to circulate Carver's report, "Some Peanut Diseases," which included both a brief description of the major diseases and preventive measures. Five
thousand copies were printed in February 1931 and sent to peanut
growers, shelling plants, county agents, newspapers, banks, and
the USDA. In a cover letter Barry referred to Carver's help and
described him as "a mycologist of International fame."[8]

That title was immediately challenged by B. B. Higgins, a botanist at a Georgia experiment station. He asserted that Carver was
not "a mycologist of any kind" and suggested that F. A. Wolfe's
Alabama experiment station bulletin was a better source of information. Barry decided to write for a copy of it and all other bulletins on peanuts and plant diseases. He was surprised at how little
attention had been paid to peanut diseases—only J. J. Taubenhaus
at a Texas station was actively involved in such research. Wolfe's
bulletin had been published in 1914, and Barry admitted that he
could not understand it. In fact he asked Carver to explain all the
various bulletins he had received.[9]

Fortunately not all station personnel were as hostile as Higgins.
A few, such as Taubenhaus, offered to cooperate with Carver, and
requested specimens. Although its accuracy was questioned, the
Carver report aroused the interest of researchers and opened
doors for Barry and Porter. They won the support of Charles
Herty, a well-known agricultural researcher, who convinced the
USDA to investigate the extent of peanut diseases, and Paul R.
Miller, a mycologist with the Bureau of Plant Industry, was dis-
patched to conduct a plant disease survey in the South.[10]

Miller was a new USDA employee and the survey was his first
assignment. It lasted two years and revealed a loss of more than 20
percent of the peanut crop. The USDA then attacked the problem,
developing measures that substantially reduced those losses. Dur-

Carver examining twig for disease

ing the survey, Miller became a close friend of Carver and was convinced that the professor had played a key role in moving the USDA to action. Their close friendship led Carver to become active once more in the field of mycology.

Miller quickly realized that Carver had neither the training nor the equipment to make accurate fungi identifications and was amazed to discover that the professor had made only one serious mistake in identification. He was even more impressed with Carver's ability to locate valuable specimens and believed he was a gifted "naturalist" with a talent for knowing the appropriate habitat for various fungi. Miller brought this talent to the attention of the USDA, and Carver was soon writing and sending specimens to various department mycologists. Some even came to Tuskegee to collect fungi with him. In 1935 the USDA recognized Carver's value by naming him a "collaborator" with the Plant Disease Survey. At that time there were two collaborators in each state, but he was designated an auxiliary collaborator and received franking privileges for his specimens. Returning to his earlier love of mycology, he remained active in this role until less than a year before his death.[11]

Of the more than eight hundred specimens he sent to Washington, several fungi were designated new species and others represented first sightings in this country. His contributions were noted in the *Plant Disease Reporter* and other mycological journals. After his death two USDA mycologists published a résumé of his specimens, which are preserved in the herbarium in Beltsville, Maryland. His peanut disease report brought him new recognition from specialists, but Barry and Porter always knew his worth. "If you had not taken two plant disease novices and made it possible for us to talk turkey to the technical men," Barry claimed in June 1932, "the matter would have been a dead issue two years ago."[12]

Huston sought ways to express his appreciation for Carver's many valuable services, since the professor would not accept compensation. He gave Carver a new typewriter, an expensive blanket, and a small gold peanut. Carver was also invited, with such prominent scientists as Charles H. Herty and Walter E. Eddy, to a luncheon sponsored by the company in 1930. The next year Huston found an outlet for his gratitude that truly delighted Carver. He commissioned Isabelle Schultz of Baltimore to sculpt a clay likeness of Carver, which was sent to Italy to be cast as a bronze bas-relief. Two plaques were made: one to hang in the laboratory at the Tom Huston Company and one to be given to Tuskegee Institute, the presentation of which was arranged to coincide with the spring commencement exercises on 28 May 1931.[13]

Carver was ecstatic. By this time his own companies were floundering and recognition by practical businessmen still meant much to him. "Tom's Peanuts" and other company products were realities, not dreams. He wrote dozens of letters to friends, mainly white, telling each of the honor and asking them to attend. "It is quite an ordeal for me to go through," he asserted, "and I want as many of my choicest friends here as possible to make the burden lighter." Apparently he still felt a need to prove himself to his Tuskegee colleagues, and a large and prestigious audience would be impressive.[14]

Bob Barry came from Columbus to preside over the unveiling, and the text of his speech indicates that he also believed that the professor was not appropriately appreciated at Tuskegee. He described Carver's contributions and noted:

> Maybe it is out of place for me to tell about him. You know him so well. But do you really know him?
>
> I see many young people here today. Do you, whom he can help so much, really know him as he is?
>
> If you live beside a mountain and see it every day, it does not seem high to you; but someone who does not see it often knows that it is high.[15]

The plaque was installed at the college chapel, and the Tom Huston Company continued to call on Carver for advice and help. For more than a decade various employees consulted him about problems ranging from rancid peanuts to the making of potato chips.[16]

Carver's efforts as a publicist were probably more important to the industry as a whole than his technical advice. All the editors of trade journals, but especially M. M. Osburn of the *Peanut Journal*, recognized the publicity value of his work. During the professor's lifetime about seventy articles by and about him appeared in various industry publications. Whenever Osburn needed an article or the answer to a question, he wrote Carver. As he declared in 1924, "Here's old man Osburn again asking for help. . . . I don't know of anyone that I have called upon any more than I have you."[17]

Significantly, Carver often cited the work of other experiment stations in his answers to questions from Osburn and others. Trade journals would seem to be a logical outlet for experiment station research on peanuts, and occasionally editors did report such work directly. But often they seemed to rely on Carver to receive or

Bronze plaque donated by the Tom Huston Company

interpret the information, just as Barry and Porter had. Thus the claim in the *Peanut Journal* that "Professor Carver is to the peanut industry what Edison is to electricity" is not entirely accurate. As an inventor he failed to make any breakthroughs that were both original and commercially valuable. He did, however, serve magnificently as an interpreter between scientists and laymen.[18]

Not only did the peanut industry benefit from the publication of Carver's work in trade journals, but a bountiful harvest of publicity also came from the coverage of his work in newspapers and popular magazines. The "lowly peanut" was prominently mentioned almost every time Carver wrote or spoke, regardless of the occasion, and by the 1930s practically every one of his utterances was widely reported. And those utterances were frequent, because in the 1920s and 1930s invitations were numerous and varied. Carver continued making yearly visits to black schools and farmers' conferences. His appearances sponsored by the CIC, the YMCA, and various other church groups led to more and more requests for his appearance at white colleges, churches, and camps. Invitations also poured in from diverse black and white civic groups, such as the Providence, Rhode Island, NAACP and the Birmingham, Alabama, Chamber of Commerce. State fair committees sought exhibits, and Carver attended fairs as far away as Tennessee, Texas, and Oklahoma. In addition individuals such as Raleigh Merritt of Philadelphia arranged lectures in their home towns. Obviously, Carver was on the road a lot between 1924 and 1938, spreading the good news of the unlimited possibilities of peanuts, sweet potatoes, native clays, and other products. Peanut industry publicists quickly realized the value of this free publicity and sometimes reprinted articles about Carver for distribution.

Although the trips were numerous and the topics similar, some were more significant than others. Aside from his interracial and religious lectures, several trips and exhibits were of special importance for a variety of reasons. The first of these was the exhibit for the Southern Exposition at New York in May 1925. The purpose of the exposition was to lure Northern capital southward by demonstrating the potential of the region. Jesse B. Hearin, the secretary of the Alabama division of the exposition, realized the appropriateness of Carver's work and wrote President Moton in June 1924 requesting that Tuskegee "reserve a liberal amount of space" in the Alabama exhibit and allow Carver to attend.[19]

Carver excitedly made preparations for the trip, asking Moton to reprint his out-of-print bulletins on the sweet potato and peanut. As the date drew nearer, however, the problem of financing the expensive exhibit arose. When Carver's attendance became doubtful, the Alabama committee insisted that the state could not be adequately represented without the Tuskegee exhibit and solicited support from civic clubs and schools around the state. Also, Richard R. Edmonds of the *Manufacturers' Record* made a plea to

Carver exhibit for the New York Exposition, 1925

the president of the exposition to "find a way to give a very conspicuous space to [Carver's] exhibit and at as small cost as possible" because "in view of the character of his work he ought to be paid for making the exhibit."[20]

These efforts paid off when Alabama won the prize for best exhibit. One of the organizers claimed that Carver's exhibit "certainly was the drawing card of the exposition, by far the most original exhibit of all." This success was important, for it firmly established Carver as a patron saint of the New South movement as well as of the peanut industry.[21]

Another significant tour was arranged in 1930. By that time the demands for Carver were so numerous that Tuskegee Institute provided a traveling secretary, H. O. Abbott, to make all arrangements and accompany Carver on his trips. A wide variety of Southwestern groups had extended invitations, so Abbott arranged a fifteen-day tour through Kansas, Oklahoma, and Texas, with talks scheduled before YMCA groups, civic organizations, scientific societies, black schools, and the Oklahoma State Teachers Association. Everywhere Carver provoked editorials on race relations and diversified agriculture, but an unscheduled speech drew the most publicity. When he reached Austin, Texas, the state legislature adopted a resolution asking him to speak to a joint session, which of course he was willing to do.[22]

In the midst of great acclaim, he also received a painful reminder that no black was exempt from racial prejudice. En route from an engagement in Oklahoma City to another meeting in Dallas, Abbott made Pullman reservations with the Wichita agent of the Atchinson, Topeka and Santa Fe Railway System, who confirmed the reservation by long-distance telephone. When it came time to leave Oklahoma City, however, the local passenger agent refused to admit Carver and Abbott to a Pullman car, and they were forced to ride in the segregated coach, which did not have special sleeping facilities.[23]*

The Oklahoma City *Black Dispatch* was quick to publicize the incident, noting that "George Washington Carver, the latches of whose shoes few white men in Oklahoma are worthy to unlatch, must warm himself in the corner of a Jim Crow coach and suffer." Reporters from the black press interviewed the Oklahoma City passenger agent, who claimed to be merely following instructions from the company's legal department, which had banned the sale of such tickets in Oklahoma, Texas, and Louisiana because of state segregation laws. This led the *Black Dispatch* to attack the hypocrisy behind the "separate but equal" accommodation laws of Oklahoma, which in application slighted the "equal" part of the clause. Noting the railroad's arguments on the expense of maintaining separate Pullman cars, the *Dispatch* went on to say, "White folk should have surveyed this phase of the question before they acted so hurriedly in 1907."[24]

---

*Under Oklahoma law the railroad companies were supposed to supply Pullman facilities to anyone, black or white, who paid for them. The railroads, however, considered separate facilities too expensive and so failed to provide any Pullman cars for blacks.

The incident also provoked an exchange of letters between Abbott and railroad officials. In response to a protest from Abbott, an official apologized and assured him the company was "instituting an investigation not only of this particular case," but also of the application of the Texas and Oklahoma accommodation laws in general and how other lines "had found a way to handle this situation more liberally." The company was distressed, the agent noted, at the unfairness of the articles in the Kansas City *Call* and other papers, since the company was only trying to avoid legal actions against it. "You of course understand," wrote the official, "that the Railways do not want the so-called 'Jim Crow' law if for no other reason than it causes them additional expense . . . and also subjects them to embarrassments such as occurred in this case."[25]

In addition, W. B. Storey, the president of the Atchison, Topeka and Santa Fe, sent Carver his personal apologies. Noting the receipt of letters from both Abbott and the NAACP, Storey assured Carver of his hopes that the company's investigation would prevent the repetition of such an incident. In closing Storey explained, "At all times we have endeavored to be guided by what will best and most certainly insure our colored passengers against disturbance and possible danger of violence or arrest and I believe that your knowledge of existing conditions . . . will enable you to understand how great is the problem and how hard it is to meet this situation wisely at all times."[26]

In his reply Carver graciously accepted the apology and expressed his approval of the company's pledge that "every courtesy possible will be extended to colored patrons." Abbott, however, brought up a few more matters. Remarking that both Carver and himself had been criticized for not suing for damages, Abbott explained that behind their restraint was the desire to see "better traveling accommodations for our people, rather than any petty gains or notoriety." He suggested that publicizing the company's new stand on the matter and a personal letter of apology from the Oklahoma City agent might further clear the air. The company politely declined both suggestions, but requested prior notification of any future Western journies by Carver so that arrangements could be made that would "leave him with a pleasant impression of Santa Fe service and of the company's desire to treat all as fairly as may be permissable [sic] under existing limitations."[27]

It required less than a month for the railroad's "new policy" to be tested—and to fail. When another black was refused Pullman accommodations in Oklahoma, the *Black Dispatch* asked why Carver had not brought suit against the company. In defense Abbott sent the editor copies of the correspondence with railroad officials, but the editor read the letters to mean that "Carver can ride in a Pullman, but the rest of the niggers can't."[28]

Enclosing clippings of the *Dispatch* editorials, Abbott again wrote the railway, saying that like "Banquo's ghost" the Oklahoma City incident would not stay down. Abbott went on to explain that both he and Carver thought the railway intended to allow Pullman service to all members of the race. Since there seemed to be a misunderstanding, Abbott suggested the matter be cleared up before the company lost any more business from the incident. A not-so-polite reply from the railroad reaffirmed that there had been no intention of singling out Carver for preferential treatment and that the company was endeavoring to do all it could, but suggested that Abbott refrain from passing on correspondence to the press. Further agitation was unwise, the letter noted, for "the same elements that caused the enactment of the separate coach laws may easily bring pressure to bear on the railways to prevent more liberal interpretation of them."[29]

The incident came to a rather unsatisfactory end, with Abbott asserting that he considered the matter closed but that he had no control over the press.[30] Carver may have believed the official explanations and promises. Most likely, however, he realized that his position at Tuskegee Institute tied his hands. He used the only leverage he felt he had available—his prestige and influence. The result was little, if any, improvement in conditions and scorn from his fellow blacks.

Although traveling exposed Carver to the degradations of racism, the reactions to his lectures also provided sustaining doses of praise that renewed and refreshed him. By 1937 he was exalted as one of the world's greatest scientists by a large segment of the general public, but the recurring skepticism of other scientists stung him deeply. For that reason, several trips in 1937 must have been especially gratifying.

In the mid-1930s a new movement known as chemurgy had arisen. The word was coined from the Egyptian "chemi" and the Greek "ergon" and meant "putting Chemistry and related Sciences to work in industry for the farmer." Under the auspices of Henry Ford and others, a national council and journal were established. The council was composed of representatives of agriculture, industry, and science, with scientists including government researchers, directors of private research foundations, and scholars from such prestigious universities as the Massachusetts Institute of Technology and Johns Hopkins.[31]

Carver's friendship with Henry Ford provided one contact with the movement, but his involvement was limited until 1937. In that year he was invited to speak at the Mississippi Chemurgic Conference, the Texas Academy of Science, and a chemurgic conference in Dearborn, Michigan, sponsored by Ford. His speeches probably did not provide any astonishing new information or ideas. Yet, as the Jackson, Mississippi, *Clarion Ledger* proclaimed, Carver was "the most human, the most appealing, and drew the best crowd" of all the speakers, including a number of prominent scientists. Soon afterwards he appeared on a nationally broadcast radio program hosted by Edgar Guest. In that broadcast and in later speeches Carver often mentioned the chemurgic movement and became its publicist and symbol, just as he had with the peanut industry and the New South movement.[32]

These trips also reflected Carver's vacillation on the issue of segregation. After the 1930 Pullman incident he often noted in replies to white invitations that "difficulties in travel accommodations" made trips very hard for a person his age. Don O. Baird, of the Texas Academy of Science, wrote that he had "taken up the matter of comfortable traveling reservations with General Passenger Agents of the three railroads over which you will travel . . . and each one had assured that they will reserve a drawing room for your use."[33]

Another problem was Carver's presence at chemurgic conference banquets. At Mississippi a special banquet was arranged for him by the state's director of colored extension agents, but Carver insisted that he did not want any banquet, declaring that "my physical strength will not allow the draft upon it." At the Dearborn conference he was invited to the main banquet but made a point of sitting outside the hall until everyone had eaten, even though Henry Ford considered him one of the most honored guests.[34]

These actions were typical of Carver's response to segregation. For apparently arbitrary reasons he gladly crossed the color line on some occasions and on others refused to do so. All through his career he ate with and in the homes of whites, even in Alabama as early as 1903. Yet he declined an invitation from a prominent white Birmingham businessman to eat together at Tuskegee.[35] On some occasions his hesitancy was undoubtedly related to his desire to protect the school he loved from criticism, as well as a genuine concern for the feelings of others and a desire to avoid humiliation. One wonders, however, if he was not sometimes rejecting an "honorary white" status as much as acquiescing to Southern customs.

Regardless of his posture, Carver's actions got welcome publicity for the peanut industry. While most of his appearances were not directly sponsored by peanut growers' associations, several trips were directly tied to the industry's promotional activities. For example, in 1926 he attended a Peanut Exposition in Windsor, North Carolina. Later the county agent in Terrell County, Georgia, solicited his aid in preparing another peanut exposition. In 1938 Carver attended a local peanut festival in Dawson, Georgia, and the National Peanut Festival in Dothan, Alabama. On each occasion his speech drew the largest crowds. The peanut industry was not unmindful of the benefit of Carver's work and publicly recognized its debt on several occasions, as in a resolution adopted at the 1932 annual meeting of the Southeastern Peanut Association.[36]

Ironically, by 1924, when Carver was widely recognized as the Peanut Man, his research work rarely focused on the peanut. Aside from his efforts to establish peanut oil massages as a treatment for the residual effects of polio, only two projects relating to the peanut appear to have absorbed much of his time between 1924 and 1938: the feeding of peanuts to swine and the commercial use of peanut hulls.

Peanut-fed pork was considered inferior because of its softness, and many customers, including Tuskegee Institute, refused to buy it. Carver believed the pork could be hardened or other uses of it found, since its flavor was often considered superior. "It means much now in dollars and cents," he declared, "to a great and growing Southern money crop." Soliciting aid from the Moultrie, Georgia, plant of Swift and Company, Carver worked on the problem periodically for at least four years. By 1941, however, his only solution was a feeding schedule for hogs that gradually increased the amount of peanuts fed them until they were eating only peanuts and then decreased peanut consumption until the hogs were eating only corn for about six weeks before marketing.[37]

In Carver's attempt to find commercial uses for peanut hulls, a waste product of peanut shellers, he suggested employing them as a mulch and as an absorbent, but most of his attention focused on making peanut shell paper. Again this was not an entirely original idea; Charles Herty had investigated the idea to some extent. Carver developed several different kinds of paper, of which the most promising was a flocked art paper. In 1938 the Velour Paper and Fabrics Company became interested and worked with him on the project. Although the preliminary work was encouraging, certain technical problems evidently could never be worked out. A major commercial disadvantage was the light but bulky nature of the shells, which prevented economical shipment. Finally, Herty's successful research using the rapid-growing slash pine in paper production made peanut shell paper even less competitive. Most peanut shellers burned the shells for fuel and continued to do so despite Carver's efforts to find other uses for the shells.[38]

Although Carver continued to add various food items to his list of peanut products, most of his research concerned nonpeanut items. Some of his experiments represented extensions of earlier projects: hybridizing amaryllis, obtaining rubber and other products from sweet potatoes, experimenting with soybeans, and developing vegetable dyes. The last effort received the most attention.

Typically, when Carver was interested in an idea he attempted to spread his enthusiasm to others. In 1924 he published a request for alligator pear (avocado) seeds in *Cleaners' and Dyers' Review*, along with a brief description of his success in obtaining a permanent dye from the seeds. He also wrote Victor H. Power, of the *Manufacturers' Record*, about his work. His interest in dyes was probably rekindled by a request from a manufacturer of artificial silk for help in developing effective vegetable dyes. The collaboration continued, but the manufacturer apparently used Carver's dyes only for experimental purposes.[39]

In the same manner, Carver's interest in sweet potato starch flowered once again when two firms began actual production in the late 1920s. He received a great deal of satisfaction from reporting the establishment of the plants, but neither appears to have been successful. However, in 1935 the USDA opened a pilot plant in Laurel, Mississippi, which produced starch and cattle food from sweet potatoes. In 1940 the plant shifted production to providing dehydrated potatoes for the army. After the war, the market demand declined and the plant was sold to the Masonite Company.[40]

In many ways all of Carver's experiments during this period were extensions of his basic idea of diversifying the Southern economy. However, a few of his ideas reflected new approaches to fulfill his dream. In the area of new crops, he became interested in growing flax. He remembered the flax on the Carver farm in Missouri and was convinced that Alabama was as well suited for its production. His initial efforts were successful, and he reported them to his former teacher, Henry C. Wallace, who was Harding's secretary of agriculture. Wallace was out of town and the acting secretary informed Carver that earlier such experiments had proved to be unprofitable from a commercial standpoint. Thus

Carver's dream of flax supplementing cotton died an even quicker death than his earlier hopes for sericulture.[41]

Another of his ideas received scant encouragement from the USDA. In 1925 he asked for information for his investigation of "the possibility of making denatured alcohol from several southern farm crops." The department expressed little interest in the idea at the time, but returned to it ten years later and requested $626,000 for research on the production of anhydrous alcohol from surplus farm crops. The request was denied because of the lack of sufficient processing plants and the "limited market outlets for fuel alcohol." As long as other fuel sources remained plentiful and cheap, Congress tried to solve the farm surplus problem in other ways.[42]

In addition to finding new uses for crops in the 1920s, Carver continued to investigate uses for waste products. Using wood shavings, he and a Chicago man developed a synthetic marble. For awhile the Chicagoan planned to open a plant in Tuskegee, but the fall of 1929 was not a propitious time to launch a new business, after the collapse of the stock market in October. The same fate befell a plan by Carver and the chief chemist of the Mid-Continent Petroleum Company to manufacture paints from petroleum sludge. His other research project that year was even less promising. From palmetto roots he made a veneer, insulation boards, black paint, and several wood stains. However, like his chicken feather experiments, these products failed to spark any commercial interest.[43]

By the end of the decade, Carver realized, many Southern farmers were still wedded to cotton and were suffering from overproduction and low prices. Therefore he began exploring possible new uses for it. His insulating board made from cotton stalks elicited interest from the Department of Commerce, but the idea was never pursued.[44] His experiments with using cotton in road paving, however, received a practical test.

By 1932 Carver had produced seventeen different paving materials, all of which included cotton. This work was publicized in the Montgomery *Journal* and aroused the interest of the Alabama Asphaltic Limestone Company, but the company's representative discovered that the idea had been tried in Louisiana, Texas, and the Carolinas and that another company was in the process of patenting it. Nevertheless, a lawyer in Montgomery attempted to interest various city and state officials in testing Carver's paving process. In 1935 cotton road paving was used in the construction of a runway at Fort McClellan, Alabama. It is unclear how much credit is due Carver for this innovation, since he told the editor of the *Alabama Public Works and Highway Journal,* "Now as to just who first thought of the idea of cotton in road building, I am not sure." At any rate, in the 1960s the runway was still in use, but cotton paving had not become widespread.[45]

Carver continued to seek relief from cotton bondage and in the mid-1930s advocated livestock raising in the South. In several newspaper articles he predicted that "cattle raising will upset King Cotton's throne." He noted that "grass, grass everywhere is the disparaging cry from many individuals without vision! They fail to see that nature is trying to teach them the fundamental principles of prosperity and permanent happiness." He believed this grass made Alabama especially suited to livestock raising and produced two bulletins on the subject in 1935 and 1936. In the latter he pointed out that farm animals could supplement the family's diet, produce salable products, and serve as "great fertilizer factories."[46]

This last comment reflected Carver's return to an emphasis on natural fertilization. In a 1936 bulletin, *How to Build Up and Maintain the Virgin Fertility of Our Soils,* he reasserted that "no fertilizer or system of fertilization . . . will build up the land as effectively, cheaply and permanently" and gave directions for making a compost pile out of muck, leaves, manure, and "wood ashes, old plaster, waste lime, rags, paper, and any other matter that will decay quickly." He was convinced that "light, upland soils" needed "just the things we are hauling away and burning" and sent reports of his success to newspapers. In one article he claimed that if farmers adopted his methods, "it would not be long before the South would have few if any non-productive areas."[47]

The Great Depression that began in 1930 had an enormous impact on all Americans, and Carver was no exception. He lost money when two Tuskegee banks failed, and the focus of his work reflected the economic changes of the era. More and more he turned from the development of products with commercial value. It was not a good time to launch new manufacturing ventures, and he was convinced that the economic collapse was a sign that Americans had become too caught up in materialistic pursuits. As he declared, "We have become ninety-nine per cent money mad." Therefore much of his work in the thirties was actually a return to his earlier projects. His bulletins on livestock raising and natural fertilization echoed past themes of self-sufficiency.[48]

Even more indicative of his changed focus was his return to dietary and nutritional work. As he noted, "The soup kitchen, bread lines, active charitable organizations, and other agencies extant to relieve suffering, all emphasize an unmistakable need which is puzzleing [sic] the wisest and most thoughtful." In response he wrote articles with such titles as "How Can We Best Fill the Empty Dinner Pail?" and "Are We Starving in the Midst of Plenty? If So Why?" He also produced a leaflet on *Some Choice Wild Vegetables that Make Fine Foods*. Such articles and leaflets did not mark a new departure, just Carver's realization that his previous food research was again relevant. His interest in diet was further stimulated in 1936 with the establishment of a chefs' school at Tuskegee. Carver developed recipes to be used in the food preparation courses, gave addresses to the group, and even helped teach two courses. In addition, he began sending articles and recipes to hotel journals.[49]

Just as the Peanut Man's research branched into nonpeanut areas, so did his consultation activities. He was besieged with requests for information from a wide variety of groups, including sweet potato growers, pecan growers, and a cotton seed cooperative. The Libby Company actually offered to pay Carver's way to Hawaii to investigate the problem of ants destroying the pineapple crop. A large number of missionaries in tropical regions also sought the professor's help. They were especially interested in improving peanut production and using peanut milk as a substitute for cow's milk to decrease the alarmingly high infant mortality rate in their areas. Letters reporting success with the milk must have been very encouraging to Carver.[50]

By the mid-1930s reports of the activities of Carver's department justifiably stressed the time consumed by consultation. He answered questions from all over the world about diverse subjects and tested samples of soils and fertilizers, among other things—in one biannual report he claimed to have tested 1,800 such samples—and after 1935 he received numerous requests for mycological specimens. In addition, he was inundated with pleas for help from polio victims. Even though he was unable to aid many of his correspondents, replying to their letters was time-consuming. His work was also continually interrupted by visitors who came unannounced to his laboratory to seek help or merely satisfy their curiosity.[51]

One result of these demands was a drastic reduction in the number of bulletins Carver produced: between 1918 and 1935 only two new ones were printed. Of course, this scarcity was also due to the fact that Moton was not as demanding on this score as Washington had been and to the Institute's perennial lack of funds. Throughout the twenties only $55 a year was budgeted to Carver's department for printing and stationery, and most of that must have been consumed by his voluminous correspondence. He was able, however, to beg funds for the reprinting of popular bulletins until the Depression, when all budgets at Tuskegee were slashed and the teachers took a 10 percent cut in pay.[52]

The situation changed in 1935 for two reasons. First of all, the Institute received a new president, Frederick D. Patterson, who infused the campus with new energy. He was convinced that Carver was Tuskegee's greatest publicity asset and encouraged all phases of his work. Financial relief came the same year from the philanthropic General Board of Education (GBE), which donated money for Carver's department as well as others. The contribution of about $5,000 a year paid for the reprinting of one bulletin and the printing of Carver's three bulletins on livestock raising and natural fertilization. By 1938, however, the GBE contribution had decreased to $2,400. To offset the costs Carver began to charge a nickel each for all copies more than one. He and Patterson also solicited contributions for the printing of bulletins from peanut organizations and others.[53]

Part of the GBE grant was earmarked for the "training of assistants to the personnel, who may be prepared to carry the work forward." After relying for so long on student help and borrowed stenographers Carver was glad to get a half-time secretary, but was dubious about the need for an assistant. Afraid that they would steal the credit for his work, Carver quickly rejected several candidates. The one who finally won his approval was Austin W. Curtis, Jr., a Cornell chemistry graduate who had taught at North Carolina Agricultural and Technical College for a few years before he received the Tuskegee offer in July 1935. Although Carver was delighted when Curtis accepted, he was disturbed that the assistant's salary of $1,800 was "nearly or quite twice as much as the person he is supposed to assist." Nevertheless, Curtis continued to receive a higher salary than his mentor.[54]

This was quickly forgiven by Carver as he grew to know Curtis. Soon after Curtis's arrival in September, Carver wrote to his assistant's father that "he seems to me more like a son than a person who had just come to work for me." During the next eight years Curtis was both son and assistant to Carver. Calling himself "Baby Carver," he relieved the professor of many routine tasks and followed up on some of Carver's earlier ideas, such as low-cost paints from oil sludge. He also branched out into new, but similar, research projects, including finding uses for magnolia seeds. His arrival in 1935 was especially fortunate, because by 1938 Carver's health had seriously deteriorated. But through Curtis, he was able to continue his work on a limited basis.[55]

By 1938, however, Carver's utilization research began to lag behind similar research being done by others. This was to some extent the result of the Depression. Secretary of Agriculture Henry A. Wallace, who succeeded his father Henry C. Wallace in that post, was one of several innovative members of Franklin D. Roosevelt's cabinet who sought to bring recovery and reform to the American economy. Farmers were among the hardest hit by the Depression, but Wallace and others realized that prior USDA activities had done little to alleviate the plight of agriculture. Most of the department's efforts had focused on increasing production, but the success of these projects had brought economic doom instead of salvation, when high crop yields glutted the markets, often pushing prices down below the cost of production.

Under the younger Wallace the USDA shifted to a policy of decreasing production and increasing demand by finding new uses for crops. Although utilization research had never been completely ignored by the USDA, the Depression marked a turning point, with more emphasis on the kind of research that Carver had focused on for forty years. But when the department turned serious attention to this field, it did so with a level of funding that quickly made Carver's work obsolete. Section 202 of the Agricultural Adjustment Act of 1938 provided for four regional research laboratories "devoted primarily to those farm commodities in which there are regular or seasonal surpluses, and their products and by products." Its enactment was a major victory for the chemurgic movement, which recognized Carver as a patron saint. After the establishment of the regional laboratory in New Orleans, however, "cookstove chemistry" could never again compete with highly trained chemists working with sophisticated equipment.[56]

Thus 1938 marked the end of one phase of Carver's career. His health and limited funds prevented any significant new research. More and more he came to see himself as a trailblazer who had shown the way and was now ready to step aside and let others follow his path. In reality, his research never again reached the level of accomplishment it had achieved before and during World War I. Instead Carver bogged down in futile projects, such as getting peanut oil massages accepted by the medical profession as a treatment for the effects of polio. Nevertheless, his contributions as a consultant and a publicist were highly valued by those he helped. Not only did he serve magnificently as an interpreter between scientists and laymen, but many of his ideas did indeed foreshadow areas of later significant research. In some ways he was a man both ahead of and behind his times.

Suffering Humanity

One constant thread in Carver's career was a concern for health and nutrition. His stay with Mariah Watkins in Neosho taught him the curative powers of native plants and herbs. Very early he was aware of the impact of diet in producing healthy bodies, and much of his work with peanuts, cowpeas, and sweet potatoes had been aimed at diversifying and improving the diet of the small farmer. He created Penol in an effort not only to expand the use of peanuts, but also to solve a serious health problem. In addition, he had recognized the therapeutic effect of massage since his days at Iowa State, where he served as a masseur to the football team.

For many years Carver treated his friends to massages to relieve tension, insomnia, poor appetite, and a variety of other ailments. He was evidently an excellent masseur, for word of his success began to circulate, bringing more people to him for help. Naturally, his interest in the nutritive value of peanuts soon led him to use peanut oil for his massages. And in the mid-1920s one patient seemed to prove the effectiveness of the peanut oil.

The Thompsons were a prominent white Tuskegee family, many of whom were close to Carver. Among the numerous Thompsons was a young boy named Foy, who was about eleven years old when he began receiving peanut oil massages from Carver. He was very frail, anemic, and underweight, and came to the professor three times a week for massages. In thirty days he gained thirty-one pounds, convincing Carver that the "muscle-building" and nutritive qualities of the peanut were being absorbed through the skin into the bloodstream.[1]

Always a dreamer, Carver believed that he had found a way to restore the wasted muscles of polio victims. Infantile paralysis is an old disease, but its cause was not known until 1908, when experiments in Austria proved that it resulted from a virus. Every summer the dreaded disease claimed thousands of victims, usually infants and children, often reaching epidemic proportions. Polio frequently caused damage to the nerve cells in the spinal cord or at the base of the brain, which sometimes brought on paralysis and the gradual wasting of muscles. It was an especially frightening disease then, for before a vaccine was developed in 1955 there was no effective treatment. All that could be done was to attempt to limit the extent of deformity through surgery, braces, and physical therapy.

In 1930 many people and institutions, such as Warm Springs, which was founded in Georgia in 1927, were experimenting with various kinds of physical therapy on polio patients. Because Carver was already convinced of the nutritive and curative properties of peanuts, he tried massaging two polio victims with peanut oil and concluded that the phenomenal results he obtained were due to those properties. Carver seldom remained silent when he believed he was on the verge of a great breakthrough. By 1931 he began to hint at his discovery in speeches. Then on 2 November 1933 a Columbus, Georgia, newspaper noted Carver's success with the two infantile paralysis patients. The United Press representative in Birmingham cabled Carver the next day for more information. Carver wired, "Do not want any further publicity at this time. Am making more demonstrations of its efficacy." Another UP agent then wrote the public relations man at Tuskegee Institute for more details. Nevertheless United Press was scooped by Associated Press writer T. M. Davenport, whose article appeared widely in AP papers on 30 December 1933.[2]

Davenport had come to Tuskegee to talk personally with Carver, and the two men immediately became friends. His article began on a cautious note, quoting Carver as saying, "It has been given out that I have found a cure. I have not, but it looks hopeful." The remainder of the article, however, belied that qualified caution. It explained how Carver had accidentally discovered the "tissue-building properties of the oil" by using it as a base for a beauty lotion. "I gave it to some ladies to use," he declared, "and those inclined to be fat brought it back to me, saying they could not use it because it made them gain weight." The article reported dramatic results on two polio victims, both boys in their early teens.

> Improvement was noted early in the test, Dr. Carver said, pink returned to the skin and the muscles increased in size by actual measurements.
>   After nine applications of the oil which was massaged into the affected limbs, one of the subjects who had been walking with crutches was able to walk with the use of only a cane.
>   The other boy less severely afflicted, had increased use of his leg and joined other boys in playing football.

Davenport then quoted Carver as saying, "I have used it on 250 persons, and it has never failed, so far as I can find out."[3] This quotation gave the mistaken impression that 250 polio patients had been cured. In reality the two boys were the only infantile paralysis victims Carver had treated. Undoubtedly he had used the oil massages on 250 people, for he believed that they helped almost any condition. Indeed, most of his male friends received at least one massage from the professor.

His massage activities fanned the fires of speculation regarding Carver's sexual orientation. It is impossible to know what Carver felt toward his male patients, but the intensity of some of these relationships suggests some degree of sexual emotion. If such feelings did exist, it is doubtful that they were ever consciously recognized by Carver. Instead the emotions were transmuted into a feeling of spiritual oneness with his friends. Some psychologists have noted a certain similarity between the emotions of sexual and religious fervor, and Carver's emotional needs appear to have been met through his religion and his religious friendships. His reluctance to accept female patients reflected a realistic appraisal of his particular circumstances rather than his sexual orientation. Rumors of his homosexuality persist but are undocumented. The letters that most seem to confirm the rumors were written to white teen-age boys, and Carver was smart enough not to risk a homosexual relationship with them in Black Belt Alabama.

After the publication of the Davenport article, the professor was swamped with requests for treatment by people of all ages, sexes, and colors with disorders ranging from the tragic to the comic. Some sufferers wrote in desperation to ask if the oil would cure such ailments as muscular dystrophy, Parkinson's disease, leprosy, multiple sclerosis, and Hodgkin's disease. Others complained of a "a bad left ovarie," excess hair, baldness, weak arches, and "small male sexual organs."

As the letters poured in by the hundreds, Carver collectively referred to the correspondents as "suffering humanity." Although he was no doubt moved by the pathos of the letters, he also appears to have enjoyed the publicity and attention, as well as the feeling of being needed. For months almost every letter he wrote contained updated counts of the pleas from "suffering humanity." Less than a month after the article appeared the count had topped eleven hundred. Many other people just came to Tuskegee. The day after the article was published a long line of cars formed on the Tuskegee campus, filled with people hoping to be treated by Carver. Six months later he was still receiving as many as fifty-six visitors in one day. Not all were patients, however. For quite some time his work had been interrupted frequently by visitors of all kinds, and he sometimes complained that he was "a regular exhibit A." But in 1934 he devoted every weekend to the various patients he accepted for treatment. By April he had accumulated fifteen regular ones.[4]

The publicity about Carver's polio work had several interesting side effects. One was the development of a peanut oil shortage in the United States. Almost every correspondent wanted to buy the "miracle oil" from Carver, so he prepared a form letter to inform people that his oil was not being manufactured commercially. Unable to get peanut oil from Carver, the writers turned to other sources, and some druggists reported a higher demand than they could meet. This demand caused problems for Carver, because, as he declared, "I myself do not attempt to extract oils because I have no presses powerful enough." All through 1934 and 1935 he frantically solicited the oil from numerous sources. Eventually supply caught up with demand, and he was able to list in another form letter seven firms from which the oil could be purchased.[5]

In that letter he stated that he modified the viscosity and limpidity of the oil to match the "absorptive power of the individual's skin," but that "any refined pure peanut oil will work in the hands of a skilled masseur." The fact that, as he declared, "anybody can get the oil" did not prevent some from trying to capitalize on the demand for a special peanut oil massage lotion. Dr. Carl S. Frischkorn, much to Carver's dismay, claimed credit for the idea of peanut oil massages and in the fall of 1934 began producing "Vitalized Peanut Oil." The next year the Rose Miller Company sought Carver's assistance in gaining approval from the Pure Food and Drug Agency for its peanut oil "bust developer." Carver's old friend J. T. Hamlin, who was having difficulty selling Penol, requested permission to market a massage oil under Carver's name. In every case the professor refused to have his name tied to any product. Nevertheless, a number of Tuskegee people entered the massage oil business; three of the seven firms listed in Carver's form letter were Tuskegee-based.[6]

Carver later claimed that his ideas had been snubbed by medical doctors because "they regard a non-practitioner the same as a patent medicine. They will not [prescribe] a patent medicine unless they tear the label off and put it in a bottle of their own." Actually, dozens of physicians and medical schools expressed interest in testing Carver's methods.[7] Apparently, however, in most cases he displayed his characteristic reluctance to discuss his discoveries in detail. Many people have noted his gift for being evasive in replying to questions of processes and procedures, a tendency that, combined with his failure to leave any detailed research notes, makes it impossible to evaluate the quality of his research.

Nevertheless, he cooperated with a few friends who were medical doctors, and his instructions to them, as well as to individual patients, give a fairly clear picture of his evolving therapy procedures. First of all, he would not accept a polio patient until the disease had run its course and any necessary corrective surgery had been performed. He also claimed that he sought a physician's statement on the extent of the disability. Next he spent about a week testing each patient's reaction to oils of varying viscosity to determine which was most easily absorbed and to be certain that no allergic reaction occurred. For some sensitive skins, Carver asserted, he had to remove much of "the oleic, leinsoleic and stearic acids." At first he placed a great deal of emphasis on finding the right oil for each patient and developed nine different oils that varied in "the Lineolic, Legnoceric, Myristic, Oleic, Palmitic, [and] fatty acids."[8] For one doctor he described the method of application in some detail.

Its proper application is equally important. The muscles needing it most should be singled out and massaged daily. Great care should be taken in the gentleness and thoroughness with which it is done. Five or six drops only of this oil should be used at a time, massaged in until every trace has disappeared. Repeat this as long as the skin and weak muscles will take it up, then stop until the next day.

If done thoroughly and properly the skin and muscles should become super-saturated in about nine days, after which it is important to stop and give only the friction massage for nine days, then use the oil again, etc.[9]

By the summer of 1935 Carver began stressing the importance of correct massaging over the need for a particular oil. He cautioned one person not to "lay too much stress upon the efficacy of the oil alone, as its method of application has much to do with it."[10] Early the next year he encouraged a Birmingham doctor to try peanut oil massages on his arthritis patients. Although he asserted that he had tested forty-four different oils, Carver explained to the doctor,

My method, which I feel is much more important than the oil itself, or certainly on a parity with it, is the thing I am attempting to work out. I make a study of the muscles, locating those that are functioning and those that are weak or that are not functioning at all as far as I can see. I let those muscles be the superficial or the deeper seated ones. Then I find the parts of greatest activity. And by graduated exercises, massages, and instructions to the patient, I have been quite successful in bringing about activity.[11]

Usually Carver's patients came in once a week for treatment, but he trained a friend or relative of each to give daily massages. In addition he recommended hot salt baths, as well as regular attempts to use the affected muscles and increasing exercise of any that showed activity. For those who could not come to see him, he suggested securing "the services of a good physio-therapist who is thoroughly trained in anatomy, blood pressure, heart action, etc., and who knows how to pick out the atrophied muscles and rejuvenate them."[12]

Under this treatment program dozens of people reported phenomenal results. In some cases the return of muscular activity might have occurred spontaneously with the passage of time. There were some cases, however, in which a considerable number of years had passed without improvement until Carver began the treatments. One example is Emmett Cox, Jr., a state employee who was stricken with polio at age two. Five years later he underwent four operations to straighten his deformed legs and was placed in two leg braces that extended to the waist. During the next seventeen years he wore the braces, and his "legs dwindled away almost to nothing and the muscular action was nearly zero." Then in September 1934 he began Carver's treatments, and by March 1935 he was able to discard both braces and to use his legs to some extent.[13]

Undoubtedly the treatment program worked for dozens of people, who were saved from being crippled invalids for life. It worked because it was founded on sound principles of therapy, namely hydrotherapy, exercise, and massage. Such a treatment regime was soon to be made famous by Sister Kinney and became widely accepted. Carver was successful in cases where other people had failed largely because of his skill as a masseur and his ability to inspire hope. His only mistake was attributing his success to peanut oil's power to nourish muscles through absorption. To many this claim raised false hopes of a miracle cure attainable without effort.

Carver's reluctance to abandon the idea that peanut oil played an important role in his treatment is understandable for two reasons. First, an admission of the dispensability of the oil was tantamount to declaring that he had made no discovery at all, since massage, exercise, and hydrotherapy were not new ideas. Second, he received support for his ideas from several prominent physicians, most significantly Dr. L. C. Fischer.

Fischer was a widely respected surgeon who founded Crawford Long Hospital in Atlanta. In 1934 he contacted Carver for more information about the treatment program, declaring, "It may be that you have discovered something the entire medical profession should know about." Fischer wrote to Carver's patients for case histories and brought one of his own patients to Tuskegee. He also encouraged Carver to develop a massage lotion with iron for anemic patients and another with mercury for syphilis patients. Fischer was very busy establishing his hospital, but he assured Carver that when that work was completed 'he was "going to do more to get your efforts before the profession."[14]

Rarely did Carver have more than one contact with anyone without causing that person to feel that he was a special friend. Fischer was no exception, and the men exchanged confidences and progress reports on their amaryllis, as well as discussions of Carver's work. On two occasions their friendship was threatened by Fischer's professional ethics, however. Once Carver mentioned a chiropractor who was trying his peanut oil massages. Fischer quickly replied that the medical profession did not recognize chiropractics and declared, "If it is your intention to have any relations whatever with this group I shall have to very reluctantly, and with much sorrow withdraw any interest that I have in your work." Carver pleaded innocence in the matter and assured Fischer that he would abide by the doctor's advice. Although this reassured Fischer, Carver in fact continued to cooperate with chiropractors.[15]

A more serious threat to their friendship came from the efforts of a journalist to have an article about Carver's polio work accepted by the *Saturday Evening Post*. T. H. Alexander's own child had benefited from the treatment, and he was eager to inform the world of it. With Carver's approval he submitted an article, which the *Post* agreed to publish if it were approved by Dr. Morris Fishbein, editor of the *Journal of the American Medical Association*. Since Fischer was mentioned in the article, Fishbein sent him a telegram that said, "Do you endorse or support the work of Carver with Peanut Oil in Poliomylelitis? Your name cited as reference." Fischer immediately wrote Carver. The tone of his letter suggested that he did not believe Carver was responsible for the use of his name, but it warned the professor to be very careful of making any statements since he could be charged with practicing medicine without a license.[16]

The same day that Fischer wrote, Carver had sent the doctor's address to Alexander so that the writer could solicit an endorsement of the polio work. Several letters crossed in the mail before the whole issue was settled. In the end Fischer categorically refused to have his name used in any way, while still expressing his opinion that Carver was correct in his assumption "that the rapid absorption of the oil is largely responsible for [the] results." Through the entire incident Fischer seems to have believed that Alexander was acting without Carver's authorization, and the professor said nothing to dispel that impression. In fact, on 16 June 1936 he asserted, "I wish it were possible for me to control the lay press and keep down just the thing that you have mentioned."[17]

Exactly one month later Carver wrote a letter of encouragement to Alexander, declaring that he was sure "that before very long that the newspapers and magazines will be more than happy to get the article you have written." Although Alexander was unable to get the article published in the *Saturday Evening Post*, he did describe Carver's work in his regular column for the Nashville

Tennessean. He also launched a campaign to win funds for support of the treatment from Governor Bibb Graves of Alabama. He made a personal appeal to the governor and enlisted the aid of the editor of the Montgomery *Advertiser*, Grover C. Hall, who wrote an editorial in July 1936 urging Graves to "lend his encouragement." His cry was picked up by Carroll Kilpatrick of the Birmingham *Age-Herald*. All these people received substantial encouragement from Carver, who continued to mention that a doctor supported the treatments, without citing Fischer by name.[18]

Carver also reassured Alexander that "you are not embarrassing me a bit in the least, as everything you have done is so safe and sane." The next day he informed Alexander that the Tuskegee paper was sending copies of the *Advertiser* editorial "to various newspapers all over the country, asking them to republish it." The professor also enclosed copies of two letters from patients, one stricken with polio from birth and the other suffering a broken back. These cases did not seem "safe and sane" to Alexander, who replied with a letter of advice and strategy. Noting that he did not believe the therapy could help such people, he suggested to Carver "just to shrug your shoulders when such cases are mentioned." He also labeled as "bad strategy" any mention of massage oil that did not include peanut oil, for "unless we stick strictly to peanut oil as a part of any formula it might be said, as Dr. Morris Fishbein did say, that the entire benefit is derived from the massage." Such precautions were necessary "to window-dress the situation for the eyes of organized medicine."[19]

By this time Alexander's article had been accepted by *Readers' Digest*, subject to an endorsement by some physician. This time Carver made sure that Fischer was not approached and warned Alexander not "to crowd [the treatment] upon the medical profession." Nevertheless Alexander and Grover Hall aggressively sought an endorsement. Hall brought a doctor to Tuskegee, who returned "not wholly convinced" but "much impressed" and willing to try the procedures himself. The difficulty in acquiring unqualified medical support was ascribed to racial prejudice by Alexander. Hall disagreed, declaring "there is no prejudice against

Carver because he is black. Most of the prejudice I see is in his favor. He seems to fascinate people."[20]

All three men explored other sources. Carver wrote his old friend John Harvey Kellogg at Battle Creek, Michigan. Alexander contacted a friend in the United States Public Health Service. Their goals were twofold: to obtain an endorsement for the Readers' Digest and to get funds for a thorough testing of the treatment by qualified physicians. Finally they pinned their hopes on Dr. J. M. Baker, the state health officer of Alabama. Their lobbying campaign produced enough pressure on Governor Graves and Baker to compel action, but in the end Baker merely brought some physiotherapists to the Institute for one day of training and asked the surgeon general of the United States to investigate Carver's work. Baker's endorsement was quite limited, stating only that he believed that the oils had "superior penetrating powers for the human skin and possibly considerable nutritive value to the tissues of the human body."[21]

Neither Carver nor Alexander believed this statement was sufficient, and Alexander recast his article, "leaving out the approval of the medical profession entirely." Soon afterwards Readers' Digest reprinted a 1925 article about Carver by James Saxon Childers from the American Magazine rather than Alexander's. This may have hurt Alexander, because afterwards his correspondence with Carver ceased.[22]

The Readers' Digest article brought Carver into the national spotlight once again, for it was reprinted in magazines together with pictures of his polio work. One photograph showing Carver beside a stack of thousands of letters from "suffering humanity" was widely circulated in June 1937. The result was predictable; he was again flooded with letters during the second half of the year.

Carver could never be accused of lacking a flair for the dramatic, so he inevitably sought to treat the most famous member of "suffering humanity"—President Franklin D. Roosevelt. As early as 1933, newspaper articles hinted that Carver might massage the president while he was at Warm Springs. When no request for treatment came, Carver sent some of his oil to the White House in 1938. The next year Roosevelt stopped by Tuskegee during a Southern tour, and a photograph of him shaking hands with Carver appeared in hundreds of newspapers. The following week Carver received an endorsement that may have relieved his disappointment over the lack of medical support. The president wrote, "I do use peanut oil from time to time and I am sure that it helps." With this encouragement, Carver sent Roosevelt a bottle of emulsion to use before his peanut oil massages, writing, "I am sending you this merely as a friendly gesture and am seeking *absolutely no publicity*." Indeed, the professor did exercise admirable restraint and discretion about his "new patient."[23]

By 1939 Carver had acquired a new lobbyist for his cause. James Hale Porter tried for over a year to get funding for Carver's work from the National Foundation for Infantile Paralysis. In his fight Porter enlisted the aid of Henry A. Wallace. As a young boy in Iowa, Wallace had followed Carver around on his trips into the woods and fields, and after he became Roosevelt's secretary of agriculture, Wallace still felt a deep affection for the professor. He corresponded with Carver, came to Tuskegee on two occasions, and sometimes mentioned their relationship in speeches. Thus he was considered a natural ally by anyone wishing to see something done for the professor and was approached numerous times while he was secretary of agriculture and later when he became vice-president.[24]

Wallace gladly responded to all requests for statements of a general nature regarding Carver. In his tributes he stressed the professor's religion and his impact on people, not his scientific contributions. "The outstanding thing to me about Carver," he once wrote, "is the depth of his faith in human beings and in God. Everything else is a by-product of this central fact in his life." If Wallace was specifically asked for explanations of Carver's research, however, he became evasive. For example, when Roosevelt asked about the advisability of issuing a Carver postage stamp, Wallace's justification for such a stamp emphasized Carver's reception by the white South and referred to his scientific work only by comparing it favorably to that of Luther Burbank, while giving the impression that neither's research was especially noteworthy. The reason for his evasiveness is clear from a confidential letter after Carver's death. "Between you and me," he wrote, "I am inclined to think that his ability as a chemist has been somewhat overrated. I have been in his chem lab at Tuskegee but frankly I doubt if much of practical value came out. [25]

In response to Porter's request, Wallace merely sent a copy of Porter's letter to the National Foundation for Infantile Paralysis with the brief statement, "If you care to make any comment I shall appreciate hearing from you concerning either the possibility of some financial aid to Dr. Carver's work or the reasons why the aid cannot be granted." Although the foundation did not specifically support Carver's work, Tuskegee Institute was granted $161,250 to establish a crippled children's clinic. The clinic was under the direction of a physician, John W. Chenault, who tried to make Carver feel that he had a vital role in it. Nevertheless, Carver remained convinced until his death that his work had not received proper credit. He did find comfort, however, in the publicity given to Sister Kinney's treatment, writing, "Her work is so similar to mine, or mine similiar to hers, it is rather remarkable." [26]

By 1941 Carver was too weak to engage in physical therapy work any longer. For ten years he had treated a variety of patients and tried to win recognition of his ideas. He failed in that endeavor, but his work with infantile paralysis did have significant consequences.

First, he undoubtedly helped dozens of persons regain some use from withered limbs. The gratitude they expressed in their letters to Carver was genuine and deserved. Even those people who were not significantly helped physically were deeply affected by their contact with the Peanut Man, and the spiritual enrichment they received helped them to deal more effectively with their handicaps. One patient eloquently expressed Carver's impact on him in a letter to the professor.

> Upon leaving your office I remarked to my wife that I could well conceive the fact that Jesus was a man of color after knowing you.

Your spirit of deep humility moved me and has made me resolve to be a better man and to attempt to live more accurately the teachings and principles of the lowly Nazarene.[27]

Carver was acutely aware that the spiritual changes he wrought were as significant as the physical changes. He saw his work as a force for better race relations and noted in 1934 that four of his patients came from "right out of the Ku Klux section."[28] Two months later he reported:

One very prominent man came last week, an avowed Negro hater. He took a massage; it did him so much good that Mr. Thompson says that he cannot talk five minutes without bringing in *so* and *so* and his work and how it is helping him.[29]

In addition, since Carver refused to take payments for his treatments, substantial numbers of contributions were made to Tuskegee Institute by grateful patients. It is also highly probable that the publicity and lobbying efforts connected with his work were responsible for the establishment of the crippled children's clinic at Tuskegee. Frequently in Carver's career his rather unorthodox research methods opened doors to fellow blacks, allowing them to pursue his visions in a more systematic and scientific way.

Undoubtedly, Carver's infantile paralysis work was not one of his sounder scientific endeavors. His relations with the press and physicians betray a streak of the charlatan, but his deceptions were committed for recognition, not material gain, and were probably not conscious lies. It is both significant and paradoxical that some of Carver's shabbier dealings brought a great deal of good to countless people. Indeed, the distortions in the "Carver myth" and the impact of his compelling personality had more positive influence than any of his research. Symbols can have more power than reality in promoting both good and evil.

Man and Symbol

Fame is immutably wedded to myth-making. All cultures must have sources of inspiration, and in many societies this need is met by popular heroes. When people become famous, parts of their life stories are embellished to serve a variety of causes. All people often subtly rearrange their memories of past events to conform to perceived self-images, and renown makes it doubly difficult to resist that tendency. The repetition of falsehoods eventually lends them credibility, and the line between myth and reality becomes blurred. People as diverse as Samuel Clemens and Sigmund Freud have succumbed to this process.

Myth-making also has a snowball effect. The public demands to be continually dazzled by its heros; yet by the time people become famous their most significant work has often already been done. So basic truths are exaggerated to make possible a constant replenishment of heroic qualities. Then publicists embroider further, until denial of the distortions would destroy all the celebrity's credibility. Moreover, people swept along by dimly understood forces of rapid social and economic change want their heroes to be uncomplicated and one-dimensional. Contradictions are ignored to make the man fit the myth, as often happened in the case of Carver.

For Carver the number of tributes grew in reverse proportion to the usefulness of his work. During the twenty years of his ill-funded attempts at harnessing the bounty of nature to improve the lives of the poor, he received no significant honors. Later, while

Carver sought to improve race relations and to aid the peanut industry, recognition increased, but from 1916 to 1936 the only widely publicized honors he received were the Royal Society invitation, the Spingarn Medal, and an honorary doctor of science degree from Simpson College. The 1928 degree was especially appreciated, since questions about the title "Doctor" had embarrassed Carver. The only thing that marred the occasion was his inability to attend because of minor injuries he received from an attack by a bull in an Institute pasture a few days before the ceremony.[1]

The winning of honors generates other honors. The year 1937 marked the beginning of what became a deluge of awards. To some extent Tuskegee Institute and Austin Curtis were responsible. In the fall of 1936 they began planning a celebration of Carver's fortieth year of service at Tuskegee. A November press release solicited contributions of "not more than $1.00" to pay for the making and presentation of a bronze bust. At first Curtis hoped for sufficient donations to build a greenhouse for Carver as well, but by February he admitted the response had been disappointing and sought the aid of the *Peanut Journal* in fundraising. The organizers also requested an "expression of appreciation" from President Roosevelt, who forwarded the request to Henry A. Wallace. Significantly, the letter Wallace drafted emphasized Carver's influence and inspiration more than his scientific contributions, declaring, "Your faith in human nature, your ability to see the good about you and to lend a directing hand to talent where it needs stimulating, are at the very basis of your life's work."[2]

Carver himself sought to ensure that the ceremony would be well attended and well publicized, enclosing circulars about the upcoming event in all his letters. He stressed what an "ordeal" the occasion would be, just as he had for the 1931 presentation of the Tom Huston plaque. The combined efforts of his colleagues at Tuskegee made the event a success. In the principal address Dr. H. E. Barnard, director of the Farm Chemurgic Council, declared, "Forty years ago [Carver] was actively developing the science of [chemurgy.]" He then gave examples of current research that had been foreshadowed by Carver's earlier work. Such recognition before the Tuskegee community was gratifying, but even more significant was the publicity the event garnered. Widely read magazines such as *Time* and *Life*, as well as many newspapers, carried accounts.[3]

That year also brought honorary membership in the National Technical Association and the Mark Twain Society, as well as a proposal by Metro-Goldwyn-Mayer to produce a short movie on Carver's life. The film offer seemed particularly lucrative to Curtis, who was trying to raise funds to establish a "Carver Creative Research Laboratory." However, after he rejected the offer of an honorarium of only $500, the studio canceled its plans.[4]

The next year the Pete Smith Specialty Company of Hollywood produced a movie about Carver. Filmed in Tuskegee, it featured several local people. Booker T. Washington III played the part of his grandfather, and Carver played himself in his later years. In the same year Carver was honored at the Seventy-fifth Anniversary of Negro Progress and received an Alumni Merit Award from the Chicago Alumni Association of Iowa State and a Distinguished Service Key from Phi Beta Sigma fraternity.[5]

In 1939 Carver's health began to decline rapidly, preventing much new research or many lecture trips. Instead Carver devoted his time to the establishment of the George Washington Carver Museum and a research laboratory at Tuskegee. When he was strong enough to travel, he usually spoke at religious gatherings and the now frequent award ceremonies. His illness even led him to decline some honors, such as membership in the New York Academy of Sciences.[6]

During 1939 Carver found the strength to accept three honors in person. The first came in April, when the Tom Huston Company presented its bronze bas-relief to a black high school in Columbus, Georgia. Then that fall he was asked to speak at the New York *Herald-Tribune* Forum. When he indicated that his health might prevent his participation, publisher William J. Schieffelin urged his attendance, noting that Carver was the first black to be asked to participate. Later Carver learned that he was to receive one of three Roosevelt Medals given by a memorial society for Theodore Roosevelt. Not only would he share the honor with Carl Sandberg and Major General Frank R. McCoy, but the presentation would be held in New York during the same week as the *Herald-Tribune* Forum. One trip would suffice for both, and he decided to go. These honors reinforced his image as one of "the foremost agricultural chemists in the country," as did his election to honorary membership in the American Inventors Society the same year.[7]

Carver later wrote, "When I arrived [in New York] I did not expect to get back at Tuskegee alive,"[8] and the next year he limited his travel considerably. One of his few trips was to Ways, Georgia, for the dedication of the George Washington Carver School established by Henry Ford on his Ways plantation. The ceremony was small and received little publicity because of Ford's concern for Carver's health. As Carver noted:

> I was with Mr. Ford the entire day. I don't think he left me fifteen minutes during the entire day. He rode with me in the car, helped me over rough places, wouldn't let me walk anywhere, and kept people away from me. In fact the dedication exercises were very quiet. . . . There were about a dozen outside people there and they right from the community. He didn't let it be known.[9]

Another honor that year received more press notice, even though Curtis had to stand in for the professor at the presentation ceremony. The International Federation of Architects, Engineers, Chemists, and Technicians gave Curtis a plaque honoring Carver at a luncheon in New York presided over by the noted anthropologist Franz Boas.[10]

By 1941 Carver's health improved enough for him to participate in two Institute ceremonies in his honor: the dedication of the Carver Museum by Henry Ford and a special exhibit of Carver's artwork. He also received two tributes by outside groups on the Tuskegee campus. In April the Catholic Conference of the South bestowed on Carver its first annual award "for outstanding service to the welfare of the South" at its meeting in Birmingham. To spare the professor a trip, the ceremony was broadcast on radio from there, with Carver's response broadcast from Tuskegee. Typically, he declared, "Why I should be so signally honored is more than I can figure out, I have just endeavored to do my little bit in the world as fast and as thoroughly as the Great Creator of all things gave me the light and strength."[11]

Later that year the University of Rochester conferred an honorary degree on Carver at Tuskegee. Not wishing to jeopardize his health, university officials broke tradition by sending the president and faculty representatives to Alabama for the ceremony.[12] While it saluted Carver's research and teaching, the major reasons for the honor were:

> Because you have opened doors of opportunity to those Americans who happen to be Negroes; because you have once again demonstrated that in human ability there is no color line; because you have helped thousands of men acquire new confidence and self-respect.[13]

Two honors in 1941 caused Carver to resume traveling. The first seems to have almost overwhelmed him. The Variety Club, an organization of entertainers, honored Carver at a banquet in Atlantic City, presenting him with a thousand-dollar check for the Carver Foundation. The award was supposed to be secret until the banquet, but Carver wrote friends that "a very special exercise" was to be held and he hoped that they could be in the city. The club took precautions to lessen the strain of the trip, and Carver asserted that the "occasion was by far the most collossal, spectacular, educational and dignified occasion that I have witnessed." His speech, which drew a standing ovation from the audience of twelve hundred, did not tax him too heavily, for he used his earlier speech for the Catholic award almost verbatim.[14]

The New Jersey trip seemed to rejuvenate Carver, and he decided to accept an invitation to deliver the baccalaureate sermon at Simpson College in June. President John O. Gross had invited him the year before and had come to visit Carver in July 1940. Again special arrangements were made to relieve the burdens of travel, and his speech was enthusiastically received by an overflow crowd of two thousand, inspiring Gross to begin a fundraising drive for a new science building named for Carver.[15]

During the last full year of Carver's life, 1942, more honors were added to the already lengthy list. He was elected a member of the Laureate Chapter of Kappa Delta Pi, an honorary education society. The Thomas A. Edison Institute conferred a fellowship on him, and he received an honorary doctorate from Selma University, a black Alabama college. Although these honors generated some publicity, much more press coverage attended another tribute by Henry Ford, who erected a Carver memorial cabin at Greenfield Village and established a nutritional laboratory in Carver's honor at Dearborn. Carver went to Michigan for several weeks, and rumors circulated that he was to spend the remainder of his life working in the new laboratory. A picture of him serving Ford a weed salad also appeared in numerous papers.[16]

The many awards and tributes helped to make Carver well known. The process was given an additional boost by the growing influence of radio. Nationwide broadcasts helped create a homogeneous culture and made possible the overnight production of national heroes. Even the nonliterate population was reached by radio, and Carver's fame grew considerably because of the miracle of wireless communication. Between 1936 and 1942 numerous national radio programs featured his story, and he appeared personally on several. Programs telling of his work included "Strange As It Seems," hosted by John Hix from Hollywood in 1936 and 1939, a Smithsonian Institute radio series aired by the National Broadcasting Company (NBC) in 1938, and "A Friend Indeed" from New York in 1942. Carver appeared personally on "It Can Be Done" with host Edgar Guest in 1937, "We the People," broadcast over Columbia Broadcasting Service in 1939, and "Freedom's People," sponsored jointly by the United States Office of Education and NBC in 1941. He was also asked to be on NBC's "Inside Story" and on "Ripley's Believe It or Not" in 1939. These national programs fostered a false impression of the value of Carver's work and made him perhaps the best known living black in America.[17]

As Carver's fame spread, so did the use of his name. As early as the 1920s schools were named for him in states from South Carolina to Oklahoma. By the mid-1930s almost every town in America seemed destined to have a Carver High School. Such schools became so numerous in Alabama that in 1938 Carver suggested that another name be found for one in Holly Wood, Alabama. During the Depression Carver's struggle to overcome obstacles seemed especially relevant, leading National Youth Administration groups and Civilian Conservation Corps camps to appropriate his name. In the last four years of his life his name was attached to almost everything even remotely connected with blacks, such as a "colored theatre" in Norfolk, a swimming pool in Indianapolis, a settlement house in Pittsburgh, a "professional building for Negroes" in Cincinnati, and a Women's Christian Temperance Union chapter in Atlanta. Eventually it became practically impossible to enter a black community anywhere in America without being reminded of the existence of a man named George Washington Carver.[18]

Other blacks made more significant scientific contributions; why did Carver become the only well-known Afro-American scientist? Indeed, why did he become one of the dozen or so best-known scientists of any color? As with most historical questions, the answer is complex. To understand it, the roots of his fame need to be reexamined.

His first national recognition came largely as a result of his connection with Tuskegee Institute and the fact that he was the only black experiment station director. By 1915 Carver's accomplishments with incredibly limited funds were widely respected among agricultural researchers and educators. In other words, his fame was both meager and justified in the years before Booker T. Washington's death in 1915. In the second half of that decade, however, two factors increased his renown. One was the realization on the part of Tuskegee administrators that Carver's recognition by fellow scientists, as evidenced by his invitation to join the Royal Society, made him a likely candidate to succeed Washington as a magnet for contributions to the Institute. Consequently, school publications began to feature his work more prominently, especially after his collaboration with federal agencies during World War I. Second, his development of peanut milk led to his discovery by peanut growers and processors, who were experiencing the same kind of postwar slump that other agriculturally related businesses were suffering. The activities of these men brought Carver his first taste of truly national recognition.

While Carver was becoming the Peanut Man, the emphasis of his work shifted toward creation of mind-boggling numbers of exotic products from "lowly" farm crops. By 1923 the significance of his earlier work was blurred, and the Carver myth was launched. Although the claims that he rescued the South from cotton dependency were extravagant, his activities were still noteworthy, especially considering the lack of concerted efforts by others in utilization research. His work failed to bear significant, practical fruit and was not totally original, but he did highlight and publicize ideas later adopted and implemented by the chemurgic movement and the USDA.

Both the peanut industry and Carver benefited from their collaboration between 1920 and 1943. Nevertheless, the initial flurry of publicity over his peanut milk and his success before Congress were only stepping stones; he would not have become a folk hero on that basis alone. To reach international prominence he had to be adopted by other groups as well. Peanuts placed Carver in the national spotlight, but it was his compelling personality, thus illuminated, that brought him real fame. That personality and the dramatic qualities of his life story were irresistible to numerous groups in search of a symbol for their cause.

Carver's commercial efforts caught the attention of New South spokesmen, but some recognized his value even earlier. Soon after Carver's appearance before the 1920 Montgomery meeting of the United Peanut Association, Richard H. Edmonds of the *Manufacturers' Record* in Baltimore published an article by Carver. In 1924 Edmonds requested another article for a special issue of his magazine on "The South's Development." After the incorporation of the Carver Products Company and Carver's exhibit at the Southern Exposition in New York, dozens of other newspapermen published articles by and about the professor. By the time of his death the roster of Carver's "New South" publicists included such people as John Temple Graves of the Birmingham *Age-Herald*, Clark Howell of the Atlanta *Constitution*, and Grover Hall of the Montgomery *Advertiser*.[19]

Articles appearing in Southern white newspapers echoed the theme of a 1929 Montgomery *Advertiser* story entitled "Negro Scientist Shows 'Way Out' for Southern Farmers," which predicted that the region's search for deliverance from its difficulties "will end in the laboratory of Dr. George W. Carver . . . if the South will show the vision and enterprise to put to practical uses the fruits of his vast research efforts." For example, the Baltimore, Maryland, *Sun* asserted, "[Carver] has opened up vistas and touched upon resources that can bring economic security where once the bonds of King Cotton kept the most bountiful half of the nation in debt and despondency."[20]

The role of Carver in uniting the races "to build a common civilization that will make for a better way of life for all human beings" was also noted. A Kentucky writer mused, "It would be strange, indeed, if a member of a liberated race should in turn liberate a large part of the South."[21] The vision of that liberated future was expressed in an Atlanta *Constitution* editorial.

> When the people below the Potomac accept that leadership outlined in part for them by Dr. Carver, they will see about them rich and productive lands, beautiful farm communities and good schools, signifying the end of an abominable and atrocious system of penury and the beginning of a new era of happiness and contentment for a much neglected people.[22]

Carver echoed these themes in speeches, articles, and letters. For example, in 1927 he wrote:

> The rapid growth of industry, the ever increasing population and the imperative need for more varied, wholesome and nourishing foodstuff makes it all the more necessary to exhaust every means at our command to fill the empty dinner pail, enrich our soils,

bring greater wealth and influence to our beautiful South land, which is synonymous to a healthy, happy and contented people.[23]

Carver definitely encouraged those who sought to use him as a New South symbol, as he had fostered the peanut promoters' efforts to publicize him as the Peanut Man. He sent unsolicited articles and letters to numerous Southern newspapers and heaped praise on writers who wrote flattering articles about him. He told one:

> And the thing that pleases me most is the fact that you are a very young man and have caught the vision, which means that you are going to keep the progressive fires burning until they act as a leaven and stir up the mass of thinkers, as it is beginning to do already.[24]

The vision of racial harmony in the South was shared by workers in the interracial movement. For them Carver became a symbol both of the fruits of tolerance and the ability of Afro-Americans. The CIC and YMCA activities in this sphere included publishing of Carver's work as well as sponsoring his speeches before white student groups. For the most part, people like Will Alexander and Robert B. Eleazer used an indirect approach. Instead of preaching the evils of discrimination to their fellow whites, they cited the example of Carver's contributions with little editorial comment. Eleazer, however, did end one press release with the observation that Carver "constitutes an unanswerable evidence of the worthwhileness of his race, and of the fact that its humblest child may possess possibilities of limitless service awaiting only a chance for development."[25]

Many church groups were also active in the fight against discrimination. Members of the missionary boards of the Southern branches of the Methodist, Episcopal, and Baptist churches used Carver's story to teach young people to appreciate "the splendid race that lives by our side" and "the struggle of the Negro for his rightful place in American life." Southern church literature usually let accounts of Carver's life speak for themselves, but Northern churches were more direct. A writer for the *American Missionary* declared, "In his own person, [Carver] answers the question, 'Can a Negro assimilate the higher education?' " To those who would deny that ability could be carried in black genes, the *Congregationalist* asserted, "No, white man, you cannot fall back on your favorite defense, 'It is due to white blood in him,' for [Carver] is so black—as a colored friend of mine says—'You have to scratch a match to see his face.' "[26]

Some New South journalists desired to increase both racial harmony and black educational funding because of the perceived costs of illiteracy. Like other Southern publicists, these writers usually let their readers draw their own conclusions from stories of Carver's accomplishments, but some were more direct. For example, an editorial in a white Macon, Georgia, paper noted:

> There is no knowing how many other Carvers the South has robbed herself of by being so niggardly with education for the Negro. We are less blind to the possibilities under a black skin nowadays, but we are still grudging our potential Carvers their chance to make this a better world.[27]

Some articles of this kind caused the writers to be branded "nigger lovers." None fought back more fervently than Hodding Carter of Mississippi in an 1937 editorial.

> Get this straight, everyone of you . . . here in the Delta we make our living, in the ultimate analysis, from the Negro. . . . Is it more revolting to try to instill in him pride in his worthwhile actions than to—hush, hush—make him think that his race is fit only for mockery by day and concubinage by night?[28]

Black journalists were also aware of the potential symbolic uses of Carver's renown. Since many whites viewed Carver as a saintly genius, they realized that discrimination towards him highlighted the inhumanity of prejudice. Thus the Pullman car incident was widely reported in the black press. Others stressed Carver's abilities to make their point, as Roscoe Dunjee of the Oklahoma City *Black Dispatch* noted to Carver.

I also take a pot-shot at white people down this way by telling them that your scientific investigations will finally isolate food products in rocks, and that when that day comes, Negroes who live in rural America and who somehow have located in the rocks and hills will have the best of their white brethern [sic] who seem to have inherited all the black land.[29]

Most black writers, however, realized that few whites read black newspapers and therefore aimed their articles at their own people, emphasizing the inspirational features of Carver's life. Editorials pleading with blacks to broaden their goals, get an education, and work hard often used him as an example of the possibilities open to all. Some blacks saw Carver's story as a means to increase black pride and to decrease the color prejudice that existed among blacks themselves. Mary Church Terrell noted, "We talk too much about complexion in our group" and told Carver that she "took special pride in emphasizing that fact that your genius can not be ascribed to Caucasian blood." One editorial decrying black attempts to look white through skin bleaching and hair straightening pointed out that "Dr. Carver has worked along the line of straightening out the kinks on the inside of the head."[30]

More militant black editors were angered by the white emphasis on Carver's humility and his refusal to join protest movements. When a white paper noted that Carver's achievements were possible because he did not waste time agitating for rights, a black journalist angrily responded.

It would have been much more logical for the editors to say that Carver achieved thus, because he did not spend all his time slinging white people's hash and washing their soiled dishes—because as a boy, and [against] the wishes of nearly the whole of white America, he chose to study chemistry rather [than] to pick cotton.[31]

Carver's color and accomplishments made him an appropriate symbol for diverse groups interested in race relations. Careful selection of the facts made it possible to prove almost any racial theory from the story of his life. However, to some groups Carver's color was irrelevant, except that it made his story more interesting and intriguing. This was true of the religious groups that adopted him in their fight against materialism and skepticism.

By the 1920s America was undergoing vast cultural changes. Technology was transforming a rural, fundamentalist society into an urban, mobile, and dynamic one. Old customs, traditions, and values were yielding to a new morality based on individualism and a scientific world view. The old order did not yield without a fight, as was evidenced by the Scopes "monkey trial." Many people, however, found themselves stranded between the old and the new, wanting desperately to reconcile the two. For these a religious scientist offered a solution. Thus when Carver's 1925 New York speech called widespread attention to his reliance on divine revelation, he was adopted by many religious groups almost overnight.

Religious writers and speakers tended to repeat and emphasize certain features of Carver's life. Most noted that he called his laboratory "God's little workshop" and always prayed before entering it. They also stressed that the professor was unconcerned with material things and never tried to get rich from his discoveries, without mentioning his patents and companies. Of the greatest importance to religious spokesmen was the fact that Carver was both religious and scientific. As one writer declared, "To me, it was a delight to meet a man of such distinction in the realm of science as Dr. Carver who enjoyed religion as he does. When we talked about the things of God his eyes sparkled and his soul caught fire."[32]

One of the most widely used stories about Carver was gleaned from his lectures. He often described his conversations with the Creator about the peanut. In one account he told the Creator, "I would like to know all about the creation of the world," to which the reply was, "Surely you have disappointed me. You are supposed to have a reasonable intelligence." Then Carver asked to know only "all about the peanut," but still the Creator declared that "all about the peanut is an infinite and you are finite." As the professor narrowed his demands, the Creator explained, "I'd be glad to give you a few peanuts. I've given you a few brains. Take the peanuts into the laboratory and pull them to pieces." Carver broke the peanuts into their constituents, and the Creator advised him to "take parts 2, 3, 4, 5, 6, and put them together anyway you wish so long as you keep the law of compatibility." When Carver asked, "Can I make milk out of the peanut?" the reply was another question, "Do you have the constituents of milk?" The professor would then note that the answer was yes, and hold up a bottle of peanut milk, followed by dozens of other products. Audiences loved the story, which revealed both his sense of humor and his belief in divine inspiration, and so he used it often.[33]

Carver's religion was mystical and nondenominational. Thus any number of religious bodies could claim him as one of their own. Leaders of diverse groups found Carver receptive to their views for two reasons: he hated to disagree with anyone and he believed that there was more than one true way to relate to the divine. He corresponded with people from all major denominations as well as with some from more unorthodox groups, such as the Divine Philosophy Group, the Theosophical Society, the Unity Farm, and the Universal Group of Intuitives. He was also in contact with a wide variety of religious spokesmen, including Frank Lauback, Gloria Dare, and E. Stanley Jones, who named Carver one of the three most influential people in his life. In addition, the professor corresponded with fellow religious scientists, such as Alexis Carrel at the Rockefeller Foundation.[34]

Carver was sometimes asked to provide a written endorsement of a religion, and he usually obliged. For example, he wrote statements of support for the Baha'i faith and the Rosicrucian Fellowship. Perhaps his most interesting statement was written in response to a letter from a follower of the black evangelist Father Divine. Born George Baker, Father Divine began preaching on Long Island in 1919 and recruited followers who called him "God." By 1930 he had thousands of disciples of all colors and fed masses of people in buildings called "heavens." As early as 1935 Carver had received literature from the movement, and in 1940 a follower wrote that Father Divine was "God incarnate," to which the professor replied, "Thank you very much for your interesting letter which contains so much information of value. I trust that I will be able to meet Father Divine some day as I am very certain we have a number of things in common." [35]

Carver's contacts with disciples of Father Divine were not widely publicized. In contrast, his work with followers of Mahatma Gandhi was frequently reported in newspapers and magazines. Gandhi's religious crusade of passive resistance to English rule in India physically weakened him, so one of his supporters came to Tuskegee in 1929 to get a vegetarian diet from Carver that would provide sufficient nourishment for the struggle. Naturally the professor complied, and then mentioned the diet in many speeches. In 1935 he was again approached by another Gandhi supporter who informed Carver that Gandhi had requested some of his bulletins. Carver was delighted to receive a personal card of appreciation from Gandhi and replied that he prayed for Gandhi's success "in this marvelous work you are doing." [36]

The social changes of the 1920s were unsettling to a number of religious beliefs, but the economic collapse that occurred in the 1930s seemed to threaten the assumptions on which American society was based. During the Depression many Americans sought proof that the system did work and that talent and effort would be rewarded. To meet this need, writers often emphasized Carver's humble origins and how he reached worldwide fame through his talents and efforts. The rags-to-riches quality of his life was often portrayed in articles with such titles as "He Never Thought of Quitting." In some minds Carver became an incarnation of the American dream. When speaking to young people, both black and white, the professor himself extolled the "unlimited possibilities" for success available to all, regardless of birth. Many of these speeches concluded with the recitation of the poem "Equipment," which ended with these words:

> You were born with all that the great have had
> With your equipment they all began,
> Get hold of yourself, and say: "I can." [37]

These articles and speeches seemed to endorse not only the value of hard work, but also the essential fairness of industrialization and the capitalist system of the United States. Carver therefore became an appropriate symbol for many patriotic groups, and his name was used by public and private agencies to foster "Americanism" during World War II. Soon after his death, the United States Treasury Department issued a Carver Victory Bond poster.[38]

Some individuals and groups even used Carver to prove the wisdom and beneficence of segregation. From the early days of slavery, many white Southerners suffered from guilt about the inhumanity of their racial policies. Assuaging these feelings and rationalizing their social system required at least one living example of the South's reasonableness and willingness to reward merit regardless of skin color. Carver seemed to serve this purpose, just as Booker T. Washington had earlier.

Editorials about Carver's accomplishments in some white papers reminded blacks that his life "should be a lesson of inspiration to all of his race tempted to despair because of supposed lack of opportunities" and that "Dr. Carver has long ago realized that there is no clash of interests between the whites and the blacks."[39] Other editorials stressed the superiority of Southern racial solutions.

> Since the first negroes were snatched from Africa and brought to America as slaves a great experiment has been going on in race relationship. The Civil War ended the slave phase. Since then it has been a period of re-adjustment for both races. The writer contends that the south has afforded the negro a fairer chance than any other section.[40]

References to Carver's humility also served the segregationist cause, although many writers, especially religious ones, emphasized it for other reasons. For example, an article entitled "He Worked With God" noted that the professor was "a humble man, he worked with humble materials, but his results were anything but humble."[41] Some stressed this quality for dramatic purposes.

Perhaps the most widely read article about Carver was the one by James Saxon Childers that appeared in both *American Magazine* and *Readers' Digest*. It opened with an account of the author's first contact with the professor.

> The stooped old Negro shuffled along through the dust of an Alabama road at a curiously rapid rate. He was carrying an armful of sticks and wild flowers. . . .
>
> When I got a little closer to him I saw that he was wearing a saggy coat which might originally have been a green alpaca, but which the sun had faded until I couldn't be sure about the color; there were so many patches that I couldn't even be certain about the material.
>
> . . . His thin body bent by the years, his hair white beneath a ragged cap, he seemed pathetically lost on the campus of a great modern educational institution.[42]

Perhaps this description reflects the bias against intellectuals and elitism common in American society. Regardless of the reasons, humility became an integral part of the Carver image. In some ways the humility was genuine, but the closely related assertion that the professor hated publicity was patently false.

As each new group or cause adopted Carver as a symbol, the mythology was expanded. In the end he was credited with almost singlehandedly remaking the South and being the world's greatest chemist, while remaining a humble old black man who looked to God for inspiration, meekly accepted segregation, and proved that merit was rewarded in the American economic system. As is usually true, these myths had some factual basis, and Carver must bear some responsibility for the distortions. His deep need for acceptance and recognition often appears to have prevented him from making more than vague and unconvincing denials of extravagant claims. Yet another facet of his personality also helped to cloud the truth. He felt a very real kindness toward his fellow human beings, which made it difficult to disagree openly with anyone. Therefore almost all visitors could come away from a meeting with him believing that he endorsed their ideas.

Very few people were met with outright rejection by Carver,

no matter how bizarre their beliefs or inventions might be. Thus correspondents received a sympathetic hearing for such products as perfume from "dog droppings" and a cement-and-peanut-hull canoe. One man who sought Carver's help in developing a language that he had learned from a hen was politely told to contact the Institute English Department with the explanation, "I can be of no help since I confine my activities to the laboratory."[43] At least some of the errors in the Carver record must be ascribed to his extreme sensitivity to the feelings of others.

Austin Curtis did not always share this reluctance to challenge parts of the Carver image, especially those that pictured the professor as a "glorified field hand." On several occasions Curtis requested changes in articles and radio programs. By 1942 even Carver became more assertive, though always in a polite way. For example, he requested the deletion of the statement "God has been mighty good to this poor old Negro" ascribed to him in a textbook published by Harcourt, Brace and Company, explaining, "That is not my language at all and I never made any such expression. I have seen various versions of it in newspapers. . . . Some even go so far as to say 'darky.' "[44]

Nevertheless, the public image was one of a benign old wizard, hardly offensive to any believer in the American dream. Even many Southerners who ardently supported white supremacy proudly hailed Carver as one of Dixie's leading citizens. His symbolic adoption by proponents of both segregation and industrial capitalism, however, tends to obscure the facts that contradict the image of him as an accommodationist achiever, who, in the words of one historian, "lived a life of undeniable usefulness while out-Bookering Booker Washington."[45]

Carver rose from slavery to world prominence in an environment of segregation, and his reluctance to publicly discuss political and racial questions made it easy to assume that he accepted the basic premises of the myth-makers. He also undeniably supported and believed in Booker Washington's approach to race relations. Carver's deep religious faith was the central focus through which he viewed the world around him, and his universalistic and mystical religion colored his approach to everything from science to race relations. To him love and truth were two of the most vital forces in the universe, the only powers strong enough to dissolve racial prejudice. His most repeated solution to prejudice was the Golden Rule, for he believed that "real Christian people speak the same language. They do unto others as they would have them do unto them. The texture of the hair, nationality, and pigment of the skin has absolutely nothing to do with it." [46] The publicity given Carver's persistent refusal to express bitterness toward the white South and his exhortations to black youth to work hard led many to assume that Carver wholeheartedly accepted Southern "racial solutions." Actually, like most Afro-Americans of the time, Carver had ambivalent feelings toward both the question of race and the capitalist system. Forced into a dual identity by the prevailing social order, he alternated between a race-conscious sense of solidarity and a denial of the validity of race as a category. His alternatives were severely circumscribed by life in the South, and actions had to be weighed against not only their social and political consequences, but also their economic results. Thus his reactions to Jim Crow varied with the circumstances.

Even before Carver moved to Black Belt Alabama he had experienced the irrationality of racial prejudice. In his hometown he was allowed to attend the white Sunday school but was barred from the regular public school. Refused admittance to one college because of race, Carver became the only black at Simpson College and Iowa State. On both campuses his unusual abilities and warm, unassuming personality won respect and the right to participate freely in extracurricular activities. Carver still encountered racial barriers but often discovered that whites supported him in the exercise of his rights. When Carver came to Tuskegee in 1896, he quickly established warm relationships with prominent whites in the town, who called upon him for advice on everything from gardening to art. Surely it must have seemed to Carver for a while that love and useful knowledge would melt away prejudice.

Several events awakened Carver's consciousness of the complexities and dangers of being black in the white South. The mob action at Ramer, Alabama, the Klan march in Tuskegee, and the Pullman car affair in Oklahoma had their lessons for Carver. He learned that he could not ignore race. He also discovered that certain kinds of actions had their costs, and while some costs were worth paying, others were not. Socializing with a white woman was less important than education for his people; a hospital manned by black doctors was worthy of a fight. Even so, in order to win in white America one had to draw battle plans carefully.

If Southern racial etiquette was irrational and confusing for the ordinary black, it was doubly so for Carver. His unique position meant that he met a wider range of responses from white Southerners. Some were truly color-blind in the presence of his genius and religious depth. Others wished to adopt him as an "honorary white." Still others sought to remind Carver that he was, after all, "just a nigger." His fame brought him greater opportunities, but also greater responsibilities. In addition, his whole past was full of contradictory experiences with whites. He had been threatened and insulted because of his color, but the only parents he ever knew were white. Is it any wonder that his response to Jim Crow was confusing and contradictory?

Despite Carver's unique position and his own cautiousness, he was sometimes denied facilities that he had requested. At least twice he refused to accommodate himself in this kind of discrimination. The first time was during the Pullman car incident in 1930. Nine years later Carver was less trusting and more prominent. By 1939 his fame had become worldwide, and during a trip to New York to appear on a national radio broadcast, another widely publicized incident of discrimination occurred. Carver had been invited to appear on "Strange As It Seems," and Curtis wrote to the New Yorker Hotel on 8 September 1939 for reservations. Confirmation of the reservations was received, but when Curtis and Carver arrived in New York they were informed that all rooms were filled. According to press accounts, Curtis refused to leave and was told that he and Carver could wait in a third floor foyer in case some guest might vacate. After Carver was offered a chair near the men's washroom, Curtis called John Woodburn of Doubleday, Doren and Company, a publishing concern that was sub-sidizing a biography of Carver. When Woodburn's pleas to the ho-tel manager to honor his commitment failed, representatives from the *New York Times*, *New York Post*, Pittsburgh *Courier*, and Chi-cago *Defender* were summoned.[47]

Several hours passed, and the hotel manager still insisted he had no rooms. At this point another representative of Doubleday, Charles Gorham, entered with baggage in hand and asked for a room. When he was told he could be accommodated immediately, Gorham refused the room and asked that it be given to Carver, but the management reverted to its position that no rooms were available. The vice-president of Doubleday then called the New Yorker and threatened legal action if Carver was not given a room at once. The *New York Post* staff also began telephoning hotel di-rectors to demand action.

Finally, more than six hours after his arrival, Carver was given rooms, and the reporters retired to the lounge for cocktails. When the headwaiter started to refuse service to the black reporters, Charles Gorham retorted, "Your hotel has just been allowed to crawl out of one nasty situation on its belly. They'd better be very careful that they don't have another one."[48]

Newspapers all over the country picked up the story, and edi-torialized on intolerance. Several noted that Carver was just one of many victims of discrimination. A New Orleans newspaper com-mented:

> There are other colored men in the same class as Tuskegee's Carver and they are meted the same treatment in their native land. They complain little, but suffer much. Just what must these servants of the general good accomplish in order to earn bed and board in the United States?[49]

In answer to the protests, the New Yorker Hotel management asserted that the incident was an absurd misunderstanding. "Every man, woman and child in these entire United States are aware of what the name Tuskegee stands for," wrote one official, who de-clared that the New Yorker was "fully aware of his identity" when

Carver's reservation was confirmed. "Is it logical to assume that we would refuse accommodations to him, when we had already confirmed said reservation?" he asked. Carver was only one of "more than a hundred awaiting room assignments, and all with reservations," in a lavishly furnished Gentlemen's Lounge built for the "express purpose of caring for our guests who are unable to obtain immediate room assignment." Indeed, he noted, Carver was given precedence over others "without coercion or force" because of his "advanced age and reputation."[50]

Regardless of what really happened, the image of the frail, almost eighty-year-old scientist sitting in a smoky corridor after twenty-two hours of travel provided grist for the editorial mills on the absurdity and inhumanity of Jim Crow. Carver never denied the press accounts, and wrote one friend, "I quite agree with the fine editorial on the ridiculous happening at the New York hotel." Some people, he asserted, "have to be made to do the right thing."[51]

It was the picture of Carver willingly sitting outside the banquet hall at the Dearborn Conference in 1937, however, rather than of him refusing to leave the New Yorker Hotel, that most white Southerners, with their almost infinite capacity for selective recollection, chose to remember. The same kind of selective process occurred when Carver was used to symbolize such things as New South boosterism, the Horatio Alger rags-to-riches myth, and the patriotism of black Americans.

Carver also had ambivalent feelings toward the prevailing economic and political system. Basically he had very little interest in or knowledge of economic or political theory, for his religion and his scientific work absorbed most of his thoughts and energy. Carver's personal success seemed to support the thesis that only hard work was needed to succeed in America. Yet Carver could see thousands of his race trapped in semislavery by economic and social conditions. His vision of the economic system was therefore tempered by his own experiences and his sense of race consciousness.

What brought Carver international fame was the publicity he

received for his efforts to find commercial uses for Southern resources. Carver himself proclaimed that a New South was dawning and had many friends among New South editors and businessmen. Because of these friendships the differences between Carver's vision and that of other boosters became obscured, probably even in Carver's own mind. The alliance, nevertheless, served to confirm the image of Carver as an accommodationist achiever. Less publicized aspects of his life, however, indicate that despite his personal success he had serious doubts about the merits of industrial capitalism.

The businessmen to whom Carver offered free advice were probably unaware that he was also serving as an unpaid consultant to the Llano Co-Operative Colony in Newllano, Louisiana. Founded near Los Angeles in 1914 by Job Harriman, the colony had moved to western Louisiana in 1917 and remained there until December 1939. Harriman, a Marxist, had intended to establish a purely collectivist society, but cooperative ownership actually extended only to the means of production, with other private property tolerated.[52]

Early in 1923 George T. Pickett, Harriman's successor as head of the colony, sought dietary advice from Carver. Carver's reply was a twelve-page letter on nutrition, including suggested daily menus, that was published in the cooperative's newspaper, the *Llano Colonist*. This exchange of letters initiated a relationship that lasted as long as the colony did. Pickett came to Tuskegee to visit Carver, and Carver suggested that a representative of the colony be sent to him for training. Although this idea was financially impossible, various colonists continued to write to Carver for advice on a wide variety of subjects. In apology for the large number of requests, Pickett wrote in 1932, "You know I never hesitate to impose upon a comrade when getting information that is being used in the interest of humanity so you may expect calls uness you throw up your hands and say 'enough.' "[53]

Carver received not only requests from but also literature about the colony, as well as the *Llano Colonist* and newsy letters from Pickett, who made it clear that he viewed America's economic system with disdain. In 1928 Carver noted, "I wish we were nearer together and racial conditions more liberal so that we could cooperate in a more effective way, but thank God they are getting better." Pickett replied that it was "only natural that those desiring to perpetuate the capitalistic system will use every means possible to keep others from working together to the best advantage, and even to the enslaving of the mind." A year later, Carver assured Pickett that he was greatly interested in the way he was working out a unique problem, "and we feel very grateful for all you are doing for my people."[54]

Carver had similar though shorter-lived ties with at least two other cooperative colonies. One of these was the United Cooperative Industries in Los Angeles, which was billed in 1936 as "a Farm and Factory Colony in the Making since 1923." The other was the Delta Cooperative Farm, established by Sherwood Eddy and his associates in 1936 to "care for the white and Negro evicted share croppers of Arkansas who had joined the [Southern Tenant] farmers union." Cy Record, a student at the University of Texas and a volunteer worker at Delta, kept Carver posted on developments within the interracial colony, as well as on his own intellectual development. Commenting on a course Record was taking at Commonwealth College on "Dialectical Materialism and Marx," Carver said that he was "pleased to know" that Record was taking "this splendid course." Carver went on to say, "I have heard quite a bit about it, and feel sure that it is something unusually good."[55]

When Carver spoke of his knowledge of Marxism, he was probably referring to what he had learned from two close friends, John Sutton and Howard Kester. Sutton's exposure to Marxism, in fact, had originally came through Carver. In late 1930 and early 1931 O. J. Golden corresponded with Carver about the desire of the Soviet Union for black agricultural specialists. Golden reported that the Soviets would pay passage and a minimum monthly salary of $150 to $200, as well as provide free medical care and a month's vacation. He urged Carver to recommend men and to come with them for a tour of Russia, asserting, "You owe it to your race. Russia is the only country in the world today that gives equill [sic] chances to black and white alike."[56]

In response to Golden's request Carver hurried a letter off to John Sutton, one of his best and closest former students, asking if Sutton would be interested in such an offer. Carver also wrote Golden that he doubted he could find fifty specialists willing to go, but that he would do the best he could "in this important matter." Noting his poor health and advanced age, Carver stated, "I appreciate the invitation to study Russia. I hope I can do it, but not until I get stronger."[57]

Although Carver never went to the Soviet Union, John Sutton accepted the offer and stayed in Russia until 1938, writing Carver glowing accounts of life and race relations under the Soviet regime. Even being forced to quit the Soviet Union in 1938, leaving his wife and child behind, did not completely disillusion Sutton with the Communist system. Since Carver was both uninterested and uneducated in politics, Sutton's words probably carried greater weight than they would have otherwise.[58]

Carver's other source of Marxist thought, Howard Kester, was one of the young white Southerners Carver met during his interracial work with the YMCA and CIC. A Christian whose faith radicalized him, Kester's work at a church for miners in the coalfields of West Virginia led him further to the left and to the Fellowship of Reconciliation in New York. Kester wrote Carver in 1929 asking whether the professor thought it advisable for the Fellowship to open a Southern office for Kester's race relations work. Carver replied:

> The surprise to me is that this has not been done before now. The beating on the tail of the snake may stop his progress a little, but more vital parts must be struck before his poisonous, death dealing venom will be wiped out. Just so with the poisonous venom of prejudice and race hatred.[59]

By 1934 Kester found himself too radical for the Fellowship of Reconciliation and joined the Committee for Racial and Economic

Justice headed by Reinhold Niebuhr. Explaining his dismissal from the Fellowship to Carver, Kester wrote:

> I am convinced that love, education, good will, moral suasion, et cetera et cetera are not enough. Something more rigorous and dynamic will be required to turn this hellish earth of ours into a fit habitation for man than these things. The force of circumstances have steadily driven me toward the left, politically and otherwise. The recent events in Germany and Austria, the breakdown of the NRA, the brutalities of white America, the stupidity of capitalistic America make of me a revolutionary socialist. There can be no peace, no security, no freedom from proverty, want, misery, disease, death as long as one group however small live on the sweat of other men's brows . . . [and] play the disinherited white and Negroes off against each other. When southern whites and southern Negroes realize that their interests are identical, that their struggle is not a racial one but a class affair then will there come a change. There is but one great struggle, that of the disinherited against the present possessors of the earth, the rich.[60]

The "good old-fashioned Southern Negro" did not appear shocked at such words. Rather than trying to dissuade Kester, Carver sent a check to the Committee to support Kester's work. As it turned out, it was the young radical and not the old professor who was to be shocked. During one of Kester's visits with Carver, the professor posited that communism was the coming religion of the world because it preached brotherhood. Kester, who was more knowledgeable about actual conditions in Russia, was horrified. In his work Kester had also met and been repelled by American Communist party leader Earl Browder, whose "duplicity and disregard for morality and ethics" had made Kester an early foe of American Communism. Gently Kester explained the Stalinist system to the naive Carver and later remarked, "I never heard him mention the matter again."[61]

Carver was never a card-carrying Communist, or a Socialist, Democrat, or Republican. He was a dreamer with a vision of a better world and a very dim grasp of political and economic reality. In response to a request from an American Legion post, Carver clearly set forth his dream for his country, describing the ideal

American as "any individual who has all the rights and privileges accorded every other American citizen, who loves freedom, hates oppression, and to the best of his knowledge and ability lives the 'Golden Rule' way of life."[62] It required little political awareness to realize that the United States fell short of this ideal.

Carver had no secret, or for that matter open, political life. He never tried to conceal his cooperation with the Soviets or his friendships with radicals. Yet the myth-makers did their work so effectively that in the McCarthy era Carver was used as a symbol by a group attempting "to offset the hatred engendered by [Paul] Robeson-type propaganda." The group planned a show featuring a movie biography of Carver that, as headlines noted, stressed "His Hatred of Commies," to be followed by live appearances of such stars as Jimmy Durante and Tallulah Bankhead.[63]

Not only did Carver have no desire to be a politician, but he did not want to be a black activist or leader any more than he wanted to be a black scientist. He merely desired to be a man, free to develop and use his talents. But this freedom was a luxury Carver's sense of responsibility would not allow him to accept. He left a secure position on the faculty at Iowa State to come South and share the fruits of his hard-earned education with his fellow blacks. If he failed to use effectively the influence his fame brought in the fight for black rights, there is no record that he ever gave any written or oral endorsement of segregation. To one group of whites who tried to convince Carver of the mutual benefit to be derived from his support of their racial policies, he merely replied, "Gentlemen, what you do speaks so loud, I can't hear what you say."[64] Unfortunately, many people were willing to ignore a lot of what Carver both said and did in order to fashion a symbol.

Labeling Carver an accommodationist was not the myth's fundamental fallacy; even Carver probably would not deny the label. The real error of the myth-makers was to expect anything more than divided loyalty from Carver. The same people who awarded him "honorary white" status supported cultural values and institutional structures that stressed the importance of skin color. How could they expect Carver not to remember at least occasionally that he was black, and to react accordingly?

Obviously the symbolic use of Carver's life and philosophy had significant but often paradoxical effects. His success both instilled black pride and soothed segregationist consciences, and also gave hope to those left out of the American dream while justifying the position of the successful. His accomplishments were magnified and the contradictions in the myth were ignored to serve a variety of causes. For the general public the Carver myth assumed more importance than the Carver reality. From historical hindsight the making of the Peanut Man might appear to have resulted from cynical exploitation by such diverse groups as the peanut industry, New South editors, religious advocates, and segregationists. Nevertheless, one fact remains—most of the people responsible for Carver's rise to fame did not consider him merely a symbol or a token black. They viewed him as a remarkable individual, and some loved him as a fellow human being.

Although strangers used Carver's life and work to support their causes, most of the professor's chief publicists were personal friends. On a one-to-one basis Carver the man was even more impressive than Carver the symbol. Few people met him and departed without becoming his disciples. His magic worked on men and women from all walks of life and all educational levels. The impact of his personality was a reality and helps to explain his fame, for most publicists did not exploit Carver; they believed in him.

Peanut industry leaders and spokesmen were the first to bring Carver national recognition. Letters from such men as M. M. Osburn of the *Peanut Journal* reveal a deep affection for the Peanut Man they helped to create. Among these men perhaps Carver's closest friend was Bob Barry of the Tom Huston Company. The grandson of a Confederate major, Barry declared that Carver proved "that the man within is greater than his skin." Barry turned to Carver for personal as well as professional help, noting, "You sure do have the knack of touching the spot that aches the most and helping to heal it." That ability led Barry to assert, "I think I will write [President] Roosevelt and ask him to make you Secretary of Inspiration."[65] Although he frequently came to Tuskegee to visit, Barry wrote that he did not see the professor often enough.

> Some of these days I am going to kidnap you and take you off in the woods where I can talk to you for about a week. . . . I talk to my wife about you quite a bit. She says I must like you better than anyone else. My reply to her is that I at least like my wife and baby better. So you see I am really getting a pretty bad case of "Carveritis" and find that it is a very enjoyable disease.[66]

Carver similarly infected a number of the newspapermen who helped to make him a symbol for the New South. He had friends on numerous Southern papers, but was especially close to Alabama editors and reporters in Tuskegee, Montgomery, Roanoke, and Birmingham. His friendship with Grover Hall of the Montgomery *Advertiser* is a good example of this kind of relationship. It began in 1928, when the professor wrote to congratulate Hall for receiving a Pulitzer Prize. Hall had never met Carver but expressed his delight that "many colored friends" had been "good enough to write." Soon afterwards, the editor came to Tuskegee, a practice he repeated often until his death in 1941. His letters to Carver reveal a warm friendship; in 1939 he wrote, "Glad you are still batting 'em out. You'll live 1000 years yet, unless you turn playboy and cut-up."[67]

No group was more profoundly affected by Carver than interracial and religious workers. Dozens of his "adopted children" from his CIC and YMCA work echoed the sentiment expressed by one who wrote, "I felt as if I were a dear possession of his while I was with [Carver] and it made me very happy—it inspired me on." For them Carver was not a token black. They shared with him their personal tragedies and joys, kidded him unmercifully, invited him to their homes, exchanged gifts with him, named their children for him, and drew strength from his love. None was more inspired than Howard Kester, who built his life on the vision they shared. As he confronted the realities of the world, the dream ex-

pressed in the charter of the George Washington Carver Fellowship moved him to accept the need for more radical solutions to
the evils of racism and poverty. At each step of his radicalization
he turned to Carver for advice and support. Through his work with
such groups as the American Civil Liberties Union, the NAACP,
the Socialist Party, the Southern Tenant Farmers' Union, and the
Fellowship of Southern Churchmen, Kester spread their shared
vision, touching dozens of lives in the same way Carver had
touched his. All the time he reaffirmed to Carver what he had
declared in 1924: "You will never, never know just what your
friendship means to me. I do not have the words to tell you all
that I feel and I often feel that words simply could not convey to
you my simple message of love."[68]

Such sentiments were also expressed by religious workers who
became Carver's personal friends. Shared religion is a powerful
bond; Carver's religious relationships were among his most intense. Some produced a genuine feeling of spiritual oneness, such
as his friendship with Glenn Clark, a literature professor at Mac-
alester College in Minnesota. The two men had a lot in common.
They were both laymen who believed in interdenominational
movements. Clark wrote and published more than a dozen religious pamphlets, spoke to church and student groups, and organized interdenominational meetings. His friendship with Carver
began in 1928 when he met Jim Hardwick at Iowa State College.
Carver's "oldest Blue Ridge boy" urged Clark to write the Tuskegean. For the next seven years Clark and Carver corresponded
and set times to pray together without ever meeting.[69] Finally in
1935 Clark came to Tuskegee and prayed with Carver in person.
Clark later claimed that he had prayed with many religious leaders,

but never have I experienced more dynamic praying than I experienced that day. He, a black man from the deep South, I, a white
man from the far North, he loving and taking into his great heart
all of the South, white as well as black, and giving them to the
Father; I, loving and taking into my heart the entire North, black
as well as white and giving them to the Father; he, approaching

God from the realm of nature and science, I, from the realm of literature and the arts; neither of us a priest, preacher or rabbi, mere lay brethren; and yet there was a power in our prayer that day that has gone with me ever since.[70]

They continued to pray together across the miles that separated them, claiming a spiritual communion that allowed them to communicate telepathically. Clark sought to bring others into this communion, forming a group called the "Minute Men of the Spirit." He also arranged for Carver to participate in two interdenominational meetings called "Crusades for Christ" in Minneapolis. There Carver shared the platform with Protestant and Catholic ministers, bishops, and deans of theology schools. These meetings and the printing of two hundred thousand copies of the pamphlet Clark wrote about Carver, *The Man Who Talks With The Flowers*, greatly spurred Carver's symbolic adoption by religious groups. However, to Clark the professor was a friend, not a symbol.[71]

Many of the black leaders and writers who publicized Carver's work also considered him a personal friend. After a visit to Tuskegee, Walter White of the NAACP wrote, "I cannot remember any experience in all my life which made me so happy nor inspired me so much." A signed picture of Carver hung in his New York office.[72] Roland Hayes, a world-renowned black tenor, spent several days with Carver and told him:

I cannot begin to say in words just how and in what ways the working of your spirit moves me. Every fibre of my being vibrates with appreciation of your efforts, and I do crave the possibility of more constant contact with you because I need the help, the benefit which your greater wisdom can give me in the work that I am called to do.[73]

Other blacks whose letters reflected a personal relationship with Carver included Claude Barnett, the founder of the Associated Negro Press; Carter G. Woodson, founder of the *Journal of Negro History;* and several black newspaper editors.

Carver's friendships with peanut industry leaders, New South editors, interracial workers, religious spokesmen, and black leaders were instrumental in his rise to fame. Another category of reported friendships—those with famous people—also brought increased publicity, but most of these were spurious. Carver's name was linked with such individuals as Edison, Gandhi, and Franklin D. Roosevelt in ways that implied more intimate relationships than actually existed. Only two of these widely publicized friendships were genuine—those with Henry A. Wallace and Henry Ford. Ford's interest in the chemurgic movement drew him to Carver, and after they finally met at the Dearborn conference they corresponded and visited each other regularly. They shared eccentric genius and an enormous mutual respect. Because of Ford's policy of hiring blacks for both skilled and unskilled jobs in his automobile plants, Carver, like many other blacks, supported the company's sometimes bloody battle against unionization. For his part, Ford promoted the image of Carver as a great scientist in interviews, through his various tributes to the professor, and through the pictures of the two men that frequently appeared in newspapers.[74]

Not all of Carver's friendships were with people who could publicize his work. The lives of dozens of Tuskegee students were profoundly influenced by their relationships with the professor. Although his contact with students diminished after he left the classroom in the 1920s, as late as 1940 one parent expressed her gratitude to Carver for his influence on her son. "I note a great change in him," she wrote. "He seems to be more settle minded now. I believe that he really wants to do something and be a credit to his race." For some students their relationship with Carver became the central focus of their lives. Clarence Hart called him "Dad" and refused an Ohio job offer because, as he wrote, "I want to be as near you as I possibly can." John Sutton felt so close to Carver that he believed the professor communicated with him telepathically while he was in Russia, giving him the solution to a difficult research problem. Hundreds of letters from other students support Washington's assertion that Carver was an "inspirer of young men."[75]

Dozens of Alabama whites also believed themselves to be spe-

Carver and Henry Ford

cial friends of Carver. To many, the professor was an exception to their assertions of white supremacy; they awarded him "honorary white" status. A good example was W. W. Thompson, who served as both sheriff and mayor in Tuskegee. During the Veterans' Hospital confrontation he wrote President Harding of his support for keeping the hospital under white management, declaring that the "negro who preaches social equality is the worst enemy to his race." However, almost twenty years later he offered to build Carver a retirement cottage next to his own on his Florida plantation.[76]

Other Alabama whites had their racial beliefs greatly altered by their contacts with Carver. One of these was Lyman Ward, the founder and principal of an industrial institute for whites in Camp Hill. His relationship with Carver spanned many years, and their shared interests were numerous. In 1921 Carver supplied him with materials for a peanut and sweet potato banquet.[77] Over the years Ward became a champion of the appointment of black principals to black schools financed by Northern philanthropists. His lack of success in this area made him very cynical about Northern supporters of the "black cause," as he indicated in a letter to Carver.

> I am not in any manner of means to be understood as thinking that the position of the Negro in the South is ideal. It is very far from it and the injustice worked upon the Negro here in the South often makes me sad beyond words. However, I feel that in the North the Negro is more or less the toy of his white friends.[78]

Carver and Ward's professions and educational backgrounds were similar. Therefore Carver's friendship with G. C. Blanks was perhaps more significant. Blanks was a small farmer from Notasulga of the type usually described as "red-neck." After Carver discovered potentially valuable clays on Blanks's land, however, the two became friends who shared more than an interest in exploiting the clay. Carver was close to the entire family, and when Blanks's son died he composed a poem of sympathy. Their friendship even caused Blanks to take a rather dangerous stand on segregation. He and Carver boarded a bus and sat together in the back. When the driver informed Blanks that he would have to move, the "red-neck" stormed off the bus, stating that he would rather walk than ride with a bigot.[79]

No summary of Carver's impact on individuals can do justice to the subject. His friendships with men and women of all colors and professions number in the hundreds. The roster of those who felt "especially close" to him would fill pages and include judges, congressmen, editors, and educators, as well as ordinary people such as Blanks. Carver's influence upon them is both intangible and significant, but his legacy of love remains one reality among the myths.

Blazing the Trail

In many ways 1938 marked a turning point in Carver's life and career. Increasing publicity made him one of the world's best-known living scientists, but worsening health led to frequent hospitalization, realizations of mortality, and an effort to reevaluate his own work. His research was limited by his poor health, and he gradually changed the focus of his interest, returning to some extent to the vision of his earlier years at Tuskegee. He also became concerned that the true significance of his work would be lost when he died. Realizing that his own career would end soon, Carver believed he still had a final, special mission—to serve as an inspiration to others. In interviews he often reiterated a 1938 description of his work. "I am not a finisher," he said. "I am a blazer of trails. Little of my work is in books. Others must take up the various trails of truth, and carry them on."[1]

After Carver became famous, exaggerated claims for his scientific achievements were made. Except for his farmers' bulletins and mycological articles, none of his work was published, and specific inquiries about his processes placed him in an embarrassing position. During the last five years, he answered these questions with restatements of his original goals.

Nothing has been issued of a very technical nature as my work is that of keeping every operation down so that the farmer and the man fartherest down can get hold of it. I do not deal very much in extreme technical processes as it takes it out of and away from the thing that will help the farmer unless it can be simplified so that he can use it.[2]

The lack of written records and Carver's failing health made him realize that special provisions had to be made immediately to preserve his work visually. He knew that without adequate funding, few blacks would be able to follow the trails he blazed. These realizations caused him to devote the largest portion of his declining years to establishing the George Washington Carver Foundation and Museum.

One of the most amazing facets of Carver's last five years was that he lived that long. He had battled recurring illness all of his life. Beginning in 1938 it appeared he would lose that battle, and his imminent death was prophesied by his doctors and friends on numerous occasions. Every time but the last he surprised everyone by not only living, but getting out of bed and resuming his work. It seems he refused to die until he was sure that his vision would be preserved.

Early in 1938 Carver began to complain of decreasing strength and proclaimed, "Physically I have been in much worse condition than most people realize." In May his doctor decided to hospitalize him for an indefinite period of rest. While in the hospital, he was found to be suffering from pernicious anemia, a serious ailment which few had survived. Carver's doctors, however, began treating him immediately with injections of liver extract rich in vitamin B_{12}. This relatively new treatment program helped to keep him alive to finish his work, but by the time the injections were started his strength had so declined that recovery was very slow.[3]

At the beginning of the next year Carver wrote, "I have been in the hospital since last May and was not expected by either the doctors or the public to come out alive." In fact he had been allowed to leave the hospital for brief periods, and in the fall had begun to live and take his meals at Dorothy Hall, the Institute's guest house, which was next door to the building in which the Carver Museum was being installed. Nevertheless, he remained under the constant care of his physicians and returned to the hospital whenever he appeared to be weakening. He tried to prove his strength by walking a mile into town, but such excursions usually sent him to bed for several days.[4]

In 1939 Carver resumed many of his activities, although he continued to receive injections and medication. This led to another major breakdown in the late fall. When he returned from a trip to New York and Michigan, he was so weakened that he remained in bed or in a wheelchair for several weeks. By February 1940 the crisis passed and he began to walk a little, a feat his doctor had never expected. He still had to receive the injections, which he found "very disagreeable." His comfort was further impaired when all his teeth were removed, for he never really adjusted to his dentures.[5]

Over the next two years Carver refused to succumb to numerous bouts of influenza and "indigestion" and remained active, even resuming shortened office hours. His physical condition was closely monitored by his doctor, by Austin Curtis, and by Carver's secretary, Jessie Abbott. Much of Carver's routine mail was handled by Curtis and Abbott, who usually rejected the numerous invitations and requests because of Carver's health. Close friends, however, were reassured that the professor was "feeling very well indeed." As Abbott noted in 1941:

> Dr. Carver has beaten up all the boys including Mr. Curtis and even Rev. Richardson. Every morning he calls himself having wash day and works on all of them as they come in. Don't you tell him I told you about how he whips the folks. In fact I'm glad that I am a lady.[6]

Despite his bursts of energy, Carver remained weak and frail. His appetite was erratic, and the foods he wanted were usually not the ones recommended by his doctors. Friends from all over the country responded to his requests for various foods. The administration at Tuskegee endeavored to meet his health and dietary needs by arranging for the preparation of special foods whenever he wanted them, but he still continued to complain frequently about the quality of his meals.[7]

Both Institute officials and personal friends sought to make Carver healthy and happy. Not surprisingly, the most dramatic gesture came from Henry Ford, who paid for the installation of an elevator in Dorothy Hall. Many individuals, especially Tuskegee's President Patterson, displayed their concern and affection. Some of the newer faculty, however, were skeptical about whether Carver deserved all the special attention. To them he appeared to be only a doddering, cranky old man. Because some faculty members and students openly ridiculed him, Carver remained convinced that he was not adequately appreciated at home. Charges made after his death that he catered to whites and ignored blacks were largely the result of his withdrawal from campus life in his last years.[8]

Carver also believed that Institute officials exploited his fame to raise funds without providing adequate support for his work. He grew tired of always "being on display" and complained to Patterson that "all want to see the 'public curiousity.' Some want to see whether he wears a dress or pants, some want to see how feeble he is, others want to see what complexion he is and whether he is black or white." Mail as well as visitors continued to flood Carver's office. Sometimes a deluge resulted from his announcement of new research, but often the inquiries concerned older work, such as sweet potato rubber, which continued to be reported by the press. After such newspaper reports, requests for more information filled his mailbox; to such queries he replied that he had moved into new fields of research that prevented his reinvestigation of earlier work.[9]

Actually Carver had little time or strength for new research after 1937. He showed brief interest in dyes, stock feed, and medicine from osage oranges, but only two new projects absorbed substantial amounts of his time. Both concerned the astringent and medical properties of persimmons. Perhaps because of the discomfort he suffered from his own dentures, in about 1938 he developed a persimmon extract for oral hygiene. Working with a Tuskegee dentist, he tested it on people with pyorrhea, and in April 1941 reports of the new drug, "still in the experimental stage," appeared in numerous newspapers. Again Carver was swamped with letters from "suffering humanity" and composed a form reply that referred all inquirers to his dentist collaborator, Dr. B. L. Jackson. Jackson presented the results of their work before a meeting of the National Dental Association, and that group of black dentists agreed to test the product and sent a $50 check to support the work. The extract was also mentioned in the July 1941 edition of *Dental Survey*, and Curtis explored the possibility of a patent. The initial success and interest led Carver to try the extract on athletes' foot, with mixed results. Soon, however, he lost interest in the product, and Curtis dropped his efforts to commercialize it, because other products were more promising.[10]

Most of Carver's other research, sometimes done in collaboration with Curtis, was devoted to expanding earlier projects. He revised his still unpublished botany text and greatly expanded his long-term efforts at cross-breeding amaryllis, lilies, and other flowers. He also continued his interest in uses for peanut hulls and investigated the possible use of peanuts in the treatment of pellagra. The conditions created by World War II brought renewed interest in some of Carver's previous research. As during World War I, wartime shortages made some of his prior work seem relevant, and the federal government sought information about various substitutes for such scarce products as rubber and fertilizer. In January 1942 Alabama senator Lister Hill asked Carver about the use of peanut oil in soap making as a replacement for Philippine coconut oil. Both men sought to interest the USDA in the idea, but discovered that peanut oil was too expensive and was more valuable as a substitute for French olive oil.[11]

The need for food conservation during the war, as well as the establishment of Ford's nutritional laboratory, rekindled Carver's interest in that area. In 1942 he distributed an article entitled "Food, What Is It? How Can It Win the War?" which listed appropriate Tuskegee bulletins on food preservation and preparation. That year he also issued Bulletin 43, *Nature's Garden for Victory and Peace*, which included illustrations of edible weeds with instructions for their preparation. Rackham Holt, who was writing a biography of Carver, used the bulletin for an article published by the *Saturday Evening Post* in June, giving it a wider audience. Thus in the last year of his life Carver returned to his earlier focus; his last leaflet, *Peanuts to Conserve Meat*, appeared a month after his death.[12]

In Carver's other two major research projects he collaborated with Curtis, and "Baby Carver" seems to have done most of the work. Both projects—fiber and paint research—were expansions of Carver's earlier projects for which Curtis was able to obtain outside funding. The fiber research investigated okra fiber and was financed by a private company but did not yield significant results. The paint project combined the two previous ideas of using clay and oil sludge to produce low-cost paint. Declaring that "we are attempting to find means whereby we can make the living conditions of the small wage earners better and more satisfying," Curtis received a grant from the Tennessee Valley Authority and hired a research assistant. The paint that was produced was used on Institute buildings and tested by the Army Corps of Engineers and the Farm Security Administration, and leaflets giving directions were printed and distributed. But when Curtis, soon after Carver's death, began negotiating for its commercial development, his efforts met with no success.[13]

Obtaining funding for these and other projects was facilitated by the establishment of the George Washington Carver Foundation. For many years Carver had dreamed of building some kind of "creative research laboratory" at Tuskegee to continue his work. As early as 1930 he talked of the plans for such a project, but until Austin Curtis arrived little concrete action was taken. Curtis was endowed with the managerial and organizational skills that his mentor lacked, and using the interest generated by the fortieth anniversary celebration, he began drafting proposals for the establishment of a laboratory. Finally in July 1937 a flyer soliciting contributions was distributed. Carver was certain that the laboratory would soon be a reality and devised a tentative schedule for its development and perpetuation in September. Nevertheless, only enough money was raised to build a greenhouse. The next year, however, Tuskegee Institute donated an old laundry building to house both a museum and laboratory. The funding for research remained dismally low, so during 1939 Carver considered incorporating a foundation based upon his life's savings. In early 1940 he had R. H. Powell, a white Tuskegee attorney, draft a certificate of incorporation for the foundation, a document transferring $32,-374.19 of Carver's government bonds and other assets to the foundation, and a will giving the rest of his estate to it.[14]

The certificate of incorporation was registered under the laws of Alabama on 10 February 1940. Carver's donation received wide coverage in United States newspapers and provided the impetus for a new fundraising campaign. With the establishment of the foundation Carver also began to hoard his assets even more than he had previously, so that by his death his estate was large enough to bring his total contribution to nearly $60,000.[15]

The size of his contribution raises questions about the sources of his income, since his salary averaged only about $1,000 for his forty-seven years at Tuskegee. The answer seems to be thrift and capitalism. In 1898 Carver deposited $295.43 in the Valley Savings Bank of Des Moines, Iowa. By 1911 he had deposited a total of about $2,500 which accumulated almost $7,000 in interest by 1940. Similar accounts existed at two Tuskegee banks which failed in 1931. When they collapsed, Carver's deposits of $2,344.29 and $31,290.51 were frozen, like those of other depositors, and he declared the failures "left me flat as a pancake." Nevertheless he appears to have recovered most of the money by 1940. After the failures he transferred most of his business to the Tuskegee Institute Savings Bank, the Valley Savings Bank, and United States savings bonds. In 1940 the bonds alone were worth $22,300. The bank failures also created an interesting side effect. To satisfy part of his claims in 1934, the Macon County Bank deeded over to him 120 acres of land that was being sharecropped. Thus Carver became a landlord, until he sold the land to the cropper in 1938.[16]

Although the accumulation of $60,000 from approximately $47,000 of salary might seem to indicate outside income or shrewd money management, neither is supported by the facts. No evidence disproves Carver's claim that he did not accept money for his consultation and lecture services. He occasionally received small honoraria and donations, but such funds seem to have gone to support the experiment station before 1940 and to the foundation afterwards. The bulk of his gift and estate appears to have come from interest earned on his savings, which was paid by banks and by individuals to whom he lent money.

Carver's one skill in financial management seems to have been not spending money on himself. His financial records were chaotic, and he often forgot to deposit checks and to return certificates of deposit for renewal. For example, when the Tuskegee banks failed, Carver was holding six monthly salary checks, drawn against one of them, which took him several years to recover. He would have lost quite a bit of interest as well if R. A. Crawford at Valley Savings had not personally seen to it that Carver returned his certificates for renewal and was not penalized for late returns. Later, R. H. Powell handled most of the professor's financial affairs and often had to request that he deposit checks.[17]

Carver's personal expenses were small because the Institute provided his room and board, although in the 1930s charges for both were deducted from his pay. His clothing was worn until it was fit only to make into rag rugs and then was often replaced by gifts. Surviving bank statements indicate that the only money he spent on himself was for medical and dental services. His frugality did not extend to his donations, however. Tax deductible contributions usually amounted to between 10 and 20 percent of his total income and did not include the numerous gifts he gave to individuals.[18]

As plans for the Carver Foundation materialized, he began to watch his money more carefully and decreased his contributions to other charities. He also requested donations for services and charged for pictures of himself. More significantly, he returned to the idea of marketing his products to finance the foundation.[19]

Soon after Curtis arrived in Tuskegee he began to explore the possibilities of commercially developing Carver's products, and in 1939 he opened a company to make peanut massage oil and a hair preparation. Early that same year several white men of Tuskegee, including C. M. Haygood, a minister, and R. H. Powell, Carver's attorney, started a small company to produce Peano-Oil, a hair preparation. A few months later a second product, Miracle Massage Oil, was added. Carver gave his blessings to both enterprises but remained aloof until Powell suggested that in return for the professor's help, the company would establish a scholarship in his honor to be financed by 2 percent of the gross sales. Haygood also proposed that the company make a "liberal voluntary contribution to the Carver Foundation" when revenues could justify it.[20]

Haygood was one of Carver's "Blue Ridge boys," and his vision for the company was compatible with the professor's. Therefore, although Carver had been reluctant to have his name attached to any product after the failure of the Carver Products Company, he allowed Haygood to rename his enterprise the Carvoline Company and became more actively involved with it. Eventually he signed a contract with the company agreeing to serve as an unofficial adviser and allowing the claim that "Carvoline Products are tested and approved in the Laboratories of Dr. George Washington Carver"; in return, the foundation received 2 percent of gross sales. Nevertheless, Carver answered all inquiries by asserting that he was "not in any way connected" with the company, and the contract never produced large revenues for the foundation. Only a few checks of about $35 were received before Carver's death, and the company did not long survive him.[21]

More money was received through various fundraising projects, such as selling Carver calendars and keys. Individual contributions were numerous but small; the largest appears to have been $1,500 bequeathed by a black physician who had never met Carver. Without Carver's personal contribution and the donation of the building by the Institute, the foundation could never have been established. Even those gifts provided only a modest beginning.[22]

The foundation was to serve two purposes: the continuation and the preservation of Carver's work. The old laundry building had to be structurally modified in 1938 to meet these needs. The basement housed a laboratory, offices, and storage space. The laboratory itself was very simple, with most of the apparatus from Carver's old facility. The only requested additions were two sinks and gas outlets. It was hardly an auspicious beginning, but Carver believed that it could be expanded later. Even after his 1940 donation, he did not seem overly concerned about laboratory facilities. Perhaps his own experience led him to believe that creative imagination was more important than sophisticated equipment. Most of the money for continuing his work was allotted for research fellowships to young men of vision, enabling them to follow his trails.[23]

From the start Carver seems to have been most concerned with preserving his work as an inspiration to others. His increasing sense of mortality made him anxious to get his work installed and arranged in a manner that would allow others to catch his vision. Curtis or someone else could continue and expand the research work of the foundation without Carver, but the museum was another matter. Without his personal supervision, Carver was afraid it would become "just a large, heterogeneous collection of 'STUFF' without any special significance attached to it."[24]

As Carver envisioned it, the museum would display all phases of his life's work, not as the diverse achievements of a multitalented man, but as parts of a coherent whole. From 1938 to the fall of 1941 most of his strength was devoted to the project. Plagued by the fear that his time was running out, he was frustrated by delays and lack of funds. The major problems were the lack of display cases and a leaky roof. Although he was convinced that many Institute people wanted to see the museum "killed in the borning," he persevered and compromised some of his original plans so that the museum could be opened on 25 July 1939 in conjunction with the unveiling of two of Carver's paintings. He mailed out hundreds of invitations, and two thousand people attended.[25]

This public enthusiasm inspired Carver, making him eager to expand the museum. More display cases were needed to house the results of his research, but he was especially concerned about the lack of hanging space for his paintings. The unveiling brought new public awareness of Carver's artistic talents, yet for him painting had always retained the fascination of a first love. He only reluctantly relinquished the idea of a full-time art career when he left Simpson College. The selection of his painting to represent Iowa at the Chicago exposition in 1893 encouraged that dream, and years after he came to Tuskegee he still hoped to return eventually to his first love, which he viewed as a way to lift "souls beyond the sordid things of life, and give them a glimpse of the creator who shapes and fashions all our destinations." During his early years at Tuskegee Carver frequently exhibited his paintings and considered sending one to the Paris Exposition of 1899. Later he claimed that a Luxembourg museum had requested his study of peaches and that individuals had sought to purchase various paintings. He always refused to break up his collection because, he declared, "You wouldn't take one bar of music out of a symphony . . . and send it away somewhere."[26]

His desire to have the entire collection displayed together was one reason for the establishment of the foundation. The delays in making the necessary structural changes to the building perturbed Carver, and he once threatened to give the collection to the state Department of Archives and History in Montgomery. His plaints finally brought action, and the art rooms of the Carver Museum were opened on 17 November 1941, during National Art Week. The event was well attended; one participant noted that "for almost two hours there was a steady stream of persons passing through the building."[27] One reporter was intrigued with the diversity of the audience.

It was a democratic crowd. There were ladies in furs, student chefs in tall white cooks caps; carpenters, with hammer heads sticking from the long pockets of their brown coveralls; student architects with rolls of drawings; white school children and grownups; farm boys in blue overalls, nurses in uniform, a washerwoman, a dressmaker, the wife of a state senator, a telephone operator, a cotton warehouseman; colored people and white people.[28]

The seventy-one pictures on display included twenty-seven works completed at Simpson, as well as many done with paints made from Alabama clays, vegetables, and magnolia seeds. The subjects were mainly flowers, fruits, and landscapes, often in simple handmade frames. One was bordered by a "frame containing more than one thousand pieces of wood, artistically whittled and woven together without nails, glue or string."[29] The paintings constituted only a part of the exhibit, as a reporter from *Time* noted.

Visitors, impressed by the simple realism and tidy workmanship of the pictures, found still more to admire in the adjoining collection of handicrafts (embroideries on burlap, ornaments made of chicken feathers, seed and colored peanut necklaces, woven textiles) which the almost incredibly versatile Carver had turned out between scientific experiments and painting.[30]

In addition to the paintings and handicrafts, the museum also housed displays representing Carver's other work. Some featured his well-known research, with products from peanuts, sweet potatoes, clays, cotton, and plant fibers. Others contained products made from such waste materials as wood shavings, rags, peanut shells, and chicken feathers. Several were educational exhibits, including animals and birds stuffed by Carver, a display of preserved fruits and vegetables, framed samples of wild vegetables with recipes, and cases for the study of plant diseases and injurious insects.[31]

The diversity of the exhibits was a testimony to Carver's wide-ranging interests and talents, but he was dismayed by the many viewers who did not look beyond the diversity to glimpse the unity of the vision he hoped to preserve. He asserted that only B. B. Walcott's article about the exhibit opening had "caught the vision." Her account closed with a description of a conversation between Carver and a museum visitor.

"How have you been able to do so many different things?" Carver was asked. . . .

"Would it surprise you," he replied gently, "if I say that I have not been doing many DIFFERENT things?"

He reached across the table for a tiny green herb. The soil still clung to its threadlike roots.

"All these years," the artist continued, looking at the weed in his hand, "I have been doing one thing. The poet Tennyson was working at the same job. This is the way he expresses it:

> 'Flower in the crannied wall
> I pluck you out of the crannies,
> I hold you here, root and all, in my hand,
> Little flower—but if I could understand
> What you are, root and all, and all in all,
> I should know what God and man is'

"Tennyson was seeking Truth. That is what the scientist is seeking. That is what the artist is seeking; his writings, his weaving, his music, his pictures are just the expressions of his soul in his search for Truth.

"My paintings are my soul's expression of its yearnings and questions in its desire to understand the work of the Great Creator." [32]

With the establishment of the George Washington Carver Foundation and the opening of the completed museum in the fall of 1941, Carver's last important work was finished.

A little over a year later he was dead. He returned from Dearborn in late 1942 in an alarmingly weakened condition, although he insisted he was "getting along fine." He stubbornly continued to come to his office and take care of his mail, even refusing assistance in getting from his room to the museum. In December he fell while trying to open the museum door. For several days he still resisted curtailing his activities, but on 19 December he admitted that "the awful tragedy of my falling has thoroughly upset me as I remain sore from head to foot yet." A little more than two weeks later, at 7:30 p.m. on 5 January 1943, Carver lost the battle with his failing body. Not expected to survive infancy, he had drawn on an incredible reservoir of will, courage, and faith for almost eighty years. [33]

Carver's entrance into life had been unheralded and unrecorded; his exit was announced in newspaper headlines around the world. Tuskegee Institute was flooded with telegrams and letters

Carver knitting in his last years

of grief and sympathy from heads of state, schoolchildren, international celebrities, domestic servants, scientists, and sharecroppers. For his funeral the Institute chapel overflowed "with people of all races and from all walks of life." Afterwards he was buried near Booker T. Washington at Tuskegee. Forty-seven years after Carver's arrival in Black Belt Alabama, his temporary mission field became his permanent resting place.[34]

Very little in Carver's life had happened as he wanted or expected. Contradiction and paradox marked his entire existence. On the surface he was a simple man, a kindly wizard who eschewed wealth and power for a life of service, working for over forty years with the same materials, at the same place, seeking the same goals, even wearing the same clothes. His experiences and emotions were far from simple, however. He experienced public adulation and discrimination, recognition and racism. He felt arrogance and humility, gratitude and bitterness. The central cause of the contradiction and complexity was a duality forced upon him by his genius and his color. The competition for dominance by these two facets of his existence dominated both his response to the world and the world's response to him.

In Diamond his white neighbors were both awed by his talents and repulsed by his color. They expressed respect for his genius, but refused to let him in their school. Obviously gifted and eager to learn, Carver spent thirty years wandering through three states to obtain a basic education. In Iowa his abilities opened new doors of opportunity. Tangible recognition of his talents in art, hybridization, and mycology offered tempting career choices. Had he been white, Carver's only dilemma would have been deciding which of these interests to pursue. Once again, however, his color intruded upon the natural course of his genius. A sense of racial responsibility, nourished by a belief that his talents were divinely given for a special purpose, led him to abandon fields to which his mind lured him.

Keenly aware of his sacrifice, Carver left an environment of white acceptance to come to Tuskegee, only to be met with resentment and skepticism by his "own people." For twenty years he dedicated his talents to enriching the lives of poor blacks and was rewarded by the humiliation of being stripped of his authority over Tuskegee's agricultural school. Succumbing to the temptation to give the public what it wanted, he finally found fame in the role of "creative chemist." His least useful work became his most recognized.

With renown came symbolic adoption by diverse groups whose goals were often contradictory with each others' and Carver's own aims. The white society that caused his genius and color to be in conflict also distorted the significance of his life by placing more emphasis on his color than his talents. Perhaps the greatest paradox was that Carver became famous as a scientist because he was black, even though his blackness diverted him from becoming a real scientist. If he had been white, he probably would have made significant contributions in mycology or hybridization and died in obscurity. Because he was black, he died famous, without making any significant scientific advances.

Since Carver's fame was based more upon what he did not do than what he actually did, evaluation of his accomplishments is difficult. Exaggerated claims for his "cookstove chemistry" and his role in remaking the South have mixed mythology with reality. These claims led his contemporaries to view him as either a charlatan or saint, a debate that has continued since his death. Any fair assessment must recognize that his legacy is mixed and not confined to the realm of specific scientific achievements. It must include his scientific work, his symbolic roles, his philosophy and values, and his impact on individuals.

On the surface, it is fairly simple to evaluate Carver's scientific contributions. He made no outstanding breakthroughs in scientific theory. Few do. Even in applied science, none of his ideas or inventions were revolutionary in the manner of Ford's mass production of automobiles. Indeed, none of his processes led directly to commercially successful products. In addition, he woefully neglected the scientific spirit. He kept no detailed records so that others could build upon his work and usually refused to share his processes even verbally. From hindsight, any claims that he was a scientist at all seem specious.

Even during Carver's lifetime some scientists questioned the legitimacy of his reputation as a chemist, but their voices were muted by the din of public support for the professor. Others, such as Henry A. Wallace, only timidly refused to endorse his work. This reluctance to dispute the value of Carver's work continued after his death. For example, in the 1960s the National Park Service commissioned a study of his scientific contributions but refused to publish the basically negative report prepared by a team of scientists from the University of Missouri. By the 1970s, however, criticism of Carver began to emerge, and historian Louis Harlan noted in 1972, "Scholars have often deplored his exaltation as the kind of black scientist white people expected, a kindly, pious man who puttered about unscientifically, while others such as Ernest Just of Howard were ignored."[35]

It is clear that Carver's chemistry did not measure up to modern standards of research and that his products did not become commercially successful. What is questionable is the appropriateness of these yardsticks to evaluate his work. Such yardsticks are based upon the Carver myth, not the reality. He was not a research chemist by training or persuasion. His original goals were not to produce marketable goods through advanced technology or to foster large-scale agriculture. At the core of his "cookstove chemistry" was the hope of providing the means for poor Southerners to enrich their lives through the use of what was available, not what was commercially superior.

Certainly Carver contributed to the erroneous interpretation of his work because of his deep need for recognition. The appeal of "cookstove chemistry" was limited in an age that worshipped the machine. Small-scale, simple technology that could be practiced by a black sharecropper was overshadowed by the lure of mass-production technology. When Carver tried to tailor his work to the spirit of the age, he failed miserably. The appearance of success was the most fallacious of the Carver myths.

An evaluation of the true significance of his research is best reserved for the discussion of his philosophy and values. Nevertheless, some observations about his scientific contributions are appropriate. First, Carver had the ability to engage in significant scientific work in the fields of mycology and hybridization, but his color diverted him from those fields. Second, he served the cause of science magnificently as an interpreter and humanizer, providing an essential link between researchers and laymen and enabling many to reap the benefits of others' work by helping them apply it to their own circumstances. Evidence that such help materially aided individuals and companies is found in the testimony of the recipients, such as the Tom Huston Company. Finally, perhaps his greatest contribution to science was the establishment of the Carver Foundation, which has grown from the small seed he planted into a research facility of significance.

The specific fruits of Carver's scientific work are meager in comparison to the myths. Was the mythology really detrimental and "deplorable," however? Carver's symbolic legacy is as contradictory and complex as the man himself. During his lifetime parts of his life story were appropriated by different groups to support conflicting goals. Some were beneficial to blacks; others were detrimental. Any attempt to assess his net impact must be subjective, for a greater frequency of one kind of symbolic usage does not necessarily mean that it had a greater impact. Nevertheless, extensive reading of Carver materials leads to the conclusion that most references were at least intended to be beneficial to blacks. The overwhelmingly predominant message of Carver's contemporary publicists was one of black achievement, regardless of the writer's motives.

The use of Carver as a symbol of black ability has continued since his death. Indeed, some of the most significant tributes occurred after 1943. His birthplace has been made a national monument. A postage stamp has commemorated his work. He has been inducted into the National Hall of Fame. His name has been attached to a naval vessel and to dozens of public buildings, and his life story has been told and retold in dozens of biographies. The net result has been to make him one of the best-known, and least-understood, blacks who ever lived. Most Americans recognize his name, but few know why. If asked what Carver actually did, many can only reply that "he did something with peanuts."

The ambiguity results from the fact that Carver's fame rests upon myth, not reality. He is known for what he did not do, not for what he did. This phenomenon raises the obvious question of why he became famous. One scholar has implied that white society was primarily responsible because of the need for an appropriate racial symbol. "By lavishing praise on a token black," Barry Mackintosh wrote, "[whites] could deny or atone for prejudice against blacks as a class."[36] While this assessment is fundamentally true, it does not take in account the personal relationship between Carver and his major publicists. Their letters to the professor prove that he was no token black to them. His warm, magnetic personality and flair for the dramatic are major keys to a full understanding of his rise to fame.

Another question is whether someone else would have been a more appropriate and desirable symbol of black ability and success. Certainly others made more contributions in science. A more forceful spokesman for black rights would have provided a clearer and more accurate image of the aspirations of Afro-Americans. Carver's perceived humility tended to reinforce stereotypes. On the other hand, there is no evidence that his fame was responsible for the lack of recognition of Ernest Just or others. These scientists, like most of their white counterparts, would probably have remained unknown to the general public if Carver had never lived. His label as one of America's greatest chemists was erroneous. However, myths often serve useful purposes. The recognition of any black scientist by a white society that believed Afro-Americans could excel only in athletics and the arts was significant. Undoubtedly the Carver myth caused many whites to reconsider their prejudices and many blacks to enter scientific careers.

A final question is whether Carver deserves continued recognition after the myth is destroyed. For some, such as Mackintosh, the answer is no. Yet this is plausible only if the real Carver was nothing more than the mythology, an assertion that ignores the significance of his true vision, or philosophy, and his impact upon individuals.

One of the greatest ironies of Carver's fame as a chemist was not that he did not deserve it, but that it has prevented his adoption by the groups for which he could be a legitimate symbol. Those groups did not exist until after Carver's death, when mythology had obscured his original ideas and goals. Those ideas were not in tune with the temper of Carver's time, and few contemporaries grasped what he was really trying to say and do. In his waning years he seemed to recognize this and sought to rectify it through the museum. Fire destroyed most of the museum in 1947, and almost twenty years elapsed before his ideas would seem relevant. Even in the 1980s the legitimacy of his philosophy is denied, but a growing number of scholars are popularizing various elements of it.

What was Carver's message? On the surface it is both simple and obvious, but its implications are profound for the modern world. He believed that truth is a unity. Nothing exists in isolation. Everything is inextricably connected and ignoring that fact can have disastrous effects. Any action must be considered in light of its overall long-term consequences, not just its immediate benefits. He also asserted that nature produces no waste. In the natural world everything is a part of the whole. What is consumed is returned to the whole in another usable form. Waste, he declared, is man-made, because of the failure to understand the unity of the universe. Expressing his ideas in religious terms, he repeatedly proclaimed that the Creator has provided all that man needed and that shortages resulted from man's failure to utilize appropriately the bounty of nature and to work with the forces of the universe. Thus both waste and shortages occur when man ignores the whole and attempts to conquer, rather than utilize, natural forces. When man realizes the unity of all, his material and spiritual needs can be met. To Carver, true progress improves the quality of existence for everyone in the present generation and the generations to come. No permanent solution to man's needs can be found outside this context.

These ideas were not original; they are almost as old as man himself. Carver simply tried to apply them to the existing conditions of the South. Translating his ideas into practice, he urged the utilization of available and renewable resources. He was not against science or technology; he sought to make them serve the "man furtherest down" by showing how to enrich life with what was already there. His clay paints were not commercially superior, but they were available to all. Organic fertilization requires time and effort. Chemical fertilizers produce quicker and more dramatic results, but those results are temporary and consume nonrenewable resources. As for the sharecropper, chemical fertilizers also consumed his scarcest commodity—money; his time and effort were free. In the same manner, vegetable protein is less nutritionally complete than meat, but vegetable matter is the cheapest, most efficient source of protein and was available to the poorest black farmer.

Carver's ultimate goal was as important as his methods. He wanted to preserve the small family farm. No one could deny that most Southern farmers' lives were bleak and dreary in the late nineteenth century. Yet Carver saw science as a way to remedy that situation, not to eliminate the small farm. Undoubtedly, his love of nature caused him to believe in the potential superiority of rural life. His view of what enhanced the human experience, however, was woefully out of tune with the time in which he lived.

Twentieth-century technology was obliterating Carver's vision, to the cheers of the general public. Mass production made luxury goods necessities. Growth became synonymous with progress. Bigger was better and brought increased productivity in agriculture and industry. More and more could be produced by fewer and fewer people. After a temporary setback in the 1930s, growth accelerated in the war years and the postwar era. Larger gross national products brought higher standards of living, and increasing productivity created more leisure time. By 1970 technology had so increased man's capacities that the USDA could point with pride to the fact that less than 5 percent of Americans were producing more food than nearly 50 percent had produced at the turn of the century. Who could question that technology was creating a plentiful harvest? Of course, there were some who did not share the plenty—they were labeled "underdeveloped," and their salvation, it was said, lay in development.

Blessed by technologically increased wealth, the United States and other developed countries sought to transfer that technology to the rest of the world. The "green revolution" in agriculture was proclaimed the answer to hunger and poverty. Those who mourned the loss of the independent craftsman and family farmer were labeled hopelessly nostalgic and impractical. All problems would be solved by consolidation and increased production when the process was complete. The American success story would become the world's success story.

American agriculture based upon monoculture and machinery was exported to such underdeveloped areas as West Africa. The results, however, were disappointing. As in the United States, farmers were displaced and moved to the cities. In Africa there were no jobs waiting there, and nations that had fed themselves for centuries had to import food to feed the unemployed masses. Expectations were raised, but prices soared for oil and other resources needed to sustain growth. Social fragmentation accompanied age-old poverty.

Finally, some development experts began to realize what Carver had preached over a half century earlier: every action has to be considered within the whole context. Agricultural efficiency that displaces farmers can create problems as bad as the ones being solved. Native African farming techniques were based on centuries of experience with an environment very different from the United States and could not be ignored without negative consequences. Coining the term "appropriate technology," scientists now said that technology had to be adapted to existing circumstances and had to build upon available resources.

The failure of earlier development policies and the recognition of limited resources has led to a reevaluation of the entire American success story. When whole species became extinct and raw materials were being rapidly depleted, the ecology movement was born, and the philosophy of Carver became relevant. Like Carver, the ecologists were ridiculed, labeled Luddites, and branded impractical, idealistic dreamers. Solar energy and organic farming are not commercially feasible, they were told. Labor-intensive agriculture was called hopelessly outdated and noncompetitive. Nevertheless, in the 1970s more people began to accept what Carver tried to say—that only short-term success can come to any system that ignores the whole, that man cannot subvert and destroy the environment without destroying himself.

By reading history backward, it can be claimed that Carver's work to provide a permanent basis for small-scale agriculture was not only doomed to failure, but should have failed. Technology and consolidation have indeed brought a better life for most Americans. Nevertheless, the huge social costs of displaced populations might have been avoided if the massive funding for agricultural research had been directed to fulfilling Carver's goals. Because it did not happen does not mean that it could not have happened. To deny the validity of his vision is to assert that any economic system dependent upon oil is feasible on a widespread and permanent basis. Only an idealistic dreamer can make that assertion given the limited supply. Perhaps in the long run a smaller scale economy based on renewable resources reflects more realism.

More a naturalist than a scientist, Carver also highlighted the problems of specialization. Significant research is dependent on such specialization and cannot be too directly influenced by utilitarian considerations. Carver was not opposed to seeking truth for its own sake, for he believed that more knowledge of all aspects of the universe enables man to find his appropriate place within the unity. The world needs its pure scientists and research chemists, but it also needs its Carvers, who try, however imperfectly, to fit the pieces together to serve both man and his environment. Without them, short-term solutions will often create new problems that are different, but not necessarily easier.

Both Carver's research and vision failed to have much impact during his lifetime and were later distorted. The symbolic uses of his story have had positive and negative results. For many, however, the professor was not merely a scientist or symbol—he was a man. His transition from educator to creative chemist changed the focus of his work, but Carver continued in one of his most important roles: he remained a "great inspirer of young men and old men." Indeed, his fame caused him to have an impact on many individuals; black and white, young and old, male and female, hundreds of people became his "children" and had their horizons expanded by his vision and love. If the public misunderstood the true significance of his life, many of his children did not, as their thousands of letters reveal. For them his legacy was a simple one of love and self-sacrifice, and some, like Howard Kester, shared that legacy with others.

Perhaps it was because his closest children understood him that Carver took so long to realize that his basic message had been blurred in his rise to fame. His eagerness to achieve greatness and to convince the skeptics at Tuskegee of his merit blinded him to the reality of what was happening until very late in his life. The public wanted proof of the commercial value of his ideas, and he embellished the truth to satisfy the demand. The key role played by the peanut industry and New South editors in making Carver famous distorted his vision and obscured his significant earlier work. His notion of the organic unity of the universe and man's need to work with, not against, the forces of nature was used to sell peanuts to the American public and industrial capitalism to doubting Southerners. His respect and love for all of the Creator's products, even men of a different skin color, were used to support the inhumane institution of segregation. He was guilty of prostituting his creative genius and of resorting to gimmickry, either consciously or unconsciously—not for monetary gain, but for recognition. Surely the materialism and racism of the society that required such actions to win its favor must share the guilt.

In his late seventies Carver began to regret the commercialization of his vision and often turned down requests for his peanut exhibit with such comments as "This technical exhibit has no value except to interest the curious, and maybe a very few factory people, but [it does not] touch the rank and file." He urged instead a return to simple cooking demonstrations within the reach of the "man fartherest down."[37] Through the museum he hoped to demonstrate the wide scope of his original vision of the universe and man's relationship to it. Through the foundation he wanted to perpetuate the search for truth by curious minds within black skins. He had wandered far, only to return to his first goals.

Notes

CHAPTER 1: WANDERING IN SEARCH OF A DESTINY

1. Booker T. Washington, *My Larger Education* (New York, 1911), pp. 225–26.
2. Anna Coxe Toogood, *Historic Resource Study and Administrative History, George Washington Carver National Monument, Diamond, Missouri* (Denver, 1973), pp. 27–28.
3. Ibid., pp. 27–28, 33–37; Paul L. Beaubien and Merrill J. Mattes, "The Archeological Search for George Washington Carver's Birthplace," *Negro History Bulletin* 18 (Nov. 1954): 33–38.
4. Toogood, *Historic Resource Study*, pp. 28–29.
5. Ibid., p. 30; "Bill of Sale," 9 Oct. 1855, President's Office, Tuskegee Institute; taped interview of Paris Boyd, 11 Feb. 1954, George Washington Carver National Monument; Jessie P. Guzman, "Investigative Trip Interview Notes," 1948, typescript, pp. 26–27, Box 100, George Washington Carver Papers, Tuskegee Institute Archives (hereafter cited as GWCNM, GWC Papers, and TIA).
6. Edwin C. McReynolds, *Missouri: A History of the Crossroads State* (Norman, Okla., 1954), p. 213; Toogood, *Historic Resource Study*, p. 26.
7. Taped interview of Ada Brock and Eva Goodwin, 12 Sept. 1957, GWCNM; Guzman, "Interview Notes," pp. 3, 6, 11–12, 16, 27; O. T. Stephenson to James Saxon Childers, 29 Sept. 1932, enc. in Childers to GWC, 18 Oct. 1932, Box 2, Jessie P. Guzman Collection of Carver Materials, TIA (hereafter cited as JPG Collection).
8. Toogood, *Historic Resource Study*, pp. 33–42.
9. GWC, untitled autobiographical sketch, ca. 1897, Box 1, GWC Papers, original in Booker T. Washington Papers, Library of Congress (hereafter cited as BTW Papers); Robert P. Fuller and Merrill J.

Mattes, "The Early Life of George Washington Carver," 26 Nov. 1957, typescript, GWCNM, pp. 5–11. (Hereafter when photocopies of documents from other archives are cited as being in the GWC Papers, the source of the original will be noted in brackets following the GWC Papers citation.)

10. Ibid.; Toogood, *Historic Resource Study*, p. 24; GWC, "A Brief Sketch of My Life," 1922, typescript, Box 1, GWC Papers (hereafter the autobiographical accounts will be cited as "1897 Sketch" and "1922 Sketch"); Guzman, "Interview Notes," p. 6. For a lengthy discussion of the controversy of Carver's birthdate see Toogood, *Historic Resource Study*, pp. 8–21.

11. *See* McReynolds, *Missouri*, pp. 187–257 and Wiley Britton, *Civil War on the Border* (Washington: 1898).

12. Britton, *Civil War*, pp. 197–99; Guzman, "Interview Notes," pp. 2–3, 6, 10; taped interview of Mattie Smith, 30 Jan. 1957, GWCNM; Mrs. W. O. Wiggins to GWC, 10 June 1927, Box 1, JPG Collection; Bessie Miller to GWC, 15 Feb. 1933, Box 22, GWC Papers.

13. Fuller and Mattes, "Early Life," pp. 12–18; Guzman, "Interview Notes," pp. 9–11; taped interview of Elza Winter, Sr., 7 June 1957, GWCNM; Richard Pilant to GWC, 8 April 1942, Box 57, GWC Papers.

14. GWC, "1897 Sketch"; GWC to Mae Carver Newlin, 16 March 1925, Box 1, JPG Collection; Lucy Cherry Crisp, undated notes of interview with GWC (hereafter cited as Crisp interview notes), Lucy Cherry Crisp Papers, East Carolina Manuscript Collection, Greenville, N. C. (hereafter cited as LCC Papers).

15. Guzman, "Interview Notes," pp. 1–2, 6; GWC, "1897 Sketch"; Edwin E. Sparks, "The Wizard of the Goober and the Yam," *American Life*, Nov. 1923, p. 14; "Home Folks" to GWC, 19 Dec. 1910, Box 1, JPG Collection.

16. GWC to L. C. Fischer, 14 Sept. 1937, Box 33, GWC Papers.

17. Guzman, "Interview Notes," p. 1; GWC, "1897 Sketch" and "1922 Sketch"; Crisp interview notes.

18. Crisp interview notes; GWC to M. L. Ross, 26 Feb. 1941, Box 52, GWC Papers.

19. Guzman, "Interview Notes," pp. 1, 5, 11, 24; Crisp interview notes; Grover to GWC, 28 April 1888, R. H. Gillmore to GWC, 11 May 1890, Box 1, JPG Collection; Richard Pilant to GWC, 8 April 1942, Box 57, GWC Papers.

20. Crisp interview notes; L. C. Crisp, "Diamond Grove," draft chapter enc. in LCC to GWC, 10 Aug. 1934, Box 26, GWC Papers.

21. Fuller and Mattes, "Early Life," p. 42; Forbes Brown to secretary of GWC, 23 June 1937, Box 32, GWC Papers; taped interview of Mattie Smith, 30 Jan. 1957, GWCNM; Crisp interview notes; GWC, "1897 Sketch" and "1922 Sketch."

22. Guzman, "Interview Notes," p. 10.

23. Taped interview of Sarah Alice Smith, 11 Aug. 1955, GWCNM; Forbes Brown to Secretary of GWC, 23 June 1937, Box 32, GWC Papers; Ethel Edwards, Carver of Tuskegee (Cincinnati, 1971), pp. 9–10; Rackham Holt, George Washington Carver: An American Biography (New York, 1943), p. 19.

24. Mrs. A. E. Lea to GWC, 6 Aug. 1939, Box 2, JPG Collection; taped interview of Mary Lou Ella Hardin, 11 Aug. 1955, GWCNM; Guzman, "Interview Notes," p. 6; GWC, "1897 Sketch" and "1922 Sketch"; Henry S. Williams, "The Development of the Negro Public School System in Missouri," Journal of Negro History 5 (April 1920): 137–65. The 1875 state constitution changed the wording regarding separate schools from "may be established" to "shall be established."

25. Sparks, "The Wizard of the Goober and the Yam," p. 16.

26. Taped interview of Harold A. Slane, 6 Nov. 1956, GWCNM; GWC, "1897 Sketch" and "1922 Sketch"; Guzman, "Interview Notes," p. 10. For a discussion of the probable dates of Carver's stay in Neosho see Fuller and Mattes, "Early Life," pp. 44–50.

27. GWC, undated written responses to questionnaire by Crisp, LCC Papers (hereafter cited as Crisp questionnaire); Calvin Jefferson to Austin W. Curtis, April 1939, Box 2, Andrew and Mariah Watkins to GWC, 5 Jan. 1906, Box 1, JPG Collection; Guzman, "Interview Notes," pp. 12–15, 19–23.

28. Crisp questionnaire; taped interviews of Amelia Thomas Richardson, 27 July 1956 and 13 Aug. 1956, GWCNM; Williams, "Development of Negro Public Schools," pp. 137–65.

29. GWC, "1922 Sketch"; Roy Garvin, "Benjamin, or 'Pap,' Singleton and His Followers," Journal of Negro History 33 (Jan. 1948): 7–23; Eugene H. Berwanger, The Frontier Against Slavery (Urbana, 1971), pp. 97–118; W. Sherman Savage, Blacks in the West (Westport, 1976), pp. 95–107, 160–64.

30. Guzman, "Interview Notes," pp. 27–34; Fuller and Mattes, "Early Life," pp. 51–54; Crisp questionnaire.

31. Elmer Coe, Fort Scott As I Knew It (Fort Scott, 1940), pp. 25–26; Mary L. Barlow, The Why of Fort Scott (n.p., 1921), p. 19; Fort Scott Daily Monitor, 27 March 1879.

32. Fuller and Mattes, "Early Life," p. 29.

33. Ibid., pp. 57–60; Guzman, "Interview Notes," pp. 100–101; taped interviews of Rashley B. Moten, Sr., 9 Dec. 1955, and William R. Moten, 14 Feb. 1956, GWCNM.

34. Fuller and Mattes, "Early Life," pp. 55–56, 61–65; Mamie Johnson to GWC, 4 April 1893, 9 Aug., 14 Dec. 1910, Box 1, JPG Collection; Mamie Johnson to Mr. Triplett, 10 March 1951, Box 82, GWC Papers; Guzman, "Interview Notes," pp. 61, 105.

35. Fuller and Mattes, "Early Life," pp. 61–65; Guzman, "Interview Notes," pp. 54–56, 62, 105–6; taped interviews of Nellie Davis, 22 March 1955, Emily Rarig, 28 March 1956, Viola Gentry, 27 March 1956, and Carlotta Nell Barker, 22 March 1956, GWCNM.

36. Fuller and Mattes, "Early Life," pp. 62–63; GWC, "1897 Sketch"; Iowa State College Bomb (Des Moines, 1896), p. 55; taped interview of Paris Boyd, 11 Feb. 1954, W. C. Rarig to Mr. McClellan, 18 Aug. 1943, GWCNM.

37. GWC, "1897 Sketch"; Guzman, "Interview Notes," pp. 102–3, 108–9.

38. Ibid.; J. F. Beeler to L. C. Crisp, 9 Aug. 1934, LCC Papers.

39. Minnie Dubbs Millbrook, Ness, Western County, Kansas (Detroit, 1955), pp. 63–64.

40. Cash entry 9431, Wakeeny, Kansas, 14 Sept. 1889, Box 1, GWC Papers [Record Group 49, National Archives]. (Hereafter originals in the National Archives will be cited [NA RG ____].)

41. Ibid.; Everett Dick, Tales of the Frontier (Lincoln, 1963), p. 304; Assessment Role Book, Eden Township, Ness City, Kansas, 1 March 1887, as cited in Fuller and Mattes, "Early Life," p. 86.

42. Fuller and Mattes, "Early Life," pp. 85–86; Highland, Kansas Vidette, n.d., clipping in LCC Papers; Guzman, "Interview Notes," pp. 44–45; taped interview of Claude Miller, 13 Feb. 1958, GWCNM; bill for "painting sessions," June 1887, Box 1, JPG Collection; Ness County Times, 15 Dec. 1887.

43. Paul I. Wellman, "Friends of Old Days in Kansas Saw Budding Genius of Negro Scientist," typed copy of article in the Kansas City Star, 9 Sept. 1942, John O. Gross–G. W. Carver Collection, Simpson College Archives (hereafter cited as JOG-GWC Papers); Ness County News, 14 Aug. 1886, 31 March 1888.

44. Fuller and Mattes, "Early Life," pp. 89–90; G. A. Borthwick to Rackham Holt, 1 July 1942, Box 2, JPG Collection.

45. Fuller and Mattes, "Early Life," p. 92; Guzman, "Interview Notes," pp. 87, 93, 95–98; GWC, "1897 Sketch"; E. R. Zeller, "Madison County Men Who Have Made Good," Winterset Madisonian, 4 Nov. 1926, clipping, Box 87, GWC Papers. See also pp. 7–10 of an untitled, undated manuscript, apparently by Mrs. Milholland, sent to

L. C. Crisp by Helen T. Closson, LCC Papers (hereafter cited as Milholland manuscript).

46. "Reminiscences of Dr. John P. Morley," enc. in Robert P. Fuller to Don L. Berry, 7 Dec. 1956, JOG-GWC Papers; taped interview of Mrs. Frank L. Townsend, 9 Nov. 1957, GWCNM; R. A. Davison to James Saxon Childers, 27 Sept. 1932, enc. in JSC to GWC, 18 Oct. 1932, Box 2, JPG Collection.

47. "Statement of Credits of Dr. George W. Carver," 18 Oct. 1938, Box 1, GWC Papers; "Reminiscences of Morley"; "President Gross's Interview with Doctor Carver at Tuskegee," 17 July 1940, typescript, Frederick Carl Sigler, "George Washington Carver," n.d., typescript, JOG-GWC Papers; Indianola *Simpsonian* 25 (Dec. 1894): 18; Lura Haun to Jessie Guzman, 16 Jan. 1949, Box 81, GWC Papers.

48. GWC to Loren C. Talbot, 8 Jan. 1925, Box 1, JPG Collection; "Reminiscences of Morley"; Guzman, "Interview Notes," pp. 92–93.

49. GWC to L. C. Talbot, 8 Jan. 1925, Box 1, JPG Collection; Milholland manuscript, pp. 11–13; Mrs. Liston to GWC, 27 Nov. 1893, 29 Oct. 1894, 20 Oct. 1932, 28 Feb. 1937, Box 1, JPG Collection.

50. Guzman, "Interview Notes," pp. 75–76; GWC to L. H. Pammel, 5 May 1922, Box 1, GWC Papers.

CHAPTER 2: TO BE OF THE GREATEST GOOD

1. Roy V. Scott, *The Reluctant Farmer: The Rise of Agricultural Extension to 1914* (Urbana, 1970), pp. 37–63; Frederick B. Mumford, *The Land Grant College Movement*, University of Missouri Agricultural Experiment Station, Bulletin 419 (Columbia, 1940), pp. 5–8; Alfred C. True, "The United States Department of Agriculture, 1862–1912," reprint from *Proceedings*, Twenty-sixth Annual Convention of the Association of American Agricultural Colleges and Experiment Stations, Atlanta, Georgia, 13–15 Nov. 1912; *An Historical Sketch of the Iowa State College of Agriculture and Mechanic Arts* (Cedar Rapids, 1920), pp. 9–16.

2. Guzman, "Interview Notes," pp. 92–93; GWC to L. H. Pammel, 5 May 1922, Box 1, GWC Papers; Fuller and Mattes, "Early Life," pp. 97–98; Milholland manuscript, pp. 15–16.

3. Lucy Cherry Crisp, "George Washington Carver," undated typescript, p. V.–12, LCC Papers; C. D. Reed to J. P. Guzman, 27 Aug. 1948, J. I. Schultz to JPG, 16 May 1949, Box 81, GWC to L. H. Pammel, 5 May 1922, Iowa State University transcript of academic work of GWC, Box 1, GWC Papers; Mrs. Sylph Sturgeon to GWC, 7 Nov. 1940, Box 2, JPG Collection.

4. *IAC Student*, 2 Sept. 1893, 28 April, 26 May 1896; Chairman of the Missionary Committee to Anna Heileman, 2 Feb. 1896, Box 1, JPG Collection; C. D. Reed to GWC, 22 Dec. 1932, GWC Papers [George Washington Carver Museum, Tuskegee Institute, hereafter cited as GWC Museum].

5. Holt, *Carver*, p. 96; James Wilson to GWC, 1 Feb. 1911, Box 46, Thomas M. Campbell Papers, TIA (hereafter cited as TMC Papers).

6. Printed brochures of YMCA of Iowa Agricultural College dated 1892 and 1893, Box 1, Arthur J. Ashby to Guzman, 23 March 1949, Box 81, GWC Papers; W. D. Weatherford to LCC, 18 Jan. 1939, LCC Papers.

7. *History and Reminiscences of I.A.C.* (Des Moines, 1897), pp. 88, 176; *IAC Student*, 25 Sept., 13 Nov. 1894; Iowa State College *Bomb* (Des Moines, 1896), pp. 64, 94, 104; Iowa State College *Bomb* (Des Moines, 1897), pp. 86, 108; Dr. Ira C. Brownlie, "Reminiscences," undated typescript, Box 101, GWC Papers.

8. *IAC Student*, 2 May 1895; J. H. Meyers to Guzman, 26 Feb. 1949, Box 81, GWC Papers; *IAC Student*, 6 March 1894, 22 Sept. 1896, 27 Aug., 4 Sept., 2 Oct. 1894, 18 Aug. 1896, 15 Aug. 1895, 24 Sept. 1892, 28 May 1895; E. M. S. McLaughlin to GWC, 22 May 1898, W. E. Long to GWC, 26 Feb. 1926, Box 1, JPG Collection.

9. Mabel Owens Wilcox to Guzman, 19 Jan. 1949, Louis B. Craig to Guzman, 23 Feb. 1949, Box 81, GWC Papers; unidentified clippings, Box 1, JPG Collection.

10. John L. Hillman to John L. Horsely, 27 January [ca. 1939], JOG-GWC Papers.

11. Mabel Owens Wilcox to Guzman, 19 Jan. 1949, Box 81, GWC Papers.

12. See numerous letters from Carver's classmates to Guzman, Box 81, GWC Papers; M. J. Orr to GWC, 2 April 1940, Mr. and Mrs. Elmer E. Isakson to GWC, 20 Dec. 1942, Box 2, JPG Collection.

13. Royal Meeker to GWC, 24 June 1898, Box 1, JPG Collection.

14. Holt, *Carver*, p. 87; *IAC Student*, 4 March 1893; GWC to L. H. Pammel, 11 June 1921, Box 11, GWC Papers [Iowa State University Archives]; *Iowa at the World's Columbian Exposition: Report of the Iowa Columbian Commission* (Cedar Rapids, 1895), p. 210, as cited in Fuller and Mattes, "Early Life," p. 100 (hereafter cited as ISUA).

15. GWC, "Grafting the Cacti," *Transactions*, Iowa Horticulture Society (1893), p. 257.

16. Iowa Horticulture Society, "Program of the 29th Annual Meeting," Box 1, GWC Papers; GWC, "Plants as Modified by Man," bachelor's thesis, Iowa State University, 1894.

17. Guzman, "Interview Notes," p. 68; 1896 *Bomb*, p. 68; GWC, "Best

Ferns for the North and Northwest," *Iowa Agricultural Experiment Station* (hereafter IAES) *Bulletin* 27 (Ames, 1894–95), pp. 150–53; GWC, "Our Window Gardens," *IAES Bulletin* 32 (Ames, 1896–97), pp. 516–25.

18. Cynthia Westcott, *Plant Disease Handbook* (New York, 1971), pp. 3–4; Wayne D. Rasmussen, *Readings in the History of American Agriculture* (Urbana, 1960), pp. 214–15.

19. L. H. Pammel to Mrs. L. B. McCullough, 3 Nov. 1928, Box 1, JPG Collection; Pammel and GWC, "Treatment of Currents and Cherries to Prevent Spot Diseases," *IAES Bulletin* 30 (Ames 1895–96) pp. 289–301; Pammel and GWC, "Fungus Diseases of Plants at Ames, Iowa," Iowa Academy of Sciences, *Proceedings* 3 (1895): 140–48; F. C. Stewart and GWC, "Inoculation Experiments with Gymnosporangium Macropus LK," Iowa Academy of Sciences, *Proceedings* 3 (1895): 162–69; Pammel, I. E. Melbus, and R. I. Cratty, "Report on the Herbarium of Iowa State College, 1927," pp. 4, 9, as cited in Guzman, "Interview Notes," p. 69.

20. Benjamin Hibbard to GWC, 5 Aug. 1941, Box 2, JPG Collection; Guzman, "Interview Notes," p. 69a.

21. H. A. Wallace (hereafter HAW) to GWC, 22 Oct. 1932, Box 21, HAW to Luzanne Boozer, 7, Dec. 1948, Box 81, GWC Papers.

22. Holt, *Carver*, pp. 95–97.

23. Louis R. Harlan, *Booker T. Washington: The Making of a Black Leader* (New York, 1972), pp. 204–88.

24. Wilson to GWC, 1 Feb. 1911, Box 46, TMC Papers.

25. GWC to BTW, 3 April, 5 April 1896, Box 4, GWC Papers [BTW]; GWC to BTW, 12 April 1896, Box 116, BTW Papers.

26. BTW to GWC, 17 April 1896, Box 4, GWC Papers [BTW].

27. GWC to BTW, 21 April 1896, Box 4, GWC Papers [BTW].

28. GWC to BTW, 6 May 1896, Box 4, GWC Papers [BTW].

29. C. D. Reed to GWC, 22 Dec. 1932, Box 22, GWC Papers [GWC Museum].

30. Joseph F. Citro, *Booker T. Washington's Tuskegee Institute: Black School Community, 1900–1915* (Ann Arbor, 1973), pp. 199–205, 210.

31. Harlan, *Washington*, pp. 113–15.

32. GWC to Pammel, 30 March 1897, Box 4, GWC Papers [ISUA].

33. GWC to Finance Committee, 11 Nov. 1896, GWC Papers [BTW].

34. GWC to BTW, 17 May 1901, Box 4, GWC Papers [BTW].

35. It was not unusual for single faculty members to live in student dormitories and serve as counselors. Carver usually supplied his dining hall table with a small tree at Christmas and once wrote a humorous letter of "suspension" to an errant tablemate. "Dr. George W. Carver

As I Knew Him," typescript of WAPI radio broadcast, 27 Feb. 1943, Box 100, GWC to Miss L. Cheeks, 29 Feb. 1908, Box 7, GWC Papers.

36. Ethel Edwards, *Carver of Tuskegee*, pp. 72–74; Crisp manuscript, VII.-18; Mrs. Liston to GWC, 3 Aug. 1905, Box 1, JPG Collection; W. N. Napier to GWC, 2 July 1905, Box 6, GWC Papers.

37. BTW, *My Larger Education*, pp. 229–30.

38. Interview with Florida Segrest, 11 Dec. 1975; Minutes of the Executive Council, 24 Nov. 1914, Box 1012, BTW Papers.

39. Charles E. Prettyman to GWC, 3 Jan. 1905, "Home Folks" to GWC, 17 Oct. 1908, 15 Nov., 19 Dec. 1910, 30 Jan. 1911, Box 1, JPG Collection; unidentified clipping [Galena, Kansas, 1908], Box 89, GWC Papers.

40. Max Bennett Thrasher, *Tuskegee: Its Story and Its Work* (Boston, 1901), p. 107; BTW, *The Story of My Life and Work* (Toronto, 1900), pp. 246–47; Anne Kendrick Walker, *Tuskegee and the Black Belt: A Portrait of a Race* (Richmond, 1944), p. 57; Harlan, *Washington*, p. 286.

41. Wilson to GWC, 12 Sept. 1898, Box 1, JPG Collection.

CHAPTER 3: TROUBLE ON THE "TUSKEGEE PLANTATION"

1. *Acts of the General Assembly of Alabama, 1896–1897* (Montgomery, 1897), pp. 945–47.

2. *Historical Sketch of Iowa State College*, p. 13; *Eighth Annual Report of the Agricultural Experiment Station of the A. & M. College, Auburn, Alabama* (Montgomery, 1896), p. 7.

3. *See* Chapter Four.

4. Allen W. Jones, "The Role of Tuskegee Institute in the Education of Black Farmers," *Journal of Negro History* 51 (April 1975): 253.

5. Citro, *Washington's Tuskegee*, pp. 153–56; Harlan, *Washington*, pp. 272–87; Minutes of the Executive Council, 5 Feb. 1901, TIA.

6. GWC to BTW, 4 July, 17 Aug. 1898, GWC to Warren Logan, 23 June 1897, BTW to GWC, 5 Jan., 17 Jan. 1901, W. J. Clayton to GWC, 7 Sept. 1899, Box 4, GWC Papers [BTW]; Minutes of the Executive Council, 12 Dec. 1901, 13 Jan. 1902, TIA.

7. Minutes of the Executive Council, 29 Dec. 1899, Box 1004, BTW Papers; Minutes of The Executive Council, 13 April 1901, TIA.

8. GWC to BTW, 13 Sept. 1897, 21 Jan. 1902, Box 4, GWC Papers [BTW]; Minutes of the Executive Council, 22 Sept. 1899, Box 1004, BTW Papers; GWC to BTW, 27 Aug. 1898, Box 4, GWC Papers

[BTW]; GWC to R. M. Attwell, 2 April 1903, GWC to J. H. Washington, 30 Oct. 1903, Box 5, GWC Papers; Minutes of the Executive Council, 6 June, 27 June 1898, Box 1004, BTW Papers.

9. GWC to BTW, 20 July 1903, 7 March 1904, Box 5, GWC Papers [BTW].

10. BTW to GWC, 23 Dec. 1899, Box 4, J. H. Washington to BTW, 10 Oct. 1901, 5 April 1902, Box 68, GWC to BTW, 29 May 1912, Box 9, GWC Papers [BTW]. John Washington was about three years older than Booker and had been considered the more intelligent of the two as a child. Booker, however, was the first to go to Hampton Institute, with financial aid from John, who later also graduated from Hampton and joined his brother at Tuskegee. There John's "somewhat nervous and irritable temperment" occasionally caused problems for Booker, who was forced to move him from commandant to superintendent of industries because of his "martinet manner." Harlan, *Washington*, pp. 10, 14, 150, 184.

11. GWC to BTW, 12 June 1898, Box 4, GWC Papers.

12. GWC to BTW, 17 Jan. 1902, Box 4, GWC Papers [BTW].

13. GWC to BTW, 17 Jan. 1902, Box 4, GWC Papers [BTW].

14. GWC to BTW, 20 Jan. 1904, Box 5, GWC Papers [BTW].

15. Citro, *Washington's Tuskegee*, pp. 132–33.

16. BTW to GWC, 28 Nov. 1898, Box 4, 23 May, 3 June 1908, Box 7, GWC Papers [BTW].

17. GWC to BTW, 9 Feb. 1897, 4 Aug. 1898, Box 4, GWC Papers [BTW]; Holt, *Carver*, pp. 144–45.

18. Interview with Georgia Poole, 15 Dec. 1975.

19. Ibid.; interview with Hariette Booth, 11 Dec. 1975; Bridgeforth to GWC, 18 Jan. 1904, Box 551, BTW Papers; Bridgeforth to BTW, 28 Feb. 1906, 30 March, 15 April 1907, Box 68, GWC Papers [BTW].

20. Bridgeforth to GWC, 2 Nov. 1904, Box 559, BTW Papers.

21. GWC to Bridgeforth, 3 Dec. 1904, Box 559, BTW Papers.

22. Bridgeforth to GWC, 6 Dec. 1904, Box 559, BTW Papers.

23. GWC to BTW, 3 Dec. 1904, BTW to GWC, 14 Dec. 1904, Box 5, GWC Papers [BTW].

24. Scott to GWC, 1 March 1905, Bridgeforth to GWC, 2 March 1905, GWC to BTW, 24 March 1905, Box 6, GWC Papers [BTW]; Minutes of the Executive Council, 8 April 1905, Box 1005, BTW Papers.

25. Bridgeforth to GWC, 18 Jan. 1904, Box 551, Committee Report on the Poultry Yard, n.d., Box 552, Committee Report on the Poultry Yard, 22 Sept. 1904, Box 552, Minutes of the Executive Council, 22 Sept. 1904, Box 1005, BTW Papers.

26. D. A. Williston, G. R. Bridgeforth, C. W. Greene, P. C. Parks, and

L. Jones to BTW, 11 Oct. 1904, Box 68, GWC Papers [BTW]; BTW to GWC, 13 Oct. 1904, Box 555, BTW Papers.

27. GWC to BTW, 14 Oct., 19 Oct. 1904, Box 5, GWC Papers [BTW]; BTW to GWC, 20 Oct. 1904, Box 555, BTW Papers.

28. BTW to GWC, 3 Nov. 1904, Box 5, GWC Papers [BTW]. This title was somewhat broader than the original one proposed by Bridgeforth et al. of "Director of Agricultural Chemistry and Experiment Station."

29. GWC to BTW, 8 Nov. 1904, Box 5, GWC Papers [BTW].

30. GWC to BTW, 14 Nov. 1904, Box 5, GWC Papers [BTW].

31. McGranahan to GWC, 8 Nov., 22 Nov., 19 Dec. 1904, 26 Jan., 22 Feb. 1905, Box 1, JPG Collection; GWC to Wilson, 11 Nov. 1904, Box 1, JPG Collection [NA RG 54]; Wilson to GWC, 21 Nov. 1904, GWC to Wilson, 28 Nov. 1904, Box 5, GWC Papers [NA RG 54]. As early as the previous summer Carver had considered leaving Tuskegee for work in Puerto Rico, but this idea was discouraged by Wilson. GWC to Wilson, 23 July 1904, Wilson to GWC, 5 Aug. 1904, Box 5, GWC Papers [NA RG 54]. Carver's seriousness about leaving in December 1904 appears in his writing to Mrs. Liston for advice. Liston to GWC, 9 Dec. 1904, Box 1, JPG Collection.

32. Ernest T. Attwell and Elizabeth A. Dugan to J. H. Washington, 22 May 1905, Box 560, Minutes of the Executive Council, 27 Jan., 25 Feb., 5 May 1908, Box 1007, E. J. Scott, Bridgeforth, and GWC to BTW, 26 Feb. 1908, Box 583, BTW Papers.

33. Minutes of the Executive Council, 5 April, 6 April 1909, Box 1007, BTW Papers; BTW to GWC, 15 April 1909, Box 7, GWC Papers [BTW]; Wilson to GWC, 29 April 1909, Box 7, GWC Papers [NA RG 16].

34. BTW to GWC, 1 May, 2 May, 12 May 1909, Box 7, GWC Papers [BTW]; Minutes of the Executive Council, 23 March, 5 April 1910, Box 1008, BTW Papers; Wilson to BTW, 16 May 1910, Box 68, Wilson to GWC, 21 May 1910, Box 8, GWC Papers [NA RG 16].

35. Charles Fearing to BTW, 20 Oct. 1910, Box 600, BTW Papers; J. H. Washington and Bridgeforth to BTW, 10 Nov. 1910, Box 68, GWC Papers [BTW]; Minutes of the Executive Council, 14 Nov. 1910, Box 1009, BTW Papers.

36. BTW to GWC and Bridgeforth, 16 Nov. 1910, Box 598, BTW Papers.

37. GWC to BTW, 19 Nov. 1910, Box 8, GWC Papers.

38. Wilson to GWC, 22 Nov. 1910, Box 8, GWC Papers [NA RG 16].

39. Committee Report, 21, Nov. 1910, Box 600, BTW Papers.

40. GWC to Bridgeforth, 1 Dec. 1910, Bridgeforth to GWC, 2 Dec. 1910, Bridgeforth to J. H. Washington, 2 Dec. 1910, JHW to Bridgeforth, 28 Nov. 1910, all enc. in Bridgeforth to BTW, 2 Dec. 1910, Box 598,

BTW Papers; GWC to BTW, 21 Feb. 1911, Box 8, GWC Papers [BTW].

41. BTW to GWC, 26 Feb. 1911, Box 8, GWC Papers [BTW].

42. GWC to BTW, 14 Sept. 1911, Box 8, 2 June 1911, 4 May, 29 Oct., 20 Dec. 1911, BTW to GWC, 8 Dec. 1911, 8 June, 8 Oct., 27 Dec. 1912, J. H. Washington to GWC, 3 May 1911, Box 9, GWC Papers [BTW]; Minutes of the Executive Council, 30 May 1911, 1 Nov. 1912, Box 1010, BTW Papers.

43. GWC to BTW, 26 May, 8 June 1914, 28 Dec. 1912, 14 Aug. 1913, Box 9, GWC Papers [BTW]. In his attempts to get away from Tuskegee, Carver turned again to James Wilson, but was disappointed by Wilson's reply that he would have to take civil service examinations. Wilson to GWC, 2 Jan. 1913, Box 9, GWC Papers.

44. Citro, *Washington's Tuskegee*, pp. 130–32.

45. BTW to GWC, 20 June 1912, Box 9, GWC Papers [BTW].

CHAPTER 4: THE NEED FOR SCIENTIFIC AGRICULTURE

1. GWC, *The Need of Scientific Agriculture in the South*, Tuskegee Institute, Farmer's Leaflet 7 (Tuskegee, 1902).

2. Theodore Saloutos, *Farmer Movements in the South, 1865–1933* (Lincoln, 1964), pp. 1–30; Pete Daniel, *The Shadow of Slavery: Peonage in the South, 1901–1969* (Urbana, 1972), pp. 19–26; C. Vann Woodward, *Origins of the New South, 1877–1913* (Baton Rouge, 1970), pp. 175–88.

3. Saloutos, *Farmer Movements*, pp. 1–30; Woodward, *Origins of the New South*, pp. 175–88.

4. GWC, *Need of Scientific Agriculture*.

5. H. C. White, "The Experiment Stations," reprint from *Proceedings, Twenty-sixth Annual Convention of the Association of American Agricultural Colleges and Experiment Stations*, Atlanta, Georgia, 13–15 Nov. 1912.

6. Jim Hightower, *Hard Tomatoes, Hard Times* (Cambridge, Mass., 1973), pp. 10–13.

7. Horace Mann Bond, *Negro Education in Alabama: A Study in Cotton and Steel* (Washington, 1939), p. 204.

8. Ibid.; Montgomery *Advertiser*, 4 Dec. 1896, 22 Jan., 23 Jan., 26 Jan., 13 Feb. 1897.

9. *Acts of Alabama, 1896–1897*, pp. 945–47; White "Experiment Stations," pp. 15–17.

10. White, "Experiment Stations," p. 15; True to GWC, 21 Sept. 1906, 16 Jan. 1909, Box 7, GWC Papers [NA RG 164].

11. *Annual Report of the Office of Experiment Stations, 1912* (Washington, 1913) (Hereafter cited as *OES Report*).

12. Wilson to GWC, 21 June 1901, Box 1, JPG Collection; Wilson to GWC, 6 Sept. 1906, Box 1, Austin W. Curtis Papers, Michigan Historical Collections, Ann Arbor (hereafter cited as AWC Papers).

13. *Acts of Alabama, 1896–1897*, pp. 945–47; GWC to A. C. True, 8 May, 14 May 1903, Box 5, GWC Papers [NA RG 164].

14. GWC, *Feeding Acorns*, Tuskegee Institute Experiment Station, Bulletin 1 (Tuskegee, 1898).

15. Frederick B. Mumford, *The Land Grant College Movement*, University of Missouri Agricultural Experiment Station, Bulletin 419 (Columbia, 1940), pp. 105–7; GWC, *Feeding Acorns*.

16. *Eighteenth Annual Report of the Agricultural Experiment Station of the A. & M. College, Auburn, Alabama* (Montgomery, 1906).

17. BTW to GWC, 1 April 1909, Box 7, GWC to J. H. Washington, 9 Feb. 1912, GWC to BTW, 30 Dec. 1913, Box 9, GWC Papers [BTW]; Minutes of the Executive Council, 27 Feb. 1911, Box 1009, 17 Feb. 1914, Box 1011, BTW Papers; "Eighty Birds of Macon County, Alabama, and Their Relation to Our Prosperity," 1914, typescript, Box 65, GWC Papers; GWC to BTW, 20 June 1912, Box 9, GWC Papers [BTW]; Tuskegee *Student*, 3 Aug. 1907.

18. C. A. Prosser to John W. Wilkinson, 4 March 1911, copy enc. in GWC to BTW, 14 March 1911, Box 8, GWC Papers [BTW]. While Washington was probably glad of any publicity that Carver's bulletin brought to Tuskegee, he was more realistic about the possible scope of the station and urged Carver to confine his work to the specific needs of Macon County. BTW to GWC, Sept. 1912?, Box 9, GWC Papers [BTW].

19. GWC to BTW, 14 March 1911, Box 8, GWC Papers [BTW]. For the most part those bulletins that do not describe the plot work of the station will be discussed in later chapters.

20. Interview with Dr. Paul R. Miller, 13 Oct. 1975.

21. *Tenth Annual Report of the Agricultural Experiment Station of the A. & M. College, Auburn, Alabama* (Montgomery, 1898), pp. 23–25; agricultural class book, Box 1, AWC Papers.

22. GWC to Warren Logan, 3 Nov. 1903, Box 5, GWC Papers; GWC, *How to Build Up Worn Out Soils*, Tuskegee Institute Experiment Station, Bulletin 6 (Tuskegee, 1905), p. 4; *OES Report, 1903*.

23. GWC, *Experiments with Sweet Potatoes*, Tuskegee Institute Experiment Station, Bulletin 2 (Tuskegee, 1898); GWC to BTW, 20 May 1897, 30 May 1898, Box 4, GWC Papers [BTW].

24. GWC to BTW, 30 March 1906, Box 7, GWC Papers [BTW]; GWC, *Successful Yields of Small Grain*, Tuskegee Institute Experiment Sta-

tion, Bulletin 8 (Tuskegee, 1906); William R. Carroll and Merle E. Muhrer, "The Scientific Contributions of George Washington Carver," mimeographed report of study supported by the National Park Service, 1962, p. 5, Box 83, GWC Papers.

26. GWC to BTW, 7 Dec., 10 Dec. 1898, 23 Dec. 1902, Box 4, GWC Papers [BTW]; Minutes of the Executive Council, 6 July, 15 Oct. 1903, Box 1005, 11 July 1911, Box 1009, BTW Papers.

27. GWC to BTW, 6 Oct. 1899, Box 4, GWC Papers [BTW].

28. BTW to GWC, 28 Sept. 1900, Box 4, GWC Papers [BTW].

29. GWC, *Fertilizer Experiments with Cotton*, Tuskegee Institute Experiment Station, Bulletin 3 (Tuskegee, 1901); GWC, *Cotton Growing on Sandy Upland Soils*, Tuskegee Institute Experiment Station, Bulletin 7 (Tuskegee, 1905); GWC, *How to Make Cotton Growing Pay*, Tuskegee Institute Experiment Station, Bulletin 14 (Tuskegee, 1908); GWC, *Cotton Growing for Rural Schools*, Tuskegee Institute Experiment Station, Bulletin 20 (Tuskegee, 1911); GWC, *A New and Prolific Variety of Cotton*, Tuskegee Institute Experiment Station, Bulletin 26 (Tuskegee, 1915).

30. Wilson to GWC, 25 Nov. 1901, Box 1, JPG Collection [NA RG Secretary's Correspondence, USDA].

31. GWC to Wilson, 25 April 1902, Wilson to GWC, 27 March 1902, Box 1, JPG Collection [NA RG Secretary's Correspondence, USDA]; GWC to Howard, 22 Oct. 1906, Box 4, GWC Papers [NA RG 7].

32. Howard to GWC, 30 Oct., 14 Nov. 1902, Box 4, GWC to Howard, 30 April 1903, Howard to GWC, 7 Aug. 1903, GWC to Howard, 3 Oct. 1903, Box 5, GWC Papers [NA RG 7].

33. GWC to Louis T. Santoro, 18 May 1940, Box 49, GWC Papers.

34. Frank H. Leavell, "The Boy Who Was Traded for a Horse," *Baptist Student* (Nov. 1938), p. 6.

35. GWC, *Some Cercosporae of Macon County, Alabama*, Tuskegee Institute Experiment Station, Bulletin 4 (Tuskegee, 1902); Ellis to GWC, 11 Jan. 1896, Box 4, GWC Papers; GWC to Pammel, 7 May, 7 Sept. 1900, 12 Feb. 1902, 6 Aug. 1907, Box 4, GWC Papers [ISUA].

36. J. B. Ellis and E. Bartholomew, "New Species of Fungi from Various Localities," *Journal of Mycology* 8 (Dec. 1902): 175; J. B. Ellis and B. M. Everhart, "New Species of Fungi from Various Localities," *Journal of Mycology* 8 (May 1902): 17; J. B. Ellis and B. M. Everhart, "New Species of Fungi from Various Localities," *Journal of Mycology* 9 (Oct. 1903): 164; J. B. Ellis and B. M. Everhart, "New Alabama Fungi," *Journal of Mycology* 8 (June 1902): 62–73. *See also* the correspondence with Ellis in Box 1, AWC Papers.

37. J. C. Arthur, "The Uredinaea Occurring Upon Phragmites, Spartina,

and Arundenaria in America," *Botanical Gazette* 34 (July 1902): 19; W. A. Ortan to GWC, 27 Nov. 1900, Box 4, 28 Feb. 1905, Box 6, Pathologist, Fruit Disease Investigation to GWC, 8 Nov. 1911, GWC to C. L. Shear, 24 Nov. 1911, C. L. Shear to GWC, 1 Dec. 1911, Box 8, GWC to Chief, Division of Plant Botany, 17 July 1915, Box 9, GWC Papers [NA RG 54].

38. GWC to BTW, 17 June 1902, Box 4, GWC Papers [BTW]; GWC to Albert E. Woods, 2 May 1902, Woods to GWC, 24 June 1902, Box 4, GWC Papers [NA RG 54].

39. GWC to BTW, 17 Oct. 1904, Box 4, GWC Papers [BTW]; *OES Report, 1904*.

40. GWC to BTW, 7 Feb. 1902, Box 4, GWC Papers [BTW]; GWC, *Cow Peas*, Tuskegee Institute Experiment Station, Bulletin 5 (Tuskegee, 1903); GWC, *How to Cook Cow Peas*, Tuskegee Institute Experiment Station, Bulletin 13 (Tuskegee, 1908); GWC, *Some Possibilities of the Cow Pea in Macon County, Alabama*, Tuskegee Institute Experiment Station, Bulletin 19 (Tuskegee, 1911).

41. GWC, *Saving the Sweet Potato*, Tuskegee Institute Experiment Station, Bulletin 10 (Tuskegee, 1906); GWC, *Possibilities of the Sweet Potato in Macon County, Alabama*, Tuskegee Institute Experiment Station, Bulletin 17 (Tuskegee, 1910).

42. GWC, *How to Grow the Peanut and 105 Ways of Preparing It for Human Consumption*, Tuskegee Institute Experiment Station, Bulletin 31 (Tuskegee, 1916).

43. Minutes of the Executive Council, 31 May 1904, Box 1005, BTW Papers; Tuskegee *Student*, 29 July 1905.

44. GWC to A. C. True, 20 Dec. 1907, Box 7, GWC Papers [NA RG 164]; GWC, *A New and Prolific Variety of Cotton*, Tuskegee Institute Experiment Station, Bulletin 26 (Tuskegee, 1915); Carroll and Muhrer, "Scientific Contributions," pp. 3–5; Tuskegee *Student*, 24 Sept. 1910.

45. GWC to Emmett J. Scott, 24 Sept. 1910, BTW to GWC, 11 Sept. 1910, Box 8, GWC Papers [BTW]; Frank Carpigiani to GWC, 1 Sept. 1910, Box 1, AWC Papers; W. A. Gayle to GWC, 3 Feb. 1912, Box 9, GWC Papers; "Experiment-Raised Cotton," Tuskegee *Southern Letter*, June 1915.

46. GWC to BTW, 31 March 1910, Box 8, 26 Nov. 1910, Box 9, GWC Papers [BTW]; Harry Simms, "A Visit to the Tuskegee Institute Experiment Station," Tuskegee *Messenger*, 20 Sept. 1912.

47. Minutes of the Executive Council, 12 May, 17 May 1909, 20 Sept. 1909, Box 1008, BTW Papers.

48. GWC to BTW, 18 Feb. 1911, Box 9, GWC Papers.

49. F. F. Bondy et al., *Dispersion of the Boll Weevil in 1921*, USDA, Departmental Circular 266 (Washington, 1923), p. 5.

50. T. N. Cowen, M. N. Work, and R. A. Clarke to BTW, 21 March 1910, Box 600, BTW Papers.

51. *OES Report, 1913*; GWC to BTW, 9 Jan., 1 Aug., 26 Nov., 29 Nov. 1912, Box 9, GWC Papers [BTW].

52. GWC to BTW, 20 Nov. 1912, 20 March 1914, Box 9, GWC Papers [BTW]; Minutes of the Executive Council, 7 Aug. 1913, Box 1011, BTW Papers.

53. *OES Report, 1912*; GWC to James Wilson, 2 July 1912, GWC Papers [NA RG Secretary's Correspondence, USDA]; Montgomery *Journal*, 9 Sept. 1914, clipping, Box 84, GWC Papers.

54. Minutes of the Executive Council, 12 Sept., 16 Sept., 18 Sept. 1913, Box 1011, BTW Papers; J. W. Washington to BTW, 2 Sept. 1913, Box 68, GWC to BTW, 17 Sept. 1913, Box 9, GWC Papers [BTW].

55. GWC to Warren Logan, 31 Oct. 1914, Box 9, GWC Papers [BTW].

56. Hightower, *Hard Tomatoes*, pp. 1–7.

CHAPTER 5: THE PROCESS OF
"UNDERSTANDING RELATIONSHIPS"

1. Scott, *Reluctant Farmer*, pp. 27–36; Woodward, *Origins of the New South*, pp. 176–78, 182.

2. John Hope Franklin, *From Slavery to Freedom* (New York, 1969), pp. 335–43; C. Vann Woodward, *The Strange Career of Jim Crow* (New York, 1966), pp. 67–109.

3. Bond, *Negro Education*, pp. 217–25.

4. BTW to GWC, 26 Feb. 1911, Box 8, GWC Papers [BTW]; Dr. L. DeLaine to GWC, 27 March 1938, Box 38, GWC Papers.

5. *A Brief Sketch of the Development of Tuskegee Institute*, Tuskegee Institute, Brochure 2 (Tuskegee, 1940), pp. 5–6; Booker T. Washington, ed., *Tuskegee and Its People: Their Ideals and Achievements* (New York, 1905), pp. 40–41.

6. GWC, "The Love of Nature," *Guide to Nature* 5 (Dec. 1912): 16–18.

7. GWC, "A Message from Dr. Carver," *World Friends* 5 (May 1932): 21; M. A. Thomas, "What Doctor Garver Taught Me," Atlanta *Daily World*, 3 April 1939, clipping, Box 93, GWC Papers; Roscoe Dunjee to GWC, 2 Feb. 1936, Box 29, GWC Papers.

8. GWC, "Suggested Outlines for the Study of Economic Plant Life," galley proof, n.d., Box 66, GWC Papers.

9. GWC to BTW, 3 April 1901, Box 4, GWC Papers [BTW].

10. "Address by Dr. G. W. Carver at Vorhees Normal and Industrial

School, Denmark, South Carolina," 19 Feb. 1919, typescript; "Address by Dr. George Washington Carver at Tuskegee Institute Chapel," 20 Oct. 1940, typescript, Box 65, GWC Papers.

11. GWC to BTW, 4 July 1898, 10 April 1902, Box 4, GWC Papers [BTW].

12. "G. W. Carver, an appreciation by one of his students," n.d., typescript, Box 100, GWC Papers; interview with Raleigh Merritt, 15 Nov. 1975.

13. Interview with Georgia Poole and Ophelia Cooper, 15 Dec. 1975.

14. Minutes of the Executive Council, 12 Jan. 1900, Box 1004, BTW Papers; GWC to BTW, 13 Sept., 2 Oct. 1902, Box 4, GWC Papers [BTW].

15. GWC, *Suggestions for Progressive and Correlative Nature Study*, Tuskegee Institute, Nature Leaflet 1 (Tuskegee, 1902); GWC, *Nature Study and Gardening for Rural Schools*, Tuskegee Institute Experiment Station, Bulletin 18 (Tuskegee, 1910).

16. GWC to BTW, 1914, Box 65, GWC Papers [BTW].

17. Wilson to GWC, 23 May 1910, Box 8, GWC Papers [NA RG 16]; GWC, "Suggested Outlines."

18. Thomas Monroe Campbell, *The Movable School Goes to the Negro Farmer* (Tuskegee, 1936), pp. 47–48.

19. Citro, *Washington's Tuskegee*, pp. 133–37.

20. GWC to BTW, 18 March 1899, Box 4, GWC Papers [BTW].

21. Wilson to GWC, 21 Dec. 1906, Box 7, GWC Papers [NA RG 16].

22. GWC to BTW, 20 Sept. 1897, 2 Nov. 1901, Box 4, GWC Papers [BTW].

23. BTW to Bridgeforth, 3 Dec. 1910, Box 598, BTW Papers; GWC to BTW, 27 Feb. 1911, Box 8, GWC Papers [BTW].

24. GWC to BTW, 1 March 1911, Box 8, GWC Papers [BTW].

25. GWC to BTW, 6 March 1911, Box 8, GWC Papers [BTW]; Logan to GWC, 29 March 1911, Box 8, GWC Papers.

26. Minutes of the Executive Council, 30 April 1912, Box 1010, BTW Papers; BTW to GWC, 8 June 1912, Box 9, Bridgeforth to BTW, 15 Aug. 1912, Box 68, GWC Papers [BTW].

27. RRM to GWC, 10 June 1916, Box 9, E. C. Roberts to GWC, 20 Feb. 1925, Box 15, GWC Papers.

28. Interview with Harold Webb, 15 Dec. 1975; "G. W. Carver, an appreciation"; GWC to BTW, 13 Dec. 1912, Box 9, GWC Papers [BTW].

29. John K. Johnson to GWC, 22 Dec. 1938, Box 40, John W. Moss to GWC, 24 Oct. 1921, Box 11, GWC to L. Robinson, 9 Jan. 1922, Box 12, GWC Papers.

30. Interview with Harold Webb, 16 Dec. 1975.

31. GWC to BTW, 19 Dec. 1898, Box 4, GWC Papers [BTW].

32. GWC to Robert Durr, 22 Oct. 1937, Box 34, GWC Papers.

33. GWC, "A New Industry For Colored Young Men and Women," *Colored American* 14 (Jan. 1908): 33.

34. L. L. Toney, "The Carver Bible Class in Tuskegee Institute—Its Origin," n.d., typescript, Box 1, AWC Papers; GWC to BTW, 28 May 1907, Box 7, GWC Papers [BTW].

35. Alvin D. Smith, *George Washington Carver: Man of God* (New York, 1954), pp. 17–18.

36. Ibid., p. 21.

37. Ibid., pp. 27–28.

38. Ibid., p. 43.

39. Tuskegee *Student*, 27 April 1907.

40. S. J. Thomas to GWC, 11 Dec. 1910, Box 8, R. R. Robinson to GWC, 28 Oct. 1918, Box 10, GWC Papers.

41. Collins Robinson to GWC, 31 July 1910, Robert L. Walker to GWC, 15 Aug. 1910, Box 8, GWC Papers; A. B. Storm to GWC, 30 June 1905, Box 1, JPG Collection.

42. Jose Figieras to GWC, 14 Jan. 1918, Samuel Richardson to GWC, 23 Sept. 1917, Box 10, GWC Papers.

43. A. W. Beck to GWC, 14 Sept. 1925, Box 15, GWC Papers.

44. Samuel Richardson to GWC, 25 June 1925, Box 15, GWC Papers.

45. "Lad of the Swamps" to GWC, 8 Aug. 1917, Box 10, GWC Papers; John Sutton, "Recollections of G. W. Carver," 1975, tape recording in possession of the author.

46. Interview with Beulah E. Cooper, 15 Dec. 1975.

47. "Dr. George W. Carver As I Knew Him," 27 Feb. 1943, typescript of WAPI radio broadcast, Box 100, GWC Papers.

CHAPTER 6: MAKING EDUCATION COMMON

1. Bond, *Negro Education*, pp. 178–94, 262–91; Louis R. Harlan, *Separate and Unequal: Public School Campaigns and Racism in the Southern Seaboard States, 1901–1915* (Chapel Hill, 1958), pp. 3–44, 248–69.

2. H. B. Bennett to GWC, 28 May, Box 8, GWC Papers [BTW].

3. Jones, "Role of Tuskegee," pp. 252–54.

4. Thrasher, *Tuskegee*, p. 163; *A Negro Conference to be Held in the Black Belt of Alabama*, handbill, 1892, Box 11, Tuskegee Institute Extension Papers, TIA (hereafter cited as TIE Papers).

5. Washington, *Story of My Life*, pp. 305–16; Booker T. Washington,

"How I Came to Call the First Negro Conference," *A.M.E. Church Review* 15 (April 1898): 802.

6. Jones, "Role of Tuskegee," pp. 255–56.

7. Anson Phelps Stokes, *Tuskegee Institute: The First Fifty Years* (Tuskegee, 1931), pp. 37–38; Washington, *Story of My Life*, p. 318.

8. GWC to BTW, 6 Jan. 1903, Box 4, GWC Papers [BTW]; Tuskegee *Student*, 18 Jan. 1903; B. W. Emery to GWC, 4 Dec. 1903, Box 5, GWC to the Tuskegee *Student*, 2 April 1910, Box 65, GWC Papers.

9. GWC to A. C. True, 18 Sept. 1902, Box 4, GWC Papers [NA RG 164]; Minutes of the Executive Council, 24 Nov. 1903, Box 1005, BTW Papers.

10. GWC, "What Chemurgy Means to My People," *Farm Chemurgic Journal* 1 (Sept. 1937): 40.

11. Tuskegee *Student*, 18 Nov. 1897; Monroe N. Work, "How Tuskegee Has Improved a Black Belt County," n.d., typescript, Box 3, Monroe Nathan Work Papers, TIA (hereafter cited as MNW Papers).

12. Jones, "Role of Tuskegee," p. 259; Tuskegee *Student*, 25 Nov. 1905, 30 June 1906, 25 May 1907; GWC to BTW, 18 March 1904, 20 April 1904, Box 555, BTW Papers; "Farmers' Institute Meeting," 21 May 1901, typed outline, Box 10, TIE Papers.

13. GWC, "What Chemurgy Means," p. 41; GWC to C. W. Greene, 19 Jan. 1903, Box 5, GWC Papers [BTW].

14. Jones, "Role of Tuskegee," pp. 259–60; T. M. Campbell, "The Relation of Extension Work to the General Economic Conditions of Country Life," ca. 1908, typescript, TMC Papers.

15. GWC, "Twelve Reasons Why Every Person in Macon County Should Attend the Macon County Fair," *Negro Farmer and Messenger*, 18 Nov. 1916.

16. Minutes of the Executive Council, 3 Dec. 1903, Box 1005, BTW Papers; Tuskegee *Student*, 12 Dec. 1903; Jones, "Role of Tuskegee," pp. 261–62.

17. Monroe N. Work, "Agricultural Training at Tuskegee Institute," n.d., typescript, Box 3, MNW Papers; "Farmers' Short Course in Agriculture Beginning January 5th and Closing January 20th 1908," n.d., Box 575, BTW Papers; Tuskegee *Student*, 20 Jan. 1906.

18. GWC to A. C. True, 18 Sept. 1902, Box 4, GWC Papers [NA RG 164].

19. GWC to BTW, 28 Nov. 1902, Box 261, R. C. Bedford to BTW, 3 Dec., 8 Dec. 1902, Box 221, BTW Papers.

20. E. J. Scott to BTW, 28 Nov., 2 Dec. 1902, Box 241, Warren Logan to BTW, 2 Dec. 1902, Box 272, R. C. Bedford to BTW, 3 Dec., 8 Dec. 1902, Box 221, N. E. Henry to BTW, 4 Dec. 1902, Box 272, BTW Papers.

21. R. C. Bedford to BTW, 3 Dec. 1902, Box 221, GWC to BTW, 28 Nov. 1902, Box 261, BTW Papers.

22. A. A. Turner, *Dairying in Connection with Farming*, Tuskegee Institute Experiment Station, Bulletin 22 (Tuskegee, 1912); GWC, *Poultry Raising in Macon County, Alabama*, Tuskegee Institute Experiment Station, Bulletin 23 (Tuskegee, 1912).

23. GWC, *Farmer's Almanac*, Tuskegee Experiment Station, Bulletin 1, 2nd. ed. (Tuskegee, 1940), first printed in 1899.

24. Atlanta *Journal*, 6 March 1923, clipping, Box 85, GWC Papers.

25. GWC, *White and Color Washing with Native Clays from Macon County, Alabama*, Tuskegee Institute Experiment Station, Bulletin 21 (Tuskegee, 1911).

26. GWC, *Some Ornamental Plants of Macon County, Alabama*, Tuskegee Institute Experiment Station, Bulletin 16 (Tuskegee, 1909).

27. Tuskegee *Student*, 30 Sept. 1905; Jones, "Role of Tuskegee," p. 266.

28. GWC, "Being Kind to the Soil," *Negro Farmer*, 31 Jan. 1914; GWC, "The Fat of the Land—How the Colored Farmer Can Live on It Twenty-One Times Each Week," *Negro Farmer*, 31 July 1915.

29. Tuskegee *Student*, 5 Oct. 1901; Calloway to GWC, 31 May 1904, Box 551, BTW Papers.

30. "George Washington Carver—The Man," mimeographed script of WAAP radio broadcast, 11 July 1948, Box 45, TMC Papers; interview with Georgia Poole, 15 Dec. 1975.

31. A. C. True, *History of Agricultural Extension Work* (Washington, 1928); Gladys Baker, *The County Agent* (Chicago, 1939), p. 7; GWC to BTW, 16 Nov. 1904, R. C. Bruce to GWC, 13 May 1904, Box 5, GWC Papers [BTW].

32. GWC to BTW, 16 Nov. 1904, Box 5, GWC Papers [BTW].

33. BTW to Jesup, 12 March 1906, Box 721, BTW Papers; Tuskegee *Student*, 17 Nov. 1906; GWC to BTW, 21 May 1906, Box 7, "Reports of the Jesup Wagon," 25 Aug. 1906, Box 108, GWC Papers [BTW]; Felix James, "The Tuskegee Institute Movable School," *Agricultural History* 45 (July 1971): 202–4.

34. Joseph C. Bailey, *Seaman A. Knapp: Pioneer Schoolmaster of American Agriculture* (New York, 1945), pp. 215–16; Seaman A. Knapp, *Demonstration Work with Southern Farmers*, USDA, Farmer's Bulletin 319 (Washington, 1908), p. 7.

35. Deborah Waldrop Austin, "Thomas Monroe Campbell and the Development of Negro Agricultural Extension Work, 1883–1956," master's thesis, Auburn University, 1975, p. 33.

36. Campbell, *Movable School*, pp. 116–20; James, "Tuskegee's Movable School," pp. 206–7.

37. Knapp to GWC, 20 Feb. 1907, Box 7, GWC Papers.

38. Baker, *County Agent*, pp. 36–40; Lewis W. Jones, "The South's Negro Farm Agent," *Journal of Negro Education* 22 (Winter 1953): 38–43; United States Commission on Civil Rights, *The Federal Civil Rights Enforcement Efforts: One Year Later* (Washington, 1971), pp. 126–27.

39. Charles S. Johnson, *Shadow of the Plantation* (Chicago, 1934), pp. 144–49.

CHAPTER 7: UNDEVELOPED SOUTHERN RESOURCES

1. In 1910, when Bridgeforth became the head of the reunified Agricultural Department, Tuskegee's extension programs were combined under the direction of an interdepartmental extension division.

2. Ms. fragment, n.d., Box 1, GWC Papers.

3. Clement Richardson, "A Man of Many Talents: George W. Carver of Tuskegee," *Southern Workman* 5 (Nov. 1916): 602; George B. Tindall, *The Emergence of the New South, 1913–1945* (Baton Rouge, 1967), pp. 276–80.

4. John Sutton to John W. Kitchens, 3 June 1975, Box 82, GWC Papers. Carver's interest in the nutritional properties of crops is evident in his major bulletins on cowpeas, sweet potatoes, and peanuts, all of which listed the protein content of the plants.

5. GWC to BTW, 7 Feb. 1902, Box 4, GWC Papers [BTW].

6. Minutes of the Executive Council, 20 Jan. 1903, TIA; Tuskegee *Student*, 17 Feb. 1906.

7. "Labels for the Montgomery Fair," n.d., Box 66, GWC Papers.

8. GWC to BTW, 8 March 1899, Box 4, GWC Papers [BTW].

9. Tuskegee *Student*, 15 March 1902; Fitzpatrick to GWC, 4 Dec. 1901, Box 4, GWC Papers.

10. Tuskegee *Student*, 15 March 1902; E. W. Menefee to GWC, 24 Jan., 18 Feb., 22 Feb. 1902, Box 4, GWC Papers.

11. Fitzpatrick to GWC, 13 Aug. 1902, Menefee to GWC, 17 Feb. 1902, Box 4, GWC Papers; Atlanta *Constitution*, 19 March 1902. Washington may have hoped to make money as a supplier for the company, since Carver was sent to investigate the possibility of the school's purchasing similiar deposits in Macon County. GWC to BTW, 26 Jan. 1904, Box 5, GWC Papers [BTW].

12. Menefee to GWC, 5 March 1902, Fitzpatrick to GWC, 28 March, 12 April, 17 May, 13 Aug. 1902, GWC to Fitzpatrick, 23 Aug. 1902, Box 4, GWC Papers.

13. Montgomery *Advertiser*, 14 Jan. 1903; Fitzpatrick to GWC, 14 Jan. 1903, Box 5, GWC Papers; Fitzpatrick to GWC, 27 July 1903, copy enc. in GWC to BTW, 28 July 1903, Box 5, GWC Papers [BTW].

14. Fitzpatrick to GWC, 27 July 1903, copy enc. in GWC to BTW, 28 July 1903, Box 5, GWC Papers [BTW]; A. Shackleford to GWC, 2 Jan. 1904, Box 5, GWC Papers.

15. Fitzpatrick to GWC, 20 Jan. 1904, J. T. Roberts to GWC, 7 March 1904, Box 5, GWC Papers.

16. GWC to BTW, 4 June 1910, Box 600, BTW Papers.

17. Committee report to BTW, 21 Nov. 1910, Box 600, BTW Papers.

18. Wilson to GWC, 10 Dec. 1910, Box 1, AWC Papers.

19. GWC to BTW, 21 Feb. 1911, BTW to GWC, 20 Feb. 1911, Box 8, GWC Papers [BTW].

20. GWC to BTW, 5 Sept., 11 Sept., 14 Sept. 1911, BTW to GWC, 7 Sept. 1911, GWC to E. J. Scott, 13 Sept. 1911, Box 8, GWC to BTW, 4 May, 20 Dec. 1912, E. T. Attwell to GWC, 29 Oct. 1912, Box 9, GWC Papers [BTW]; Minutes of the Executive Council, 29 March 1912, Box 1010, BTW Papers. As late as the mid-1930s Paul R. Miller was amazed to discover that Carver did not have an autoclave for sterilizing equipment and induced a company to donate one. Interview with Paul R. Miller, 3 Nov. 1975.

21. E. T. Attwell to GWC, 15 Aug. 1911, Box 8, R. R. Taylor to GWC, 20 Jan. 1912, Box 9, GWC Papers; Minutes of the Executive Council, 3 July 1913, Box 1011, BTW Papers; GWC to T. M. Campbell, 1 Sept. 1911, Box 8, E. J. Scott to GWC, 5 Aug. 1913, GWC to C. W. Greene, 18 Aug. 1914, J. B. Logan to GWC, 4 Oct. 1913, Box 9, GWC Papers.

22. Bridgeforth to J. H. Washington, 3 Aug. 1910, Box 600, Minutes of the Executive Council, 7 Dec. 1912, Box 1010, BTW Papers; GWC to BTW, 20 Dec. 1913, GWC to J. H. Washington, 11 July 1914, Box 9, GWC Papers [BTW].

23. GWC to BTW, 24 June 1912, 31 Aug. 1912, Box 9, GWC Papers [BTW]; GWC, A Study of the Soils of Macon County, Alabama, and Their Adaptability to Certain Crops, Tuskegee Institute Experiment Station, Bulletin 25 (Tuskegee, 1913).

24. GWC to BTW, 3 April 1911, JHW to GWC, 27 May 1911, Box 8, GWC Papers [BTW].

25. GWC to BTW, 29 May 1911, Box 8, GWC Papers [BTW].

26. GWC to BTW, 13 June 1911, Box 8, GWC to Warren Logan, 16 March 1912, GWC to BTW, 25 March 1912, John H. Drakeford to GWC, 25 March 1912, Box 9, GWC Papers [BTW]. As of 1980 the church still retained Carver's original stains.

27. GWC to J. H. Washington, 7 Aug. 1912, GWC to Mr. Fearing, 22 Aug. 1912, GWC to H. E. Thomas, 2 July 1912, GWC to Miss S. M. Russell, ca. 1912, Box 9, GWC Papers; BTW to GWC, 8 Sept. 1913,

GWC to BTW, ca. 1913, 10 Dec. 1913, 23 Jan., 24 Jan. 1914, GWC to E. J. Scott, 4 June 1914, Box 9, GWC Papers [BTW].

28. Montgomery *Advertiser*, 4 April 1912; GWC to BTW, 5 April 1912, Box 9, GWC to Scott, 7 Sept., 9 Sept. 1911, Box 8, GWC Papers [BTW].

29. GWC to Scott, 16 Nov. 1911, Box 8, GWC to Scott, 19 Feb. 1912, Aug. 1912, 5 Sept. 1912, 29 Nov. 1912, E. T. Attwell to GWC, 29 Oct. 1912, Box 9, GWC Papers [BTW].

30. Fitzpatrick Drug Company to GWC, 20 May, 31 May 1912, Box 9, GWC Papers [BTW].

31. GWC to J. H. Washington, 5 April 1911, Box 8, GWC Papers [BTW]; Minutes of the Executive Council, 18 Dec. 1912, Box 1010, BTW Papers.

32. J. Howard Fore to GWC, 31 Jan. 1912, GWC to E. J. Scott, 15 March 1912, GWC to BTW, 7 May 1912, form letter signed by GWC, 4 Sept. 1912, Edward L. Snyder to GWC, 4 Sept. 1912, GWC to BTW, 17 June 1913, J. B. Ramsey to GWC, 16 Sept. 1913, Box 9, GWC Papers; Minutes of the Executive Council, 15 June 1915, Box 1012, BTW Papers; Minutes of the Executive Council, 26 Aug. 1919, TIA.

33. GWC to BTW, 24 Aug., 27 July 1914, Box 9, GWC Papers [BTW].

34. GWC to BTW, 5 April 1911, Box 617, Minutes of the Executive Council, 19 Nov. 1913, Box 1011, 3 June 1915, 9 Dec. 1915, Box 1012, BTW Papers.

35. GWC, *Saving the Sweet Potato Crop*, Tuskegee Institute Experiment Station, Bulletin 10 (Tuskegee, 1906); GWC, *Saving the Wild Plum Crop*, Tuskegee Institute Experiment Station, Bulletin 12 (Tuskegee, 1907).

36. J. H. Washington to GWC, 20 Sept. 1911, BTW to GWC, 9 Oct. 1911, Box 8, GWC Papers [BTW].

37. BTW to Bridgeforth, 9 Dec., 13 Dec. 1911, Box 68, GWC Papers [BTW].

38. BTW to J. H. Washington, 2 Aug. 1912, Box 9, GWC Papers; Minutes of the Executive Council, 3 Aug., 1 Oct. 1912, Box 1010, BTW Papers; GWC, *The Pickling and Curing of Meat in Hot Weather*, Tuskegee Institute Experiment Station, Bulletin 24 (Tuskegee, 1912); GWC to BTW, 2 Feb. 1912, Box 9, GWC Papers [BTW].

39. GWC, *When, What and How to Can and Preserve Fruits and Vegetables in the Home*, Tuskegee Institute Experiment Station, Bulletin 27 (Tuskegee, 1915); GWC, *How to Dry Fruits and Vegetables* (Tuskegee, 1917).

CHAPTER 8: THE WIZARD OF TUSKEGEE

1. Earle to GWC, 23 Feb. 1910, Box 1, AWC Papers; Cary to GWC, 4 Jan. 1898, Box 4, GWC Papers.

2. Tuskegee *Student*, 11 Oct. 1902; GWC to BTW, 8 June 1904, Box 5, GWC Papers [BTW].

3. Tuskegee *Student*, 6 May 1911, 2 March 1901.

4. Ibid., 7 Jan. 1911; Kolb to GWC, 20 April 1914, Smith to GWC, 1 July 1903, Box 5, GWC Papers [BTW].

5. W. M. Hays to GWC, 17 Dec. 1904, Box 4, GWC Papers; GWC to BTW, 19 Jan. 1903, Box 5, GWC Papers [BTW].

6. Tuskegee *Student*, 7 Feb. 1903; GWC to BTW, 3 Feb. 1903, Box 5, GWC Papers [BTW].

7. GWC to E. J. Scott, 16 Sept. 1910, Box 8, GWC Papers [BTW]; Tuskegee *Student*, 24 Sept. 1910.

8. GWC to BTW, 9 Dec. 1897, 12 Nov. 1898, Box 4, GWC Papers [BTW].

9. GWC to BTW, 19 Nov. 1903, Box 5, GWC Papers.

10. For a listing of some of the "little Tuskegees" *see* Stokes, *Tuskegee Institute*, pp. 33–34.

11. Akron (Ohio) *Times*, 12 April 1925, clipping, Box 87, GWC Papers.

12. Jackson (Tenn.) *Christian Index*, 2 July 1908.

13. Enclosure in Jessie O. Thomas to GWC, 11 April 1918, Box 10, GWC Papers; *see* printed programs in Box 2, GWC Papers; E. J. Scott to GWC, 1 March 1915, Box 9, GWC Papers [BTW].

14. GWC to BTW, 3 March 1903, Box 5, GWC Papers [BTW]; Tuskegee *Student*, 14 March 1903; New York *Evening Post*, 6 March 1906, clipping, Box 1, AWC Papers.

15. *See* printed programs in Box 2, GWC Papers.

16. *Southern Letter*, Aug. 1904, clipping, Box 84, GWC Papers.

17. *See* clippings, Box 87, GWC Papers; Minutes of the Executive Council, 20 Jan. 1903, TIA.

18. GWC to BTW, 3 Feb. 1903, Box 5, GWC Papers [BTW]. In 1907 Carver was asked to prepare a permanent exhibit for the state capitol. Minutes of the Executive Council, 7 Nov. 1907, Box 1006, BTW Papers.

19. Montgomery *Advertiser*, 21 Oct. 1911.

20. GWC to BTW, 10 May 1915, 25 Dec. 1914, Box 9, GWC Papers [BTW].

21. GWC to BTW, 16 Nov. 1914, Box 9, GWC Papers [BTW]; Tuskegee *Student*, 13 Nov. 1915.

22. Montgomery *Advertiser*, 8 March 1903; Tuskegee *Student*, 15 Aug.

1900; "Gave Up Art Career for His Race," *Technical World Magazine* 17 (May 1912): 15.

23. Tuskegee *Student*, 11 March 1911.

24. GWC, "A Few Hints to Southern Farmers," *Southern Workman*, Sept. 1899, pp. 351–52; Review of Reviews Company to GWC, 28 Feb. 1902, Box 4, GWC Papers, GWC to BTW, 29 Feb. 1904, Box 5, 15 Dec. 1913, Box 9, GWC Papers [BTW]; A. W. Rayward to GWC, 10 Nov. 1904, Box 5, GWC Papers.

25. Sir Harry Johnston, *The Negro in the New World* (London, 1910), p. 416.

26. Crisp interview notes.

27. Washington, *My Larger Education*, pp. 223–31.

28. "The Latest Contribution to Negro Progress," *Tuskegee Alumni Bulletin* 1 (Jan.–March 1914): 1–2.

CHAPTER 9: THE END OF AN ERA

1. GWC to BTW, 27 Aug. 1898, Box 4, 1 April 1911, Box 8, 25 Sept. 1912, GWC to Scott, 15 Feb. 1916, 3 April 1916, Box 9, GWC Papers [BTW].

2. GWC to RRM, 18 July 1919, Box 11, GWC Papers.

3. RRM to GWC, 10 June 1916, Box 9, GWC Papers.

4. RRM to GWC, 7 Sept. 1917, Box LC 11, Robert Russa Moton Papers, TIA (hereafter cited as RRM Papers).

5. GWC to E. J. Scott, 7 Sept. 1916, Box 9, GWC Papers; Tuskegee *Student*, 16 Sept. 1916; Royal Society for the Encouragement of Arts, Manufactures and Commerce, *List of Fellows* (London, 1924), p. 9.

6. E. J. Scott to GWC, 21 Dec. 1916, Box 9, GWC Papers; G. K. Menzier to Robert B. Eleazer, 13 Nov. 1925, Box 31, Commission on Interracial Cooperation Papers, Atlanta University (hereafter cited as CIC Papers).

7. Minutes of the Executive Council, 16 March 1916, TIA; RRM to GWC, 21 July 1919, Box 11, GWC Papers; "Thirteen Highest Salaries List," typescript, 1914, Box 654, BTW Papers.

8. James B. Dudley to GWC, 22 Feb. 1919, Box 1, AWC Papers.

9. Sutton, "Recollections."

10. Ezella M. Carter to GWC, 29 Aug. 1918, P. B. Speer to GWC, 22 June 1917, Box 10, GWC Papers.

11. GWC to L. H. Pammel, 15 July 1921, Box 11, GWC Papers [ISUA].

12. GWC to RRM, 3 Dec. 1919, Box 11, GWC Papers; Tuskegee *Student*, 27 Nov. 1920; John Reed to GWC, 12 Oct. 1917, Box 10, GWC Papers.

13. Harry L. Lightbourne to GWC, 25 Jan. 1919, Walter L. Hutcherson to GWC, 7 April 1919, Box 10, GWC Papers.

14. GWC to RRM, 5 Sept. 1916, GWC to Warren Logan, 18 Oct. 1916, Box 9, GWC Papers.

15. Tuskegee *Student*, 3 Feb. 1917; GWC to RRM, 6 June 1924, Box 14, GWC Papers.

16. GWC to Business Committee, 14 Dec. 1925, Box 15, GWC Papers; Matthew Woods to T. M. Campbell, 28 Feb. 1940, Box 14, TMC Papers.

17. Warren Logan to GWC, 1 June 1922, Box 12, Secretary to the Principal to GWC, 2 Sept. 1920, Box 11, GWC Papers.

18. GWC to RRM, 1 Feb. 1917, GWC to Warren Logan, 6 Feb., 20 Feb., 26 Feb. 1917, E. J. Scott to GWC, 3 Feb. 1917, Box LC 3, RRM Papers; William Holtzclaw to GWC, 31 Dec. 1921, Box 11, GWC Papers.

19. GWC, *How to Grow the Peanut and 105 Ways for Preparing It for Human Consumption*, Tuskegee Institute Experiment Station, Bulletin 31 (Tuskegee, 1916); GWC, *Three Delicious Meals Every Day for the Farmer*, Tuskegee Institute Experiment station Bulletin 32 (Tuskegee, 1916); GWC, *43 Ways to Save the Wild Plum Crop*, Tuskegee Institute Experiment Station, Bulletin 34 (Tuskegee, 1917); GWC, *How to Grow the Cow Pea and Forty Ways of Preparing It as a Table Delicacy*, Tuskegee Institute Experiment Station, Bulletin 35 (Tuskegee, 1917); GWC, *Twelve Ways to Meet the New Economic Conditions Here in the South*, Tuskegee Institute Experiment Station, Bulletin 33 (Tuskegee, 1917).

20. GWC, *How to Grow the Tomato and 115 Ways to Prepare It for the Table*, Tuskegee Institute Experiment Station, Bulletin 36 (Tuskegee, 1918); GWC, *How to Make Sweet Potato Flour, Starch, Sugar, Bread and Mock Cocoanut*, Tuskegee Institute Experiment Station, Bulletin 37 (Tuskegee, 1918).

21. EJS to GWC, 20 Dec. 1916, Box 9, GWC Papers; GWC to EJS, 22 Dec. 1916, Box LC 6, RRM Papers.

22. GWC to RRM, 1 Feb. 1917, Box LC 6, RRM Papers.

23. GWC to RRM, 27 Feb. 1918, Box LC 11, RRM Papers; Littell McClung, "A Glimpse of the Remarkable Works of George W. Carver, the Negro Scientist," Montgomery *Advertiser*, 25 Nov. 1917; David Fairchild to GWC, 20 June 1920, Box 1, AWC Papers.

24. Tuskegee *Student*, 9 Feb. 1918.

25. GWC to A. L. Holsey, 24 Jan. 1918, Box LC 11, RRM Papers.

26. GWC to RRM, Box LC 11, RRM Papers. Evidently Carver correctly assessed his impact on the men at the meeting. In 1942 W. A. Lloyd

of the Association of Land Grant Colleges and Universities wrote that he still remembered how Carver "contributed so much at that time." Lloyd to GWC, 16 May 1942, Box 57, GWC Papers.

27. C. E. Mangels to GWC, 27 March 1919, S. T. Prescott to GWC, 29 March 1919, W. S. Moore to GWC, 30 May 1918; H. C. Gore to GWC, 10 May, 14 May 1918, Box 10, George Hoffman to GWC, 18 Sept. 1919, H. C. Gore to GWC, 24 Nov. 1919, Box 11, GWC Papers.

28. "Tuskegee's War Work," *Southern Letter* 35 (July 1918); Orangeburg (S.C.) *Record*, 2 March 1918; GWC, *How to Dry Fruits and Vegetables* (Tuskegee, 1917); GWC, *How to Make Sweet Potato Flour, Starch, Sugar, Bread and Mock Cocoanut*, Tuskegee Institute Experiment Station, Bulletin 37 (Tuskegee, 1918), p. 3; Bamberg County (S.C.) *Times*, 12 Feb. 1920, clipping, Box 85, GWC Papers.

29. GWC to RRM, 22 Sept. 1919, GWC to Grubbs, 1 Oct. 1919, Grubbs to GWC, 30 Nov. 1919, Box 11, GWC Papers.

30. Grubbs to GWC, 30 Nov., 12 Dec. 1919, Box 11, GWC Papers.

31. Carrol and Muhrer, "Scientific Contributions," pp. 22–23; *Principal's Annual Report, 1919–1920* (Tuskegee, 1920), p. 2; interview with Mrs. Milton Kerensky, 1980; "Convention of the United Peanut Association of America, Montgomery, Alabama, September 13th and 14th, 1920," Box 2, AWC Papers.

32. "Peanut Milk," *Good Health*, Oct. 1920, pp. 589–91; "Close Counterpart of Milk Made from Peanuts," *Popular Mechanics*, May 1920; "Cows Milk from Peanuts, Work of Colored Genius," *Liberty Bell*, May 1920, p. 2; interview with Helen Dibble, 14 Dec. 1975.

33. "Distinguished Negro's Plea," *Southern Nut Growers Journal*, April 1921; *Hearings Before the Committee on Ways and Means. House of Representatives on Schedule G, Agricultural Products and Provisions, January 21, 1921. Tariff Information, 1921* (Washington, 1921), pp. 1543–51 (hereafter cited as *Tariff Hearings*); Garner to GWC, 31 Aug. 1939, Box 45, GWC Papers.

34. *Tariff Hearings*, pp. 1544, 1548, 1546–47.

35. "Distinguished Negro's Plea"; "Peanuts to Be Basis for New Foods— Prof. Carver," *Peanut Journal*, April 1921, p. 11.

36. "Newspapers Talking About the Peanut Exhibit of Prof. Carver," *Peanut Promoter*, April 1921, p. 54; numerous clippings, Box 85, GWC Papers; "The Potential Uses of the Peanut," *Peanut Promoter*, May 1921, p. 20; J. Frank Fooshe to GWC, 21 April 1922, Lem Jordan to GWC, 29 Aug. 1922, Box 12, GWC Papers; Norfolk *Journal and Guide*, 4 Nov. 1922.

37. GWC to Rogers Co., 18 Aug. 1922, GWC to E. M. DePencier, 29 Nov., 12 Dec. 1922, Box 12, GWC Papers.

38. "Peanuts: How Scientist's 145 Varieties Helped Lowly Goober to Rise," *Popular Science Monthly*, May 1923, p. 68.

39. St. Louis *Globe-Democrat*, 3 April 1921, clipping, Box 85, GWC Papers.

40. Musher & Co. to GWC, 28 Nov. 1919, GWC to Lyman Ward, 29 Nov. 1921, Box 11, GWC Papers.

41. George F. King, "North Carolina Negro Farmers Present Dr. Carver Loving Cup," *Rural Messenger*, April 1922, p. 1; Jno D. Wray to GWC, 17 Feb. 1922, Box 12, GWC Papers.

42. Tougaloo College (Miss.) *News*, March 1917, clipping, Box 84, Savannah *Press*, 17 Feb. 1923, clipping, Box 85, GWC Papers.

43. GWC to Pres. Murphy, 24 Sept. 1934, Box 26, Norman Speiden to GWC, 9 June 1937, Box 32, GWC Papers.

44. GWC to Speiden, 12 June 1937, Box 32, GWC Papers.

45. Edison to Agricultural School, Tuskegee Institute, 27 May 1927, Box 17, GWC Papers.

CHAPTER 10: DAWNING OF THE NEW SOUTH

1. Edwards, *Carver of Tuskegee*, pp. 36–37, 76–77.

2. Atlanta *Journal*, 6 March 1923; G. W. Ridout, "Kingdom of God Notes," *Pentacostal Herald*, 17 July 1935.

3. *Tariff Hearings*, p. 1544.

4. Harold O. Winter to GWC, 22 April, 30 April, 8 May 1919, Box 10, Winter to GWC, 10 June 1919, Box 11, Danforth to GWC, 24 April 1922, GWC to Danforth, 5 May 1922, Box 12, GWC Papers.

5. GWC to Blodgett, 15 May, 12 July, 22 Nov. 1922, Blodgett to GWC, 6 July, 15 Nov. 1922, Box 12, Blodgett to GWC, 9 Aug., 20 Aug. 1923, Box 13, GWC Papers; Savannah *Press*, 17 Feb. 1923, clipping, Box 85, GWC Papers.

6. Interview with Florida Segrest, 11 Dec. 1975; GWC to BTW, 11 June 1913, Box 9, GWC Papers.

7. EWT to GWC, 18 Oct. 1921, Box 11, GWC Papers.

8. GWC to EWT, 19 Dec. 1921, Box 11, GWC Papers.

9. EWT to GWC, 20 May 1922, Box 12, GWC Papers.

10. EWT to GWC, 7 Jan., 14 Jan., 16 Jan., 10 Feb., 15 Feb., 20 Feb., 7 March, 8 March, 13 March, 21 March, 1 May, 22 May, 8 June, 10 July 1922, Box 12, GWC Papers.

11. Sam W. Wilkes to J. P. Billups, 9 March 1923, Box 68, GWC Papers; Atlanta *Journal*, 6 March 1923.

12. Ibid.

13. Woodward, *Origins of the New South*, pp. 142–234; Paul M. Gaston,

The New South Creed: A Study in Southern Mythmaking (New York, 1970).

14. Atlanta *Journal*, 6 March 1923.

15. EWT to GWC, 1 March 1923, Box 12, GWC Papers.

16. Atlanta *Journal*, 22 May 1927; Scott W. Allen to GWC, 12 May 1923, Box 12, GWC Papers.

17. EWT to GWC, 21 March 1923, GWC to Martin A. Menefee, 20 April 1923, GWC to Lyman Ward, 23 April 1923, Box 12, GWC Papers.

18. EWT to GWC, 27 April 1923, S. W. Allen to GWC, 12 May 1923, Box 12, GWC Papers; *see also* copies of patents in Box 2, GWC Papers.

19. EWT to GWC, 27 April 1923, Box 12, GWC Papers.

20. EWT to GWC, 10 Oct. 1923; Baltimore *Afro-American*, 11 July 1925, clipping, Education 1925, Scholarship and Other Distinctions, Department of Records and Research Files, TIA (hereafter cited as DRR Files).

21. EWT to GWC, 26 June 1923, Atlanta *Journal*, 26 Aug. 1923.

22. Atlanta *Constitution*, 26 Aug. 1923.

23. EWT to GWC, 13 Aug., 21 Aug. 1923, Box 13, GWC Papers; *see also* pamphlet and flyer in Box 83, GWC Papers.

24. Atlanta *Journal*, 26 Aug. 1923; *Manufacturers' Record*, 6 Sept. 1923.

25. EWT to GWC, 10 Oct., 2 Nov., 4 Nov., 9 Nov. 1923, GWC to C. E. Gross, 13 Nov. 1923, Box 13, GWC Papers; Atlanta *Journal*, 21 Feb. 1924; *see also* undated invitation in Box 2, GWC Papers.

26. EWT to GWC, 11 March, 30 Sept. 1923, Box 12, 9 April, 21 April, 27 May 1924, Box 13, GWC to EWT, 4 Jan. 1925, Box 15, GWC Papers; GWC to C. E. Rarig, 15 Oct. 1924, Box 1, JPG Collection; GWC to L. H. Pammel, 22 May 1924, Box 13, GWC Papers [ISUA].

27. EWT to GWC, 17 July, 19 July, 24 July, 31 Aug. 1924, J. B. Clarke to GWC, 27 Sept. 1924, EWT to GWC, 24 July, 13 Aug., 1 Oct. 1924, Box 14, EWT to GWC, 13 July 1925, Box 15, GWC Papers.

28. GWC to Mr. McDuffie, 14 Sept. 1925, GWC to Business Committee, 14 Dec. 1925, Box 15, GWC Papers.

29. GWC to C. A. Goodwin, 12 Feb. 1927, Box 17, Sam W. Wilkes to GWC, 21 June 1926, Box 16, Carrie Kirtley to GWC, 15 Dec. 1930, Box 19, GWC to Raleigh Merritt, 16 Dec. 1928, Box 18, GWC Papers.

30. New York *World*, 19 Nov. 1924; GWC to Albert Logette, 22 Nov. 1924, Box 16, GWC Papers.

31. A. J. King to GWC, 18 Feb. 1925, Charles W. Watts to GWC, 18 April 1925, Box 15, H. W. Pope to GWC, 28 Nov. 1924, Box 14, GWC Papers.

32. Printed stock offering, n.d., Box 106, GWC Papers; "Carver Penol Company," *Peanut Journal* 5 (Oct. 1926): 28; GWC to Courtney DeKalb, 1 April 1926, GWC to Love Joy Smith, 15 Oct. 1926, Box 16, GWC Papers.

33. GWC to Raleigh Merritt, 25 May 1926, Box 16, GWC Papers; Rebecca Caudill, "A Scientist in God's Workshop," *Our Young People*, Jan. 1927, p. 7.

34. GWC to Edmond J. Cleveland, 20 Sept. 1926, Box 16, Penol pamphlet, n.d., Box 106, GWC Papers.

35. George B. Philips to GWC, 20 June 1929, Friday [1929], Box 19, GWC Papers; form letter, 23 April 1930, Box 46, TMC Papers.

36. GWC to Raleigh Merritt, 5 Nov. 1931, Box 21, Powell to Hamlin, 24 Sept. 1937, Box 68, GWC Papers.

37. Hamlin to GWC, 20 Oct. 1932, Box 21, A. P. Durham to GWC, 17 Oct. 1933, Box 23, Hamlin to GWC, 17 Jan. 1934, Box 24, GWC Papers.

38. Powell to Hamlin, 24 Sept. 1937, Box 68, reprint from *Drug Topics*, Aug. 1933, Box 90, Hamlin to GWC, 23 Aug. 1937, Box 33, GWC Papers.

39. Powell to Hamlin, 24 Sept. 1937, Box 68, GWC Papers.

40. Hamlin to Powell, 29 Sept. 1937, Box 68, GWC Papers.

41. Interview with Mrs. G. C. Thompson, 27 July 1977.

42. Hamlin to GWC, 29 Sept. 1937, GWC to Hamlin, 6 Oct. 1937, Box 33, Hamlin to GWC, 12 Feb., 21 Feb. 1938, GWC to Hamlin, 17 Feb. 1938, Box 37, GWC Papers.

43. GWC to EWT, 25 Feb. 1938, Box 37, GWC Papers.

44. Hamlin to GWC, 29 Sept. 1937, Box 33, GWC Papers.

45. Hamlin to GWC, 12 Oct. 1937, Box 33, 7 Oct. 1940, Box 50, GWC to Hamlin, 12 Oct. 1940, Box 50, GWC Papers.

46. Hamlin to GWC, 4 Dec. 1941, Box 55, GWC Papers.

47. GWC to A. L. McLendon, 5 Feb. 1938, Box 36, GWC Papers.

48. Patent 1,522,176, "Cosmetic and Process of Producing Same," 6 Jan. 1925, Box 2, GWC Papers.

CHAPTER 11: BREAKING DOWN BARRIERS

1. Franklin, *From Slavery*, pp. 475–86; Arthur I. Waskow, *From Race Riot to Sit-In, 1919 and the 1960s* (New York, 1967), pp. 1–208.

2. Mrs. Will C. King to GWC, 7 March 1923, Box 12, GWC Papers; Atlanta *Constitution*, 10 March 1923.

3. William H. Holtzclaw to GWC, 24 Dec. 1917, Box 10, 21 May 1922,

Box 12, GWC Papers; John Hurst to GWC, 11 June 1923, Box 1, AWC Papers.

4. DuBois to GWC, 29 June 1923, Box 1, AWC Papers.

5. *14th Annual Report of the N.A.A.C.P. for the Year 1923* (New York, 1924), p. 38.

6. GWC to Pammel, 24 Aug., 5 May 1923, LHP to GWC, 5 March 1923, Box 12, GWC Papers [ISUA].

7. For further information on the organization and program of the CIC see Edward Flud Burrows, "The Commission on Interracial Cooperation: A Case Study in the History of the Interracial Movement in the South," Ph.D. dissertation, University of Wisconsin, 1954; Ann Wells Ellis, "The Commission on Interracial Cooperation, 1919–1944: Its Activities and Results," Ph.D. dissertation, Georgia State University, 1975; Wilma Dykeman and James Stokely, *Seeds of Southern Change: The Life of Will Alexander* (Chicago, 1962).

8. New York *Age*, 31 July 1920, clipping in Race Relations: Cooperation—Discussions, 1920, DRR Files.

9. Hot Springs *Sentinel-Record*, 29 Aug. 1920; Utica Institute *News*, 15 April 1921; GWC to Lyman Ward, 24 April 1920, GWC to F. J. Hubbard, 16 Aug. 1920, GWC to RRM, 11 Feb. 1921, Box 11, Alexander to GWC, 13 July 1922, GWC to Mrs. Luke Johnson, 20 Nov. 1922, GWC to Alexander, 23 Nov. 1922, Box 12, GWC Papers; Ashville *Citizen*, 23 June 1923; Atlanta *Constitution*, 7 Dec. 1922.

10. Alexander to GWC, 16 March 1923, George E. Haynes to GWC, 23 March 1923, Weatherford to GWC, 5 May 1923, Box 12, GWC to Alexander, 4 June 1923, Box 13, GWC Papers; Edwards, *Carver of Tuskegee*, p. 115.

11. Edwards, *Carver of Tuskegee*, p. 121–22.

12. Ibid.

13. GWC to JTH, 29 Oct. 1923, Box 13, GWC Papers [GWCNM].

14. Pete Daniel, "Black Power in the 1920s: The Case of the Tuskegee Veterans Hospital," *Journal of Southern History* 36 (Aug. 1970): 368–88.

15. EWT to GWC, 6 July, 18 July 1923, Box 13, GWC Papers; Edwards, *Carver of Tuskegee*, p. 131.

16. GWC to John D. Mayhew, 15 Oct. 1923, GWC to Alexander, 16 Oct. 1923, Box 13, GWC Papers.

17. GWC to J. E. Johnson, 12 Nov. 1923, GWC to Alexander, 1 Dec. 1923, Box 13, Hodges to GWC, 16 June 1925, Box 15, GWC Papers.

18. GWC to M. A. Menefee, 14 Nov. 1923, Box 13, "Expense Account," 18 Nov. 1923, Box 13, Hodges to GWC, 16 June 1925, Box 15, GWC Papers.

19. W. M. Riggs to J. E. Johnson, 5 Dec. 1923, R. C. Grier to Johnson, 30 Nov. 1923, Box 68, GWC Papers.

20. D. M. Douglass to Johnson, 28 Nov. 1923, Box 68, GWC Papers; Edwards, *Carver of Tuskegee*, p. 153; GWC to JTH, 7 Jan. 1924, Box 13, GWC Papers [GWCNM].

21. GWC to Bergthold, 18 Feb. 1924, Box 13, GWC Papers; Robert B. Eleazer, "The Goober Wizard," *Intercollegian* 41 (March 1924): 10–11; A. R. Elliot to GWC, 12 April, 25 April 1924, GWC to Elliot, 19 April 1924, Box 13, GWC Papers.

22. Howard Kester, "Recollections of G. W. Carver," 2 Nov. 1975, typescript in possession of author (hereafter cited as Kester, "Recollections").

23. Bergthold to GWC, 3 June 1924, GWC to Bergthold, 6 Aug. 1924, Box 14, GWC Papers.

24. Kester, "Recollections"; Walter Nickell to GWC, 29 Oct. 1931, Box 21, GWC Papers.

25. Bergthold to GWC, 4 July, 20 Oct. 1924, Alexander to GWC, 30 July 1924, GWC to Bergthold, 29 Oct. 1924, Bergthold to RRM, 1 Nov. 1924, Box 14, GWC Papers.

26. Bergthold to GWC, 29 Nov., 3 Dec. 1924, Edith Allen to GWC, 7 May 1924, GWC to Edith Allen, 22 Oct. 1924, Box 14, GWC Papers.

27. New York *World*, 19 Nov. 1924.

28. *New York Times*, 19 Nov. 1924.

29. GWC to *New York Times*, 24 Nov. 1924, Box 46, TMC Papers; New York *World*, 20 Nov. 1924; Columbus (Ga.) *Inquirer*, 20 Nov. 1924, clipping, Box 86, GWC Papers.

30. GWC to Lyman Ward, 15 Nov. 1925, Box 15, GWC Papers.

31. Bergthold to GWC, 3 Dec. 1924, Box 14, Vera L. Ward to GWC, 30 Jan. 1925, Alexander to GWC, 30 Jan. 1925, Box 15, New York *Age*, 31 Jan. 1925, clipping, Box 87, GWC Papers; Greensboro *News*, 21 Jan. 1925, clipping in Education: Scholarship and Other Distinctions, 1925, DRR Files.

32. GWC to Hyne, 10 Feb. 1924, Box 15, Ithaca *Journal-News*, 19 Feb. 1925, clipping, Box 87, GWC Papers.

33. Hyne to GWC, "Monday night," Box 14, "Monday night," Box 15, GWC Papers.

34. GWC to RRM, 16 March 1926, Box 16, GWC Papers.

35. Copy enc. in Arthur Faucett to GWC, 4 April 1926, Box 16, GWC Papers.

36. "Introductory Statement Concerning the George Washington Carver Fellowship, Containing Historical Statement, Purpose, Organization and Concluding Statement," 10 July 1926, Box 100, GWC Papers.

37. GWC to RRM, 16 March 1926, Bergthold to GWC, 19 April, 14 June 1926, Jack E. Boyd to GWC, 8 Oct. 1926, Eleazer to GWC, 24 Nov. 1926, Box 16, "Expense Account," 5 Nov. 1926, Box 2, GWC Papers.

38. "Student Interracial Work in the Southern Region" [1926?], typescript, Box 103, GWC Papers; "Students White and Colored," *World Tomorrow*, Aug. 1924, clipping in Race Relations: Improvement of, 1924, DRR Files; Charlotte *Presbyterian Standard*, 3 March 1936, clipping in Race Relations, Improvement of, 1926, DRR Files.

39. Chicago *Christian Century*, 7 May 1925, clipping in Race Relations: Improvement of, 1925, DRR Files.

40. GWC to Sue Hill, 30 April 1927, Hill to GWC, 13 June 1927, Box 31, CIC Papers; Brown to GWC, 20 Dec. 1927, Box 17, GWC Papers. There are other letters regarding the aborted Mississippi tour in Box 31, CIC Papers.

41. Brown to Eleazer, 13 March, 30 April 1928, Karl Terfors to Sue Hill, 22 April 1928, GWC to Eleazer, 28 April 1928, Brown to GWC, 30 April 1928, Marysville *Highland Echo*, 27 April 1928, reprint, Box 31, CIC Papers; Norfolk *Journal and Guide*, 12 May 1928.

42. Eleazer to L. R. Reynolds, 22 Jan. 1929, Box 31, CIC Papers; Wilson Newman to GWC, 1 Feb. 1929, Box 18, GWC Papers; Brown to Eleazer, 8 Oct. 1930, Box 31, CIC Papers; GWC to JTH, 7 Dec. 1930, Box 19, 6 April 1931, Box 20, Ashville *Citizen*, 1 May 1931, Atlanta *World*, 22 April 1931, clippings, Box 89, GWC Papers.

43. GWC to JTH, 3 March 1932, CIC press release, 5 May 1932, Box 31, CIC Papers; Washington *Tribune*, 13 May 1932, New Orleans *Times-Picayune*, 17 May 1932, clippings, Box 89, GWC Papers; Edwards, *Carver of Tuskegee*, pp. 175–77.

44. This editorial was reprinted in the Tuskegee *Messenger*, July 1932. *See also* Edwards, *Carver of Tuskegee*, p. 177.

45. GWC to JTH, 16 June 1933, Box 21, JTH to "Dear Friend," 14 Oct. 1932, mimeographed letter, Box 68, GWC Papers.

46. GWC to JTH, 3 Jan., 9 Jan. 1933, Box 21, GWC Papers.

47. Johnnie Pickle to GWC, n.d., in "George Washington Carver: Lover of Men, Master of Things," GWC Museum (hereafter cited as "Lover of Men").

48. Howard Frazier to GWC, 6 Oct. 1932, Kester to GWC, 2 Nov. 1932, in "Lover of Men."

49. "George W. Carver: Apostle of Interracial Appreciation," Tuskegee *Messenger*, Jan. 1934; Benjamin F. Hubert to GWC, 26 Sept., 29 Sept. 1933, GWC to JTH, 23 Dec. 1933, Box 23, GWC Papers. *See also* the copy of Philip Wener to Heads of Institutions, 2 Jan. 1933, Box 31, CIC Papers.

50. GWC to JTH, 19 Oct. 1933, Box 23, GWC Papers [GWCNM].
51. Billy Fielder to GWC, 24 Sept. 1932, Box 21, GWC Papers.
52. Wilson Newman to GWC, 20 Nov. 1929, Box 19, GWC Papers.
53. JTH to GWC, 28 Dec. 1932, in "Lover of Men."
54. Edwards, *Carver of Tuskegee*, p. 182; Al Zissler to GWC, 15 Dec. 1935, Box 28, GWC Papers.
55. JTH to GWC, 28 Dec. 1932, in "Lover of Men"; Jim Boysell to GWC, 1 May 1928, Box 17, GWC Papers.
56. Lucy Cherry Crisp to GWC, 6 Oct. 1933, Box 23, GWC Papers.
57. Jack E. Boyd to GWC, 18 Nov. 1930, Box 19, GWC Papers.
58. Gilbert W. Weiting to GWC, 15 Feb. 1939, Box 41, Tom B. Hyder to F. D. Patterson, 10 Jan. 1943, Box 73, GWC Papers; interview with John B. Stevenson, 14 Nov. 1975; Kester, "Recollections."

CHAPTER 12: THE PEANUT MAN

1. L. D. Shuford to GWC, 8 Jan. 1924, D. D. Breese Jones to GWC, 14 May 1925, GWC to Albon Holsey, 7 May 1924, Box 13, GWC to RRM, 30 Sept. 1927, Box 17, GWC Papers.
2. Huston to GWC, 18 Oct. 1924, GWC to Huston, 23 Oct. 1924, Huston to GWC, 25 Oct. 1924, Box 14, GWC to Huston, 12 April 1926, Box 16, Huston to GWC, 5 March 1928, Box 17, GWC to Huston, 6 Oct. 1928, Box 18, GWC Papers.
3. GWC to Walter A. Richards, 1 July 1929, Box 19, GWC Papers.
4. Barry and Porter, "Report on the Culture of the Virginia Type Peanut in the Southeastern States in 1930," mimeographed report, 30 Jan. 1931, Box 104, pp. A-1–A-6, C-1–D-3, GWC papers.
5. Ibid., pp. F-1–F-9.
6. Ibid., p. F-2; Barry to GWC, 20 Aug. 1930, Box 19, GWC Papers.
7. Barry to GWC, 16 Sept. 1930, Box 19, GWC Papers.
8. Barry to GWC, 3 Feb. 1931, Box 20, Barry to Arthur M. Hyde, 16 Feb. 1931, Box 68, GWC Papers [NA RG 16].
9. B. B. Higgins to Barry, 19 Feb. 1931, Barry to GWC, 16 March 1931, Barry to Higgins, 14 March 1931, Barry to GWC, 25 March 1931, Box 20, GWC Papers.
10. GWC to Taubenhaus, 11 April, 22 June 1931, Barry to GWC, 15 July 1931, Box 20, GWC Papers.
11. Interview with Paul R. Miller, 3 Nov. 1975.
12. Barry to GWC, 2 June 1932, Box 21, GWC Papers.
13. GWC to Huston, 7 Jan. 1930, Box 19, GWC Papers; interview with Paul R. Miller, 3 Nov. 1975; Columbus *Enquirer-Sun*, 13 March 1930, clipping, Box 85, GWC Papers; Huston to GWC, 7 May 1931,

Box LC 53, RRM Papers; "The Tom Huston Placque," Box 2, GWC Papers; Birmingham *News*, 26 May 1931.

14. GWC to Huston, 13 May 1931, GWC to Lyman Ward, 22 May 1931, Box 20, GWC Papers.

15. Montgomery *Advertiser*, 29 May 1931.

16. GWC to RRM, 16 Nov. 1931, Box LC 53, RRM Papers; GWC to Mr. Usher, 8 Aug. 1935, Box 28, Grady Porter to GWC, 10 Jan. 1938, Box 35, Walter Richards to GWC, 28 Jan. 1938, Box 36, Porter to GWC, 29 Nov. 1939, Box 17, 15 Feb. 1940, Box 48, GWC Papers.

17. Osborn to GWC, 7 Aug. 1924, Box 14, GWC Papers.

18. GWC to Osborn, 15 Feb. 1924, Box 13, 6 June 1929, Box 19, GWC Papers; "Peanut Diseases and Their Control," *Peanut World* 1 (May 1931): 15–17; *Peanut Journal* 8 (May 1929): 9.

19. Hearin to RRM, 9 June 1924, Box 68, GWC Papers.

20. GWC to RRM, 26 Feb., 28 April 1925, Box 15, GWC Papers; "Carver's Exhibit at the New York Exposition," *Peanut Journal* 6 (July 1925): 9–10; Edmonds to William G. Sirrine, 4 May 1925, enc. in Edmonds to GWC, 4 May 1925, Box 15, GWC Papers.

21. GWC to RRM, 22 May 1925, Box 15, John H. Baird to E. W. Thompson, 15 July 1925, Box 68, GWC Papers; "Exhibit of Sweet Potato and Peanut Products by Professor Carver of Tuskegee," *Manufacturers' Record*, 7 May 1925. Hearin noted that "nothing contributed more to our success than your splendid exhibit." Hearin to GWC, 26 May 1925, LCC Papers. The governor of Alabama shook hands with Carver at the exhibit and said, "You are an asset to the whole South." Crisp interview notes.

22. Press release, n.d., Box 88, GWC Papers; Tuskegee *News*, 27 Feb. 1930; W. E. Long to GWC, 12 Feb. 1930, LCC Papers.

23. Oklahoma City *Black Dispatch*, 13 Feb. 1930.

24. Ibid.

25. W. J. Black to HOA, 8 March 1930, Box 19, GWC Papers.

26. W. B. Storey to GWC, 20 June 1930, Box 19, GWC Papers.

27. GWC to Storey, 27 June 1930, Box 19, GWC Papers; HOA to Black, 2 July 1930, Black to HOA, 31 July 1930, Box 1, AWC Papers.

28. Oklahoma City *Black Dispatch*, 14 Aug., 21 Aug. 1930.

29. HOA to Black, 29 Aug. 1930, Box 68, GWC Papers; Black to HOA, 8 Sept. 1930, Box 1, AWC Papers.

30. HOA to Black, 14 Sept. 1930, Box 1, AWC Papers.

31. *National Farm Chemurgic Council*, n.d., pamphlet, Box 106, GWC Papers.

32. J. C. Holton to GWC, 22 Feb., 2 March 1937, Box 31, 5 April 1937, Box 32, Don O. Baird to GWC, 5 Oct. 1937, Carl B. Fritsche to

GWC, 27 March 1937, Box 31, GWC Papers; Tuskegee *News*, 20 May 1932; Montgomery *Advertiser*, 19 July 1937; Jackson *Clarion Ledger*, 14 April 1937.

33. Baird to GWC, 3 Oct. 1937, Box 31, GWC Papers.

34. Holton to HOA, 26 March 1937, Box 68, GWC to Holton, 18 March 1937, Box 31, GWC Papers; Crisp interview notes.

35. GWC to BTW, 19 Nov. 1903, Box 5, GWC Papers; Forrest Brown to GWC, 30 April 1928, Box 31, CIC Papers; GWC to JTH, 1 Nov. 1923, Box 13, GWC [GWCNM]; *see also* clippings in Box 92, GWC Papers.

36. Dallas Spurlock to GWC, 29 Aug., 25 Sept., 5 Oct. 1935, Box 28, GWC Papers; Albany (Ga.) *Herald*, 30 Oct. 1938; Dothan *Eagle*, 13 Nov. 1938; GWC to M. L. Ross, 18 Nov. 1938, Box 40, Slaughter Linthicum to GWC, 5 July 1932, Box 21, GWC Papers.

37. GWC to Bob Barry, 19 Sept. 1930, GWC to John M. Powell, 24 Sept. 1930, GWC to H. McDowell, 26 Sept. 1930, Box 19, McDowell to GWC, 24 Aug. 1934, Box 26, GWC Papers; James Wilson to GWC, 19 Oct. 1932, Box 2, JPG Collection; GWC to M. J. Stacey, 24 Sept. 1941, Box 1, AWC Papers.

38. GWC to Bob Barry, 26 Oct. 1930, Box 19, GWC to J. W. Watson, 13 Aug. 1931, Box 20, Richard M. Payson to GWC, 7 Feb. 1938, Box 36, GWC to Payson, 9 March, 21 March, 5 May 1938, Payson to GWC, 2 May 1938, Box 37, GWC to W. A. Richards, 8 March 1941, Box 52, GWC Papers.

39. *Cleaner's and Dyer's Review*, Sept. 1925, p. 30, clipping, Box 87, GWC to Power, 8 Sept. 1925, GWC to Bertrand R. Clarke, 6 Aug., 25 Aug., 9 Oct. 1925, Box 15, GWC Papers.

40. F. O. P. Theoander to GWC, 31 Aug. 1928, Box 18, 7 June 1929, Ira L. Griffin to GWC, 20 Sept. 1929, Box 19, H. S. Paine to A. W. Curtis, 21 Feb. 1938, Box 69, GWC Papers; Carroll and Muhrer, "Scientific Contribution," pp. 46–47.

41. GWC to Wallace, 7 June 1923, Acting Secretary to GWC, 21 June 1923, Box 1, JPG Collection [NA RG 16].

42. GWC to Chief, Bureau of Chemistry, 26 Jan. 1925, Box 15, GWC to Roosevelt, 21 Oct. 1935, A. J. S. Weaver to GWC, 1 Nov. 1935, Box 28, GWC Papers [NA RG 145].

43. W. Paul Shook to GWC, 10 Sept., 16 Sept., 5 Oct., 19 Nov. 1929, Box 1, AWC Papers; GWC to H. T. Bennett, 18 July, 4 Sept. 1929, GWC to R. L. Phillips, 25 May 1929, Newport (R.I.) *Herald*, 13 Sept. 1928, clipping, Box 88, GWC Papers.

44. GWC to Jack Thorington, 15 July 1929, Box 19, GWC Papers.

45. *See* the notes on the experiments, 26 Sept.–10 Dec. 1931, Box 66,

GWC Papers; Montgomery *Advertiser*, 9 Oct. 1931; J. H. Conzelman to GWC, 8 June 1932, Jack Thorington to GWC, 30 July 1932, Box 21, GWC Papers; Roanoke (Ala.) *Leader*, 11 Sept. 1935; W. Roy Brown to GWC, 3 Sept. 1935, GWC to Brown, 6 Sept. 1935, Box 28, GWC Papers; Carroll and Muhrer, "Scientific Contributions," p. 48.

46. Montgomery *Advertiser*, 10 Aug., 6 Sept. 1935, 2 Oct. 1936; GWC, *The Raising of Hogs, One of the Best Ways to Fill the Empty Dinner Pail*, Tuskegee Institute Experiment Station, Bulletin 40 (Tuskegee, 1935); GWC, *Can Livestock be Raised Profitably in Alabama?*, Tuskegee Institute Experiment Station, Bulletin 41 (Tuskegee, 1936).

47. GWC, *How to Build Up and Maintain the Virgin Fertility of Our Soils*, Tuskegee Institute Experiment Station, Bulletin 42 (Tuskegee, 1936); GWC to F. D. Patterson, 23 Aug. 1937, Box 33, GWC Papers; "Top Soil and Civilization," Montgomery *Advertiser*, 21 June 1938.

48. GWC to M. M. Osborn, 15 Dec. 1931, Box 21, GWC Papers.

49. GWC, "Action Needed Now More Than Anything Else," *Peanut Journal*, Jan. 1934; GWC, "How Can We Best Fill the Empty Dinner Pail?", *Peanut Journal and Nut World*, Feb. 1933; GWC, "Are We Starving in the Midst of Plenty? If So Why?", *Peanut Journal and Nut World*, Jan. 1932; GWC, *Some Choice Wild Vegetables that Make Fine Foods*, Tuskegee Institute, Special leaflet 1 (Tuskegee, 1938); W. T. Wilson to L. B. Whitfield, 16 July 1936, Box 68, GWC Papers.

50. GWC to McNeill and Libby, 4 March 1929, GWC to RRM, 27 Feb. 1929, Box 18, GWC Papers; F. J. Rossiter to GWC, 30 Oct. 1922, Box 1, AWC Papers; Hilda Cooper to GWC, 18 Sept. 1925, Box 15, GWC to Julia S. Rea, 10 May 1927, Box 17, W. E. Jabb to GWC, 16 Feb. 1929, Box 18, Alice D. Musselman to GWC, 4 May 1936, Box 29, GWC Papers.

51. GWC to FDP, 3 April 1936, Box 29, 5 Aug. 1936, Box 30, GWC to W. T. B. Williams, 17 May 1937, Box 32, 29 Nov. 1937, Box 34, GWC Papers.

52. GWC, *How the Farmer Can Save His Sweet Potatoes and Ways of Preparing Them for the Table*, Tuskegee Institute Experiment Station, Bulletin 38 (Tuskegee, 1922); GWC, *How to Make and Save Money on the Farm*, Tuskegee Institute Experiment Station, Bulletin 39 (Tuskegee, 1927); William H. Carter to GWC, 23 July 1924, Box 14, 5 Aug. 1925, Box 15, 13 March 1926, Box 16, GWC Papers.

53. GWC to FDP, 23 May 1936, Box 29, Edmund H. Burke to GWC, 27 Sept. 1938, GWC to T. M. Bell, 10 Oct. 1938, GWC to Helen Porter, 12 Sept. 1938, Box 39, GWC to FDP, 25 July 1938, FDP to GWC, 29 Aug. 1938, Box 38, GWC Papers.

54. G. L. Washington to GWC, 12 July 1937, Box 33, FDP to GWC, 19

July 1935, GWC to FDP, 23 July 1935, Box 28, L. H. Foster, Jr. to Administrative Officer, 1 June 1942, Box 72, GWC Papers.

55. GWC to Austin W. Curtis, Sr., 14 Oct. 1935, Box 28, GWC Papers.

56. H. A. Wallace to GWC, 19 March 1938, Box 38, GWC Papers.

CHAPTER 13: SUFFERING HUMANITY

1. Interview with Foy Thompson, 25 July 1977.

2. Atlanta *Journal*, 8 Nov. 1931; Columbus *Ledger*, 2 Nov. 1933; McGinnis to GWC, 3 Nov. 1933, Harver to R. S. Darnaby, 5 Nov. 1933, Box 23, Davenport to GWC, 12 Jan. 1934, Box 24, GWC Papers.

3. *See* numerous clippings of article, Box 90, GWC Papers.

4. GWC to Mr. Chisolm, 21 Jan. 1934, Box 25, GWC Papers; Norfolk *Journal and Guide*, 13 Jan. 1934; GWC to Raleigh Merritt, 12 July 1934, Box 26, Mrs. A. S. Steele to "Dear Friend," 31 Jan. 1925, Box 15, GWC to M. L. Ross, 19 April 1934, Box 26, GWC Papers.

5. GWC to William F. Rae, 20 Feb. 1939, Box 41, GWC Papers.

6. Form letter [1935?], Box 28, GWC to L. C. Fischer, 8 March 1937, Box 31, GWC to M. L. Ross, 10 Sept., 22 Sept. 1934, Box 26, 11 Oct. 1934, Box 27, E. Tunkle to GWC, 9 Sept., 19 Nov. 1935, Box 28, E.Tunkle to GWC, 31 March 1936, Box 29, Hamlin to GWC, 22 April, 28 April 1939, GWC to Hamlin, 25 April 1939, Box 43, GWC Papers.

7. GWC to James Hale Porter, 6 Jan. 1939, Box 41, GWC Papers.

8. GWC to Mrs. Mayes, 19 March 1935, Box 27, GWC to M. L. Ross, 19 April, 24 May 1934, Box 26, 11 Nov. 1934, Box 27, GWC Papers.

9. GWC to Dr. Dibble, 3 Dec. 1934, Box 27, GWC Papers.

10. GWC to T. L. Hoshell, 14 Aug. 1935, Box 28, GWC Papers.

11. GWC to Hardee Johnson, 28 Jan. 1936, Box 28, GWC Papers. *See also* GWC, "Results of Experiments with Peanut Oil as an Aid in the Treatment of Wasting Diseases," Box 65, GWC Papers.

12. GWC to J. E. Cotton, 30 Aug. 1937, Box 33, form letter [1935?], Box 28, GWC Papers.

13. Kenneth V. James to W. S. Sherrill, 17 Feb. 1935, Box 68, GWC Papers [Franklin Delano Roosevelt Library]; Emmett Cox to GWC, 20 March 1935, Box 27, Cox to W. M. Wellman, 25 March 1936, Box 29, GWC Papers.

14. LCF to GWC, 14 Dec. 1934, 20 June, 26 June 1935, Box 27, LCF to GWC, 5 July, 11 July, 15 July, 18 July 1935, GWC to M. L. Ross, 30 July 1935, GWC to LCF, 20 July 1935, LCF to GWC, 28 Aug. 1935, Box 28, 3 Sept. 1936, Box 30, 4 April 1936, Box 29, GWC Papers.

15. LCF to GWC, 16 March 1936, GWC to LCF, 21 March 1936, Box 29, GWC to Leo S. Whitaker, 10 Oct. 1938, Box 39, GWC Papers.

16. Alexander to GWC, 17 March, 19 May 1936, GWC to Alexander, 20 May 1936, Alexander to GWC, 31 May 1936, Box 29, Fishbein to LCF, 3 June [1936], Box 68, LCF to GWC, 4 June 1936, Box 29, GWC Papers.

17. GWC to Alexander, 4 June 1936, LCF to GWC, 6 June, 12 June 1936, GWC to LCF, 10 June 1936, LCF to GWC, 1 June 1936, GWC to LCF, 16 June 1936, Box 29, GWC Papers.

18. GWC to Alexander, 16 July 1936, Box 29, GWC Papers; *see* clippings, Box 91, GWC Papers; Alexander to Graves, 13 July 1936, Alexander to GWC, 18 July, 19 July 1936, Box 29, GWC Papers; Montgomery *Advertiser*, 18 July 1936; Birmingham *Age-Herald*, 22 July 1936; GWC to Kilpatrick, 20 July 1936, GWC to Hall, 20 July 1936, GWC to Graves, 23 July 1936, Box 29, GWC Papers.

19. GWC to Alexander, 21 July, 22 July 1936, Alexander to GWC, 26 July 1936, Box 29, GWC Papers.

20. Alexander to GWC, 18 July 1936, GWC to Alexander, 28 July 1936, Hall to Alexander, Tuesday, enc. in Alexander to GWC, 30 July 1936, Box 29, GWC Papers.

21. GWC to Kellogg, 10 Aug. 1936, Box 30, Alexander to GWC, 27 July 1936, Box 29, GWC to LCF, 17 Sept. 1936, Box 30, Baker to Thomas Parran, 17 Aug. 1936, enc. in Baker to GWC, 17 Aug. 1936, Box 30, GWC Papers.

22. GWC to Alexander, 18 Aug., 21 Aug., 31 Aug. 1936, GWC to Childers, 2 Nov. 1936, Box 30, GWC Papers.

23. Columbus *Ledger*, 2 Nov. 1933, clipping, Box 90, Thomas H. R. Clarke to GWC, 6 Jan. 1938, Box 35, GWC to FDR, 4 April 1939, FDR to GWC, 7 April 1939, Box 42, GWC to FDR, 27 April 1939, Box 43, GWC Papers.

24. Porter to GWC, 21 March 1938, Box 38, GWC to Porter, 17 Jan. 1939, Box 41, GWC Papers.

25. HAW to Clarence Poe, 27 July 1942, Box 42, GWC Papers, HAW to FDR, 13 Nov. 1939, Box 69, GWC Papers [FDR Library]; HAW to Don, 25 June 1965, Box 82, GWC Papers.

26. HAW to Keith Morgan, 23 March 1939, Box 69, GWC Papers [NA RG 16]; GWC to Porter, 6 Jan. 1939, Box 41, 25 May 1939, Box 44, Chenault to GWC, 1 June 1939, Box 44, FDP to GWC, 6 Feb. 1940, GWC to FDP, 8 Feb. 1940, Box 47, GWC to Porter, 22 June 1942, Box 56, GWC Papers.

27. Arthur Stovall to GWC, 23 July 1935, Box 28, GWC Papers.

28. GWC to J. T. Hardwick, 24 Feb. 1934, Box 25, GWC Papers [GWCNM].

29. GWC to Hardwick, 18 April 1934, Box 26, GWC Papers [GWCNM].

CHAPTER 14: MAN AND SYMBOL

1. John L. Hillman to GWC, 10 March, 16 March 1928, GWC to C. W. Emmons, n.d., Simpson College Archives.

2. Press release, 18 Nov. 1936, Box 91, AWC to Foley Greenhouse Mfg. Co., 5 Jan. 1937, AWC to T. Byron Cutchin, 9 Feb. 1937, Box 68, GWC Papers; B. B. Walcott to FDR, 11 Dec. 1936, William D. Hassett to HAW, 16 Dec. 1936, J. D. Crow to Hassett, 29 Dec. 1930, FDR to GWC, 30 Dec. 1936, Box 30, GWC Papers [FDR Library].

3. *See* brochures in Box 2, GWC Papers; Montgomery *Advertiser*, 4 June 1937.

4. William J. Orr to GWC, 17 May 1937, Box 32, Orr to GWC, 20 Sept. 1937, Box 33, AWC to Orr, 25 May 1937, Box 68, GWC Papers.

5. Pittsburg *Courier*, 27 May 1938, clipping, Box 94, GWC Papers; Wallace E. Barron to GWC, 18 June 1938, Box 2, JPG Collection; Oklahoma City *Black Dispatch*, 26 Feb. 1938.

6. Eunice Thomas Miner to GWC, 28 March 1938, GWC to Miner, 31 March 1938, Box 38, GWC Papers.

7. Columbus *Enquirer*, 17 April 1938, clipping, Box 93, William Jay Schieffelin to GWC, 13 Oct. 1939, A. R. Reid to GWC, 21 Oct. 1939, Box 46, Norfolk *Journal and Guide*, 14 Oct. 1939, Chattanooga *Times*, 9 Oct. 1939, clippings, Box 94, GWC Papers.

8. GWC to Lucius Boomer, 7 Aug. 1940, Box 50, GWC Papers.

9. GWC to H. O. Abbott, 25 April 1940, Box 48, GWC Papers [GWCNM].

10. E. L. Dimitry to GWC, 3 May 1940, Box 49, GWC Papers; GWC to H. O. Abbott, 1 June 1940, Box 49, GWC Papers [GWCNM]; New York *Daily Worker*, 21 April 1940, Oklahoma City *Black Dispatch*, 15 June 1940, clippings, Box 94, GWC Papers.

11. Paul D. Williams to GWC, 15 Feb. 1941, Box 52; "Dr. George Washington Carver: A Catholic Tribute," Box 84; *International Review*, n.d.; Vincent Warren, "An Appreciation of Dr. George Washington Carver," *Colored Harvest* 29 (June–July 1941): 8–9, clippings, Box 84; GWC, "Response to the Presentation of the Catholic Plaque," 22 April 1941, Box 65, GWC Papers.

12. Alan Valentine to GWC, 6 March 1941, Box 52, GWC Papers.

13. "Citation: George Washington Carver, for the honorary degree of

Doctor of Science, The University of Rochester," 18 June 1941, Box 2, GWC Papers. Carver was delighted by the fact that the action was unprecedented. GWC to Eugene L. Connelly, 13 June 1941, Box 53, GWC Papers.

14. Chicago *Defender*, 31 May 1941; GWC to Harvey J. Hill, 19 April 1941, Box 52, GWC to John Harris, 26 May 1941, GWC to Glenn Clark, 27 May 1941, Box 56, "Speech of Dr. George W. Carver at Atlantic City," 17 May 1941, Box 65, GWC Papers.

15. JOG to GWC, 12 April 1940, GWC to JOG, 20 July 1940, JOG to GWC, 18 Feb. 1941, GWC to JOG, 5 June 1941, JOG-GWC Papers; Des Moines *Bystander*, 5 June 1941, clipping, Box 94, GWC Papers; JOG to GWC, 16 June 1941, JOG-GWC Papers.

16. E. I. F. Williams to GWC, 3 March 1942, Robert Hofday to GWC, 27 Jan. 1942, Box 56, "Extracts from the 1942 Commencement Program of Selma University," Box 65, GWC to Walter G. Crump, 25 Sept. 1942, Box 59, GWC Papers.

17. GWC to Cleo Foster, 15 Jan. 1936, Box 28, Nashville *Globe*, 22 Sept. 1939, clipping, Box 94, Nashville *Globe*, 20 May 1938, clipping, Box 93, Stanford M. Mirkin to GWC, 13 May [1942], Box 57, "A Negro Slave Who Became a Great Scientist," *Look*, 26 Oct. 1937, Atlanta *World*, 2 Oct. 1939, New York *Age*, 18 Oct. 1941, clippings, Box 94, Jack Sensenly to GWC, 2 June 1939, Box 44, Don McClure to GWC, 14 Sept. 1939, Box 45, GWC Papers.

18. GWC to F. F. Holton, 1 Dec. 1938, Box 40, GWC Papers.

19. GWC, "Vast Possibilities Offered in the Development of the Sweet Potato and Peanut Industry," *Manufacturers' Record*, 6 Jan. 1921; "Marvels of Chemistry in Food Production," *Manufacturers' Record*, 6 Sept. 1923; Edmonds to GWC, 2 Oct. 1924, Box 14, GWC Papers.

20. Montgomery *Advertiser*, 22 Dec. 1929; Baltimore *Sun*, 16 May 1937, clipping, Box 92, GWC Papers.

21. Brewton (Ala.) *Standard*, 17 Nov. 1938, Louisville *Courier-Journal* n.d., clippings, Box 93, GWC Papers.

22. Atlanta *Constitution*, 17 May 1936.

23. GWC to Marlin E. Penn, 18 June 1927, Box 17, GWC Papers.

24. GWC to Carroll Kilpatrick, 4 Dec. 1935, Box 28, GWC Papers.

25. Eleazer, "One Time Slave, Now Scientific Wizard," n.d., press release, Box 84, GWC Papers.

26. Estelle Haskins to GWC, 4 Feb. 1922, Box 12, Una Roberts Lawrence to GWC, 19 Jan. 1942, Box 56, GWC Papers; "Possibilities of the Peanut," *American Missionary*, 76 (June 1921); George L. Cady, "Negro Evolution and Tuskegee," *Congregationalist*, 27 April 1922.

27. Macon *News*, 30 May 1931, clipping, Box 89, GWC Papers.

28. Oklahoma City *Black Dispatch*, 31 July 1937.

29. Dunjee to GWC, 11 July 1941, Box 53, GWC Papers.

30. Jacksonville *Florida Sentinel*, 26 May 1923, Pittsburgh *Courier*, 22 Sept. 1923, clippings, Box 86, Terrell to GWC, 17 April 1929, Box 18, Indianapolis *World*, 10 May 1929, clipping, Box 88, GWC Papers.

31. Baltimore *Herald*, 26 Sept. 1923, clipping, Box 86, GWC Papers.

32. G. W. Ridout, "The Kingdom of God Notes," *Pentacostal Herald*, 17 July 1935, clipping, Box 83, GWC Papers.

33. "The Story the Peanut Tells," Box 65, GWC Papers.

34. D. R. Miller to GWC, 18 March 1940, Box 48, GWC to Carrel, 6 Feb. 1939, Carrel to GWC, 19 April 1939, Box 43, GWC Papers.

35. GWC, "The Baha'i Movement," 4 April 1941, Box 66, GWC to Estelle Durral, 18 Aug. 1941, Box 54, *Spoken Word* to GWC, 6 July 1935, Box 28, Lula Slatzell to GWC, 17 Nov. 1940, GWC to Slatzell, 30 Nov. 1940, Box 51, GWC Papers.

36. GWC to C. F. Andrews, 24 Feb. 1929, Box 18, Andrews to GWC, 11 Nov. 1929, Box 19, Tulsa *Eagle*, 27 Dec. 1930, clipping, Box 88, Richard B. Gregg to GWC, 24 May 1935, Box 27, GWC to Gandhi, 27 July 1935, Box 28, GWC Papers.

37. Carver had copies of this anonymous poem printed and sometimes enclosed one in letters.

38. Official U. S. Treasury Poster, 1945, Box 100, GWC Papers.

39. Montgomery *Advertiser*, 25 Nov. 1917; Valdosta *Daily Times*, 22 Feb. 1940.

40. Brewton (Ala.) *Trade Record*, clipping, Box 84, GWC Papers.

41. Thelma Pearson, "He Worked with God," *St. Joseph Magazine* 50 (June 1949): 23.

42. James Saxon Childers, "A Boy Who Was Traded for a Horse." *American Magazine*, Oct. 1932, p. 24.

43. Provine McKinley Fagin to GWC, 2 Jan. 1939, GWC to Fagin, 6 Jan. 1939, Box 41, GWC Papers.

44. GWC to James M. Reid, 8 April 1942, Box 57, GWC Papers.

45. Harlan, *Washington*, p. 227.

46. GWC to Richard Therrell, 28 Nov. 1941, Box 55, GWC Papers.

47. AWC to Hotel New Yorker, 8 Sept. 1939, Lloyd A. Fitzgerald to AWC, 14 Sept. 1939, Box 69, GWC Papers; Pittsburgh *Courier*, 30 Sept. 1939.

48. Pittsburgh *Courier*, 30 Sept. 1939; AWC, "Reminiscences of George W. Carver," Jan. 1976, taped responses to questions by author.

49. Washington *Tribune*, 14 Oct. 1939; Des Moines *Tribune*, 30 Sept. 1939; Norfolk *Journal and Guide*, 4 Nov. 1939; Chicago *Defender*, 30 Sept. 1939; New Orleans *Louisiana Weekly*, 4 Nov. 1939.

50. Leo A. Maloney to Harvey J. Hill, 18 Oct. 1939, enc. in Hill to GWC, 22 Jan. 1940, Box 47, GWC Papers.

51. GWC to H. A. Mueller, 5 Oct. 1939, Box 2, JPG Collection.

52. Henrik F. Infield, *Cooperative Communities at Work* (New York, 1945), pp. 37–52.

53. GWC to GTP, 18 July 1922, Box 12, *Llano Colonist*, 26 Aug. 1922, clipping, Box 83, GTP to GWC, 8 Aug., 27 Oct. 1924, Box 14, Helene Morgane to GWC, 21 Feb. 1924, Box 13, GTP to GWC, 7 Nov. 1927, Box 17, 12 April 1929, Box 18, GWC to H. B. Clark, 17 June 1930, Box 19, H. E. Walton to GWC, 6 June 1932, GTP to GWC, 6 June 1932, Box 21, GWC Papers.

54. GTP to GWC, 26 April 1939, Box 43, GWC to GTP, 23 Jan. 1928, GTP to GWC, 28 Jan. 1928, Box 17, GWC to GTP, 19 April 1929, Box 18, GWC Papers.

55. Walter Millsap to GWC, 17 June 1936, Cy Record to GWC, 24 June, 8 July, 14 July 1936, GWC to Record, 26 June, 13 July 1936, Record to GWC, 7 Aug.; 15 Aug. 1936, GWC to Record, 22 Aug. 1936, Box 30, GWC Papers.

56. O. J. Golden to GWC, 12 Dec. 1930, 18 April 1931, Box 1, AWC Papers.

57. GWC to Sutton, 26 Jan. 1931, GWC to Golden, 24 Jan., 7 May 1931, Box 20, GWC Papers.

58. Golden to GWC, 19 Aug. 1931, Sutton to GWC, n.d., Box 1, AWC Papers; Sutton to GWC, 1 July 1932, Box 21, 4 March 1938, Box 37, GWC Papers.

59. GWC to Kester, 2 April 1929, Box 18, GWC Papers.

60. Kester to GWC, 13 March 1934, Box 25, GWC Papers.

61. Elisabeth Gilman to GWC, 30 May 1936, Box 29, GWC Papers; Kester, "Recollections."

62. GWC to T. N. Carswell, 9 Dec. 1941, Box 55, GWC Papers.

63. New York *World Telegram*, 5 April 1951, clipping, Box 97, GWC Papers.

64. Interview with Jessie Abbott, 17 Dec. 1975.

65. Barry to GWC, 1 June 1931, Box 20, Barry to GWC, n.d., Box 61, Barry to GWC, 8 March 1933, Box 23, GWC Papers.

66. Barry to GWC, 18 Dec. 1930, Box 19, GWC Papers.

67. GWC to Hall, 15 May 1928, Hall to GWC, 15 May, 18 May 1928, Box 17, Hall to GWC, 22 June 1939, Box 44, GWC Papers.

68. Al [Zissler] to Jim [Hardwick], 17 July 1934, LCC Papers; Kester to GWC, 4 July 1924, Box 14, GWC Papers.

69. GWC to Clark, 27 Feb. 1928, Box 17, GWC Papers.

70. Glenn Clark, *The Man Who Talks with Flowers* (St. Paul, n.d.), p. 19.
71. GWC to Clark, 4 Jan. 1939, Box 41, Clark to GWC, 28 Feb., 11 April 1940, Box 48, 14 May 1940, Box 49, Minneapolis *Journal* 5 May 1938, clipping, Box 95, GWC Papers; program, Box 1, AWC Papers.
72. White to GWC, 30 Dec. 1940, Box 51, Ralph N. Davis to GWC, 23 Jan. 1942, Box 56, GWC Papers.
73. Hayes to GWC, 2 March 1931, Box 20, GWC Papers.
74. GWC to Ford, 17 April 1941, 12 Feb. 1941, Box 52, GWC Papers.
75. Mrs. Velma Lewis to GWC, 9 Sept. 1940, Box 50, Hart to GWC, 1 April 1924, Box 13, GWC Papers; Sutton, "Recollections."
76. William W. Thompson to the President of the United States, 9 April 1923, Box 13, GWC Papers; interview with Mrs. G. C. Thompson, 27 July 1977.
77. GWC to BTW, 9 April 1902, Box 4, GWC Papers [BTW]; Ward to GWC, 28 Nov. 1921, Box 11, 8 Feb. 1923, Box 12, GWC Papers.
78. Ward to GWC, 16 Oct. 1939, Box 46, GWC Papers.
79. GWC to Blanks, 10 Aug. 1925, Box 15, GWC Papers; interview with Mrs. G. C. Blanks, 7 July 1978.

CHAPTER 15: BLAZING THE TRAIL

1. Leavell, "Boy Traded," p. 6.
2. GWC to Leo F. Collier, 29 March 1940, Box 48, GWC Papers.
3. GWC to H. O. Abbott, 28 April 1938, Box 38, GWC Papers [GWCNM]; Emile Hooker to H. O. Abbott, Box 69, GWC Papers.
4. GWC to Hattie F. C. Caper, 24 Jan. 1939, GWC to Mrs. Lee, 2 Jan. 1939, Box 41, GWC to M. L. Ross, 28 Sept. 1938, Box 39, GWC to Ida L. Jackson, 26 Nov. 1938, Box 40, GWC Papers.
5. GWC to H. O. Abbott, 22 Feb. 1940, Box 48, GWC Papers [GWCNM]; GWC to H. A. Wallace, 9 Jan. 1940, Box 47, GWC Papers [NA RG 16]; GWC to Lucy C. Crisp, 15 Nov. 1939, Box 46, GWC to Helen Chisholm, 19 Jan. 1940, Box 47, GWC to R. Beecher Costa, 16 April 1940, Box 48, GWC Papers.
6. Jessie Abbott to M. L. Ross, 11 Nov. 1941, Box 71, GWC Papers.
7. GWC to Mrs. Doobs, 7 Aug. 1942, Box 59, GWC Papers.
8. Frank Campsall to FDP, 21 May 1941, Box 71, GWC Papers; interview with Paul R. Miller, 3 Nov. 1975.
9. GWC to FDP, 5 May 1942, Box 57, GWC Papers.
10. GWC to J. R. Boxley, 3 April 1937, Box 42, clippings, Box 94, GWC to Whom It May Concern, 19 April 1941, Box 52, Robert H. Thomp-

son to AWC, 11 June 1942, Box 71, Jackson to GWC, 17 Feb. 1942, Box 56, GWC to M. L. Ross, 25 June 1941, GWC to Dr. Gomez, 16 July 1941, Box 53, GWC to Gomez, 30 July, 1 Aug. 1941, Box 54, GWC Papers.

11. Allen Eaton to GWC, 13 Jan. 1940, Box 47, GWC to Mr. Yates, 22 Oct. 1940, Box 50, GWC to C. R. Stephens, 14 April 1942, Box 57, GWC to H. Harold Hume, 23 Sept. 1942, Box 59, Mary Emma Barnes to GWC, 29 July 1941, V. P. Sydenstricker to GWC, 8 Aug. 1941, Box 54, Charles W. Greenleaf to GWC, 10 Sept. 1942, Box 59, Sherman Briscoe to FDP, 27 April 1943, Box 75, Hill to GWC, 15 Jan., 21 Jan. 1942, GWC to Hill, 19 Jan., 6 Feb. 1942, Box 56, Henry A. Knight to H. A. Wallace, 28 Jan. 1942, Grover B. Hill to Hill, 14 March 1942, Box 71, GWC Papers.

12. GWC, *Nature's Garden for Victory and Peace*, Tuskegee Institute Experiment Station, Bulletin 43 (Tuskegee, 1942); Rackham Holt, "How to Have Fun with Weeds," *Saturday Evening Post*, 20 June 1942, pp. 18,90; GWC, *Peanuts to Conserve Meat*, Tuskegee Institute Experiment Station, Leaflet 14 (Tuskegee, 1943).

13. Reuben E. Blumenfield to GWC, 11 Sept. 1941, Box 54, "Proposal for Renewal of Fiber Research Project," 15 June 1942, Box 113, AWC to R. H. Baum, 11 July 1939, R. Brooks Taylor to AWC, 21 Nov. 1939, Box 69, FDP to GWC, 12 Feb. 1940, Box 48, AWC, untitled memo, 22 Sept. 1941, Box 71, AWC to Thomas M. Searles, 19 Jan. 1943, AWC to Edgar Melvin, 29 Jan. 1943, Box 73, GWC Papers.

14. GWC to Ceresine International Products Co., 15 Aug. 1930, Box 19, AWC, "Background, Plan and Objectives fo the Proposed Carver Creative Research Laboratory," Jan. 1937, "Some Facts of Interest about Dr. George W. Carver," July 1937, Box 111, GWC to AWC, 13 Sept, 1937, GWC to F. W. Peterson, 9 Aug. 1937, Box 33, GWC to FDP, 25 April 1938, Box 38, GWC Papers.

14. GWC to Powell, 2 Jan. 1939, Box 41, Powell to GWC, 12 Jan. 1940, GWC to Powell, 27 Jan. 1940, Box 47, GWC Papers.

15. Powell to GWC, 17 Feb. 1940, Box 48, clippings, Box 94, GWC Papers.

16. R. A. Crawford to GWC, 31 March 1898, Box 1, JPG Collection; Crawford to GWC, 21 July 1911, Box 8, Lloyd Isaacs to F. M. Morrison, 21 Aug. 1940, Box 70, claim form, 31 June 1931, Box 2, E. C. Meredith to GWC, 6 July 1931, Box 20, GWC to M. L. Ross, 7 Jan. 1933, Box 22, Addie Lee Farish to GWC, 28 June 1938, Box 38, Meredith to GWC, 13 Oct. 1934, Box 27, Powell to GWC, 19 Oct. 1935, Box 28, 3 Dec. 1936, Box 30, 7 April 1938, Box 38, GWC Papers.

17. William H. Cork to GWC, 21 Jan. 1932, Box 21, 8 Nov. 1934, Box

27, Crawford to GWC, 26 Jan. 1904, Box 5, Powell to GWC, 3 Dec. 1936, Box 30, GWC Papers.

18. *See* tax and bank records, Box 2, GWC Papers.

19. GWC to Miss M. Kuchanshas, 3 July 1937, Box 44, AWC to R. J. Combs, 27 March 1939, Box 69, GWC Papers.

20. Haygood to GWC, 4 Jan. 1939, Powell to GWC, 14 Jan. 1939, Box 41, Haygood to Herb-Juice Co., 20 April 1939, Box 69, Powell to GWC, 15 May 1940, Box 49, Haygood to GWC, 14 March 1940, Box 48, GWC Papers.

21. Haygood to GWC, 11 July 1940, Box 49, Powell to GWC, 25 June 1941, Box 53, GWC to E. L. Allen, 2 Sept. 1941, Box 54, GWC to Haygood, 31 Oct. 1941, Box 55, 22 July 1942, Box 59, R. W. Brown to Eva T. Maguire, 12 Sept. 1944, Box 80, GWC Papers.

22. B. B. Walcott, "Meet George Washington Carver, American Artist," *Service* (Jan. 1942), p. 10.

23. GWC to FDP, 16 Aug. 1938, Box 38, GWC Papers.

24. GWC to FDP, 27 Feb. 1940, Box 48, "The Why of the George Washington Carver Museum," n.d., Box 110, GWC Papers.

25. GWC to H. O. Abbott, 8 Nov., 12 Nov. 1938, Box 40, GWC Papers [GWCNM]; GWC to FDP, 7 July 1939, GWC to Dear Friend, 28 June 1939, GWC to D. A. Williston, 27 July 1939, Box 44, GWC Papers.

26. GWC to J. J. Lewis, 15 Aug. 1939, Box 45, GWC to BTW, 5 June 1899, Box 4, GWC Papers; Tuskegee *Student*, 2 Feb., 21 Dec. 1901; Crisp interview notes.

27. GWC to Lloyd Isaacs, 19 July 1940, Box 49, GWC to Lyman Ward, 27 Oct. 1941, Box 55, GWC Papers; "The Carver Art Collection," JOG-GWC Papers.

28. Tampa *Bulletin*, 29 Nov. 1941, clipping, Box 94, GWC Papers.

29. *The Carver Art Collection*, pamphlet, 15 Oct. 1941, Box 110, GWC Papers.

30. "Black Leonardo," *Time*, 24 Nov. 1941.

31. Untitled typed description of the museum, n.d., Box 110, GWC Papers.

32. Walcott, "Meet GWC," p. 30.

33. GWC to C. R. Walwryn, 16 Dec. 1942, Box 60, Jessie Abbott to H. O. Abbott, 2 Jan. 1943, Box 72, GWC to Betsy Graves Reyneau, 19 Dec. 1942, Box 60, GWC Papers.

34. AWC to Mary T. Scott, 12 Jan. 1943, Box 73, GWC Papers.

35. Harlan, *Washington*, p. 277.

36. Barry Mackintosh, "George Washington Carver: The Making of a Myth," *Journal of Southern History* 42 (Nov. 1976): 525.

37. GWC to H. G. Ritchie, 7 Oct. 1938, Box 39, GWC Papers.

INDEX